The Essential Poet's Glossary

The

ESSENTIAL

Poet's Glossary

Edward Hirsch

An *Imprint* of HarperCollins*Publishers*

ecco

An Imprint of HarperCollins Publishers, registered
in the United States of America and/or other jurisdictions.

www.harpercollins.com

Library of Congress Cataloging-in-Publication Data is available.
ISBN 978-0-544-93123-7

Book design by Greta D. Sibley

Printed in the United States of America

23 24 25 26 27 LBC 9 8 7 6 5

To Poetry

Don't desert me
just because I stayed up last night
watching *The Lost Weekend.*

I know I've spent too much time
praising your naked body to strangers
and gossiping about lovers you betrayed.

I've stalked you in foreign cities
and followed your far-flung movements,
pretending I could describe you.

Forgive me for getting jacked on coffee
and obsessing over your features
year after jittery year.

I'm sorry for handing you a line
and typing you on a screen,
but don't let me suffer in silence.

Does anyone still invoke the Muse,
string a wooden lyre for Apollo,
or try to saddle up Pegasus?

Winged horse, heavenly god or goddess,
indifferent entity, secret code, stored magic,
pleasance and half wonder, hell,

I have loved you my entire life
without even knowing what you are
or how — please help me — to find you.

Acknowledgments

My dear friend and colleague André Bernard first convinced me to write a glossary for *How to Read a Poem and Fall in Love with Poetry*. Everything here flows from that initial idea. Special thanks to Jenna Johnson, Deanne Urmy, Jenny Xu, Laura Brady, and their exemplary team at Houghton Mifflin Harcourt. Susanna Brougham did an excellent job copyediting the manuscript. I am also eager to acknowledge my agent, Liz Darhansoff. I am grateful to the many poets, near and far, who have talked over so many of the topics of poetry with me over the years. Their impress is everywhere apparent. My deep gratitude goes out to Lauren Watel, my love, for her keen intelligence and high standards.

Introduction

This is a book for writers and readers. It lays out, defines, and characterizes the essential terms of poetry. It has grown, as if naturally, out of my lifelong interest in poetry, my curiosity about its vocabulary, its forms and genres, its histories and traditions, its small devices and large mysteries — how it works. I hope it will be a companion, pleasurable to read, useful to study. It's intended for both initiated and uninitiated readers, something to keep at hand, a compendium of discoveries that has befriended me. It's a book of familiar and unfamiliar terms, old and new, some with long and complicated histories, others freshly minted. The alphabetical format may feel cool, but the hand that made the art was warm, and this book is animated by the practitioners who made poetry their own: the rational and the irrational, the lettered and the unschooled, those who would storm the barricades and tear down the castle, those who would rebuild it, the high priests of art, the irreverent tricksters, the believers and the skeptics, the long-lived purists and the doomed romantics, the holy eccentrics, the critics, the craftsmen, and the seers (singers, chanters, listeners, readers, writers); my quarrelsome friends, an extended family of makers. I've tried to figure out what they've been up to over the centuries.

This book is culled from the much larger book *A Poet's Glossary*. That book was as definitive, inclusive, and international as I could make it. This volume is shorter and more focused. It drills down to what I deem the most crucial terms for understanding and appreciating poetry. It is meant to be manageable, though the reader will still find terms from a wide variety of poetries, oral and written, lyric and epic. It is selective and international. I've also added a few items and rectified some mistakes. Even in its shorter format, this project has something of the madness of a Borgesian encyclopedia, since every culture has its own poetry, usually in its own language. It would be impossible to include all the central terms in all the languages. I've explained what I can. I'm grounded in our moment, in the history of English and American literature, but I've continued to look for guidance to Hebrew and Arabic poetry, to Greek and Latin poetry, to the European poetries, east and west, to Irish, Welsh, and Scottish poetry, to Russian and Scandinavian poetry, to Chinese and Japanese poetry, to African, South Asian, and Latin American poetry. I've relied on many different sources — literary, historical, folkloric, anthropological, linguistic, and philosophical — and built on the work of others, but the mistakes are my own. I take responsibility for what's here and what's not. This is the result of a lifetime of engagement.

I've learned a tremendous amount in doing my reseach. As I've worked, I've often found myself transported to different time periods and countries, placing myself here and there, wondering what it would have been like to be a poet in the heady days of eighth-century China, or twelfth-century Provence, or thirteenth-century Florence, or fourteenth-century Andalusia, or fifteenth-century Wales, or seventeenth-century Japan, or early nineteenth-century England, or late nineteenth-century Ireland, or early twentieth-century Russia ... I move freely among the bards, scops, and griots, the tribal singers, the poets of courtly love who sang for their mistresses, the court poets who wrote for their supper, the traveling minstrels, the revolutionaries, the flâneurs, the witnesses. I've encountered a series of recurring questions and debates about style and language, like the unresolved argument about the merits of the plain and the baroque style, or about the role of poetry in culture and society. There has been an ongoing quarrel, played out in many different countries, between tradition and innovation, the local and the international, the home-grown and the cosmopolitan. What language does one use, what forms does one employ? To whom is the poet responsible, and to what? Poetry too takes part in conversations about identity and nationalism. I've been surprised in my research by the sheer number of poetic contests throughout history. We may think of poetry as a noncompetitive activity, or as a competition with oneself, a struggle between the poet and the poem, but poetry competitions have kept cropping up over the years. The aesthetic debates, seldom good-natured, have also been fierce. I've tried to understand the intensities, to figure out what's at stake, and welcomed the contestants into the tent.

The devices work the magic in poetry, and a glossary gives names to those devices. It unpacks them. I believe its purpose is to deepen the reader's initiation into the mysteries. Here, then, is a repertoire of poetic secrets, a vocabulary, some of it ancient, which proposes a greater pleasure in the text, deeper levels of enchantment.

The Essential Poet's Glossary

A

abecedarian The word derives from the names of the first four letters of the alphabet plus the suffix "-arius" (*abecedarius*). An alphabetical acrostic in which each line or stanza begins with a successive letter of the alphabet. The abecedarian, which generally starts with the first letter of the alphabet and runs to the final letter, is an ancient form often employed for sacred works. Most of the acrostics in the Hebrew Bible are alphabetical; Psalm 119, for example, consists of twenty-two eight-line stanzas, one for each letter of the Hebrew alphabet. The first eight lines all begin with the letter *aleph,* the next eight lines begin with the letter *beth,* and so on, for 176 verses until the final *tav.* The completeness of the form enacts the idea of total devotion to the law of God.

The abecedarian originally had powerful associations with prayer. In 393, Saint Augustine composed an alphabetical psalm against the Donatists, "Psalmus contra partem Donati." Geoffrey Chaucer was probably familiar with some Vulgate translations of Psalm 119 into Medieval Latin, and he employed the abecedarian in his twenty-four-stanza poem titled "An A.B.C." (ca. 1370), a translation of a French prayer ("The Prayer of Our Lady"). Each stanza begins with a letter of the Medieval Latin alphabet, progressing from A to Z. Ronald Knox adapts the biblical precedent in his re-creation from the Hebrew of the "Lamentations of the Prophet Jeremiah: An Alphabet of Patience in Misery" (1950).

The Japanese *iroha mojigusari* (literally "character chain") is a specialized version of the abecedarian. The first letter of the alphabet kicks off the first line and the second letter of the alphabet concludes it. The third letter starts the second line and the fourth letter finishes it. This continues until all the letters of the alphabet have been used in order.

SEE ALSO *acrostic.*

abstract, abstraction An abstract is a summary of any piece of written work. In poetry, abstraction refers to the use of concepts or ideas, things that come to us not through the senses but through the mind. Abstraction strips away the context and employs the immaterial properties of language. To employ abstraction is the opposite of embracing concrete particulars. Abstractions were a central feature of Victorian and symbolist poetry, one reason modern poets reacted against them. "Go in fear of abstractions," Ezra Pound declared in "A Retrospect" (1913): "Don't use such an expression as 'dim lands *of peace.*' It dulls the image. It mixes an abstraction with the concrete." But a postsymbolist modern poet such as Wallace Stevens, who claimed that "It Must Be Abstract" ("Notes Toward a Supreme Fiction," 1942), found ways to embrace abstraction by employing ideas and thinking in poetry. For Stevens, reality itself was an abstraction with multiple perspectives: "The major abstraction is the idea of man." Abstraction means the act of withdrawing. It is an act of moving away, a form of distancing and removal.

abstract poetry Dame Edith Sitwell coined this term to describe her own poems. Describing her 1922 book, she writes, "The poems in *Façade* are abstract poems, that is, patterns in sound." They try to use sound in much the same way that abstract painters use color, shape, and design. Abstract poetry never became a movement, though Lewis Carroll's nonsense poetry and Gertrude Stein's prose poems create some of the same effects.

SEE ALSO *nonsense poetry, sound poetry.*

accent From the Latin word *accentus,* meaning "song added to speech." The vocal stress or emphasis placed on certain syllables in a line of verse. Stress varies from weak to strong. Some poetries, such as Anglo-Saxon, count only accents, the number of stresses in a line. Other poetries, such as English, count both accents and syllables. Vocal stress is crucial to how we speak and hear the English language, how we say, scan, and sing poems in our language.

SEE ALSO *beat, meter, prosody, scansion.*

accentual-syllabic verse, see *meter.*

accentual verse, see *meter.*

acrostic From the Greek: "at the tip of the verse." The acrostic reads down as well as across. The initial letters of each line have a meaning when read vertically. The abecedarian is possibly its oldest form.

The acrostic may initially have been used as a mnemonic device in the transmission of sacred texts. Its origin and history suggest that words have magical, incantatory, and religious power. In written poetry, the acrostic became a way of both hiding and revealing mysterious information, such as the names of lovers, authors, and titles. The writer engages the reader as the solver of a puzzle, inviting a more intimate bond. Thus Edgar Allan Poe spells out the name of his beloved in "Enigma" (1848), and Ben Jonson prefaces a play with an acrostic that spells out its name (1610):

The Argument

T he sickness hot, a master quit, for fear,
H is house in town, and left one servant there.
E ase him corrupted, and gave means to know
A Cheater and his punk, who now brought low,
L eaving their narrow practice, were become
C oz'ners at large; and, only wanting some
H ouse to set up, with him they here contract,
E ach for a share, and all begin to act.
M uch company they draw, and much abuse,
I n casting figures, telling fortunes, news,
S elling of flies, flat bawdry, with the Stone;
T ill it, and they, and all in fume are gone.

A different type of acrostic (the mesostich) focuses on the middle letter of each line; another (the telestich) uses the final one. A double acrostic employs both the first and last letters of the lines. A compound acrostic spells one word down the left-hand margin and another down the right-hand one. A word square consists of a set of words, all of which have the same number of letters as the total number of words. Written out in a grid, the words can be read both horizontally and vertically.

SEE ALSO *abecedarian, palindrome.*

adonic In Greek and Latin poetry, an adonic verse is a five-unit metrical foot that consists of a dactyl and a spondee (or trochee): / u u | / / or

/ u u | / u. The last line of the Sapphic stanza is an adonic. Ezra Pound concludes his poem "The Return" (1912) with an accentual-syllabic adonic: "pállĭd thĕ léash mén."

SEE ALSO *dactyl, meter, Sapphic stanza, spondee, trochee.*

Aeolic Two of the inventors of lyric poetry, Sappho and Alcaeus (late seventh to early sixth century B.C.E.), wrote in a Greek dialect known as Aeolic. The Greek colonies of Aeolis, a district of Mysia in Asia Minor, were one of the traditional birthplaces of lyric poetry. Aeolic subsequently became the name for a class of meters that brings dactyls and iambs close together to form a choriamb, a pattern of four syllables: long-short-short-long. In English prosody, this became two stressed syllables enclosing two unstressed ones. Horace responded to the themes of Sappho and Alcaeus by employing their meters, thus claiming, "I, passing from humble to mighty, / first found for Aeolic song a home / in Italian melodies" (*Odes,* book 3, 23–13 B.C.E.).

SEE ALSO *Alcaic, choriamb, dactyl, iamb, meter, Sapphic stanza, trochee.*

air, ayre A song, a tune, or a melody. It can also suggest all three together. The English ayre derived from the French *air de cour* and referred to a solo song accompanied by a lute, which is why it is called the lute-song or lute-air. It was a subgenre of the lyric that flourished in the first two decades of the seventeenth century. The earliest publication of ayres was John Dowland's *The first Booke of Songs or Ayres* (1597). The lute-song hits its most beautiful notes in Thomas Campion's *Two Books of Ayres* (ca. 1613). "In these English Ayres," Campion wrote, "I have chiefly aymed to couple my Words and Notes lovingly together." He sets his program in "Now Winter Nights": "Let well-tun'd words amaze / With harmony divine."

SEE ALSO *lyric, song, songbook.*

aisling From the Irish: "dream" (plural *aislingí*). The *aisling* (pronounced "ashling") is a vision or dream poem, which developed in Gaelic poetry in Munster during the late seventeenth and eighteenth centuries. It has its origins in the Old French *reverdie,* which celebrates the arrival of spring, often in the form of a beautiful woman. The *aislingí* present and personify Ireland in the form of a woman, who can be young or old, haggard or beautiful, lamenting her woes. The woman is usually referred to as a *spéir-bhean* ("sky-woman"). Aodhagán Ó Raithille inaugurated the tradition of the political *aisling* with his eighteenth-century poem "The Merchant's Son." In *The Hidden Ireland* (1924), Daniel Corkery calls the *aisling* an "intimate expression of the hidden life of the people among whom it flourished."

SEE ALSO *reverdie*.

Alcaic A classical Greek stanza named for and possibly invented by Alcaeus, a poet of the late seventh and early sixth centuries B.C.E. It consists of four lines: the first two lines have eleven syllables each, the third, nine, and the fourth, ten. It has a complicated metrical scheme. Rosanna Warren points to "the principal beauty of the Alcaic, its shifts in rhythm in mid-course, its calculated imbalance as the iambic and choriambic first two lines yield to iambs in the third and resolve in racy dactyls in the fourth. An exemplum of poetry's task, it acts out the dynamic equilibrium between order and disorder."

Horace honored Alcaeus by adapting the Alcaic to Latin poetry; two-thirds of his *Odes* (23–13 B.C.E.) are written in it. The stanza was later adapted to Italian, French, German, Hungarian, and English poetry. There are no true English equivalents of this quantitative meter, but there have been imitations by the Countess of Pembroke (the sixteenth-century "Psalm 120"), Arthur Clough ("Alcaics," 1849), Robert Bridges ("Song: Chorus to Demeter," 1914), Thomas Hardy ("The Temporary the All," 1898), and Alfred, Lord Tennyson, who called it "the grandest of all measures." W. H. Auden took a Horatian stance and employed the stanza in "In Memory of Sigmund Freud" (1939). In *Greek Lyrics* (1955), Richmond Lattimore used Alcaics to translate Alcaeus himself.

SEE ALSO *iamb, choriamb, dactyl, meter*.

alexandrine A twelve-syllable poetic line used primarily in French poetry until the advent of *vers libre* ("free verse") in the nineteenth century. It is the standard line of traditional French poetry since the sixteenth century and has an importance comparable to blank verse in English poetry. It was invented in the twelfth century — the name may have derived from a poem about Alexander the Great — and circulates in the bloodstream of anyone classically educated in French poetry. The traditional alexandrine divided the line into two groups of six syllables with a fixed medial pause, or caesura. There are strong stresses on the sixth and the last syllables. The *Alexandrin classique* was perfected by the dramatists Pierre Corneille (1606–1684) and Jean Racine (1639–1699), its greatest exponent. The twelve-syllable *vers romantique,* or *Alexandrin trimètre,* divides the line into three parts. The twelve-syllable *tétramètre* divides the line into four parts, with a caesura after the sixth syllable. Victor Hugo and other nineteenth-century poets challenged and reformed the alexandrine to give it greater rhythmic fluidity. Paul Verlaine expanded it so that it bordered on free verse.

The six strong accents of the English alexandrine give it a particularly sprawling, drawn-out feeling. In English poetry, Edmund Spenser employs an alexandrine as the last line of each stanza of *The Faerie Queene* (1590–96), and Milton cannily imitates him in his nativity ode (1629). Alexander Pope evokes what he criticizes in the second line of this couplet from "An Essay on Criticism" (1711):

> A needless Alexandrine ends the Song,
> That like a wounded Snake, drags its slow length along.

Robert Bridges employs what he calls "neo-Miltonics" or "loose alexandrines" for his long philosophical poem, *The Testament of Beauty* (1929):

> *What is beauty? saith my sufferings then.* — I answer
> the lover and poet in my loose alexandrines . . .

The Very Reverend William Ralph Inge (1860–1954), dean of Saint Paul's Cathedral in London, reputedly said that he hated "loose alexandrines" worse than loose living.

SEE ALSO *caesura, free verse, hexameter, meter, vers libre.*

allegory From the Greek word *allēgoria,* which comes from *állos* ("other") and *-ēgorein* ("to speak"): that is, "speaking otherwise." Isidore of Seville (d. 636) wrote, "Allegory is other-speech. One thing is spoken, another is meant." An allegory operates on two levels simultaneously. The narrative acts as an extended metaphor, with a primary or surface meaning that continually discloses a secondary or representational meaning. The two levels provide a parallel experience: one entertains; the other instructs.

Allegory is a postclassical idea. Plutarch noted in *Moralia* (ca. 100 C.E.) that what was called *allēgoria* in his time had been previously called *huponoia* ("under-meaning"). It was a thought or meaning that existed underneath the surface of a text. The sense of hidden meaning expanded into a full-fledged method of "speaking otherwise." The characters in an allegory are often personifications; that is, abstract ideas incarnated as persons. There is a one-to-one correspondence between what they are and what they mean. Think of the characters Death, Fellowship, Good-Deeds, and Beauty in the medieval morality play *Everyman,* or the characters Christian, Faithful, and Mr. Worldly Wiseman in John Bunyan's *Pilgrim's Progress* (1678). The characters of the great allegories go beyond merely representing their designated vices and virtues; they become them.

We are in the range of allegory whenever a writer explicitly indicates the relationship of the image to the precept. Northrop Frye writes, "A writer is being allegorical whenever it is clear that he is saying 'by this I *also* (*allos*) mean that.'" The hero of an allegory is a cipher or a designated figure for the reader, since it's understood that the action takes place in the mental landscape of the audience. Allegory, a distinctive form, treats the story as a means to an end and channels our affective responses. As William Empson explains in *The Structure of Complex Words* (1948), "Part of the function of an allegory is to make you feel that two levels of being correspond to each other in detail and indeed that there is some underlying reality, something in the nature of things, which makes this happen ... But the effect of allegory is to keep the two levels of being very distinct in your mind though they interpenetrate each other in so many details."

Allegory is a method of critical analysis as well as a literary model. Critics interpret works allegorically when they perceive coherent analogies behind living characters and abstract ideas (hence psychoanalytic criticism). In *The Well Wrought Urn* (1947), Cleanth Brooks allegorizes the poems he explicates insofar as they become "parables about the nature of poetry." Frye suggests in *Anatomy of Criticism* (1957) that all criticism is covert allegorizing.

SEE ALSO *metaphor, personification.*

alliteration The audible repetition of consonant sounds at the beginning of words or within words. Listen to the letter *m* and the letter *d* in Gerard

Manley Hopkins's ecstatic evocation of a kestrel in "The Windhover" (1877): "I caught this <u>m</u>orning <u>m</u>orning's <u>m</u>inion, king<u>d</u>om of <u>d</u>aylight's <u>d</u>auphin, <u>d</u>apple-<u>d</u>awn-<u>d</u>rawn Falcon . . ."

Alliteration is part of the sound stratum of poetry. It predates rhyme and takes us back to the oldest English and Celtic poetries. It is known as *Stabreim* in the ancient Germanic languages. Alliterative meter was the principal organizing device in Anglo-Saxon poetry and resounded through the fourteenth century, as in the opening line of *Piers Plowman*: "In a <u>s</u>omer <u>s</u>eason, whan <u>s</u>oft was the <u>s</u>onne . . ." The repetitive *s* here ties four words together and urges their interaction upon us. Alliteration can reinforce pre-existing meanings (summer season) and establish effective new ones (soft sun). A device of phonic echoes, of linked initial sounds, alliteration reverberates through most of the poetries of the world. It didn't predominate in later metrical verse, but it forms a rough current in the work of Sir Thomas Wyatt (1503–1542) and thereafter becomes a subterranean stream in English-language poetry. It comes bubbling to the surface in such modern Welsh poets as David Jones and Dylan Thomas.

SEE ALSO *assonance, consonance.*

allusion A passing or indirect reference to something implied but not stated. The writer refers to something recognizable — a historical or fictional character, a specific place, a particular event or series of events, a religious or mythological story, a literary or artistic work. Allusion may serve as a compact between writer and reader, a means of summoning a shared world or tradition, a way of packing a work with meaning. Thus Dante alludes throughout the *Inferno* (1304–9) to Virgil's *Aeneid* (29–19 B.C.E.), especially the sixth book, which charts Aeneas's descent into the underworld, even as Virgil alludes to Homer's *Odyssey* (ca. eighth century B.C.E.), especially book 11, in which Odysseus gathers the shades at the edges of the known world. Some contemporary readers consider allusion an elitist device, especially since so little shared literary knowledge now exists, and yet allusion provides a crucial way for poems to talk to each other and create meaning for us.

SEE ALSO *tradition.*

ambiguity An ambiguous word or sign is open to more than one explanation or interpretation. In rhetoric, ambiguity has been treated as a stylistic fault (the Latin *ambiguitas*) and a potential literary virtue. William Empson introduced this term to modern critical discourse in *Seven Types of Ambiguity* (1930). Empson defines ambiguity as "any verbal nuance, however slight, which gives room for alternative reactions to the same piece of language." Empson's consideration of ambiguity, which moves from the least ambiguous (double meanings) to the most ambiguous (contradictory meanings), suggests the linguistic plenitudes of verbal art. The division into exactly *seven* types of ambiguity now seems arbitrary, but Empson enlarged the reading of poetry by close verbal analysis and careful textual consideration of the multiple meanings of words and passages. Following Empson, the formalist New Critics treated ambiguity as one of the crucial features of poetry.

amoebean verses From the Greek: "responsive verses." These verses in dialogue are found primarily in pastoral poetry, especially in the work of Theocritus and Virgil. Here two speakers chant alternate lines, couplets, or stanzas. In Virgil's *Georgics* (book 3, ca. 29 B.C.E.), the shepherd Menalcus asks the shepherd Dametas, "Do you want us to try alternately to see what each of us is capable of?" The speakers try to match, debate, and outdo each other according to specified rules. Edmund Spenser imitated the form in *The Shepheardes Calender* (1579). Responsive verses were rooted in the singing competitions of local peasant communities. As the pastoral genre developed, these responsive verses were modeled not on oral verses but on literary texts. The literary pastoral created fictions about rural life that were eventually critiqued by poets writing counter-pastorals. Thus George Crabbe in *The Village* (1783):

> Fled are those times, when, in harmonious strains,
> The rustic poet praised his native plains:
> No shepherds now, in smooth alternate verse,
> The country's beauty or their nymphs' rehearse.

SEE ALSO *débat, georgic, pastoral, poetic contest.*

amphibrach From the Greek: "short at both ends." A classical metrical foot consisting of one long syllable enclosed by two short ones. The pronunciation of a word like *remember* approximates the effect; it is literally short at both ends. As Coleridge describes it in his poem "Metrical Feet" (ca. 1806), "One syllable long, with one short at each side, / Ămphĭbrăchўs hāstes with ă stātelў strīde; —."

SEE ALSO *cretic, foot, meter.*

Anacreontic Anacreon (ca. 570–485 B.C.E.) was a Greek lyric poet who lived in Teos, in Asia Minor. Mere fragments survive of his graceful, light-hearted poems, which deal with wine, women, and song. The *Carmina Anacreontea* (*Anacreontic Poems*) consists of sixty texts in the manner of Anacreon on the simple pleasures of life. They survive from an appendix to the tenth-century codex of *The Palatine Anthology.* Abraham Cowley brought the word into English when he called a section of his poems "anacreontiques" because they were paraphrased out of the work of Anacreon or his imitators (*Miscellanies,* 1656). They supposedly mimicked the Greek meter, which combined long (—) and short (u) syllables in the seven-syllable pattern u u — u — u —. Robert Herrick cultivated the Anacreontic and suggested that his mistress would bring him to Anacreon in the afterlife ("The Apparition of His Mistresse Calling Him to Elizium. Dezunt Nonulla —," 1648). In 1800, Thomas Moore published a collection of erotic Anacreontics (*Odes of Anacreon,* 1800) that try to catch "the careless facility with which Anacreon appears to have trifled." The Anacreontic now refers to any easygoing lyrical poem that mixes and serves wine with love.

anagram From the Greek: "transposition of letters." A word or phrase rearranged to form another word or phrase. Lying awake one November night in 1868, Lewis Carroll transposed "William Ewart Gladstone" into "Wilt tear down *all* images." He later came up with an even better one, "Wild agitator! Means well." The anagram is not a poetic form per se, but it can yield anagrammatic poems, such as David Shulman's sonnet "Washington Crossing the Delaware" (1936), in which every line is an anagram of the title. The Greek poet Lycophron (third century B.C.E.) was the first known practitioner of onomastic anagrams, or anagrams relating to names. Anagrams were a common literary amusement in the Latin Middle Ages, when it was discovered that the letters comprising the words of the Annunciation, "Ave Maria, gratia plena, Dominus tecum" ("Hail Mary, full of grace, the Lord is with you"), could be rearranged as "Virgo serena, pia, munda et immaculata" ("Virgin serene, holy, pure and immaculate"). George Puttenham tried to define the rules for the formation of anagrams in "Of the Anagrame, or Posy transposed" (*The Art of English Poesie*, 1589), and so did the Scottish poet William Drummond of Hawthornden in his essay "Character of a Perfect Anagram" (written ca. 1615, collected in 1711). The historian William Camden gathered many samples of anagrams in *Remains Concerning Britain* (1605). "Perhaps partly because of a continuing, post-Gutenberg fascination … with how words and letters looked in print, and how readily they could be rearranged into movable type," R. H. Winnick speculates, "English interest in onomastic anagrams, especially in court circles, reached a level of intensity by the late sixteenth century that would later surpass sonnet mania."

SEE ALSO *palindrome, pun.*

analogy A resemblance between two different things, frequently expressed as an extended simile. William Blake talks back to ecclesiastical authority with this analogy from "Proverbs of Hell" (1790–93): "As the caterpillar chooses the fairest leaves to lay her eggs on, so the priest lays his curse on the fairest joys." The reader participates in the making of an analogy, especially an extended analogy, by testing the proposition against experience. Try this one: Paul Valéry states that poetry is to prose as dancing is to walking. To what extent is that analogy true?

Analogies and metaphors are modes of relational thinking. An analogy works by suggesting similarity. A metaphor creates an identity between two different things. Some philosophers consider analogies and metaphors the same thing, with a grammatical difference, while others think of them as two different forms of reasoning. Analogical thinking is nonlinear, nonconsecutive, indirect. It is an extended associative process. Thomas Aquinas believed that the fact that God created the world points to a fundamental "analogy of being" between God and the world. Henry David Thoreau concluded, "All perception of truth is the detection of an analogy."

SEE ALSO *conceit, metaphor, simile.*

anapest A metrical foot consisting of three syllables, two unaccented followed by one accented, as in the phrase "ĭn ă wár." The anapest was originally a Greek martial rhythm and often creates a galloping sense of action, a catchy, headlong momentum, as in these lines from the beginning of Lord Byron's "The Destruction of Sennacherib" (1815):

> Thĕ Ăssýr | iăn căme dówn | lĭke thĕ wólf | ŏn thĕ fóld,
> Ănd hĭs có | hŏrts wĕre gléam | ĭng ĭn púr | plĕ ănd góld;
> Ănd thĕ shéen | ŏf thĕir spéars | wăs lĭke stárs | ŏn thĕ séa,
> Whĕn thĕ blúe | wăve rŏlls níght | lў ŏn déep | Gălĭlée.

My own anthology of eighteenth- and nineteenth-century anapestic poems in English would include Blake's "Ah! Sun-flower" (1794), Shelley's "The Cloud" (1820), Poe's "Annabel Lee" (1849), and Swinburne's "Before the Beginning of Years" (1865). The momentum of anapests has mostly been employed for comic or ironic effects in modern poetry, as in Thomas Hardy's "The Ruined Maid" (1901). David Rakoff used anapestic tetrameter, which trots along at four feet per line, for his posthumously published novel, *Love, Dishonor, Marry, Die, Cherish, Perish* (2013).

SEE ALSO *foot, meter.*

anaphora From the Greek: "a carrying up or back." Anaphora is the repetition of the same word or words at the beginning of a series of phrases, lines, or sentences. In the first century, Longinus treated anaphora as an imitative action and a key feature of the sublime. Thomas Wilson dubbed anaphora "the marcher" (*The Arte of Rhetorique,* 1585), and George Puttenham deemed it the "figure of report" (*The Arte of English Poesie,* 1589). Anaphora serves as an organizing poetic strategy for long lists or catalogs, as in the Hebrew Bible. The piling up of particulars is a joyous poetic activity, a way of naming and claiming the world. Open to almost any page of *Leaves of Grass* (1855) and you encounter Walt Whitman's anaphoric method, his ecstatic iterations. Take this excerpt from "A Broadway Pageant":

For I too raising my voice join the ranks of this pageant,
I am the chanter, I chant aloud over the pageant,
I chant the world on my Western sea,
I chant copious the islands beyond, thick as stars in the sky,
I chant the new empire grander than any before, as in a vision it comes to me,
I chant America the mistress, I chant a greater supremacy,
I chant projected a thousand blooming cities . . .

The key to anaphora is that each line is a repetition with a difference. Robert Alter calls it "a productive tension between sameness and difference, reiteration and development." Something is reiterated, something else added or subtracted. Our attention keeps shifting from the phrasing that is repeated to the phrasing that is freshly introduced. What recurs is changed. Anaphora is a self-conscious and repeated turn back to beginnings.

The counterpart of anaphora is epiphora, or epistrophe: the repetition of a word or phrase at the end of successive clauses, sentences, or lines. Whitman uses the epiphora "it shall be you" fourteen times in seventeen lines of a passage from "Song of Myself" (1855), which begins with "If I worship one thing more than another it shall be the spread of my own body, or any part of it," and concludes with this:

Sun so generous it shall be you!
Vapors lighting and shading my face it shall be you!
You sweaty brooks and dews it shall be you!
Winds whose soft-tickling genitals rub against me it shall be you!
Broad muscular fields, branches of live oak, loving lounger in my winding
     paths, it shall be you!
Hands I have taken, face I have kiss'd, mortal I have ever touch'd, it shall be you!

The repetition of the first words at the end of a sequence is called epanalepsis. Elizabeth Barrett Browning declares, "Say over again, and yet once over again, / That thou dost love me"; Robert Frost writes, in "The Gift Outright" (1941), "Possessing what we still were unpossessed by, / Possessed by what we now no more possessed."

SEE ALSO *catalog poem, parallelism, the sublime.*

anthology From the Greek: "collection of flowers." A collection of poetry or prose. The earliest compilation of Greek poems dates to the fourth century B.C.E. Sometime around 90 B.C.E. Meleager of Gadara collected a "bouquet" of short epigrams, which represented some fifty poets, from Archilochus (seventh century B.C.E.) to himself. In the tenth century, Constantinus Cephalas, a Byzantine Greek, drew on previous anthologies and put together *The Palatine Anthology,* also known as *The Greek Anthology,* the first major anthology of poems, one of the sourcebooks of lyric poetry.

antiphon A song, hymn, or poem in which two voices or choruses respond to each other in alternate verses or stanzas, as is common in verses written for religious services. Antiphonal poetry has the quality of call and response, of liturgy. In George Herbert's "Antiphon (I)" (1633), for example, the chorus begins:

> Let all the world in ev'ry corner sing,
> > *My God and King.*

The leader or minister calls back:

> The heav'ns are not too high,
> His praise may thither fly:
> The earth is not too low,
> His praises there may grow.

And the congregation responds:

> Let all the world in ev'ry corner sing,
> > *My God and King.*

antistrophe The middle section of a classical ode, following the strophe and preceding the epode. The structure of the classical ode is based on the odes of Pindar (early fifth century B.C.E.), who adapted this characteristic pattern from the songs chanted by the chorus in Greek drama. The chorus moved to the left during the strophe and to the right during the antistrophe.

SEE ALSO *epode, ode, strophe.*

antithesis, antithetical A rhetorical contrast or opposition between ideas, often enacted through parallel structure. Antithesis is one of the favorite strategies of biblical poetry, as in these wisdom proverbs: "When pride comes, then comes shame: but with the lowly is wisdom" (Proverbs 11:2) and "The Lord is far from the wicked: but he hears the prayer of the righteous" (15:29). Aristotle singled out antithesis as a pleasing device:

> When the style is . . . antithetical, in each of the two members . . . an opposite is balanced by an opposite, or two opposites are linked by the same word. For example . . . "By nature citizens, by law bereft of their city . . ." This kind of style is pleasing, because things are best known by opposition, and are all the better known when the opposites are put side by side; and is pleasing also because of its . . . logic — for the method of refutation is the juxtaposition of contrary conclusions. (*Rhetoric,* book 3, chap. 9, ca. 335–330 B.C.E.)

In *Paradise Lost* (1667), John Milton effectively contrasts Adam and Eve through the use of antithesis:

> For contemplation he and valour formed,
> For softness she and sweet attractive grace;
> He for God only, she for God in him.

In philosophy, antithesis is a second argument raised to oppose a first proposition, as in Hegel's dialectic of thesis, antithesis, and synthesis. Poetic contests are also founded on the debate principles of argument and counterargument.

SEE ALSO *parallelism, poetic contest, rhetoric.*

aoidos From the Greek: "singer" (plural *aoidoi*). The Greek *aoidos* was a singing poet, a professional bard who performed at court or traveled from town to town. Homer gives us the name Phemius ("man of fame"), the *aoidos* at Odysseus's palace in Ithaca, who sang the return of the Achaeans: "And the famous bard [*aoidos*] sang to them, and they sat quietly listening." Homer also tells of Demodocus ("received by the people"), a blind *aoidos* at the palace of Alcinous, who sang about the quarrel of Achilles and Odysseus. Homer declares they are "like gods in their *audê* [human voice]." He would most likely have considered himself an *aoidos.*

Aoidean poetry is sometimes used as a technical term for early Greek oral epic poetry, but the Homeric corpus consistently refers to epic poems as *aoidê*, "singing." Homer deemed poetry *thespis aoidê*, "divine song."

SEE ALSO *bard, epic, oral-formulaic method.*

apostrophe From the Greek: "to turn away." Apostrophe is a poetic mode of direct address. Quintilian, speaking of oratory in the first century, defines apostrophe as "a diversion of our words to address some person other than the judge." Unlike the ideal orator, the poet turns away from the audience to address one or more gods, the Muse, an absent person, the dead, a natural object, a thing, an imaginary quality or concept. One of the distinctive marks of poetry is that it can address anything. Geoffrey Chaucer playfully addresses his purse in "The Complaint of Chaucer to His Purse" (ca. 1399); Anne Bradstreet addresses a book she has written in "The Author to Her Book" (1678); John Donne speaks to the sun in "The Sun Rising" (1633). Think of the fervor with which William Blake cries out, "O Rose thou art sick" ("The Sick Rose," 1794) or the unhinged grief with which Alfred, Lord Tennyson, proclaims, "Ring out, wild bells" (*In Memoriam*, 1849). Apostrophe seems to take us back to the realm of magic ritual, to the archaic idea that the dead can be contacted and propitiated, the absent recalled, the inanimate and nonhuman formally humanized and invoked, called upon for help.

SEE ALSO *invocation.*

Arcadia, Arcady Arcadia is an isolated mountainous region of Greece in central Peloponnese. In the ancient world, the sparsely populated region was known for its rustic simplicity, which became associated with the traditional singing and pipe playing of herders, whose native god was Pan. It became famous throughout the ancient world as a utopian ideal of pastoral harmony and simplicity. Theocritus set his idylls (third century B.C.E.) in Arcadia. Virgil imagined Arcadia in his *Eclogues* (42–39 B.C.E.), where it bears a striking resemblance to northern Italy. Raymond Williams explains the transformation from the Arcadia of the Greek poet to the Arcadia of the Latin one in *The Country and the City* (1973):

The pastoral landscape of Theocritus had been immediate and close at hand just outside the city … A transformation occurs, in some parts of Virgil, in which the landscape becomes in fact more distant, becomes in fact Arcadia, and the Golden Age is seen as present there, at once summoned and celebrated by the power of poetry … It is only a short step from a natural delight in the fertility of the earth to this magical invocation of a land which needs no farming.

Virgil's *Eclogues* were widely imitated in the pastoral poetry of the Italian, French, Spanish, and English Renaissance, from the fourteenth to the seventeenth century. The landscape was the setting for Sir Philip Sidney's romance *Arcadia* (1580). The French painter Nicolas Poussin (1594–1665) employed the tradition in his painting of four shepherds, which is known as *The Arcadian Shepherds*. The art historian Erwin Panofsky wrote an influential essay on the inscription in Poussin's painting, ET IN ARCADIA EGO ("I too am in Arcadia"), showing that the statement was meant to be spoken by death itself, thus asserting the presence of mortality in the seemingly timeless pastoral world.

In 1690, a group of Italian poets named their association the Arcadian Academy. The members wrote pastoral poetry and often dressed in shepherds' costumes for their meetings. They sought "to exterminate bad taste and see to it that it shall not rise again," but bad taste survived, while the group produced little of lasting merit. The name Arcadia continues to be associated with an ideal place of rustic simplicity and tranquility.

SEE ALSO *eclogue, ecopoetry, idyll, nature poetry, pastoral.*

archaism A deliberately old or outdated use of language. To use an archaism is to resuscitate a word, an expression, or a form that has fallen out of use. Words are continually changing in meaning. Using an archaism is a way of holding on to or renewing something ancient, evoking an older style of speech and writing. In *Poetic Diction* (1928), Owen Barfield suggests that true archaism implies "not a standing still, but a *return* to something older."

In the history of poetry, one function of archaism was to maintain metrical regularity. The older form of a word sometimes has a different metrical weight. Thus poets continued to use the word *morn* for "morning" or treated the word *loved* as a two-syllable word. At a deeper level, older words have been used because of their associations with the past. Thus Edmund Spenser employs archaic words, "strange inkhorn terms," to evoke the age of chivalry in *The Faerie Queene* (1590–96). In turn, Spenser and other Elizabethan poets became a source of archaisms for the Romantic poets. In "The Rime of the Ancient Mariner" (1798) Samuel Taylor Coleridge uses archaic words to give the feeling that his work belongs to the past of the ballad poets:

> He holds him with his skinny hand,
> "There was a ship," quoth he.
> "Hold off! unhand me, grey-beard loon!"
> Eftsoons his hand dropt he.

Sir Walter Raleigh said that the language of poetry always has "a certain archaic flavor." Poetry looks backward but it also looks forward, and the archaizing impulse wars with the equally powerful impulse for poets to use common speech and naturalize poetic diction. The use of archaism is at odds with the modern impulse to, in Pound's phrase, "make it new," though Pound's own work is filled with archaisms. Sometimes poets make poetry new by reviving something old.

archetype An original pattern or model, a prototype. Carl Jung pioneered the idea of the archetype as a "primordial image," a common psychic form that structures human experience. In Jungian theory, the archetype is a universal theme or idea, a "psychic residue" found in dreams and myths, in poems and other works of art, in different religions and philosophies. Archetypes belong to the "collective unconscious" of all peoples. The "outcast," who has been thrown out of society, the "scapegoat," who gets blamed for everything, "the star-crossed lovers," who are destined for doom — all are common archetypal figures. The idea of the archetype, especially the fundamental concept of the quest, has been stimulating for many American poets — Theodore Roethke, Stanley Kunitz, Robert Bly, David Bottoms — who have tried to tap a primordial imagery for their poems. Literary critics adopted the Jungian notion of archetypes to consider permanently recurring symbols and patterns of action, images and character types, such as youthful heroes setting off to battle dragons and journey to other worlds.

ars poetica "Poetry is the subject of the poem," Wallace Stevens declares in "The Man with the Blue Guitar" (1937), and the ars poetica is a poem that takes the art of poetry as its explicit subject. It proposes an aesthetic. Self-referential, uniquely conscious of itself as both a performance and a treatise, the great ars poetica embodies what it is about.

Horace's *Ars poetica* is our first known poem on poetics and the fountain-head of the Western tradition. Horace introduces himself as both poet and critic in what was probably his final work (ca. 19–18 B.C.E.), a combination of the formal epistle and the technical treatise. Written when freedom was imperiled in Rome, it eloquently defends liberty. Horace speaks of art and ingenuity, of the poet's need to fuse unity and variety, to offer what is delightful (*dulce*) and useful (*utile*). He defends the value of artistic constraints and the necessity of artistic freedom, and he writes on behalf of both the writer and the reader, the poet and the audience: "it is not enough for poems to be beautifully crafted, let them be attractive and drive as they wish the audience's emotion . . . if you want me to weep, you must first yourself feel grief: only then will I share the pain of your disasters."

My anthology of the ars poetica would include Alexander Pope's "Essay on Criticism" (1711), the exemplary treatise of the Enlightenment; passages from William Wordsworth's *Prelude* (1805, 1850), which traces the growth of the poet's mind, and from Walt Whitman's "Song of Myself" (1855); Emily Dickinson's poem number 1129 ("Tell all the Truth but tell it slant —" ca. 1868); Wallace Stevens's "Of Modern Poetry" (1940); and Hugh Mac-Diarmid's "The Kind of Poetry I Want" (1961). It would take into account Marianne Moore's adversarial ars poetica "Poetry," first published in 1921 ("I, too, dislike it") and Czeslaw Milosz's conditional "*Ars Poetica?*" ("The purpose of poetry is to remind us / how difficult it is to remain just one person," 1968). The ars poetica, like the defense of poetry, becomes a necessary form when poetry is called into question and freedom is endangered.

assonance From the Latin word *assonare,* meaning "to answer with the same sound." The audible repetition of vowel sounds within words encountered near one another. Robert Latham defines assonance as the "resemblance of proximal vowel sounds." Listen to the interplay of vowels in these lines from "The Lotos-Eaters" (1833) by Alfred, Lord Tennyson:

And round about the keel with faces pale,
Dark faces pale against that rosy flame,
The mild-eyed melancholy Lotos-eaters came.

Notice the repetition of the letters *ou* in the words *round about;* the recurrence of the vowels *a* and *e* in "fac̲e̲s̲ pal̲e̲," which is repeated twice; how the soft *a* reverberates from the words *and* to *about* to *dark* to *against;* how the hard *a* is picked up again in the words *flame* and *came;* how the letter *o* moves as a hard sound from the word *rosy* to the first syllable of the word *Lotos* and as a soft sound from the word *melancholy* to the second syllable of the word *Lotos;* and how the letter *e* echoes from *mild-eyed* to *Lotos-eaters.* This is "vocalic rhyme."

John Keats was especially compelled by technical problems of assonance, of vowel music. "One of his favorite topics of discourse was the principle of melody in Verse," Benjamin Bailey remembered in 1849: "Keats's theory was, that the vowels should be so managed as not to clash one with another so as to mar the melody, — & yet that they should be interchanged, like differing notes of music." Keats's verbal tactics of repetition and variation, his subtle way of mixing long and short vowels, enabled him to fashion a sonorous music, and his vowels dilate the line into a numinous presence, creating a feeling both of intensity and spiritual easefulness.

Assonance preceded rhyme in the early verse of the Romance languages, Old French, Provençal, and Spanish, where it was a characteristic coordinating element. For example, each strophe, or *laisse,* closes with the same vowel sound in the epic *Chanson de Roland* (*The Song of Roland,* ca. 1090), the oldest surviving major work of French literature. As a binding element, assonance was later replaced by rhyme in European poetry. Nonetheless, poets have continued to experiment with assonance as an echo chamber within a poem. Assonance remains a key aural device, subtle and unsystematic, a form of internal vowel play that pleases the ear.

SEE ALSO *alliteration, consonance, rhyme.*

aubade A dawn song expressing the regret of parting lovers at daybreak. The earliest European examples date from the end of the twelfth century. The

Provençal, Spanish, and German equivalents are *alba, albada,* and *Tagelied.*
Some scholars believe the aubade, which has no fixed metrical form, grew
out of the cry of the medieval watchman, who announced from his tower the
passing of night and return of day. Ezra Pound renders the Provençal "Alba
Innominata" as "Ah God! Ah God! That dawn should come so soon!" In *The
Spirit of Romance* (1910), he points out that romance literature dawned with
a Provençal "Alba" from around the tenth century:

> Dawn appeareth upon the sea,
>> from behind the hill,
> The watch passeth, it shineth
>> clear amid the shadows.

The dawn song is found in nearly all early poetries; its poignancy crosses
cultures.

The aubade recalls the joy of two lovers joined together in original dark-
ness. It remembers the ecstasy of union. But it also describes a parting at dawn.
With that parting comes the dawning of individual consciousness; the sepa-
rated, day-lit mind bears the grief or burden of longing for what has been lost.
The characteristic aubade flows from the darkness of the hour before dawn
to the brightness of the hour afterward. It moves from silence to speech, from
the rapture of communion to the burden of isolation, and the poem itself be-
comes a conscious recognition of our separateness. This is evident in Shake-
speare's *Romeo and Juliet* (act 3, scene 5, 1597), which includes a debate about
whether the two lovers hear the song of a nocturnal bird or a morning one:

JULIET: Wilt thou be gone? it is not yet near day:
It was the nightingale and not the lark,
That pierc'd the fearful hollow of thine ear;
Nightly she sings on yon pomegranate tree:
Believe me, love, it was the nightingale.

ROMEO: It was the lark, the herald of the morn,
No nightingale: look, love, what envious streaks
Do lace the severing clouds in yonder east:
Night's candles are burnt out, and jocund day
Stands tiptoe on the misty mountain tops.

The aubade concludes with Romeo's heartfelt cry, "More light and light — more dark and dark our woes!" John Donne rebels against the convention of separation in his aubade "The Sun Rising" (1633), which begins by chiding the sun. There is no beloved at all in Philip Larkin's last poem, "Aubade" (1977), a terrifying spiritual confrontation with oblivion. The direction of the aubade is irreversible. It moves from the song of the nightingale to the song of the lark and thus flows into time.

automatic writing, automatism The Surrealist poets advocated writing automatically without any conscious control. The method was a kind of Freudian free association, and the goal was to free the unconscious from the constraints of the ego or conscious mind. Poetry would be liberated by trance-like states, startling images. André Breton and Philippe Soupault created the first automatic book, the novel *Les champs magnétique* (*The Magnetic Fields*, 1919). Breton equated automatic writing with "pure psychic automatism" in his first *Manifeste de surréalisme* (1924) and dreamed of magical dictation. Maurice Blanchot summarizes the breakthrough of automatic writing:

> Automatic writing tended to suppress constraints, suspend intermediaries, reject all mediation. It put the hand that writes in contact with something original; it made of this active hand a sovereign passivity, no longer a means of livelihood, an instrument, a servile tool, but an independent power, over which no one had authority any more, which belonged to no one and which could not, which knew not how to do anything — but write . . .

William Butler Yeats conducted experiments in automatic writing with his bride, Georgie Hyde-Lees, which eventuated in *A Vision* (1925). He described the experience: "On the afternoon of October 24th, 1917, four days after my marriage, my wife surprised me by attempting automatic writing. What came in disjointed sentences, in almost illegible writing, was so exciting, sometimes so profound, that I persuaded her to give an hour or two day after day to the unknown writer, and after some half-dozen such hours offered to spend what remained of life explaining and piecing together those scattered sentences. 'No,' was the answer, 'we have come to give you metaphors for poetry.'"

SEE ALSO *Surrealism.*

avant-garde *Avant-garde* literally means the "advance-guard," the most forward-facing troops. It dates back to the Middle Ages as a term of warfare. In the nineteenth century, it was aggressively imported from the military into the realm of art and literature to blur the distinction between art and life, to challenge the social order and "shock" the bourgeoisie. It suggests something new and advanced, a revolutionary vanguard. In 1845, Gabriel-Désiré Laverdant declared, in *De la mission de l'art et du rôle des artistes,* that

> art, the expression of society, manifests, in its highest soaring, the most advanced social tendencies: it is the forerunner and the revealer. Therefore, to know whether art worthily fulfills its proper mission as initiator, whether the artist is truly of the avant-garde, one must know where Humanity is going, what the destiny of the human race is . . .

There is a paradox in the cultural idea of the avant-garde, which borrows a military notion to express its nonconformism. Charles Baudelaire showed disdain for the "predilection of the French for military metaphors" (*My Heart Laid Bare,* 1887). A political vocabulary infiltrated avant-garde notions of culture in the nineteenth century, as when Stéphane Mallarmé told an interviewer in 1891 that the modern poet is "on strike against society." The avant-garde set out to destroy and invent. Matei Călinescu points out that Mikhail Bakunin's anarchist maxim — "To destroy is to create" — applies to most of the activities of the twentieth-century avant-garde.

During the first decades of the twentieth century, the concept of the avant-garde widened to include all the new antitraditional schools of art, music, and poetry (futurism, Cubism, etc.). Ever since, it has committed itself to rupture and change, to novelty. The avant-garde moved from modernism to postmodernism, and since the 1960s it has drawn its energy from a cross-pollination of genres, playfulness in style, a commitment to experimentation. But ever since the late 1950s, critics such as Roland Barthes have also been declaring the death of the avant-garde. "It was dying," Călinescu summarizes, "because it was recognized as artistically significant by the same class whose values it so drastically negated." In *Postscript to "The Name of the Rose"* (1984), Umberto Eco argues that the avant-garde hostility toward the past leads to silence:

The historic avant-garde ... tries to settle scores with the past. "Down with the moonlight" — a futurist slogan — is a platform typical of every avant-garde; you have only to replace "moonlight" with whatever noun is suitable. The avant-garde destroys, defaces the past: *Les Demoiselles d'Avignon* is a typical avant-garde act. Then the avant-garde goes further, destroys the figure, cancels it, arrives at the abstract, the informal, the white canvas, the slashed canvas, the charred canvas. In architecture and the visual arts, it will be the curtain wall, the building as stele, pure parallelepiped, minimal art; in literature, the destruction of the flow of discourse, the Burroughs-like collage; silence, the white page in music, the passage from atonality to absolute silence (in this sense, the early Cage is modern). But the moment comes when the avant-garde (the modern) can go no further.

SEE ALSO *Cubist poetry, Dadaism, modernism, postmodernism, Surrealism.*

B

ballad The traditional British ballad is a narrative song, a poem that tells a story, preserved and transmitted orally. It unfolds in four-line stanzas and customarily alternates four- and three-stress lines. The second and fourth lines rhyme. Here is the opening of "Earl Brand":

> Rise up, rise up, my seven brave sons,
> And dress in your armour so bright;
> Earl Douglas will hae Lady Margaret awa
> Before that it be light.

The word *ballad* derives from the Middle English *balade,* from the Old French *ballade,* from the Provençal *balada,* a dancing song. As the linguist Edward Sapir writes, "Poetry everywhere is inseparable in its origins from the singing voice and the measure of the dance." Over time, the ballad lost whatever connection it once may have had to dance, though Robert Graves believed that "when the word 'ballad' was adopted by English singers, though the association with dancing did not survive, there remained latent in it the sense of *rhythmic group action* whether in work or in play." Iceland is well known for its heroic ballads, the sagas, which were passed down orally for centuries. Once they were written down, their form was fixed and they were perceived as written poetry. The *rímur,* or sung ballads, were epic heroic songs. The English-language ballad originated in the fourteenth century — its most popular hero was Robin Hood. The most important collection is the Child ballads; it consists of 305 ballads from England and Scotland (and their American variants) collected by Francis James Child: *English and Scottish Popular Ballads* (1882–98). The European ballad developed out of an earlier epic tradition. Medieval epic songs were transformed into shorter dramatic songs, such as the *romance* (a poem in octosyllabic meter) in France, Portugal, and Spain, which in turn crossed the ocean and became the Mexican *cor-*

rido. Whereas epics were heroic songs sung by men, ballads were often sung by women and told different kinds of stories.

As a form of great antiquity, the ballad has been built up and scoured down by oral transmission to a work of eloquent simplicity. It often opens abruptly, focuses on a single crucial episode, and moves decisively toward a tragic conclusion. Dialogue carries the story and the narration is rapid, elliptical, and impersonal, though it retains vestiges of ritual participation. The individual singer serves as the deputy of a public voice. The high degree of repetition is mnemonic, the refrain a way of creating and discharging emotion.

The broadside ballad was a poem printed on a broadside, a single sheet of paper, and sold in the streets. It was popular during the eighteenth century. "I love a ballad in print," Shakespeare writes in *The Winter's Tale* (act 4, scene 4, 1623). The written literary ballad, which emerged at the end of the eighteenth century as a viable and widely practiced subgenre, echoes the spirit, and often the language and form, of the traditional folk ballad. Thomas Percy's *Reliques of Ancient English Poetry* (1765) and Sir Walter Scott's collection *The Minstrelsy of the Scottish Border* (1802–3) helped create the vogue. The ballad especially appealed to the Romantic poets because it is an authentically popular form practiced by ordinary people, because of its "medieval" subject matter and "Gothic" taste, because it calls up deep feeling in the audience. Whitman loved Scott's offering of old ballads precisely because it seemed to take him back to the primitive origins of all poetry and thus offered a bardic model for his own "barbaric yawp." The writer of literary ballads seeks to transcend isolation and express a primordial collective will. The ballad writer also tends to be in quest of an archaic way of knowing, and thus the form of the ballad becomes a way of attaining what Daniel Hoffman calls "barbarous knowledge."

SEE ALSO *broadside ballad, epic, folk song, incremental repetition, oral poetry, refrain, romance, Romanticism.*

ballade From the Old French: "dancing song." The most important of the fixed forms (*formes fixes*) of Old French poetry. A musical form, it consists of three eight-line stanzas with a strict rhyme scheme (*ababbcbc*) and a four-line envoi (*bcbc*). The last line repeats in all three stanzas as well as the envoi.

The entire poem turns on three rhymes, which build to the refrain. The lines are usually eight or ten syllables long. In English, the meter is customarily iambic tetrameter or pentameter. The envoi is a summary statement, traditionally an apostrophe to a head of state. Originally, this may have been the judge (the so-called prince) of a poetic competition. In these competitions, the host would often supply the first line and the poets would improvise from there. There are fifteen surviving poems, for example, that begin with the line that François Villon used so powerfully, "I die of thirst beside the fountain" ("Je meurs de soif auprès de la fontaine").

The ballade rose to prominence in the fourteenth and fifteenth centuries when it was popularized by troubadour poets (Guillaume de Machaut, Eustace Deschamps, Christine de Pisan, Charles d'Orléans), but reached its zenith in sixteenth-century France. Villon mastered the form in such works as "Ballade des pendus" ("Ballade of the Hanged," published 1489) and "Ballade des dames du temps jadis" ("Ballade of Dead Ladies," 1450), with its sorrowful refrain, translated by Dante Gabriel Rossetti as "But where are the snows of yester-year?"

In Germany, the ballade was a narrative poem or song, akin to the folk ballad, which flourished in the last quarter of the eighteenth and the first half of the nineteenth century. The French ballade was imported into English poetry by both John Gower (ca. 1325–1408), whose surviving ballades are written in French, and Geoffrey Chaucer — for example, "The Complaint of Chaucer to His Purse" (ca. 1399). The form had a vogue in late nineteenth-century England when it caught on with Austin Dobson, W. E. Henley, Alfred Noyes, and especially Algernon Charles Swinburne and Dante Gabriel Rossetti, both of whom translated Villon.

There are some variations on the original ballade formula. The ballade supreme consists of three ten-line stanzas that rhyme (*ababbccdcd*), with an envoi of five lines that rhyme (*ccdcd*). It turns on four rhymes. The refrain repeats as the last line of each stanza and of the envoi. The double ballade and the double ballade supreme have six stanzas of eight and ten lines, respectively, and follow the rhyme schemes of the ballade and the ballade supreme. The hutain, sometimes called the Monk's Tale stanza, is a complete poem composed of a single ballade stanza (*ababbcbc*). One form of the dizain is a complete poem composed of a single ballade supreme stanza (*ababbccdcd*).

The ballade is now mostly a form of light verse, as in Dorothy Parker's "Ballade at Thirty-Five" (1924) and "Ballade of Unfortunate Mammals" (1931).

SEE ALSO *chant royal, formes fixes, meter, Monk's Tale stanza, octave.*

bard The word *bard* originally referred to the ancient Celtic order of minstrel-poets who composed verses celebrating the laws and heroic achievement of the people, of chiefs and warriors. The bards carried necessary cultural information and underwent rigorous technical training. Ted Hughes noted that "tradition dwells on the paranormal, clairvoyant, somewhat magical powers of the Bards." The professional literary caste of the bardic order in Ireland lasted from the thirteenth to the seventeenth century. It was serious business to become a poet and the training period could extend for as long as twelve years. In *The Book of Irish Verse* (1998), John Montague says that one way of describing the training is as "seven winters in a dark room," and quotes an early eighteenth-century memoir:

> Concerning the poetical Seminary or School ... it was open only to such as were descended of Poets and reputed within their Tribes ... The Structure was a snug, low Hut, and beds in it at convenient Distances, each within a small Apartment ... No windows to let in the Day, nor any Light at all us'd but that of Candles, and these brought in at a proper Season only ... The reason of laying the Study aforesaid in the Dark was doubtless to avoid the Distraction which Light and the variety of Objects represented thereby commonly occasions.

The poets who came through this strict regimen were technical virtuosos. Some of their most poignant poems mourn the passing of their order. Some songs in the Irish language are a legacy of the bardic tradition, especially the repertoire of *sean nós* ("old style"). As Emerson writes in "The Poet" (1844), "The ancient British bards had for the title of their order, 'Those who are free throughout the world.' They are free, and they make free." In "Merlin I" (1846), he declares, "Great is the art, / Great be the manners, of the bard."

The bardic poet in ancient Greece was called an *aoidos*: "And the famous bard [*aoidos*] sang to them, and they sat quietly listening," Homer states in the *Odyssey* (ca. eighth century B.C.E.). Medieval bards in Wales were frequently composers and not performers. They employed a harpist and a *datgeiniad*, who declaimed the bard's words. Since the eighteenth century, the term *bard* has often been used as a synonym for *poet*. One legacy of the Celtic bardic order is to preserve language, another to embody imaginative freedom. The creative use of technical poetic skill and wide literary and cultural knowledge makes for our greater freedom. The poet offers us thought schooled by intuition, emotion deeper than thought, and soulfulness deeper than emotion. Such archaic ways of knowing go all the way down to the roots of being.

SEE ALSO *aoidos, fili.*

baroque Probably from the Portuguese word *barroco*, a jeweler's term for a rough, irregular pearl imported from Goa to Portugal in the sixteenth century. In the eighteenth century, the French started using the word *baroque* as an adjective meaning "bizarre" or "odd." The term was first used in a pejorative sense to describe the art and architecture of the preceding era; their exuberance and superabundant ornamentation were perceived as bad taste in the eighteenth century. The baroque was contrasted with the sober clarity and classicism of the Renaissance. In the nineteenth century, the art historian Heinrich Wölfflin rehabilitated the term to describe any art that has become fully elaborated. In 1934, Erwin Panofsky argued that the Baroque era was not the end of the Renaissance, but "the beginning of a fourth era, which may be called 'Modern' with a capital M."

The term *baroque* refers both to an antinaturalistic style and to a period in art, architecture, music, and literature. The baroque style is eccentric, excessive, extravagant, and lavishly ornate. The Baroque era in the visual arts refers to a European style of art and architecture that developed in the seventeenth century. The Baroque era in music refers to the period roughly from 1600 to 1750. In poetry, the term is often used to refer to the elaborate poetic styles of the early seventeenth century, especially Gongorism, which derives from the work of the Spanish poet Luis de Góngora, and Marinism, which derives from the work of the Italian poet Giovanni Battista Marini. The mannerisms of the English metaphysical poets are often considered baroque.

The baroque style is colorful, decorative, and flamboyant. In *A Universal History of Infamy* (1935), Jorge Luis Borges defines it as "that style which deliberately exhausts (or tries to exhaust) all its possibilities and which borders on its own parody."

SEE ALSO *metaphysical poets.*

beat The main rhythmic pulse in metrical verse. Sometimes called *ictus* (the Latin word for "beat"), sometimes stress, it is also referred to as dynamic, intensive, or expiratory. It is a way of keeping time. The oldest meaning of the word *beat* is "to strike repeatedly," and thus it carries the vestiges of repeated physical action.

SEE ALSO *meter.*

blank verse Unrhymed (hence "blank") iambic pentameter. The five-beat, ten-syllable line was established in English over the fourteenth through sixteenth centuries, its emergence coterminous with the rise of Renaissance humanism. Blank verse was initially employed by Henry Howard, Earl of Surrey, in his translation (ca. 1594) of Virgil's *Aeneid.* Christopher Marlowe (1564–1593) was the first English poet and playwright to explore the full potential of blank verse. The English dramatists used blank verse to move fluently between normal conversation and high rhetoric, and it became the standard form of drama in the era of Elizabeth I and James I. Many of the speeches in William Shakespeare's plays are written in blank verse, as in this famous soliloquy from *Macbeth* (1611):

> Tomorrow, and tomorrow, and tomorrow,
> Creeps in this petty pace from day to day,
> To the last syllable of recorded time;
> And all our yesterdays have lighted fools
> The way to dusty death. Out, out, brief candle!
> Life's but a walking shadow, a poor player
> That struts and frets his hour upon the stage
> And then is heard no more: it is a tale
> Told by an idiot, full of sound and fury,
> Signifying nothing.

John Milton used blank verse in *Paradise Lost* (1667) to liberate poetry from the "troublesome and modern bondage of rhyming," thus establishing it as the pattern with the greatest equilibrium in English. Such eighteenth-century poets as James Thomson (*The Seasons*, 1730) and William Cowper (*The Task*, 1785) took up the mantle of Miltonic blank verse. Samuel Taylor Coleridge's "conversation poems" ("The Aeolian Harp," 1795; "Frost at Midnight," 1798) introduced the short blank-verse poem into English. William Wordsworth, Percy Bysshe Shelley, John Keats, and Alfred, Lord Tennyson, all wrote major poems in blank verse. The American Romantics Hart Crane and Wallace Stevens are also notable for their use of the noble blank-verse line.

It has been estimated that three-fourths of all English poetry until the twentieth century is written in blank verse, which suggests that blank verse is the modal pattern in English, the one closest to natural speech, and therefore, as Allen Grossman puts it in "Summa Lyrica" (1992), "the form speech takes when it depicts the speech of persons in social situations." Blank verse has most often been used — from Shakespeare's plays to Robert Frost's dramatic monologues — to evoke the spoken word, to create a speaker in a dramatic situation.

SEE ALSO *conversation poem, decasyllable, dramatic monologue, iambic pentameter, meter, rhyme.*

blazon, blason From the French: a heraldic term meaning "coat of arms." In literature, a blazon is a catalog, traditionally written by a man, of his beloved's physical features or attributes. The convention dates to the thirteenth century. The blazon relies on a series of comparisons, usually drawn from nature, that tend to come from a stock of images in the biblical Song of Songs. Petrarch made the blazon a prominent part of his *Rime sparse* (*Scattered Rhymes*, 1374) and it thus became central to the Petrarchan tradition. Elizabethan lyricists especially liked to detail a mistress's physical beauty. Spenser provides an example in *Epithalamion* (1595):

> Her goodly eyes like sapphires shining bright,
> Her forehead ivory white,
> Her cheeks like apples which the sun hath rudded,
> Her lips like cherries charming men to bite,
> Her breasts like to a bowl of cream uncrudded,
> Her paps like lilies budded,
> Her snowy neck like to a marble tower,
> And all her body like a palace fair . . .

Ernst Robert Curtius uses the term *recipes* for medieval codes prescribing head-to-toe descriptions of the body. Mikhail Bakhtin speaks of the "dual fact, complete ambivalence, and contradictory fullness" of the blazon. Clément Marot launched a literary fashion with his erotic "Blazon du beau tétin" ("Blazon of the Beautiful Breast," 1536), which inaugurated the vogue for "anatomical blazons" (*blasons anatomiques*), descriptive poems in praise of the parts of the female body. John Davies of Hereford's poem "Some blaze the precious beauties of their loves" critiques those who write blazons for their hyperbolic comparisons, and then proceeds to praise his beloved with a sense of wordless wonder (*Wit's Pilgrimage*, 1605). The convention inevitably became clichéd and thus led to parody, the contreblazon (antiblazon). Robert Greene mocks the traditional blazon in *Menaphon* (1589):

> Thy teeth like to the tusks of fattest swine,
> Thy speech is like the thunder in the air:
> Would God thy toes, thy lips, and all were mine.

SEE ALSO *catalog poem, conceit, Petrarchism.*

blues A secular form of African American folk song. Sung solo, the blues often express a deep stoic grief and despair, a dark mood of lamentation, but also a wry and ribald humor, a homemade political philosophy, a proverbial wisdom. Within the African American community, the blues have traditionally been contrasted to spirituals, and thus likened to devil's music. "You can bury my body down by the highway side / So my old evil spirit can catch a Greyhound bus, and ride," Robert Johnson sings in "Me and the Devil Blues." The color blue was associated with the devil as early as the sixteenth century, hence the expression "blue devils."

The blues were first arranged, scored, and published early in the twentieth century, but have their roots in much earlier work songs, field hollers, group seculars, and sacred harmonies. The blues have retained a flexible style and structure, but classically tend toward a twelve-bar, three-line stanza with an *aab* rhyme pattern: a couplet stretched to three lines. The first line establishes the premise and scene; the second repeats (sometimes with slight variations) and hammers it in. This allows the singer to emphasize and modify the first line while improvising the next one. The third line punches, develops, or turns the premise. Each line is an intact entity, each stanza a complete unit.

> I'm goin' to the river, take my rockin' chair,
> Goin' to the river, take my rockin' chair,
> If the blues overcome me, I'll rock on away from here.

The trick to singing the blues is to flatten the third, fifth, and seventh notes of the major scale, thus creating the "blue notes." Here is a durable vocal art, a living tradition, a foundational form, a shaping influence on American music, such as jazz and rock-and-roll. The blues have also been a major influence on African American written poetry from Langston Hughes and Sterling Brown to Michael S. Harper and Yusef Komunyakaa.

SEE ALSO *spirituals, work song.*

bob and wheel A metrical device of five short, rhyming, tightly metrical lines found mainly in Middle Scots and Middle English poetry, most notably in *Sir Gawain and the Green Knight* (late fourteenth century). The bob is a short line, usually only two syllables long, and the wheel is a set of four slightly longer lines at the end of a stanza. Each one of the 101 stanzas of uneven length in *Sir Gawain and the Green Knight* ends with a bob and wheel. The bob serves as a bridge from the alliterated to the rhyming lines; the wheel concludes the stanza with four three-stress lines; the rhyme scheme is *ababa*. Here is the first instance:

> wyth wynne,
> Where werre and wrake and wonder
> Bi sythes has wont therinne,
> And oft bothe blysse and blunder
> Full skete has skyfted synne.

broadside ballad The eighteenth century popularized the broadside ballad, a ballad printed on a single sheet of paper (broadside) and sold in the streets. It may have developed as early as the fifteenth century. It thrived as a popular form of doggerel until the rise of the daily newspaper in the 1860s. Folk songs were sometimes written as broadsides, broadsides sometimes refashioned into folk songs. John Skelton's "A Ballade of the Scottysshe Kynge"

(1513) may be the earliest printed broadside. Skelton mercilessly mocks the Scottish king, James IV, for his challenge to the English king, Henry VIII. Purists have frequently denigrated broadside ballads, preferring ballads created anonymously and transmitted orally. Francis James Child expressed this point of view in an appendix to *The English and Scottish Popular Ballads:*

> The vulgar ballads of our day, the "broadsides" which were printed in such large numbers in England and elsewhere in the sixteenth century or later . . . are products of a low kind of *art,* and most of them are, from a literary point of view, thoroughly despicable and worthless.

Despite these negative connotations, the broadside ballad was a popular form of street poetry, a metrical form of journalism, in its topical vulgarity a forerunner of the tabloid.

SEE ALSO *ballad, doggerel, folk song.*

burden, burthen The common name for the refrain or chorus of a song until the seventeenth century, the burden carries a repetitive power, reinforcing a theme and feeling. Shakespeare plays on the meaning of *burden* in one of Ariel's songs in *The Tempest* (ca. 1611): "Foot it featly here and there, / And, sweet sprites, the burden bear." Songs and ballads with refrains were themselves sometimes called burdens. A burden can also be the leading idea or principal feeling of a poem or song.

SEE ALSO *refrain.*

burlesque From the Italian word *burlesco,* which comes from *burla,* meaning "ridicule" or "joke." A burlesque is a satirical imitation, an exaggerated send-up of a literary work. "The rhapsodists who strolled from town to town to chant the poems of Homer," Isaac D'Israeli writes in *Curiosities of Literature* (1823), "were immediately followed by another set of strollers — buffoons who made the audiences merry by the burlesque turn which they gave to the solemn strains."

Samuel Johnson said, "Burlesque consists in a disproportion between the style and the sentiments, or, between the adventitious sentiments and the fundamental subject." Burlesque most commonly applies to drama and other stage entertainment, as in the play of Pyramus and Thisbe that Bottom and his friends perform in Shakespeare's *Midsummer Night's Dream* (ca. 1595), which sends up earlier dramatic interludes, or *The Beggar's Opera* (1728), John Gay's satirical take on Italian opera. In 1648, the French dramatist Paul Scarron wrote a burlesque in verse titled *Virgile travestie*. Nicolas Boileau-Despréaux burlesqued the classical epic in *Le lutrin* (*The Lectern*, 1674) — the mock epic is a burlesque form — and John Dryden made fun of the animal fable in *The Hind and the Panther* (1687). The burlesque sonnet was a rich comic take on the sonnet form.

SEE ALSO *Hudibrastic verse, mock epic, parody, satire.*

C

cacophony Jarring, discordant sound. The opposite of euphony, cacophony is generally associated with harsh consonants, rather than with vowels. The discordant sounds of poetry are often marshaled from Anglo-Saxon and other alliterative Germanic verses for special effect, as when Lord Byron writes of "Bombs, drums, guns, bastions, batteries, bayonets, bullets, — / Hard words, which stick in the soft Muses' gullets" (*Don Juan*, 1819– 24).

SEE ALSO *dissonance, euphony.*

cadence (1) Balanced, rhythmic flow; (2) the measure or beat of movement; or (3) the general inflection or modulation of the voice, especially a falling inflection, as at the end of a sentence. The term *cadence* describes the rhythmic movement of non-metrical poetry, of free verse, biblical poetry, highly charged prose. In "A Retrospect" (1918), Ezra Pound exhorted his contemporaries to write by the musical cadence: "As regarding rhythm: to compose in the sequence of the musical phrase, not in sequence of a metronome." F. S. Flint characterized free verse in 1920 as "unrimed cadence" and spoke of "the natural cadence of our emotion."

SEE ALSO *free verse, measure, rhymed prose, rhythm.*

caesura From the Latin word *caedere,* meaning "to cut." A pause in the poetic line. The caesura comes at the end of a unit of sense and is signaled either by a comma or a period. It is marked in scansion by a double vertical line (||). For example, there is a caesura after the semicolon in the first line and after the comma in the second line of this sonnet by William Wordsworth (ca. 1802): "The world is too much with us; || late and soon, / Getting and spending, || we lay waste our powers."

SEE ALSO *meter.*

calligrammes, see *concrete poetry.*

canon A standard body of writings, a group of creative works that have been deemed authoritative. The word *canon* derives from a Greek word that meant either a measuring rod or a list. The first meaning was the basis for the idea of a model, a standard employed as a rule or principle. This was applied to the idea of "canon law" (ecclesiastical law). The second meaning forms the basis for the Roman Catholic concept of canonization, the practice of adding an individual to a "list" of saints. The idea of a definitive canon was developed in the fourth century in relationship to the Hebrew Bible and the New Testament. It was a way of safeguarding a tradition. The biblical canon, which was formed over the centuries, comprised the books that the Christian church considered Holy Scripture. Books related to the scriptural canon that were not officially recognized in this way became known as the Apocrypha ("hidden books"). A reading of the Bible that emphasizes the unity of the biblical texts tends to be called a canonical interpretation. By contrast, a historical interpretation suggests that the different books of the Bible were authored by different writers working under different circumstances in different times.

In late sixteenth-century England, the idea of canon was applied to secular writings. In "The Canonization" (1633), for example, John Donne expresses the hope of being canonized, thus achieving a fame comparable to that of the Catholic saints, but of a secular nature. In his tract *Polimanteia* (1595), William Covell advocated canonizing literary works under the auspices of English universities. Critics later began to employ the idea of a canon in reference to the definitive works attributed to a given author, as in "the Shakespeare canon." Works outside that established canon were considered apocryphal.

The word *canon* is now most frequently used as a collective term for the totality of the most esteemed works in a culture. A church canon is determined by an institutional authority. A secular literary canon is more amorphous, less official. Literary canons determine which writers are "major" and "minor," what works are "classics." Often perceived as static, canons are always in flux, under revision. New works force us to reconsider old ones. Since the 1970s, literary theorists have drawn attention to canon formation, the social processes that determine how certain authors and not others become recognized as standard. Pressure to revise and open up the canon continues.

SEE ALSO *tradition.*

cante fable   The cante fable, a narrative form common in folktales, tells a story partly in song. The term was coined in the only extant medieval (twelfth or thirteenth century) European cante fable, *Aucassin and Nicolette,* which contains the line "Our cante fable is coming to a close." The distinguishing feature of the cante fable is the juxtaposition between the spoken sections, which set the scene and explain the story, and the lyrical song sections, usually in dialogue, which are emotionally charged and often contain magical statements, animal calls, riddles, the sayings of poets. The cante fable is a hybrid form. Verse is embedded in *One Thousand and One Nights* and the *Panchatantra* (third century B.C.E.), in early Celtic literature and old Scandinavian sagas, in classic fairy tales. Listen to a traditional English ballad sung by descendants of Africans in the West Indies, or, for that matter, in the southern United States, and you'll most likely hear a cante fable form. In the early 1960s, the folklorist Roger Abrahams found a profusion of cante fables in an African American neighborhood in west Philadelphia (*Deep Down in the Jungle,* 1964).

SEE ALSO *folk song, narrative poetry.*

canto   From the Latin: "song." One of the major divisions of a long poem. The cantos of a narrative or epic poem are like the chapters of a novel, except more lyrical. The division into separate cantos gave bards and minstrels the chance to structure a performance, to mark units within a longer work, and to rest between sections. Both oral and written poets use the canto to time a plot, to linger over individual sections, and to examine particular themes within an overarching structure. Dante's decision to divide his *Commedia* (*The Divine Comedy,* ca. 1304–21) into one hundred cantos, instead of breaking it into long books as Virgil does in the *Aeneid* (29–19 B.C.E.), suggests commitment to a new lyricism, a vernacular epic. Ariosto, Tasso, Pope, and Byron all divided their work into cantos. Ezra Pound spent much of his life working on his modernist epic, *The Cantos* (1915–69).

canzone From the Italian: "song" (plural *canzoni*). The term *canzone* suggests both art and popular music. A *canzoniere* is a maker of songs and/ or a singer of songs. The canzone also refers to various kinds of medieval Provençal and Italian lyric poems, usually on the subject of love. Petrarch established the canzone as a form comprising five- or six-line stanzas and a concluding envoi (half-stanza). In *De vulgari eloquentia* (*Concerning Vernacular Eloquence,* ca. 1302–5), Dante called the canzone "the self-contained action of one who writes harmonious words to be set to music." He considered it the most perfect species of lyric. He composed a maddeningly difficult form of the canzone modeled on the Provençal *chanso* — a poem that uses the same five end-words in each of the five twelve-line stanzas, intricately varying the pattern. There is also a five-line envoi (a *tornada*) that uses all five of the words. It operates with mathematical precision.

Stanza one: 1, 2, 1, 1, 3, 1, 1, 4, 4, 1, 5, 5
Stanza two: 5, 1, 5, 5, 2, 5, 5, 3, 3, 5, 4, 4
Stanza three: 4, 5, 4, 4, 1, 4, 4, 2, 2, 4, 3, 3
Stanza four: 3, 4, 3, 3, 5, 3, 3, 1, 1, 3, 2, 2
Stanza five: 2, 3, 2, 2, 4, 2, 2, 5, 5, 2, 1, 1
Envoi: 1, 2, 3, 4, 5

Dante knew that his rigorous philosophical poems could be challenging and relied on beauty to make them enchanting. Here he concludes the first canzone of the *Convivio* by radically addressing his own poem, which Shelley translates in *Epipsychidion* (1821):

My song, I fear that thou wilt find but few
 Who fitly shall conceive thy reasoning
  Of such hard matter dost thou entertain.
 Whence, if my misadventure chance should bring
Thee to base company, as chance may do,
  Quite unaware of what thou dost contain,

> I prithee comfort thy sweet self again,
> My last delight; tell them that they are dull,
> And bid them own that thou art beautiful.

The Dantescan form of the canzone has been keenly employed by W. H. Auden, L. E. Sissman, James Merrill, Anthony Hecht, and Marilyn Hacker. John Hollander explains two versions of the traditional canzone by enacting them in his handbook, *Rhyme's Reason* (1981). Ezra Pound titled his fifth book of poems *Canzoni* (1911).

SEE ALSO *chanso, chanson, sestina, song, songbook.*

canzonet, canzonetta From the Italian: "a little song." The English composer Thomas Morley adopted this term to title his first collection of works in the madrigal style: *Canzonets, or Little Short Songs in Three Voyces* (1593). Another Renaissance usage of this term was to denote short and light songlike poems, such as Michael Drayton's "To His Coy Love: A Canzonet" (1619), which concludes with these lines:

> Clip me no more in those dear arms,
>   Nor thy life's comfort call me;
> O these are but too powerful charms,
>   And do but more enthrall me.
> But see how patient I am grown,
>   In all this coil about thee;
> Come, nice thing, let my heart alone;
>   I cannot live without thee.

Both Shakespeare and Ben Jonson employed the term to mean a ditty. Oscar Wilde penned a canzonet in 1888, and the American poet A. Bronson Alcott affected an Italian manner in *Sonnets and Canzonets* (1882). In the 1940s, Umberto Saba boasted about his twelve canzonettas: "Saba's *Canzonettas* are to common canzonettas what a Chopin waltz or a Bach gavotte was to the waltzes and gavottes that couples used to dance to."

SEE ALSO *ditty, madrigal.*

carmen The Latin word *carmen,* which means "song" or "lyric" (plural *carmina,* as in Catullus's *Carmina,* first century B.C.E.), has attracted

English-language poets because of its closeness to the word *charm*. It is ety-mologically connected to *canere* ("sing"). In older Latin texts it also means a magic formula, an incantation to make things happen. Horace uses it in the *Odes* (23–13 B.C.E.) to suggest divine inspiration, the song of the poet as an instrument of the Muse.

SEE ALSO *charm, incantation, muse.*

carmen figuratum, see *pattern poetry.*

carol   A lighthearted religious song. The etymology of the word *carol* traces back to choric music, to a circle dance accompanied by singers. Originally a folk song, the carol seems to have traveled to England from France during the Middle Ages. It was apparently an ancient church practice to sing carols, but medieval clerics sought to curtail their use in religious celebrations, most likely because of their association with earlier pagan rites and their often erotic lyrics. The medieval carol had a more or less fixed form. The metrical style reflected its close connection with dance. But as that association faded, so did the carol's formal strictures. Since the sixteenth century, the word *carol* has come to mean any festive religious song. It follows secular rather than re-ligious musical traditions. It is now mostly sung at Christmas in honor of the birth of Christ (in this sense it is akin to the French *Noël* and the German *Weihnachtslied*). Some examples: "Joy to the World" (1719), the seventeenth-century "I Saw Three Ships (Come Sailing In)," the Old English "Seven Joys of Mary," and "The Twelve Days of Christmas" (1780). John Milton, Henry Vaughan, George Herbert, Robert Southwell, and Ben Jonson all contrib-uted to the carol genre. Though they aren't actually sung, many poems by Romantic and modern poets borrow motifs from the traditional carol. Some examples: Samuel Taylor Coleridge ("A Christmas Carol," 1799), C. Day Lewis ("A Carol," 1935), R. S. Thomas ("Carol," 1985), Donald Hall ("A Carol," 1987–90), W. S. Merwin ("Carol of the Three Kings," 1952), and Joseph Brodsky ("A Martial Law Carol," 1983).

SEE ALSO *folk song, song.*

carpe diem   From the Latin: "seize the day." The notion of carpe diem is a recurring motif in poetry. Horace employs the motto in his *Odes* (23–13

B.C.E.), but the idea has been present in poetry from its inception. It is found in ancient Egyptian poetry (in what are called "harper's songs" — mortuary poems inscribed on tombs) and Persian poetry (by Omar Khayyám, 1048– 1131). The idea that we are going to die is at the heart of lyric poetry, and carpe diem encapsulates an epicurean response to the ephemeral nature of life with an injunction: make the most of time, take seriously the pleasures of life. Religious poetry in general and Christian poetry in particular often appropriate the carpe diem theme to contrast the temporality of human life on earth with the eternal nature of the divine.

Carpe diem has often been associated with sexuality, especially a fruitless chastity. An underlying cynicism toward the motif is detectable from Catullus (84–54 B.C.E.) to the English Cavalier poets. Thus Andrew Marvell, "Had we but World enough, and Time, / This coyness, lady, were no crime" ("To His Coy Mistress," ca. 1650s), and Robert Herrick, "Gather ye Rosebuds while ye may, / Old time is still aflying: / And this same flower that smiles today / To morrow will be dying" ("To the Virgins, to Make Much of Time," 1648). Billy Collins playfully captures the spirit of the motif in his poem "Carpe Diem" (2008): "I knew this was one morning I was born to seize."

catalog poem, catalog verse   A list, or catalog poem, takes inventory of people, places, things, or ideas. Writing started with the making of practical lists around 3200 B.C.E. in ancient Mesopotamia. "The list is, perhaps, the most archaic and pervasive of genres," Jonathan Z. Smith explains. This ancient device, a structure of parallelism, is found in literatures around the world. One thinks of the genealogical lists in oral and written poetry, such as Genesis 10. "The Catalogue of Ships" in book 2 of the *Iliad* (ca. eighth century B.C.E.) served as a model for innumerable poetic catalogs to follow. Poets such as Christopher Smart and Walt Whitman give the catalog an incantatory quality and often use it to praise the diversity and unity of the universe. It thus becomes a form of praise poem. Randall Jarrell describes the pages of ecstatic listing in *Leaves of Grass* as "little systems as beautifully and astonishingly ordered as the rings and satellites of Saturn." The greatest catalogs in poetry instill a sense of wonder.

SEE ALSO *anaphora, blazon, incantation, litany, parallelism, praise poems.*

cento From the Latin: "patchwork" (plural *centos, centones*). A type of pastiche, the cento is a poetic composition that consists entirely of lines or passages from other poems. Centos have been composed since at least the first century and may have begun as school exercises. Later they became occasional pieces, sometimes humorous and off-color. They were also used to create Christian narratives out of pagan texts, as in the *Cento virgilianus* of Proba (fourth century). Homer (eighth century B.C.E.) was the most popular source of the Greek cento and Virgil (90–19 B.C.E.) of the Latin one. Two contemporary examples: John Ashbery's "The Dong with the Luminous Nose" (1998), which takes its title from an Edward Lear poem (ca. 1876), and Peter Gizzi's "Ode: Salute to the New York School" (2012), which works both as homage and bibliography.

SEE ALSO *collage.*

chain rhyme, chain verse A type of verse that interlinks lines or stanzas through rhyme or repetition, as in Dante's terza rima (*aba bcb cdc*) or Robert Frost's interlocking rubaiyat, "Stopping by Woods on a Snowy Evening" (1923), which takes the unrhymed line in one stanza (*aaba*) and rhymes it with three lines in the next stanza (*bbcb*). These rhyme schemes and verse forms create a chain that connects the stanzas, like the rooms of a house.

SEE ALSO *rhyme, rhyme scheme, rubaiyat stanza, terza rima, villanelle.*

chanso, canso A love song. The *chanso* became the premier genre of Provençal poetry (the other main branch was the sirventes, or satire). It has been estimated that the *chanso* accounts for about one thousand poems, some 40 percent of the troubadour canon. The theme of the *chanso* was the troubadour ideal of courtly love. The typical structure consisted of four or five symmetrical stanzas and an envoi, or *tornada.* Each troubadour tried to mark the form with his own stanzaic structure and tune. The *chanso* was the model for the Italian *canzone. Vers* was the older term for *chanso,* though it was used loosely and designated poems on almost any subject.

The *retroencha* essentially seems to have been a *chanso* or love song with a refrain at the end of each stanza, often with a satirical twist. Only a few examples of this form survive; it apparently did not have a rigidly fixed structure.

Jay Wright employs the *retroencha* in "The Hieroglyph of Irrational Space" (2000).

SEE ALSO *canzone, courtly love, troubadour.*

chanson   Ever since the Middle Ages, the French term for *song* has been used to refer to a wide variety of poetry and music, including the medieval epic songs (chansons de geste), the early story songs (*chansons d'histoire*), and the repertoires of the Provençal troubadours and the French trouvères. The troubadour Guillaume de Machaut (ca. 1300–1377), a great composer-poet, set the course for the French secular polyphonic songs of the fourteenth and fifteenth centuries.

SEE ALSO *chanso, chansons de geste, song, troubadour, trouvère.*

chansons de geste   The term for the more than eighty Old French epic poems, "songs of heroic deeds," that date from the twelfth to the fifteenth century. The word *geste* carries an additional meaning of "history" or "historical document," suggesting that these poems were also songs of lineage. A large number of the chansons de geste, which were performed by jongleurs, revolve around the deeds of Charlemagne, who is accompanied by his Twelve Noble Peers and celebrated as the champion of Christendom. These legends are known as "the matter of France." The greatest chanson de geste is *La chanson de Roland* (*The Song of Roland,* ca. 1090). A group of twenty-four poems center on Guillaume d'Orange. The tales about Roland and Oliver circulated widely and culminated in two Renaissance epics: Matteo Bolardo's *Orlando inamorato* (ca. 1478–86) and Ludovico Ariosto's *Orlando furioso* (1516).

SEE ALSO *epic, jongleur, laisse.*

chant   From the Latin word *cantare,* meaning "to sing." The term *chant* may refer to any song or melody; it may denote the particular melody to which a psalm or canticle is sung; it may refer to the actual psalm or canticle itself; it may suggest any religious recitative with a refrain. The Gregorian plainsong (*cantus firmus*) is the most influential form of religious chant. The chant may be part of special rites, as in the Navajo *yerbichai* ("night chants").

   Chanting also refers to a way of reciting a poem, giving it liturgical emphasis that is something between speaking and singing. William Hazlitt wrote,

"There is a *chaunt* in the recitation both of Coleridge and Wordsworth, which acts as a spell upon the hearer and disarms the judgment." Chanting is a stylized mode of recitation that subordinates the musical element to the verbal one. It gives verse an oracular quality. One thinks of the many oral epic poets who composed and chanted their poems aloud: the Greek rhapsodists and Celtic bards, the Old English scops and Scandinavian skalds, the French trouvères and jongleurs. There are still *guslari* ("minstrels") in Bosnia, Serbia, and Macedonia who chant heroic poems aloud.

SEE ALSO *bard, jongleur, rhapsode, rune, scop, skald, troubadour, trouvère.*

chant royal A rich and difficult Old French verse form, the chant royal is a sixty-line poem. It is similar to, but even more demanding than, the ballade. The chant royal typically consists of five stanzas of eleven lines, each rhyming *ababccddede,* and a five-line envoi rhyming *ddede.* The last line of the first stanza repeats as a refrain at the end of each succeeding stanza, including the envoi. Sixty lines rhyme on five sounds. This regal form was mostly used for elevated subjects, though it was probably considered "royal" because it was addressed to the "prince" who presided over a *puy,* a poetic contest.

The chant royal was first mentioned by Nicole de Margival around 1300. In his poem "Story of the Panther" he narrates a dream experienced by a lover who speaks in the first person. When the lover wakes up, he reports that he composed a series of poems in six types, including the chant royal. The form flourished in the fourteenth century. Some of those who excelled at it were Guillaume de Machaut (ca. 1300–1377), Eustache Deschamps (1340–1406), Christine de Pisan (1364–ca. 1431), Charles d'Orléans (1394–1465), and Jean Marot (1457–1526). It was briefly revived in the nineteenth century by Théodore de Banville (1823–1891) and others. Paul Valéry claimed that "compared with the chant royal, the sonnet is child's play."

SEE ALSO *ballade, poetic contest.*

charm A spell or incantation (a word, a phrase, a verse, a song) spoken or sung to invoke and control supernatural powers. Charms are among the earliest forms of recorded written literature. They carry the resonance of magic rites in archaic cultures. The Old English charms (against wens, against the theft of cattle, for taking a swarm of bees, for a land remedy) stand as some of the first written works in our language. A charm, such as *abracadabra,* which was used throughout the Middle Ages, gave the individual a feeling of protection through contact with higher powers. Charms can be used for positive or negative ends, to ward off the spirit of evil or invoke it, to destroy an enemy or attract a beloved, to enchant objects, to ensure good luck with supra-normal power. Here is the beginning of a charmed and charming poem by Thomas Campion:

> Thrice tosse these Oaken ashes in the ayre,
> Thrice sit thou mute in this inchanted chayre;
> Then thrice three times tye up this true loves knot,
> And murmur soft; shee will, or shee will not.

SEE ALSO *incantation, spell.*

Chaucerian stanza, see *rhyme royal.*

chivalric romance   A major type of medieval romance. From the twelfth century onward, there were literary works, usually in verse, that described the adventures of legendary knights and celebrated an idealized code of behavior. As children, many of us read watered-down versions of the Arthurian romances that recount the adventures of Lancelot, Galahad, Gawain, and other knights of the Round Table. Chrétien de Troyes's *Lancelot* (late twelfth century), the anonymous *Sir Gawain and the Green Knight* (late fourteenth century), Sir Thomas Malory's *Le morte d'Arthur* (1484), and Edmund Spenser's *Faerie Queene* (1590–96) are all chivalric romances.

SEE ALSO *courtly love.*

choriamb, choriambus   A Greek metrical foot in which two long syllables enclose two short ones. This has been converted in accentual-syllabic or qualitative verse into a foot in which two stressed syllables enclose two unstressed ones. A choriamb unites one trochee and one iamb into a single four-syllable metrical unit (/ u u /). "Few of us who burst out with 'Son of a bitch!' realize they have just given utterance to a classic choriamb," John Frederick Nims notes in a piece on "maverick meters." Sappho was fond of choriambic meters, as in her poem about a woman of little culture (number 55), which Horace adapted to deride superstitions five hundred years later. The choriamb was frequently employed in Latin poetry. It is somewhat herky-jerky in English and rarely used, though Swinburne experimented with it in "Choriambics" (1878), which he modeled on Catullus. Each line consists of one trochee, three choriambs, and one iamb. It begins, "Lóve, whăt | aíled thĕe tŏ léave | lífe thăt wăs máde | lóvely, wĕ thóught, | wĭth lóve? —"

SEE ALSO *Aeolic, foot, iamb, meter, trochee.*

cinquain From the French: "a grouping of five." It is also called a quintet and refers to any five-line stanza or poem in five lines. Adelaide Crapsey developed a special form of five-line syllabic poem that was published in her posthumous book *Verse* (1915). It consists of twenty-two syllables: a two-syllable line followed by a four, a six, an eight, and ending with a two. It is akin to the five-line Japanese tanka. Here is "November Night":

> Listen ...
> With faint dry sound,
> Like steps of passing ghosts,
> The leaves, frost-crisp'd, break from the trees
> And fall.

There is something asymmetrical in the five-line stanza; the imbalance often enacts a feeling of something beyond reason, an out-of-kilter comedy, as in the limerick, or a deeper solemnity of feeling, as in Philip Larkin's "Home Is So Sad" (1964).

SEE ALSO *limerick, quintet, tanka.*

classic, classical, classicism   Matthew Arnold argues in *The Study of Poetry* (1888) that "the true and right meaning of the word *classic, classical*" is that the work of art "belongs to the class of the very best." The classic work is the standard-bearer, worthy of imitation, fit to be studied for generations. The word *classicus* originated as a Roman tax term for a member of the highest income bracket. It was distinguished from *proletarius,* a wage-earner below the taxable minimum. The scholars of Alexandria invented the classic status of early Greek literature, a system inherited by the Romans. In literary study, the term *classical,* which appeared in English criticism around the mid-eighteenth century, came to refer to ancient Greek and Roman writing. The word *classicism* designated later writing influenced by the ancient models. T. S. Eliot notes in "What Is a Classic?" (1945) that a true classic can be determined "only by hindsight and in historical perspective." Frank Kermode adds that "the doctrine of classic as model or criterion entails, in some form, the assumption that the ancient can be more or less immediately relevant and available, in a sense contemporaneous with the modern."

Classicism in poetry represents a belief in order, in reason and rule. It emphasizes clarity, proportion, and restrained feeling. The classically minded poet looks forward by looking backward and building on the traditions of ancient Greece and Rome. Jacques Barzun characterizes classicism as "stability within known limits." In the eighteenth century, a new or revived classicism — a return to first principles — became a fundamental neoclassicism. Robert Herrick proposes a neoclassical attitude when he writes, in "Rules for Our Reach" (1648), "Men must have Bounds how farre to walk; for we / Are made farre worse, by lawless liberty." The classically minded artist is committed to objectivity and impersonality. As Heinrich Wölfflin pointed out, "The word 'classic' has a somewhat chilly sound."

SEE ALSO *neoclassicism, Romanticism.*

clerihew   The British detective writer Edmund Clerihew Bentley (1875–1976) invented this form of comic poetry. It consists of a skewed quatrain — two rhyming couplets (*aabb*) of unequal length that whimsically encapsulate a person's biography. The form spoofs metrical smoothness. There is usually something ludicrous in the deadpan send-up of a famous person, whose name appears as one of the rhymed words in the first couplet:

> Geoffrey Chaucer
> Could hardly have been coarser,
> But this never harmed the sales
> Of his *Canterbury Tales.*

G. K. Chesterton (1874–1936) and W. H. Auden (1907–1973) were devotees of the clerihew.

SEE ALSO *light verse, limerick.*

cliché A trite, stereotyped expression or idea. In his *Dictionary of Clichés* (1940), Eric Partridge characterizes clichés as phrases that have become hackneyed, outworn, and tattered, though, as Christopher Ricks points out, "what, as a metaphor, could be more hackneyed than *hackneyed,* more outworn than *outworn,* more tattered than *tattered*?" Alexander Pope takes aim at the stereotypical phrases of eighteenth-century poets in "An Essay on Criticism" (1711):

> Wher'er you find "the cooling western breeze,"
> In the next line it "whispers through the trees";
> If crystal streams "with pleasing murmurs creep,"
> The reader's threatened (not in vain) with "sleep."

Clichés deaden and abuse language. Yet the cliché, often banished by literary arbiters, also has creative uses. Marshall McLuhan takes the contrarian position that a cliché presents an opportunity, for it is, as he puts it in *From Cliché to Archetype* (1970), "an active, probing, structuring feature of our awareness. It performs multiple functions from release of emotion to retrieval of other clichés from both the conscious and unconscious life." In *Structure & Surprise* (2007), Michael Theune identifies a "Cliché-and-Critique Structure" in poems that "strategically incorporate clichés to make their meanings." Such poems as Walt Whitman's "Death's Valley" (1892) and John Ashbery's "And *Ut Pictura Poesis* Is Her Name" (1987) begin with a cliché, which they then critique.

climax The apex, the moment when a crisis reaches its greatest peak of intensity, which is then resolved. A climax can appear in any form of narrative—a poem, a play, a story.

closet drama A dramatic work, usually written in verse, that is not intended for theatrical performance. It is meant to be read in one of two ways: experienced by a solitary reader or read aloud in a group. The tradition of closet drama reaches its peak in Milton's *Samson Agonistes* (1671) and Goethe's *Faust* (1808–32), in Byron's *Manfred* (1817), Shelley's *The Cenci* (1819) and *Prometheus Unbound* (1820), Browning's *Pippa Passes* (1841), and Hardy's *The Dynasts* (1904–8). James Merrill reinvented the genre in his trilogy, *The Changing Light at Sandover* (1976–82). Richard Howard's *Two-Part Inventions* (1974) takes the dramatic monologue in the direction of the closet drama, though these five highly performative pieces for reading, especially "Wildflowers," a dialogue between Oscar Wilde and Walt Whitman, are a long way out of the closet.

SEE ALSO *drama*.

collage From the French word *coller,* meaning "to glue." The first meaning of *collage* is an artistic composition made of various materials glued onto a surface. As an assembly of different forms, the collage made a dramatic entry into modern art early in the twentieth century. In 1912, Georges Braque and Pablo Picasso started making paper collages according to the principles of Cubism. The subversive and creative strategy spread to other modernist movements — the futurists used collage to create works of dynamic speed, the Surrealists to make unconscious connections — and to the other arts as well. Here's the principle: you don't just make art, you find it. A literary collage is a creative work that incorporates various materials or elements; it puts together disparate scenes in rapid succession without transitions.

Works such as Ezra Pound's *Cantos* (1915–69) and T. S. Eliot's "Waste Land" (1922) are based on principles of collage, which David Antin defines as "the dramatic juxtaposition of disparate materials without commitment to explicit syntactical relations between elements." Many poets and critics have argued that the collage technique was the most crucial innovation in twentieth-century art.

SEE ALSO *cento, Cubist poetry, found poem, fragment, futurism, Surrealism.*

comedy "Comedy has been particularly unpropitious to definers," Samuel Johnson cautioned in 1755, and no single definition can encompass the wide scope of what is considered comic. Comedy and tragedy are the two most common kinds of drama. The term *comedy* derives from the Greek word *komos,* "a processional celebration," which suggests that comedies date back to festivals of revelry. The primal archaic drive of comedy is the power of renewal. The first recorded performance of a comedy took place in March 486 B.C.E. in the Theater of Dionysus, an open-air structure located on the southern slope of the Acropolis in Athens. Five comic poets competed in the five-day festival City Dionysia. Thus, as George Meredith puts it, "comedy rolled in shouting under the divine protection of the Son of the Wine-jar, as Dionysius is made to proclaim himself by Aristophanes."

Historically, in Greek drama, comedies were stage plays with happy endings. Comedies end well, whereas tragedies end badly. Aristotle argues in the *Poetics* (350 B.C.E.) that, whereas tragedy presents "noble actions" of "noble personages," comedy presents "actions of the ignoble." Comedy was initially devoted to "invective" or to "the ridiculous," which Aristotle calls "a species of the ugly," that is, "a mistake or deformity not productive of pain or harm to others." Both tragedy and comedy originated in "improvisations," he says, but tragedy derives from "dithyrambs" and comedy from "phallic songs." There was always an element of the low mimetic in comedy.

Old Comedy was essentially topical satire directed against individuals. Aristophanes (ca. 450–ca. 388 B.C.E.) embodies the spirit when he skewers Socrates (ca. 470–399 B.C.E.) as the worst kind of sophist in *The Clouds* (423 B.C.E.) and makes fun of his rival tragic playwrights, Sophocles (ca. 496–406 B.C.E.), Aeschylus (525–456 B.C.E.), and Euripides (ca. 480–406 B.C.E.) in *The Frogs* (405 B.C.E.). The New Comedy of Menander (342–291 B.C.E.) ridiculed types of characters rather than well-known figures. It treated human foibles by mocking ordinary people. This comedy of manners became the model for Roman playwrights, such as Terence and Plautus (both second century B.C.E.), who in turn transmitted a typical structure to Renaissance playwrights, including Shakespeare (1564–1616). In the medieval era, comedy expanded beyond drama to include any narrative that ends positively, as in Dante's *Commedia* (*The Divine Comedy*, ca. 1304–21). In Christian literature, comedy is enacted as a theme of salvation. The Renaissance brought the term *comedy* back to the theater, but without a connotation of satire.

The Italian *commedia dell'arte* ("comedy of art" or "comedy of the profession") was a type of unwritten drama, a form of improvised "sketches," that flourished in the sixteenth and seventeenth centuries. Performed by traveling players, it gave us stock characters, such as Pierrot the sad clown and Harlequin the sly servant, that have had a strong afterlife in poetry and other genres.

The *commedia erudita* was the written comic drama of the Italian Renaissance.

The comedy of manners was the dominant form of Restoration comedy (1660–1700). It depicted the manners, customs, and outlook of a particular society. Often satirical, it sent up the fashionable members of a social set, as in William Congreve's *Way of the World* (1700).

The comedy of humours was a form of drama inspired by the theory of "humours." The humours were believed to be the fluids that regulated the body and thus the human temperament. There were four main ones: blood, phlegm, black bile, and yellow bile. In the comedy of humours, each character embodied a particular humour and what it represented, as in Ben Jonson's *Every Man in His Humour* (1598). It was a satirical mode. Molière, the leading comic dramatist of seventeenth-century France, writes, "I am telling you that I now abandon you to your poor constitution, to the intemperance of your bowels, to the corruption of your blood, to the bitterness of your bile and to the starchiness of your humours" (*Le malade imaginaire [The Imaginary Invalid]*, act 3, scene 5, 1673).

Comedy, especially satirical comedy, is generally more topical than tragedy. It tends to exploit a local situation. William Hazlitt suggested that the satirical impulse in comedy inevitably dissipated itself: "Comedy naturally wears itself out — destroys the very food on which it lives; and by constantly and successfully exposing the follies and weaknesses of mankind to ridicule, in the end leaves itself nothing worth laughing at." Yet comedies too can reach beyond the local moment, as in Samuel Beckett's *Waiting for Godot* (1952). Over the centuries, comic absurdity has increasingly taken over some of the subject matter of tragedy.

Comedy is a form of playfulness. The comedy of errors was a type of play heavily dependent on coincidences, as in Shakespeare's early comedies, such as *The Comedy of Errors* (1592–94), which drew on two Latin farces by Plautus (ca. 254–184 B.C.E.). Kenneth Burke follows Nietzsche and argues that comedy takes a humane attitude toward existence. In *Attitudes Toward History* (1937), he defends comedy by saying that "the progress of humane enlightenment can go no further than in picturing people not as vicious, but as mistaken. When you add that people are necessarily mistaken, that *all* people are exposed to situations in which they must act as fools, that *every* insight contains its own special kind of blindness, you complete the comic circle." Comedy becomes a mode of enlightened thinking concentrated on human folly.

SEE ALSO *satire, tragedy, tragicomedy.*

common measure, common meter, see *ballad, hymn.*

complaint　The complaint goes against Robert Frost's dictum of "grief without grievance." It is a plaintive poem, which defines itself by its grievance, often wistful, sorrowful, or sad. In the history of poetry, the complaint has frequently operated as a poem to an inconstant or unresponsive mistress, as in the Earl of Surrey's "A Complaint by Night of the Lover Not Beloved" (1557). The medieval love-complaint turned into a staple of Renaissance love poetry. The pastoral complaint, a popular Elizabethan genre, stressed the dangers of ambition and the virtues of the simple life. The Elizabethans often referred to epistolary poems of love or complaint as elegies, as in Christopher Marlowe's translation of Ovid's *Amores* (16 B.C.E.), which he called *Ovid's Elegies* (1594–95).

There are poetic complaints that mourn the general state of the world as well as pointed political complaints, such as the Scottish poet David Lyndsay's "The Dreme" (1528), an allegorical lament on the misgovernment of Scotland, which includes an epistle to the king, "Complaynt to the King" (1529), and "Complaynt of Our Soverane Lordis Papyngo" (1530), a bird poem that is by turns mournful, exhortatory, satirical. Thomas Sackville's "Complaint of Henry, Duke of Buckingham" (1563) attributes the duke's misery to his ruthless ambition. There are lighthearted complaints, such as Chaucer's "Complaint of Chaucer to His Purse" (ca. 1399), but at times the complaint is indistinguishable from the lament, as in "Deor's Lament" (ninth or tenth century), the complaint of a scop fallen from favor. Thomas Percy included the song "The Complaint of Conscience" in *Reliques of Ancient English Poetry* (1765). There will be complaints as long as the poet has a conscience and the world is flawed.

SEE ALSO *elegy, pastoral, Petrarchism, scop.*

computer poetry　Poets started experimenting with computers in the 1950s, the decade when the computer revolution began. Poets first used computer programs to synthesize databases. They fed the computer a series of instructions, which established a work's shape and content. "Labeled by its authors as 'Computer Poetry' and 'computer-poems' (among other terms)," C. T. Funkhouser explains, "these works are generated by computer algorithm, arranged as a sequence of words, or signs and symbols according to a programming code":

> All works of text generation, or archetypal computer poetry, can be seen as performing some type of permutation in that they transform or reorder one set of base texts or language (word lists, syllables, or pre-existing texts) into another form … I measure the permutation procedures of algorithmically generated poems into three classifications. Works are either permutational (recombining elements into new words or variations), combinatoric (using limited, preset word lists in controlled or random combinations), or slotted into syntactic templates (also combinatoric but within grammatical frames to create an image of "sense").

Charles O. Hartman lays out the basics of programming and poetry in *Virtual Muse: Experiments in Computer Poetry* (1996).

conceit From the Italian word *concetto,* "conception." An elaborate figure of speech comparing two extremely dissimilar things. A good conceit discovers or creates a surprisingly apt parallel between two otherwise unlikely things or feelings. It is an arresting mental action that draws attention to the artificial process of figuration. "Shall I compare thee to a summer's day?" Shakespeare asks in a sonnet that goes on to develop and extend the analogy. The process invites the reader to participate in the making of the analogy, playfully developing and extending it.

The Petrarchan conceit, borrowed from Italian poetry, compares the beloved to a rose, the sun, a statue, a summer day. Shakespeare employs these conceits even as he satirizes them in the first eight lines of "Sonnet 130" (1609):

> My mistress' eyes are nothing like the sun;
> Coral is far more red than her lips' red;
> If snow be white, why then her breasts are dun;
> If hairs be wires, black wires grow on her head.

I have seen roses damasked, red and white,
But no such roses see I in her cheeks,
And in some perfumes is there more delight
Than in the breath that from my mistress reeks.

T. S. Eliot defined the metaphysical conceit as the elaboration "of a figure of speech to the furthest stage to which ingenuity can carry it." Since its ingenious employment by the English metaphysical poets, the conceit has often been associated with poems about erotic love or the most intense spiritual or sensual experiences.

SEE ALSO *analogy, metaphor, metaphysical poets, simile.*

concrete poetry   A poem of visual display, a form of spatial prosody. Each concrete poem presents itself in a different physical shape — a lyric typed out to look like a typewriter, the word *SHRINK* printed in letters that gradually decrease in size, and so forth. All written poems have a spatial dimension, but the concrete poem foregrounds the visual configuration and pushes the pictorial boundaries of poetry.

The term *concrete poetry* was coined in the 1950s, but the desire to bring together literary and visual impulses into a shaped poem is ancient. There are poems in the shape of objects, such as a shepherd's pipe or a pair of wings, which date to the Hellenistic era (third to second century B.C.E.) in Greece. Guillaume Apollinaire's *calligrammes* are a lively avant-garde manifestation of what was once known as *technopaignia,* or pattern poetry, verses arranged in distinctive shapes on the page. The pioneers of the 1950s international movement were the Bolivian-born Eugen Gomringer, who initially called his poems "constellations" (the visual poem is a "constellation" in space), and three Brazilian poets, Haroldo de Campos, Augusto de Campos, and Décio Pignatari, who formed the avant-garde group Noigrandes. The concrete poetry movement, launched at the National Exhibition of Concrete Art in São Paulo in 1956, was international in scope. In 1965 the German concrete poet Max Bense said, "Concrete poetry does not separate languages; it unites them, it combines them."

Anyone interested in environmental poetry should wander through Little Sparta, Ian Hamilton Finlay's five-acre garden near Edinburgh, where his poems are inscribed on stones. Mary Ellen Scott suggests that "the pure concrete poem extracts from language an essential meaning structure and arranges it in space as an ideogram or a constellation — as a structural word design — within which there are reticulations or play-activity." The most powerful concrete poems still follow the example of Renaissance figure poems, in which the words are arranged to form a design on the page that mimics or enacts the subject.

SEE ALSO *pattern poetry.*

confessional poetry   Reviewing Robert Lowell's book *Life Studies* in 1959, M. L. Rosenthal claimed that the poems invoked "the most naked kind of confession." Rosenthal considered the word *confessional* appropriate "because of the way Lowell brought his private humiliations, sufferings, and psychological problems" into his poems, which were thus "one culmination of the Romantic and modern tendency to place the literal Self more and more at the center."

The controversial term *confessional poetry* applies most appropriately to Lowell and a group of three younger poets associated with him: W. D. Snodgrass (*Heart's Needle,* 1959), Anne Sexton (*To Bedlam and Part Way Back,* 1960, and *All My Pretty Ones,* 1962), and Sylvia Plath (*Ariel,* 1965). These poets reacted against the New Critical focus on impersonality, which fetishized technique, as well as the modernist separation between, in T. S. Eliot's words, "the man who suffers and the mind which creates." They collapsed the distinction between the persona and the writer so that readers felt they were getting "the real Robert Lowell" or "the real Sylvia Plath," an enabling fiction. These poets, along with Theodore Roethke (1908–1963), John Berryman (1914–1972), and Randall Jarrell (1914–1965), introduced a raw sensibility and a broken subjectivity into their poems.

The narrow definition of "confessional poetry" equates poetry too closely with psychological trauma and defines it too restrictively as a way of writing about such illicit subjects as sexual guilt, alcoholism, and mental illness. There is a more honorific sense of confession, which goes back as far as *The Book of the Dead* and other ancient Egyptian literary texts. It can be traced to autobiographical writing from Saint Augustine (354–430) to Jean-Jacques

Rousseau (1712–1778). Confessional writers in the autobiographical vein declare, disclose, and defend the individual self as a representative figure, who writes not just about the inner self but also about the outer world. Thus in the 1860s Charles Baudelaire exposes "Mon coeur mis à nu" ("My Heart Laid Bare") in a book that was meant to gather all his rage, but which he never completed.

SEE ALSO *impersonality.*

congé A farewell poem. There are two distinct types of medieval French goodbye poems. One type, the *congé d'amour* (the troubadour *conjat*), was a consolation poem about the separation of lovers. The poet takes reluctant leave of his lady, a cruel or withholding mistress. The military *congé d'amour* was written on the occasion of departing for military service. Giving a miniature image of oneself as a pledge of love played a part in these poems.

The second type of farewell poem, the *congés d'Arras,* consists of three poems by trouvères in the city of Arras in the thirteenth century. Jean Bodel (d. 1210) and Baude Fastoul (d. 1272), both forced into exile because of leprosy, wrote their fellow citizens a poem "to ask for permission to leave." Bodel's congé said goodbye to forty-two friends in forty-two stanzas. Ironically, one of the friends was Fastoul, who would later write his own leave-taking poem from the same hospice. Adam de la Halle (ca. 1237–1288), who left Arras by choice, turned the lyric congé into a satirical genre.

connotation, see *denotation.*

consolations The Latin *consolatio* (plural *consolationes*) was a work spoken or written to expound religious or philosophical themes as comfort and aid amid the misfortunes of life. The *consolatio* literary tradition encompasses poems, speeches, personal letters, and essays. Crantor of Soli (ca. 325–ca. 375 B.C.E.) inaugurated the genre, which became famous in Latin through Cicero's now lost treatise consoling himself on the death of his daughter Tullia in 45 B.C.E. Seneca (ca. 4 B.C.E.–65 C.E.) wrote three consolatory works, which characterize his Stoic teachings. Plutarch's *Consolatio ad uxorem* (*Consolation to His Wife,* early 90s C.E.) is a letter that he wrote to his wife when he received news of the death of their two-year-old daughter. Boethius's treatise *The Consolation of Philosophy* (ca. 524), in which philosophy consoles the author for his misfortunes, claims a strong connection with the *consolatio*.

The Oxford Classical Dictionary summarizes the typically recurring arguments, or topoi, that characterize the consolation genre: "All are born mortal; death brings release from the miseries of life; time heals all griefs; future ills should be prepared for; the deceased was only 'lent' — be grateful for having possessed him. Normally grief is regarded as natural and legitimate, though not to be indulged in." One *consolatio* in verse form that has survived is the *Consolatio ad Liviam* (ca. 9 B.C.E.), a lament on the death of Drusus, which was once attributed to Ovid but now considered the work of an anonymous poet working in the Ovidian vein.

consonance The audible repetition of consonant sounds in words encountered near each other whose vowel sounds are different. Thus W. H. Auden presses the consonants from "rider to reader" and from "farer to fearer" and from "hearer to horror" in the last stanza of his 1930s poem "'O where are you going?'" Consonance is seldom a structuring device in poetry. Rather, it is a strategic way of enforcing relation. It has an echo effect. Consonance overlaps with alliteration. Whereas alliteration repeats the first letter of a word, consonance repeats sounds within a word. Listen to the letters *f* and *l* woven through these lines from Wilfred Owen's World War I poem "Insensibility" (posthumously published in 1920):

> The front line withers,
> But they are troops who fade, not flowers
> For poets' tearful fooling:
> Men, gaps for filling:
> Losses, who might have fought
> Longer; but no one bothers.

SEE ALSO *alliteration, assonance.*

convention An implicit agreement between a writer and a reader, or a speaker and an audience; an accepted device, procedure, principle, or form. "What we mean by a 'convention' in art ranges from an accepted distortion of reality, as when a character speaks in meter, to an expected system of feeling," David Perkins writes in *A History of Modern Poetry* (1987). Art is a form of play, and to accept a convention is to accept the rules of a game. What would be madness in life can be playfully serious and seriously comic in poetry. Samuel Johnson explains the convention of dramatic illusion in *Preface to Shakespeare* (1765):

> Delusion, if delusion can be admitted, has no certain limitation; if the specta-tor can be once persuaded, that his old acquaintance are Alexander and Caesar, that a room illuminated with candles is the plain of Pharsalia, or the bank of Granicus, he is in a state of elevation above the reach of reason, or of truth, and from the heights of empyrean poetry, may despise the circumscriptions of ter-restrial nature. There is no reason why a mind thus wandering in ecstasy should count the clock, or why an hour should not be a century in that calenture of the brains that can make the stage a field. The truth is, that the spectators are always in their senses, and know, from the first act to the last, that the stage is only a stage, and that the players are only players.

Conventions change over time to accommodate innovations and chal-lenges, new types of work, new eras. Some conventions continue mostly un-changed, others become outmoded, but there is no ongoing poetry without them. As Paul Fussell explains it, "The notion that convention shows a lack of feeling, and that a poet attains 'sincerity' . . . by disregarding [convention], is opposed to all the facts of literary experience and history."

SEE ALSO *decorum, sonnet.*

conversation poem   A type of poem that is intimate, informal, and se-rious. Like the verse epistle, it addresses a particular person, and probably has its origins in Horace's epistles and satires. The subtitle of a poem by Coleridge — "The Nightingale. A Conversation Poem" (1798) — inspired George Harper to coin the term *conversation poems* in 1928. Also taking a lead from the Horatian motto in *Sermoni propriora* (*Satires,* book 1, satire 4, ca. 36 B.C.E.), "more fitted to conversation or prose," Harper gave a name to the kind of poem that Coleridge developed and mastered in "The Aeolian Harp" (1795), "Reflections on Having Left a Place of Retirement" (1796), "This Lime-tree Bower My Prison" (1797), "Frost at Midnight" (1798), "The Nightingale" (1798), "Fears in Solitude" (1789), "Dejection: An Ode"

(1802), and "To William Wordsworth" (1807). Coleridge's conversation poems introduced the short blank-verse poem into English literature.

The conversation poem simulates a speaking voice, usually in blank verse, but does not record a conversation per se because it is animated by only one speaker. It tends to be a poem of friendship addressed to a specific living person who is not a lover. Readers are positioned to overhear one side of a conversation that is meant to be overheard.

SEE ALSO *blank verse, letter poem.*

correlative verse   Verse in which relationships among the words in one group balance and parallel relationships among the words in a second group. This kind of symmetry dates to some of the epigrams in *The Greek Anthology* (tenth century). Listen to the opening stanza of George Herbert's "The Call" (1633):

> Come, my Way, my Truth, my Life:
> Such a Way, as gives us breath:
> Such a Truth, as ends all strife:
> And such a Life, as killeth death.

Each of the three presiding nouns that describe Christ in the first line ("Way," "Truth," "Life") becomes the subject of one of the three following lines ("Such a Way," "Such a Truth," "And such a Life").

counted verse   In this type of poem, lines are made up of set numbers of words, as in May Swenson's self-explanatory "Four-Word Lines" (1967). William Carlos Williams's "The Red Wheelbarrow" (1923) consists of eight lines broken into four stanzas. The first line of each stanza contains three words and the second line has one word. Counted verse purposely does not count accents or syllables. It has an arbitrary mathematical orderliness.

counterpoint, counterpoint rhythm   In the second half of the nineteenth century, Gerard Manley Hopkins coined the term *counterpoint rhythm* to describe two simultaneous rhythms operating in one poetic line: "two rhythms are in some manner running at once and we have something answerable to counterpoint in music, which is two or more strains of tune going on together." Hopkins considered Milton the great master of counter-point, especially in the choruses of *Samson Agonistes* (1671). An example:

> Or do my eyes misrepresent? Can this be he,
> That heroic, that renowned,
> Irresistible Samson? whom, unarmed,
> No strength of man, or fiercest wild beast, could withstand; . . .

Hopkins was accounting for changes of rhythm, multiplicities and cross-rhythms, formal substitutions and irregularities, "which all natural growth and motion shews."

SEE ALSO *organic form, sprung rhythm.*

counting-out rhymes   Some bits of poetry hide in childhood memories. Remember the game of It? Someone stands in the middle and counts, "Eeny, meeny, miny, mo . . ." The self-appointed leader points to each player in turn, one child per word, until the end, the last syllable. Someone is It. You may have balked, but you accepted your fate.

The rhyme starts the game and marks it as a type of play, which is why it is removed from ordinary speech. It is a form of gibberish or near-gibberish that signals the roles in the upcoming game. In England and America, this children's game is called counting-out or telling-out. It was once called rim-bles. In Scotland it is called chapping-out or titting-out. Some British children call it dips or grace. The one who is It is called the Wolf in Germany, and likewise the Loup in France; the Pupule, or Crazy One, in Hawaii; the Boka, or Leper, in the Malagasy tribe of Madagascar; the Oni, the Devil or Evil Spirit, in Japan. An ancient terror lurks in these childhood rhymes.

Counting-out rhymes are one of many types of traditional rhymes passed on by children to each other in games, such as ball-bouncing rhymes and jump-rope rhymes, which subdivide into different rhymes for different jumps. These ancient rhymes come down to us through the schoolyard, bearing relics of the past, some of them religious. Children love nonsense and preserve these charms and chants, some of which are holy phrases smoothed down by quick, frequent repetition.

SEE ALSO *charm, nonsense poetry.*

country-house poem This subgenre of Renaissance poetry typically praises the virtues of a powerful patron's country estate, which represents life in retirement, far from the city. Ben Jonson provided the model "To Penshurst" (1616), which compliments Robert Sidney and openly alludes to Horace's *Odes* (book 2, ode 18, 23–13 B.C.E.):

> Thou art not, Penshurst, built to envious show,
> Of touch or marble, nor canst boast a row
> Of polished pillars, or a roof of gold;
> Thou hast no lantern, whereof tales are told,
> Or stair, or courts; but stand'st an ancient pile,
> And, these grudged at, art reverenced the while.

Two other key examples: Thomas Carew's "To Saxham" (1640) and Andrew Marvell's "Upon Appleton House" (ca. 1650). Alastair Fowler suggests the term *estate poems* to account for those poems that do not deal with the architecture of a country house but promote the values of a country-house ethos. The country-house poem typically contrasts the "natural" world of the country, the uncorrupted natural realm, to the worldliness of the city, the corrupted urban realm. It carries a set of social values and morals related to aristocracy. Raymond Williams argues that there is a mystification of actual social relations, especially in regard to rural laborers, in the country-house poem.

SEE ALSO *topographical poetry.*

couplet Two successive lines of poetry, usually rhymed (*aa*). It has been an elemental stanzaic unit — a couple, a pairing — as long as written rhyming poetry has existed in English. It can stand as an epigrammatic poem on its own, as in Pope's "Epigram Engraved on the Collar of a Dog which I gave to his Royal Highness" (1734): "I am his Highness' Dog at Kew; / Pray tell me Sir, whose Dog are you?" The couplet also serves as an organizing pattern in long poems (Shakespeare's "Venus and Adonis," 1592–93; Marlowe's "Hero and Leander," 1593) or part of a larger stanzaic unit. It stands as the pithy conclusion to the ottava rima stanza (*abababcc*), the rhyme royal stanza (*ababbcc*), and the Shakespearean sonnet (*ababcdcdefefgg*).

The rhyming iambic pentameter or five-stress couplet — later known as the heroic couplet — was introduced into English by Chaucer in "The Prologue to the Legend of Good Women" (1386), in imitation of French meter, and employed for most of *The Canterbury Tales* (ca. 1387–1400). It has been nicknamed "riding rhyme," probably because the pilgrims reeled off rhyming couplets while they were riding to Canterbury. It was taken up and used with great flexibility by the Tudor and Jacobean poets and dramatists. Nicholas Grimald's pioneering experiments with the heroic couplet should be better known (*Tottel's Miscellany*, 1557). Christopher Marlowe employed the heroic couplet for his translation of Ovid's *Amores* (16 B.C.E.), which he called *Ovid's Elegies* (1594–95). The mighty two-liner was used by William Shakespeare, George Chapman, and John Donne, and then stamped as a neoclassical form by John Dryden, Alexander Pope, and Samuel Johnson, who wrote, "Let Observation with extensive View / Survey Mankind, from China to Peru." This closed form of the couplet is well suited to aphoristic wit.

The octosyllabic or four-stress couplet, probably based on a common Latin meter, became a staple of English medieval verse (such as *The Lay of Havelok the Dane,* ca. 1280–90), then was virtually reinvented by Samuel Butler in his mock-heroic satire *Hudibras* (1663–80), whose couplets became known as Hudibrastics and were raised to a higher power by Milton ("L'Allegro" and "Il Penseroso," both 1645), Marvell ("To His Coy Mistress," ca. 1650s), and Coleridge ("Christabel," 1797–1800).

We call a couplet closed when the sense and syntax come to a conclusion or strong pause at the end of the second line, thus giving a feeling of self-containment and enclosure, as in the first lines of "To His Coy Mistress": "Had we but world enough, and time, / This coyness, Lady, were no crime." We call a couplet open when the sense carries forward past the second line into the next line or lines, as in the beginning of Keats's *Endymion* (1818):

A thing of beauty is a joy for ever:
Its loveliness increases; it will never
Pass into nothingness, but still will keep
A bower quiet for us, and a sleep
Full of sweet dreams . . .

Ben Jonson told William Drummond that he deemed couplets "the bravest Sort of Verses, especially when they are broken." All two-line stanzas in English carry the vestigial memory of closed or open couplets.

SEE ALSO *end-stopped line, enjambment, meter, octosyllabic verse, stanza.*

courtly love "The history of love is the history of a passion but also of a literary genre," Octavio Paz writes in *The Double Flame* (1996). In the Middle Ages, the troubadour poets invented the idea of courtly love — a fantasy love, a noble passion in which the courtly lover idolizes a sovereign lady, his true beloved. He longs for union with her. The poet or knight is ennobled by his passion for an ideal beauty, a paragon of virtue married to another. Thus his ideal love is also extramarital and so inevitably thwarted, illicit, adulterous. The historian Barbara Tuchman describes the stages of courtly love:

> The chivalric love affair moved from worship through declaration of passionate devotion, virtuous rejection by the lady, renewed wooing with oaths of eternal fealty, moans of approaching death from unsatisfied desire, heroic deeds of valor which won the lady's heart by prowess, [very rarely] consummation of the secret love, followed by endless adventures and subterfuges to a tragic denouement.

The troubadour concept of courtly love, the exaltation of an untouchable beloved, owes something both to the feudal courts and to medieval Christianity, especially the cult of the Virgin. The troubadours were probably influenced by Ovid (43 B.C.E.–18 C.E.) as well as by the Arabic poets of Andalusia and elsewhere in the Islamic world. The passionate ideal — masochistic, spiritual — traveled like wildfire to Europe. In Italy, one thinks of Cavalcanti (ca. 1250–1300), Guinizelli (ca. 1230–ca. 1276), and especially Dante (1265–1321). In northern France, courtly love became central to the trouvères and to the romances, such as Chrétien de Troyes's *Le chevalier de la charrette* (*The Knight of the Cart,* ca. 1170s). In Germany, it was a staple of the minnesingers. In England, Chaucer transformed it into *Troilus and Criseyde* (ca. 1380s). Courtly love had a tremendous influence on Petrarch, and thus on subsequent love poetry influenced by him. It became one of the formative influences on sixteenth-century English poetry.

Courtly love was a prevailing literary ideal, but there is scant evidence that it was ever practiced. As a term, *courtly love* is a relatively late invention. It derives from the phrase *amour courtois,* which was coined by Gaston Paris in 1883 to describe the medieval experience. The medieval terms were *amor honestus* ("honest love") and *fin'amor* ("refined love"). A. J. Denomy writes, in *The Heresy of Courtly Love* (1947), that "the novelty of Courtly Love lies in three basic elements: first, in the ennobling force of human love; second, in the elevation of the beloved to a place of superiority above the lover; third, in the conception of love as ever unsatisfied, ever increasing desire." He calls these three things the "skeleton framework" of courtly love because they distinguish it from all other kinds of love.

SEE ALSO *allegory, minnesingers, Petrarchism, romances, troubadour, trouvère.*

cretic From the Greek: "long at both ends." A Greek quantitative foot, which consists of one short syllable between two long ones. It is the opposite of the amphibrach. William Blake's poem "Spring" (1789) imitates the meter by substituting two stressed syllables for long syllables and an unstressed syllable for the short one.

> Sóund thĕ Flúte!
> Nów ĭt's múte.
> Bírd's dĕlíght
> Dáy ănd Níght.

Coleridge imitates the meter he describes: "First and last being long, middle short, Amphimacer / Strikes his thundering hoofs like a proud high-bred Racer" ("Metrical Feet," ca. 1806).

SEE ALSO *amphibrach, foot, meter.*

crown of sonnets, see *sonnet.*

Cubist poetry Guillaume Apollinaire defined Cubism in 1913 as "the art of painting new structures out of elements borrowed not from the reality of sight, but from the reality of insight." Cubist poetry was an experimental attempt to create in language something equivalent to the work of the Cubist painters, especially Pablo Picasso (1881–1973), Georges Braque (1882–1963), and Juan Gris (1887–1927). The Cubist painters shattered surfaces, analyzed broken objects, and reassembled the fragments in a non-objective or abstracted form. Every subject was depicted from a multitude of perspectives. The planes interpenetrated. Cubism in poetry was, as Kenneth Rexroth characterized it, "the conscious, deliberate dissociation and recombination of elements into a new artistic entity made self-sufficient by its rigorous architecture."

The French poets associated with Analytical and Synthetic Cubism are Apollinaire (1880–1918), Pierre Reverdy (1889–1960), Blaise Cendrars (1887–1961), Jean Cocteau (1889–1963), André Salmon (1881–1969), and Max Jacob (1876–1944). In the United States, one thinks of Parker Tyler (1904–1974); Charles Henri Ford (1913–2002); Walter Conrad Arensberg's last works, especially "For Shady Hill" (1917); and the early poems of Rexroth, collected in *The Art of Worldly Wisdom* (1949). William Carlos Williams (1883–1963) moved beyond the pictorialism of imagism and experimented with Cubist techniques, especially in *Al Que Quiere!* (1917). Gertrude Stein's *Tender Buttons* (1914) is the most sustained literary work of Analytical Cubism. Stein describes objects without naming them and approaches each subject from a multiplicity of perspectives, like a Cubist painter.

SEE ALSO *ekphrasis.*

cynghanedd From the Welsh: "harmony." In Welsh poetry, *cynghanedd* is a highly elaborated system of sound arrangements and correspondences, involving stress, alliteration, and rhyme. *Cynghanedd* as a poetic art was well developed by the fourteenth century, but was not codified until the Caerwys Eisteddfod, or Bardic Assembly, of 1524. These consonant chimes show up in the definitions of all traditional Welsh forms. The sound patterns are impossible to reproduce accurately in English. In *The White Goddess* (1948), Robert Graves defines *cynghanedd* as "the repetitive use of consonantal sequences with variations of vowels," and invents this example:

Billet spied,
Bolt sped.
Across field
Crows fled,

Aloft, wounded,
Left one dead.

There are three types of *cynghanedd*: (1) consonantal; (2) *sain*, which involves both rhyme and alliteration; and (3) *lusg* (dragging), which involves internal rhyme. The consonantal type divides into three prevalent kinds: "crossing" (*groes*), "leaping" (*draws*), and "interlinked" crossing. In crossing, or cross-harmony, the alliteration connects two stressed vowels: the last before the medial caesura and the last in the line. In *groes*, the consonants in the first half of the line are repeated in the second part, in the same order. In *draws*, the middle consonants are ignored, and there are consonants in the second half of the line that are not part of the echoed consonants. In *sain*, the line divides into three parts, each with a primary stress. The first two parts rhyme, and the second part is linked to the third by consonance or alliteration. In *lusg*, the last unaccented syllable in the first half of the line rhymes with the stressed penultimate syllable of the line.

These complicated meters took years for poets to master in the bardic orders. In "The Wreck of the Deutschland" (1875–76), Gerard Manley Hopkins employed, as he said, "certain chimes suggested by the Welsh poetry I had been reading (what they call *cynghanedd*)." Dylan Thomas (1914–1953) followed Hopkins's example and experimented with using *cynghanedd* in modern English-language poetry. The Scottish poet Hugh MacDiarmid (1892–1978) desired a "poetry full of *cynghanedd*, and hair-trigger relationships, / With something about it that is plasmic" ("The Kind of Poetry I Want," 1961). In the 1970s, Alan Llwyd and other Welsh poets formed a society called Barddas (Poetic Art), which brought new energy to the study of *cynghanedd*.

SEE ALSO *alliteration, bard, cywydd, rhyme.*

cywydd From the Welsh: "harmony" or "song." A traditional Welsh metrical form that has been employed from the fourteenth century to the present day. It was developed by the medieval poet Dafydd ap Gwilym, who assimilated Welsh verse into European poetry, and it became the favorite meter of the Poets of the Nobility (ca. 1350–ca. 1600), who were also called the Cywyddry, the masters of the *cywydd* meter. It is a flexible form with four variations. The type most commonly practiced by the Celtic bards was the *cywydd deuair hirion*. It consists of a series of seven-syllable lines in rhyming couplets. In each couplet, one of the end-rhymes is stressed and one unstressed. Each line employs the devices of *cynghanedd*. It is this meter that is usually meant when one refers to the *cywydd*. The other three meters are *awdl-gywydd, cywydd deuair fyrion,* and *cywydd llosgyrnog.* The *cywydd* has no set length, but generally runs to sixty or seventy lines.

The *cywydd* has proved wily, flexible, and suited to all kinds of purposes. It has been employed for love poetry, whether joyous or despairing. It has served for prayers to the Virgin and appeals to patrons. As Gwen Jones states, in *The Oxford Book of Welsh Verse in English* (1977), "It was a jousting spear or switch of nettles for poetic rivals; *conte,* homily, beast-fable, social comment, friendly invitation, autobiography, tribute, elegy — whatever the need the *cywydd* supplied it. Stylistically it lent itself perfectly to such poetic devices as description by comparison (*dyfalu*), allegory, the break in syntactic flow (*sangiad*), or between what in English are words so closely related as to be inseparable (*trychiad*)."

SEE ALSO *cynghanedd, strict-meter poetry.*

D

dactyl From the Greek: "finger." A metrical foot consisting of three sylla-bles, one accented syllable followed by two unaccented ones, as in the word *póĕtrў*. Tennyson's "Charge of the Light Brigade" (1854) deploys dactyls, as do many nursery rhymes. Here is the haunting opening of Thomas Hardy's dactylic poem "The Voice" (1912): "Wómăn mŭch / míssed, hŏw yŏu / cáll tŏ mĕ, / cáll tŏ mĕ."

SEE ALSO *double dactyl, foot, meter.*

Dadaism, Dada Surrealism grew directly out of the flamboyantly self-conscious and joyously nihilistic movement known as Dada, which began in the Café Voltaire in Zurich in 1916 when a group of young writers and art-ists, including Tristan Tzara (1896–1963), Hans Arp (1886–1966), Richard Huelsenbeck (1892–1974), Hugo Ball (1886–1927), Emmy Hennings (1885–1948), and Sophie Taeuber (1889–1943), showered contempt on the decadent values of bourgeois society and the moral insanity of World War I. The word *dada,* chosen at random from a dictionary, is baby talk for "hobby-horse" in French. "This is the song of a dadaist / who had dada in his heart," Tzara chants in "Chanson Dada": "he tore his motor apart / he had dada in his heart."

The Dadaists' favorite word was *nothing*. There is a subversive, childlike energy in their manifestoes, sound poems, simultaneous lyrics, noise music, and provocative public spectacles aimed at destroying rational logic, social restraints and conventions, traditional art and literature. Dada was subsumed by Surrealism and formally laid to rest in a mock funeral service in Paris in 1923, though sightings have been reported wherever nonsense thrives and the spirit of anarchy reigns.

SEE ALSO *sound poetry, Surrealism.*

dead metaphor A metaphor used so often it has lost its capacity to describe one thing in terms of another, and no longer operates as a metaphor. Do we think of the heart when we say that this definition strikes *the heart of the matter*? The question of whether or not a dead metaphor is still a metaphor has been debated in recent years. Metaphors may not be surprising, but they can still work as metaphors. As Zoltán Kövecses explains it, "The 'dead metaphor' account misses an important point ... The metaphors ... may be highly conventional and effortlessly used, but this does not mean that they have lost their vigor in thought and that they are dead. On the contrary, they are 'alive' in the most important sense — they govern our thought — they are 'metaphors we live by.'" Some poets, such as Samuel Johnson in "The Vanity of Human Wishes" (1749), make a point of invigorating dead metaphors. Giambattista Vico contended, in *The New Science* (1725), that all language begins with metaphor and that the first metaphors were drawn from the human body. A great deal of what we think of as literal speech consists of dead metaphors: "the mouth of a river," "veins of minerals," "murmuring waves," "weeping willows," "the bowels of the earth," and "smiling skies."

SEE ALSO *cliché, convention, metaphor, personification.*

débat A popular literary genre of the twelfth and thirteen centuries, the *débat* dramatizes a quarrel or debate between two opposing perspectives. For example, the twelfth-century Middle English poem *The Owl and the Nightingale* sets up a debate between a somber owl, who represents the didactic or religious poet, and a merry nightingale, who represents the love poet. The owl sings in the mood of winter, the nightingale in the mood of summer. The allegorical *débat* poem sets up a dramatic model for a verbal contest of wits; its outcome is decided by a judge.

There are pastoral contests of wit in the eclogues of Theocritus and Virgil, and many examples in Old French and Provençal literature, such as the fifteenth-century "Débat du cors et du l'âme" ("Debate Between Body and Soul"). Later, François Villon wrote the great "Débat du coeur et du corps" ("Debate Between Heart and Body," 1461). The theme of the soul versus the body has a pedigree that dates to Old English literature. Andrew Marvell presents two examples in "A Dialogue, Between the Resolved Soul and Created Pleasure" (1681) and "A Dialogue Between the Soul and Body" (1681). In the latter poem the soul inquires:

> What magic could me thus confine
> Within another's grief to pine,
> Where, whatsoever it complain,
> I feel, that cannot feel, the pain,
> And all my care itself employs,
> That to preserve, which me destroys:
> Constrained not only to endure
> Diseases, but, what's worse, the cure:
> And ready oft the port to gain,
> Am shipwrecked into health again?

And the body responds:

> But physic yet could never reach
> The maladies thou me dost teach:
> Whom first the cramp of hope does tear,
> And then the palsy shakes of fear;
> The pestilence of love does heat,
> Or hatred's hidden ulcer eat;
> Joy's cheerful madness does perplex,
> Or sorrow's other madness vex;
> Which knowledge forces me to know,
> And memory will not forgo.
> What but a soul could have the wit
> To build me up for sin so fit?
> So architects do square and hew
> Green trees that in the forest grew.

SEE ALSO *dialogue, dit, poetic contest.*

decadence From the Latin word *decadere*, "to fall down or away." The word *decadent* was used for centuries to characterize conditions of decline, as in the corruption that led to the fall of the Roman Empire. It wasn't until the mid-nineteenth century in France that a pejorative turned into an honorific, and decadence was put forward as a full-fledged aesthetic stance. It opposed any notion of "normalcy" or the triumphalist idea of progress and its associated bourgeois optimism. Charles Baudelaire (1821–1867) was the initial poet of decadence, and his masterpiece *Les fleurs du mal* (*The Flowers of Evil*, 1857) represented its moral and spiritual side. Decadence is both a style and an attitude.

During the 1880s and '90s *decadence* and *decadents* came to be used as proper nouns. In England, the poet Algernon Charles Swinburne (1837–1909), the artist Aubrey Beardsley (1872–1898), and the aesthete Walter Pater (1839–1894) were all affiliated with the decadent stance. Oscar Wilde (1854–1900) became the "High Priest of the Decadents." The fatalistic mood, languorous glamour, and feverish thinking of decadence were taken up by the poets Lionel Johnson (1867–1902), who said that decadence occurs "when thought thinks upon itself, and when emotions become entangled with the consciousness of them," and Arthur Symons (1865–1945), who said that "what decadence in literature really means is that learned corruption of language by which style ceases to be organic and becomes, in the pursuit of some new expressiveness or beauty, deliberately abnormal." In 1898, William Butler Yeats lyrically described the decadent movement as a reflection of "the autumn of the body."

SEE ALSO *symbolism*.

decasyllable　A ten-syllable line, as in "Where are the songs of Spring? Ay, where are they?" (John Keats, "To Autumn," 1820). The decasyllable line appeared in French poetry (*décasyllabe*) in the eleventh century and in Italian poetry (*decasillabo*) in the twelfth century. It was often called "heroic verse" because it was used for the medieval French heroic epics, the chansons de geste, such as *La chanson de Roland* (*The Song of Roland,* ca. 1090). An oddity: because French and Italian lines often have multisyllabic, or feminine, endings, the decasyllable itself often has eleven or twelve syllables. One classic formulation divides the line into two parts of four and six syllables, with a strong caesura after the fourth syllable. In French poetry, the decasyllable was essentially replaced by the twelve-syllable alexandrine, in Italian by the eleven-syllable hendecasyllable.

The decasyllable is the basic unit of the rhythmical epic poetry of South

Slavic epic poetry. The linguist Roman Jakobson points out that the basic type of the decasyllable not only exercises "a complete hegemony over contemporary Serbocroatian epic lore, but it survives to this day in the oral tradition of other Slavic areas, while remaining alien in a non-Slavic environment." He finds it a living element in the Slovenian, Macedonian, and West Bulgarian epic traditions.

The decasyllable has usually been treated in English as a five-stress iambic pentameter line, the standard-bearer for English poetry until the twentieth century.

SEE ALSO *alexandrine, blank verse, chansons de geste, epic, hendecasyllabics, iambic pentameter.*

decorum   Propriety; an appropriate sense of form, subject matter, language. Aristotle used the word *propon* to describe propriety of style (*Rhetoric,* ca. 335–330 B.C.E.), and Cicero claimed that decorum was the Latin equivalent of *propon* (*Orator,* 46 B.C.E.). Horace illustrated the purposefulness of decorum as a concept in poetry in his *Ars poetica* (ca. 19–18 B.C.E.), where he argues that each style should find its proper place. It matters who speaks — a slave, a hero, or a god — and comic and tragic themes are distinct and should be kept separate. The doctrine of decorum was aesthetically influential throughout the Renaissance and beyond. Hence John Milton's recognition of poetry, in his *Tractate on Education* (1644), as "that sublime art which in Aristotle's *Poetics,* in Horace, and the Italian commentaries of Castelvetro, Tasso, Mazzoni, and others, teaches what the laws are of a true epic poem, what of a dramatic, what of a lyric, what decorum is, which is the grand masterpiece to observe." The neoclassical theory of decorum emphasized a hierarchy of styles (plain, moderate, grand) and a distinct division of poetic genres. One of the primary impulses of Romanticism was the breaking of these rules, especially in relationship to language. In the preface to *Lyrical Ballads* (1798), William Wordsworth explained how he changed decorum by using situations from "humble and rustic life" in a "selection of language really used by men."

Decorum is outdated, no longer an influential concept. Yet it still functions in the social constraints and usages of poetry, even if writers and readers are little aware of it. Occasional poems, for example, are deemed appropriate (or not) and fitted to their occasions. Some genres — the epithalamium, the elegy — work within social norms, with a related sense of decorum.

SEE ALSO *elegy, epithalamium, neoclassicism, occasional poem.*

deep image   Robert Kelly coined this term in "Notes on the Poetry of Deep Image" (1961) to identify a new energy entering American poetry. Deep imagism was never a movement, but the term is associated with the poetry of Robert Bly, James Wright, Louis Simpson, William Stafford, Donald Hall, W. S. Merwin, Galway Kinnell, David Ignatow, and other poets of "the emotive imagination" working in the 1960s and '70s. These poets deployed the image to concentrate inner and outer energies, to unite the psyche and the cosmos.

In his magazine *The Fifties,* Robert Bly argued that American poetry after Pound and Eliot had exalted the conscious mind at the expense of the unconscious. He sought a more passionate, irrational poetry modeled after earlier twentieth-century Spanish-language poets such as Pablo Neruda (1904–1973), César Vallejo (1892–1938), Antonio Machado (1875–1939), and Federico García Lorca (1898–1936). In "A Wrong Turning in American Poetry" (1963), Bly differentiated the Spanish poets from the American modernists ("the phrase 'objective correlative' is astoundingly passionless") and distinguished the kind of image he was seeking from that of the imagist movement, which he dismissed as "Picturism." The deep imagists sought to unite the conscious and unconscious mind through "psychic leaps."

SEE ALSO *image, imagism, objective correlative, Surrealism.*

denotation   From the Latin: "to mark out." **connotation**   From the Latin: "to mark [a thing] with or in addition [to another]." Denotation is the exact meaning of a word, what you would find in the dictionary. The denotative qualities of a word are stated, explicit, and definable. Connotation is the force of a word's associations. It is suggestive and reflects the emotional and cultural meanings radiating from a word beyond its lexical meaning.

descriptive poetry   Poetry that describes something, that pictures and represents it in words. *Wasf,* or descriptive verse, was one of the four main categories of medieval Arabic poetry. The *wasf* tradition was highly developed, and poets elaborately described single subjects, such as hunting for animals or observing different kinds of flowers. They described natural scenes and memorable occasions. The medieval Hebrew poets adapted this tradition and used poetry to describe gardens and palaces, the pleasures of wine, the beauties of young men and women.

Descriptive verse also flourished in Europe in the sixteenth, seventeenth, and eighteenth centuries, especially in landscape and topographical poetry. James Thomson's *The Seasons* (1730) is one of the defining classics of descriptive poetry. Description can seldom be sustained as an end in itself in poetry — Thomson's many imitators seemed to prove this — and thus descriptive poetry gave way in the nineteenth century to description *in* poetry. Critics have often derided the descriptive impulse. John Keats's ode "To Autumn" (1820) was once condescended to as "mere description." But for poets ranging from William Wordsworth to Elizabeth Bishop, everything starts with description, the visual representation of the world.

SEE ALSO *nature poetry, topographical poetry.*

dialogue   In a general sense, we think of dialogue as a verbal exchange between two or more imaginary speakers in fiction, drama, or poetry. This kind of exchange is at the heart of drama. A literary dialogue, either in prose or poetry, is also a genre; characters discuss a subject at length, as in Plato's celebrated *Dialogues,* which may have their origins in the mimes of the Sicilian poets Sophron and Epicharmus (fifth century B.C.E.). This sort of dialogue is not intended for the stage. Poetic contests are essentially dialogues. Two speakers go back and forth and, in many traditions, respond to each other by matching poetic forms. The dialogue poem written by a single poet tends to stand between the conversation poem, which has one speaker, and the play, which has any number of speakers. Narrative poems, such as ballads and epics, often employ dialogue.

The *débat* poem, popular in England and France in the medieval era, depicts a dialogue between two opposing forces, such as sun and moon, winter and summer, and, especially, body and soul. Andrew Marvell's "A Dialogue Between the Soul and Body" (1681) stands behind such modern poems as T. S. Eliot's "First Debate Between the Body and Soul" (1910) and W. B.

Yeats's "A Dialogue of Self and Soul" (1928). The dialogue poem can also simulate speech, two people talking to each other, which is how it is used in William Barnes's nineteenth-century dialect poems and the verse dialogues in Robert Frost's *North of Boston* (1914).

SEE ALSO *conversation poem, drama, dramatic monologue, flyting, pastoral, poetic contest.*

didactic poetry From the Greek word *didak,* "apt at teaching." Didactic poetry, which seeks to instruct, probably originated in the proverb. The Book of Proverbs in the Hebrew Bible is an anthology of didactic poetry whose goal is to teach wisdom. The ancient Greeks established a traditional model for didactic poetry, which operated in one of two ways. It taught *how* to do something, such as keep bees or handle a plow, or it taught *what* to know about something, such as mathematics or philosophy. Hesiod, the father of didactic poetry, signals his pedagogical vocation in two ways. He conveys practical information and teaches about farming in *Works and Days* (ca. 700 B.C.E.), whereas he explains the genealogy and myths of the gods, the origins of the cosmos, in *Theogony* (ca. 700 B.C.E.). Virgil's *Georgics* (29 B.C.E.) teaches "how to farm" and thus follows the practical model; Lucretius's *De rerum natura* (*On the Nature of Things,* 50 B.C.E.) is an exposition of science, ethics, and the nature of materialism, and follows the philosophical model.

From the second millennium B.C.E., Sumerian poetry had a central role in the educational system, and thus was didactic. Christian poetry of the Middle Ages is almost entirely didactic. The fable, which often employs speaking animals, is a didactic genre and so is the *conte dévot* ("pious tale"). The eighteenth century turned one type of didactic poetry, which teaches a moral, into a predominant mode. Alexander Pope's "Essays" ("An Essay on Criticism," 1711; *Moral Essays,* 1731–35; "An Essay on Man," 1733–34) epitomize the best argumentative moral verse. Much political poetry has a didactic intention.

John Keats rebelled against didactic poetry when he declared in 1818, "We hate poetry that has a palpable design upon us — and if we do not agree, seems to put its hand in its breeches pocket. Poetry should be great and unobtrusive." Yet Keats also spoke of "doing the world some good" through poetry.

In *The Didactic Muse* (1989), Willard Spiegelman observes that "even those who try to evade the didactic impulse embrace it." To examine the didactic impulse in poetry is to study strategies of instruction.

SEE ALSO *fable, proverb, rhetoric, verse essay, wisdom literature.*

dirge From the first word of the Latin antiphon, adapted from Psalm 5:9, in the Christian Office of the Dead: "Dirige, Domine, Deus meus, in conspectu tuo viam meam" ("Direct my way in your sight, O Lord my God"). A song of grief, a lament commemorating the dead. The dirge is close to the elegy, but less consoling, less meditative. The genre comes from the Greek *epicedium,* a song sung over the dead, and the Greek threnody, a song sung in memory of the dead. In fifth-century Greece, lyric dirges were sung not just at funerals and other ceremonies commemorating the dead, but also at festivals. The dirge was also an ancient Near Eastern literary form used to memorialize disasters.

The Latin meter was the hexameter (elegiac distich). In English, the mournful tones of the dirge can be heard in Henry King's *Exequy* (1624) on his young wife, in Percy Shelley's "Autumn: A Dirge" (posthumously published in 1824), in Thomas Lovell Beddoes's "Dirge" (1825–44), and in George Meredith's "Dirge in Woods" (1870). In American poetry, a leitmotif of ritual grief runs through Ralph Waldo Emerson's "Dirge" (1838), Herman Melville's "A Dirge for McPherson" (1864), and Walt Whitman's "Dirge for Two Veterans" (1867). G. M. T. Emezue calls the African dirge "one of the elevated forms of poetry."

SEE ALSO *distich, elegy, epicedium, hexameter, keening, lament.*

discursive A poetry that moves from topic to topic, digressing, relying on argumentation, is called discursive. This essayistic movement of a text puts things in more than it takes them out. Often it is a reaction against a radically stripped-down poetry, such as imagism. In "The Discursive Mode" (1965), the Australian poet A. D. Hope characterized the discursive as "that form in which the uses of poetry approach closest to the uses of prose, and yet remain essentially poetry." Robert Pinsky champions discursive poetry in *The Situation of Poetry* (1978), arguing for poetry as speech, "organized by its meaning, avoiding the distances and complications of irony on one side and the ecstatic fusion of speaker, meaning, and subject on the other. The idea is to have all of the virtues of prose, in addition to those qualities and degrees of precision which can be called poetic."

SEE ALSO *imagism, verse essay.*

dissonance   A harsh sound or rhythm. It is nearly equivalent to cacophony. To distinguish between them, it can be said that cacophony refers to conflicting sounds, whereas dissonance denotes a deliberate lack of harmony among disparate things. In *Paradise Lost* (1667), Milton writes of "the barbarous dissonance / Of Bacchus and his revellers, the race / Of that wild rout that tore the Thracian bard / In Rhapsode."

SEE ALSO *cacophony.*

distich   A stanzaic unit of two metrical lines, which usually rhyme and express a complete thought. It was commonly used in Greek and Latin elegiac poetry. The two-line epigram, for example, is a distich. At Pembroke College, Cambridge, a student named Penlycross included this Latin motto with an essay he thought would be rejected for a contest:

> Distichon ut poscas nolente, volente, Minerva,
> Mos sacer? Unde mihi distichon? En perago.

> Without a distich, vain the oration is;
> Oh! for a distich! Doctor, e'en take this.

SEE ALSO *couplet, epigram.*

dit   From the French: "something said." In medieval French poetry, the *dit* was literally a poem meant to be spoken, not sung. The term applied to a wide variety of poetic forms, and seems closely related to other forms, such as the fabliau, the *débat,* and the *lai.* Commonly written in octosyllabic couplets, it could be either narrative or expository, and ranged in length from one hundred to several thousand lines. It could be a love poem or a eulogy, a political satire, a spiritual testament. According to *The New Oxford Companion to Literature in French* (1995), certain traits can nonetheless be associated with the *dit:* "It is always constructed on first-person discourse. Thus the narrative *dits,* in which a narrator identified with the author recounts events that he or she experienced or observed, can be distinguished from the *lai,* narrated in the third person and often set in the distant past." Some medieval examples: Rutebeuf's "Le dit de l'herberie" ("The Tale of the Herb Market"), Guillaume de Machaut's "Le livre dou voir dit" ("The Book of the True Poem"), and Christine de Pisan's "Ditié de Jehanne d'Arc" ("The Tale of Joan of Arc").

SEE ALSO *débat, fabliau, lai.*

dithyramb   The dithyramb began as a frenzied choral song and dance in honor of Dionysus, the god of wine, fertility, and procreation. It was a processional danced song. What we think of as three distinct genres — poetry, music, and dance — were intertwined. Archilochus (seventh century B.C.E.) first used the term *dithyramb* to describe the "beautiful song of Dionysus"; Plato (ca. 427–ca. 347 B.C.E.) mentioned "the birth of Dionysus called, I think, the dithyramb"; and Aristotle (384–322 B.C.E.) argued that the dithyramb evolved into Greek tragedy. C. M. Bowra suggests that Arion "seems to have found in existence an improvised, ecstatic song to Dionysus and to have transformed it into a formal, choral hymn attached to definite festivals and accompanied by regular dancing." The dithyramb was a narrative in lyric form.

The first dithyrambs were probably composed in Athens around the seventh century B.C.E. Lasus of Hermione is said to have introduced dithyrambic competitions into Athens. As Aristophanes reports in *The Wasps* (422 B.C.E.), "A contest rose 'twixt Lasus and Simonides / (The day has long gone by) who show'd most mastery / In music." These large-scale compositions were performed at festivals in Athens, Delphi, and Delos. The dithyramb reached its peak in the work of Simonides (ca. 556–468 B.C.E.), Bacchylides (fifth century B.C.E.), and Pindar (ca. 522–443 B.C.E.). A. W. Pickard-Cambridge describes the Pindaric dithyramb as "an anti-strophic composition dealing with special themes taken from divine and heroic legend, but still maintaining its particular connection with Dionysus, who is celebrated, apparently at or near the opening of the song, whatever its subject."

Today any wild, vehement, and enthusiastic piece of writing may be considered a dithyramb. Dithyrambs are relatively rare in English, though John Dryden composed one called "Alexander's Feast" (1697).

SEE ALSO *chorus, paean, poetic contest, tragedy.*

ditty   A short, simple song. The ditty can refer to a composition to be sung, sometimes a *lai,* occasionally even a ballad, as in Rudyard Kipling's *Departmental Ditties & Barrack-Room Ballads* (1899). The ditty can also suggest the words of a song, its burden or theme. The term *ditty* now has a disparaging connotation, but that was not always so. Thomas Campion's chapter "Of Ditties and Odes" in *Observations in the Art of English Poesy* (1602) suggests that for him the ditty and the ode were essentially the same thing.

SEE ALSO *ballad, burden, lai, ode, roundelay.*

doggerel   A derogatory term for bad poetry, used since the thirteenth century. A trivial form of verse, loosely constructed and rhythmically irregular, it often has forced rhymes, faulty meters, and trite sentiments. Doggerel has been employed as a source of comedy and a type of satire. In German, it is known as *Knittelvers* ("cudgel verse"). Northrop Frye states that "doggerel is not necessarily stupid poetry; it is poetry that begins in the conscious mind and has never gone through the associative process. It has a prose initiative, but tries to make itself associate by an act of will, and it reveals the same difficulties that great poetry has overcome at a subconscious level."

   In "The Nature and Phenomena of Doggerel" (1906), George Saintsbury distinguishes between two different kinds of doggerel: "there is doggerel which is doggerel, and doggerel which is not." The doggerel "which is doggerel" is merely bad verse, a lyric that aspires to a certain standard and fails. The doggerel "which is not," on the other hand, consists in "the using of recognized forms of verse, and of diction recognized and unrecognized, with a willful licentiousness which is excused by the felicitous result. The poet is not trying to do what he cannot do; he is trying to do something exceptional, outrageous, shocking."

   Chaucer uses the term *rhyme doggerel* in the mock-courteous "Tale of Sir Thopas" (ca. 1387–1400), and Shakespeare often puts doggerel into the

mouth of a comic character. Jonathan Swift (1667–1745) is one of its satiri-
cal masters and so is John Skelton (1460–1529), who writes,

> For though my rhyme be ragged,
> Tattered and jagged,
> Rudely rain-beaten,
> Rusty and moth-eaten,
> If ye take well therewith,
> It hath in it some pith.

Doggerel is one of the staples of comic verse, from Samuel Butler (1612–
1680) to Ogden Nash (1902–1971). Easily memorized, it is present in limericks
and nonsense poetry, in children's games, popular songs, and advertising jingles.

SEE ALSO *jingle, Knittelvers, light verse, limericks, nonsense poetry, Skeltonics.*

double dactyl   Two dactyls in a row (/ / u / / u), as in the word
mónŏmăníăcăl. The double dactyl is a comic verse form, an offshoot of the
clerihew invented by Anthony Hecht and Paul Pascal (1961). This elaborate
form of doggerel, also known as Higgledy Piggledy, consists of two four-line
stanzas. Most of the lines are double dactyls. The first line is usually a jingle or
nonsense phrase, often "Higgledy Piggledy" or "Jiggery-pokery." The second
line is the name of a person, who is the subject of the poem. The truncated
fourth and eight lines rhyme. One line in the second stanza should consist of
a single word.

SEE ALSO *clerihew, dactyl, doggerel, light verse.*

the dozens   An African American verbal street game of escalating in-
sults. In different communities, it is also called woofing, sounding, joning,
screaming, cutting, capping, and chopping, among other things. The rules
shift from place to place. Played by both males and females, it is sometimes
"clean," more often "dirty." In *The Dictionary of Afro-American Slang* (1970),
Clarence Major defines the Dirty Dozens as "a very elaborate game tradition-
ally played by black boys, in which the participants insult each other's rela-
tives, especially their mothers. The object of the game is to test emotional
strength. The first person to give in to anger is the loser."

No one knows the origins of the dozens, which probably derives its name from an eighteenth-century meaning of the verb *dozen,* "to stun, stupefy, daze." Lawrence Levine points out that all the ingredients of the dozens were present in the slaves' environment. He quotes the earliest documentation of the dozens in a Texas song collected in 1891:

> Talk about one thing, talk about another;
> But if you talk about me, I'm gwain to talk about your mother.

The dozens is a way of using language to stun someone in front of an audience, as in this opening rhymed couplet:

> I don't play the dozens, the dozens ain't my game,
> But the way I fucked your mama is a god damn shame.

There is a structural turn in the couplet: the first line disclaims the game, and the second line contradicts the disclaimer.

In *Die Nigger Die!* (1969), H. Rap Brown remembers that in school his teachers tried to teach him "poetry" in the classroom when he was actually talking poetry in the streets. "If anybody needed to study poetry," Brown says, "[my teacher] needed to study mine. We played the Dozens for recreation, like white folks play Scrabble." He grew up in Baton Rouge and distinguishes between the dozens, a "mean game because what you try to do is totally destroy somebody else with words," and "Signifying," which was "more humane." Claudia Mitchell-Kernan recalls that in Chicago, games of verbal insult were generally called sounding. The dozens was a specific subcategory; it broadened the target from an individual adversary to include the person's relatives and ancestors, especially the mother. Direct insults were called sounds, and indirect insults were called signifying.

drama, dramatic poetry Drama applies to the entire corpus of work written for the theater. We speak of English drama and Russian drama. We classify plays by their content or style, as in Restoration drama and the drama of the absurd. In general, a drama is a work performed by actors on a stage, for an audience. The fundamental situation of a drama or play, then, is that actors take the role of characters, uttering dialogue, performing actions. The audience participates with the actors in the realm of make-believe. The pact between them relies on dramatic convention, the way that literary practice simulates reality — that time is compressed, that masks or personas represent real people, and so forth. All this helps to simulate a play world. There is a perceptible psychic distance between the performers and the audience. A play is different from a game because the outcome is predetermined. The *dramatis personae* (Latin for "persons"; literally, "masks") are the characters in a play. The dramatic structure is the plan that creates and resolves conflict in a literary piece. For example, the Elizabethan dramatists borrowed from the Roman playwrights the idea of dividing their plays into five acts, beginning with an introduction, proceeding through a rising action, then a climax and a falling action, and concluding with a final resolution. Lyric poetry borrows from dramatic poetry the idea of a dramatic situation — that is, a situation that brings into contention different conflicting forces. At the core, drama represents conflict.

The drama, which dates to the fifth century B.C.E. in Greece, has its roots in religious practice and ritual. Comedy developed from festivals of revelry, tragedy from ritual hymns sung during an animal sacrifice at Dionysian festivals. Drama, which retains elements of ritual, initially served as a way of honoring the divine. A verse drama, sometimes called a poetic drama, is a play in which the dialogue is written in verse.

Literary works have conventionally been divided into three types, based on who is doing the speaking:

epic or *narrative:* the narrator speaks in the first person, then lets the characters speak for themselves.
drama: the characters do all the talking.
lyric: a first-person speaker utters the words.

This useful but flawed textbook taxonomy evolved from Aristotle's definitions of the three genres of poetic literature: epic, drama, and lyric. "Like all well-conceived classifications," the Portuguese poet Fernando Pessoa writes (ca. 1915),

this one is useful and clear; like all classifications, it is false. The genres do not separate out with such essential facility, and, if we closely analyze what they are made of, we shall find that from lyric poetry to dramatic there is one continuous gradation. In effect, and going right to the origins of dramatic poetry — Aeschylus, for instance — it will be nearer the truth to say that what we encounter is lyric poetry put into the mouths of different characters.

Pessoa conceived different "heteronyms" for himself, and thus considered himself "a dramatic poet writing in lyric poetry." In *A Common Stage* (2007), Carol Symes demonstrates that "the generic definition of a play as such was in flux for most of the Middle Ages." The distinction between lyrics, dialogues, and plays is permeable.

Elements of drama spill over into everyday life. In fact, the term *drama* applies to any situation in which there is conflict. We keep playing roles and acting out, putting or finding ourselves in situations framed with a beginning, middle, and end. In *Frame Analysis* (1976), the sociologist Erving Goffman demonstrates some ways in which we frame experience, how drama operates in ordinary life.

SEE ALSO *closet drama, comedy, dialogue, dramatic monologue, monologue, tragedy.*

dramatic monologue "Everything written is as good as it is dramatic," Robert Frost declared in *A Way Out* (1929). Poems become dramatic when we get the sensation of someone speaking, when we hear a poem, in Frost's words, "as sung or spoken by a person in a scene — in character, in a setting." A monologue presents a single person speaking alone, but a dramatic monologue presents an imaginary or historical character speaking to an imaginary listener or audience, as in Robert Browning's "Andrea del Sarto" (1853), "My Last Duchess" (1842), and "The Bishop Orders His Tomb at St. Praxed's Church" (1844). Browning termed such poems "dramatic lyrics." Browning and Tennyson inaugurated this type of poem.

The speaker of the dramatic monologue is decidedly *not* the author, and thus the poem requires a high degree of impersonation. It enacts the displacement of the poetic self into another being. The utterance tends to take place in a specific situation at a critical moment, the speaker addresses and sometimes interacts with one or more listeners (this is revealed by what the speaker *says*), and the speaker gradually reveals his or her character to the reader. The dramatic monologue imagines a speaker into being over the course of a poem. It engages us in the act of poetic making and reminds us that the poem is an artificial utterance.

E

echo   A recurrence of the same sound or combination of sounds. The repetitions of rhymes and near rhymes, the patterns of alliteration, of assonance and consonance, of refrains, are all varieties of echo, part of the sound chamber of lyric poetry. An echo can also be a means of allusion, a way of evoking an earlier text. Thus John Milton echoes the Hebrew Bible at the beginning of *Paradise Lost* (1667): "In the beginning how the heav'ns and earth / Rose out of chaos ..." In *The Figure of Echo* (1984), John Hollander points out that the sonic origin of the term creates an association between a written echo and "a lurking and invisible vocal presence."

SEE ALSO *alliteration, assonance, consonance, echo verse, refrain, rhyme.*

echo verse   A lyric in which lines conclude with (or are followed by) a word or phrase that echoes the preceding syllable, word, or phrase. The echo verse dates to *The Greek Anthology,* which spans the classical and Byzantine periods of Greek literature. Ovid tells the story in *Metamorphoses* (8 C.E.) of how the nymph Echo, who keeps vainly repeating the words of Narcissus, dwindles to a mere voice. This bodiless sense of missed connection haunts the tradition of echo poems, which flourished in sixteenth- and seventeenth-century Italian, French, and English verse. Pastoral poetry employed the figure of echo when the shepherds delight in hearing their voices resounding through the natural world.

The echo can be used for light effects, as in Barnabe Barnes's "Sestine 4" from *Parthenophil and Parthenophe* (1593), which begins,

> *Eccho,* what shall I do to my Nymphe, when I goe to behold her?
> *Eccho,* hold her.

It can create a sense of crossed dialogue, as in George Herbert's "Heaven":

O who will show me those delights on high?
> *Echo.   I.*
Thou Echo, thou art mortal, all men know.
> *Echo.   No.*

SEE ALSO *pastoral.*

eclogue From the Greek word *eklegein,* "to choose." The word *eclogue* orig-
inally suggested "a choice poem," the title given to choice collections of ex-
tracts from longer works. An eclogue is a short dialogue or soliloquy. The
term defines the structure and not the content of this type of poem, though
almost all eclogues are pastorals. The name was first applied to Virgil's
Bucolics, which date from the mid-30s B.C.E., and later became known as
the *Eclogues.* These formal pastoral poems extend a pattern, first established
by Theocritus in his idylls (third century B.C.E.), in which urban poets turn
to the countryside for sustenance.

In the Middle Ages and the Renaissance, the term *eclogue* was often mis-
construed as "goat song," falsely derived from *aix,* "goat," and *logos,* "speech."
As a genre, the eclogue was revived by Dante (1265–1321), Petrarch (1304–
1377), and Boccaccio (1313–1375), and flourished throughout the early
modern era. It often has a coded or allegorical dimension. In *The Art of
English Poesie* (1589), George Puttenham recognized that the eclogue was
devised "not of purpose to counterfeit or represent the rustical manner of
loves or communications, but under the veil of homely persons and in rude
speeches, to insinuate and glance at great matters, and such as perchance
had not been safe to have been disclosed of any other sort." He contended
that the eclogue makes it possible for writers to consider "great matters" that
would otherwise be unacceptable for them to take on more directly.

Some English poems descend from Virgil's *Eclogues:* Edmund Spenser's
Shepheardes Calender (1579), Sir Philip Sidney's double sestina "Ye Goat-
herd Gods" (1593), Christopher Marlowe's "The Passionate Shepherd to
His Love" (1599, 1600), Andrew Marvell's "Mower" poems (1681), John
Milton's "Lycidas" (1638), Alexander Pope's "Pastorals" (1709), book 8 of
William Wordsworth's *The Prelude* (1805, 1850), Percy Shelley's "Adonais"
(1821), and Matthew Arnold's "Thyrsis" (1866). Robert Frost's "Build Soil
— A Political Pastoral" (1936) illustrates the artistic difficulty of reviving the

eclogue in modern poetry. Jonathan Swift wrote the greatest nonpastoral eclogue, *A Town Eclogue. 1710. Scene, The Royal Exchange* (1710).

SEE ALSO *ecopoetry, georgic, nature poetry, pastoral.*

ecopoetry Nature poetry is as old as poetry itself, but since the 1960s the modern environmental crisis has given new urgency to the poetry of the natural world. The poetry that responds to this crisis has come to be called ecopoetry. It shows great sensitivity to the natural world itself, to the world that is other-than-human, and it challenges our dominion over nature. It puts us in our place. Ecopoetry is environmentally oriented, ecologically minded. It values biodiversity and views the world as an ecosystem. It seeks to heal the contemporary divorce between humanity and the rest of nature, to cherish and imagine a livable earth. It is a poetry of intervention, a series of human cries and calls that respond to our endangered world.

SEE ALSO *Arcadia, eclogue, georgic, idyll, nature poetry, pastoral, topographical poetry.*

Edda The Edda encompasses two collections of Old Norse literature and stands as the fountainhead of Germanic mythology. The Icelandic poet and historian Snorri Sturluson (1179–1241) put together a mythographic treatise, largely a handbook of poetics or book of instruction for skalds, which he termed the Edda, a word that in fourteenth-century Icelandic came to mean "poetics," seemingly derived from the word for poetry, *odr*. The nineteenth-century philologist Jacob Grimm later defined the word *edda* somewhat nostalgically as "great-grandmother," based on its usage in the *Rigsthula* (*The Song of Rig*, fourteenth century). He skewed the Edda into the folkloristic "Tales of a Grandmother." The Icelandic scholar Eiríkr Magnússon determined that the term *edda* derives from the proper name Oddi, a settlement in southwest Iceland, the home of Snorri Sturluson and Saemund the Wise (1056–1133). Snorri's treatise was thus conventionally named *The Book of Oddi*.

Snorri's Edda, written in the thirteenth century, is now referred to as the *Younger Edda* or the *Prose Edda*. It consists of a prologue and three distinct sections. The *Gylfaginning* (*The Tricking of Guilfi*) tells how Guilfi, the king "of the land men now call Sweden," travels to find out about the origin and destruction of the world of the Nordic gods. This survey of Old Norse mythology is written in prose, but contains lines and stanzas from skaldic poetry. The next section, *Skáldskaparmál* (*Poetic Diction* or *The Language of Poetry*), lists specifically poetic words, kennings for various people, places, and things, and explains them by retelling many of the old mythological stories. The last section, *Háttatal* (*List of Verse-Forms*), is Snorri's ars poetica, a poem consisting of 102 stanzas in 100 different meters. It systematizes the material with a practical commentary in prose.

In 1643, Brynjólfur Sveinsson discovered a manuscript of twenty-nine poems (ca. 1270), some partial and some complete, which contained lines and stanzas referenced in Snorri's Edda. The collection, referred to as the *Codex Regius,* was attributed to Saemund the Wise, Snorri's predecessor and compatriot, and thus was called *Saemund's Edda.* It is now named the *Elder Edda,* or the *Poetic Edda.* The evidence suggests that these poems were orally transmitted between 900 and 1100 and were written down in the thirteenth century. They were circulated in many different regions (Denmark, Germany, Iceland, Norway) and composed by different hands.

The *Poetic Edda* and a similar group of poetry fragments from other manuscripts, the *Eddica minora,* suggest that the language of Eddaic poetry is simpler, more direct, and less adorned than the later Old Icelandic poetry and prose of the skalds. The *Poetic Edda* fevered the imagination of such English-language poets as Thomas Gray (1716–1771), William Morris (1834–1896), and W. H. Auden (1907–1973).

SEE ALSO *alliteration, ars poetica, kenning, lai, saga, skald.*

ekphrasis (adjective *ekphrastic;* alternative spellings *ecphrasis, ecphrastic*). *The Oxford Classical Dictionary* defines *ekphrasis* as "the rhetorical description of a work of art." The prototype of all ekphrastic poetry is Homer's description of the shield that Hephaestus is making for Achilles in the *Iliad* (ca. eighth century B.C.E.). This description is a "notional ekphrasis," the representation of an imaginary work of art. The long Western tradition of ekphrasis includes the Greek, Latin, and Byzantine anthologists. Homer's description of the shield of Achilles leads directly to Virgil's account of Aeneas's shield in the *Aeneid* (29–19 B.C.E.) and Dante's description of the sculptures on the terrace of the proud in the *Purgatorio* (1308–12). The tradition extends in a more or less unbroken line from the rhapsodists of late antiquity to Keats and Shelley, Baudelaire and Gautier, Rilke and Yeats; it extends from Horace (whose famous phrase *ut pictura poesis* — "as in painting, so in poetry" — has had a controversial history) to Marianne Moore, William Carlos Williams, E. E. Cummings, W. H. Auden, Randall Jarrell, Elizabeth Bishop, and John Ashbery. Ekphrastic modes address — and sometimes challenge — the divide between spatial and temporal experience, eye and ear, visual and verbal mediums.

SEE ALSO *ut pictura poesis.*

elegy From the Greek word *élegos,* "funeral lament." A poem of mortal loss and consolation. The elegy was among the first forms of the ancients, though in Greek literature it refers to a specific verse form as well as the emotions conveyed by it. Any poem using the particular meter of the elegiac couplet or elegiac distich was termed an elegy. It was composed of a heroic or dactylic hexameter followed by a pentameter. Here are two lines from Henry Wadsworth Longfellow's "Elegiac Verse" (1882): "So the Hexameter, rising and singing, with cadence sonorous, / Falls; and in refluent rhythms back the Pentameter flows." There were elegies, chanted aloud and traditionally accompanied by the flute, on love (amatory complaints) and war (exhortatory martial epigrams) as well as death. But, as Peter Sacks puts it, "behind this array of topics there may have lain an earlier, more exclusive association of the flute song's elegiacs with the expression of grief."

Since the sixteenth century, the elegy has designated a poem mourning the death of an individual (as in W. B. Yeats's "In Memory of Major Robert Gregory," 1918) or a solemn meditation on the passing of human life (as in Thomas Gray's "Elegy Written in a Country Churchyard," 1751). The elegy does what Sigmund Freud calls "the work of mourning." It ritualizes grief into language and thereby makes it more bearable. The great elegy originates in the unspeakable, unacceptable loss and touches the unfathomable. It turns loss into remembrance and delivers an inheritance. It opens space for retrospection and drives wordless anguish toward the consolations of verbal articulation and ceremony.

The sense of overwhelming loss that powers the poetry of lamentation exists in all languages and poetries. It has roots in religious feeling. The process, the action of mourning, of doing something to release the dead, thus clearing a space between the dead and the living, has residual force in the ceremonial structure of the elegy. Classical antiquity had several literary vehicles for the formal expression of sorrow. The dirge was a song of lament deriving from the Greek *epicedium*, a mourning song sung over the body of the dead. The threnody was a Greek "wailing song" sung in memory of the dead. Originally a choral ode, it evolved into the monody (from the Greek: "alone song"), an ode sung by a single actor in a Greek tragedy or a poem mourning someone's death. John Milton described "Lycidas" (1638) as a monody; Matthew Arnold also termed "Thyrsis" (1866) a monody. These poems, along with Edmund Spenser's "Astrophel" (1586) and Percy Bysshe Shelley's "Adonais" (1821), belong to a subspecies of the tradition called the pastoral elegy. The laments of three Sicilian poets writing in Greek — Theocritus (third century B.C.E.), Moschus (second century B.C.E.), and Bion (second century B.C.E.) — inspired the pastoral conventions of the later English elegy. Their highly elaborated conventions (the invocation to the Muse, the representation of nature in the lament, the procession of mourners, and so forth) become the formal channel of mourning. "The elegy follows the ancient rites in the basic passage from grief or darkness to consolation and renewal," Sacks writes. The pastoral conventions are dropped in a poem like Alfred, Lord Tennyson's *In Memoriam* (1849), but the ritualistic feeling remains. The dignified formality opens out into elegies commemorating a public figure, such as Walt Whitman's poem for Abraham Lincoln, "When Lilacs Last in the Dooryard Bloom'd" (1865), and W. H. Auden's "In Memory of Sigmund Freud" (1939).

Samuel Taylor Coleridge was thinking of the elegy as a de-particularized form, a poem with a meditative mood or style, when he described it as "the form of poetry natural to the reflective mind." The definition of the elegy as a serious reflection on a serious subject applies to the so-called Anglo-Saxon elegies, some of the earliest poems in the English tradition, such as "The Wanderer" (tenth century) and "The Seafarer" (tenth century). This sense of the elegy carries forward through Thomas Nashe's "A Litany in Time of Plague" (1600), Samuel Johnson's "The Vanity of Human Wishes" (1749), Gray's "Elegy Written in a Country Churchyard" (1751), Edward Young's *Night Thoughts* (1742–46), and Rainer Maria Rilke's *Duino Elegies* (1923).

The sense of a highly self-conscious dramatic performance, a necessary and sometimes reluctant reentry into language, continues to power the elegy, but its traditional consolations have often been called into question. The American elegist in particular seems to suffer from what Emily Dickinson calls a "polar privacy," a dark sense of isolation, of displacement from the traditional settings of grief and the consolations of community. This is accompanied by a more naked experience of grief.

SEE ALSO *dirge, epicedium, keening, lament.*

elision From the Latin: "striking out." *Elision* is a metrical term for the blurring or omission of an unstressed vowel or syllable to preserve the regular meter of a line of verse. This line from Shakespeare's "Sonnet 129" provides an example: "Th'expense of spirit in a waste of shame." So too Robert Burns deliberately substitutes "o'er" for "over" in "Tam o' Shanter" (1791): "Whiles holding fast his guid blue bonnet, / Whiles crooning o'er an auld Scots sonnet..."

ellipsis From the Greek: "leaving out." An ellipsis is a form of compression, the intentional omission or non-expression of something understood, an expected word or phrase in a sentence. It is secondly a sudden leap from one topic to another. Ellipsis goes back to the ancient Greek and Hebrew poets, but it was an especially favored device of the modernists, such as T. S. Eliot, who made it one of the disjunctive strategies of "The Waste Land" (1922).

The ellipsis is also a three-point punctuation mark (... or ***) used in writing and printing to indicate an intentional omission or pause.

SEE ALSO *collage, elliptical poetry, modernism.*

elliptical poetry In *The Idiom of Poetry* (1946), Frederick Pottle used the term *elliptical* for a kind of pure poetry that omits prosaic information. He recognized ellipticism in various historical works, but contended that "the modern poet goes much farther in employing private experiences or ideas than would formerly have been thought legitimate." To the common reader, he says, "the prime characteristic of this kind of poetry is not the nature of its imagery but its obscurity, its urgent suggestion that you add something to the poem without telling what that something is." He names that something "the prose frame." Robert Penn Warren used the term *elliptical* in "Pure and Impure Poetry" (1943) to summarize T. S. Eliot's notion that some poets "become impatient of this meaning [explicit statement of ideas in logical order] which seems superfluous, and perceive possibilities of intensity through its elimination." Stephen Burt redeployed the term *elliptical poetry* to characterize a kind of oblique, gnomic poetry. He calls elliptical poets "post-avant-gardist" or "post-postmodern."

SEE ALSO *ellipsis.*

emblem   An image accompanied by a motto and a brief verse. The emblem, which was intended as a moral lesson, was a pictorial representation of an idea. *The Oxford English Dictionary* defines it as a verbal form, a "fable or allegory that might be constructed pictorially," or an image, "a drawing or picture expressing a moral fable or allegory." It is both image and text. There is a hieroglyphic element to the emblem, which is related to the epigram. The dialogue or tension between the picture and the words creates a space for the audience to interpret the meaning.

The emblem emerged as a distinct literary form in the sixteenth century. It is also known in vernacular as *device,* or *impresa* in Italian, *empresa* in Spanish. The first European emblem book was Andrea Alciati's *Emblematum liber* (1531), which inspired several episodes in Spenser's *Faerie Queene* (1590–96); the first English emblem book was George Whitney's *A Choice of Emblemes* (1586); the most well-known Protestant emblem book was Francis Quarles's *Emblemes* (1635). Quarles called the emblem a "silent parable." Henri Estienne described it as "a sweet and morall Symbole, which consists of pictures and words" (1646). Both as a form in and of itself and as a fund of imagery, the emblem influenced not only Spenser and Shakespeare, but also Ben Jonson, Richard Crashaw, John Donne, and George Herbert, whose pattern poems, such as "The Altar" (1633), have an emblematic quality. William Blake's illuminated books evoke the tradition of emblem books. Robert Louis Stevenson playfully revived the form in *Moral Lessons* (1881). The emblem book slows the pace of reading and invites associations between image and word.

SEE ALSO *epigram, pattern poetry.*

encomium From the Latin word *encomium,* which derives from a Greek word meaning "in revel"; originally meant "revel songs," then "songs of praise" (plural *encomia*). A formal expression of praise, the encomium was a Greek choral song in celebration of a hero. It was sung at a joyous procession, the *komos,* which praised the victor of athletic matches. Pindar (ca. 522–443 B.C.E.) and Simonides (ca. 556–468 B.C.E.) wrote the great early encomia. Aristotle (384–322 B.C.E.) remembered the encomium as part of all early poetry, but considered it a subdivision of declamatory oratory. He also argued that praise is one of the two essential forms of poetry (the other is blame). Later, the term *encomium* came to suggest any laudatory composition in poetry or prose.

SEE ALSO *praise poems.*

end-stopped line A poetic line in which a natural grammatical pause, such as that occurring at the end of a phrase, clause, or sentence, coincides with the end of a line. An end-stopped line, the alternative to an enjambed or run-on line, halts the movement of the verse and creates the sensation of a whole syntactical unit, which gives the line additional rhetorical weight and authority, a meaning unto itself. It imparts a feeling of completeness, though that feeling is temporary, since the poem then proceeds onward until its end. The end-stopped line gains additional force by its relationship to the whole. The halting effect is increased when each end-stopped line concludes with an emphatic punctuation mark, as in the first eight lines of Gerard Manley Hopkins's sonnet "The Starlight Night" (1877):

> Look at the stars! look, look up at the skies!
>   O look at all the fire-folk sitting in the air!
>   The bright boroughs, the circle-citadels there!
> Down in dim woods the diamond delves! the elves'-eyes!
> The grey lawns cold where gold, where quickgold lies!
>   Wind-beat whitebeam! airey abeles set on a flare!
>   Flake-doves sent floating forth at a farmyard scare!
> Ah well! it is all a purchase, all is a prize.

SEE ALSO *enjambment, line.*

enjambment   Enjambment (or what the French call *emjambement*) is the carryover of one line of poetry to the next without a grammatical break. A runover or enjambed line is the alternative to an end-stopped line. Enjambment creates a dialectical motion of hesitation and flow. The lineation bids the reader to pause at the end of each line even as the syntax pulls the reader forward. This creates a sensation of hovering expectation. In 1668, John Milton called enjambment "the sense variously drawn out from one verse into another."

SEE ALSO *end-stopped line, line.*

envelope   A pattern of repetition, the envelope is a line or stanza that encloses the rest of the poem. It recurs in the same form or with a slight variation. The structural pattern of recurrence gives the line or stanza deeper resonance by being brought back propitiously at the end of the poem. This strategy was one of the favorites of the biblical poets. For example, Psalm 8 begins and ends with the line "O Lord our Lord, how excellent is thy name in all the earth!" Robert Alter explains that "the repetition of this vertically ordered poetic review of cosmic hierarchy is felt as a climactic completion, a symmetric framing-in by praise of the panorama of creation." It is called an envelope rhyme when a pair of outer rhymes encloses a pair of inner ones, as in Tennyson's In Memoriam stanza (*abba*), based on the stanzas of his poem of 1849.

SEE ALSO *In Memoriam stanza, refrain, repetition, rhyme.*

envoi, envoy   A "send-off." The half-stanza that concludes certain French forms, such as the ballade and the sestina. The troubadours called their envois *tornadas* ("returns"). The envoi is a final return to the subject, a valedictory summing up, and a clever send-off.

SEE ALSO *sestina, troubadour.*

epic   A long narrative poem, exalted in style, heroic in theme. The earliest epics focus on the legendary adventures of a hero against the backdrop of a historical event: think of the Trojan War and Odysseus's action-packed journey home in the Homeric epics the *Iliad* and the *Odyssey* (ca. eighth century B.C.E.), the models for epic poetry ever since; or the territorial battles of a warrior culture in the Anglo-Saxon epic *Beowulf* (eighth to eleventh century); or the preservation of a city and a civilization in the Babylonian *Gilgamesh* (ca. 1600–1000 B.C.E.). These epics seem to be the written versions of texts long sung and retold, composed and recomposed by many epic singers over time, all telling the tale of a tribe. The first audiences for the epics were listeners, the later ones readers. Aristotle (384–322 B.C.E.) considered the Homeric epic the prototype of tragedy. The epic carried important cultural truths but, as M. I. Finley puts it, "Whatever else the epic may have been, it was *not history*. It was narrative, detailed and precise, with minute description of fighting and sailing, and feasting and burials and sacrifices, all very real and vivid; it may even contain, buried away, some kernels of historical fact — but it was not history." The epic is inherently nostalgic. It looks back to greater and more heroic times — the emergence of tribes, the founding of countries, the deeds of legendary figures. It is removed from the contemporary world of the audience and looks back to what Goethe and Schiller called the *vollkommen vergangen* ("perfect past"). It moves beyond individual experience and binds people to their communal past.

The epic singer brings together a powerful memory and strong improvisatory technique, using formulaic phrases, lines, and half-lines; propulsive rhythms; stock descriptions; and recurrent scenes and incidents, to build a tale with encyclopedic range and cyclical action. The epic is purposely recited in segments. In the epic, Mikhail Bakhtin writes, "it is, therefore, possible to take any part and offer it as the whole . . . the structure of the whole is repeated in each part, and each part is complete and circular like the whole." The epic poets who worked at the same time as Homer are called the Cyclic poets because they covered the entire war cycle. "The cyclical form of the classical epic is based on the natural cycle," Northrop Frye explains. "The cycle has two main rhythms: the life and death of the individual, and the slower social rhythm which, in the course of years . . . brings cities and empires to their rise and fall."

Some examples: the great Sanskrit epics of ancient India are the Mahabharata (ninth to eighth century B.C.E.) and the Ramayana (fifth to fourth century B.C.E.); the major epic poem in Persian is the Iranian epic Shahnameh (ca. 977–1010). The epics of Mesopotamia survived in tales written in Sumerian and Akkadian. The *Nibelungenlied* (ca. 1180–1210) is the epic of Middle High German. *La chanson de Roland* (*The Song of Roland,* ca. 1090) is the pinnacle of the French epic tradition of chansons de geste ("songs of heroic deeds [lineage]"), which influenced the most complete example in the thriving Spanish epic tradition, *Poema de mío Cid* (*Poem of My Cid,* twelfth century). The Irish epic *Táin Bó Cúailnge* (*Cattle Raid of Cooley*) was written down by monks in the ninth century, but the story dates to the La Tène period of civilization, possibly about 100 B.C.E. It intersperses lyrics and verse dialogues with the main tale told in prose. Vladimir Nabokov calls *The Song of Igor's Campaign: An Epic of the Twelfth Century* (1960) "a harmonious, many leveled, many hued, uniquely poetical structure created in a sustained and controlled surge of inspiration by an artist with a fondness for pagan gods and a percipience of sensuous things." In the early nineteenth century, a group of medieval German texts were grouped together as *Spielmannsepen* ("minstrel epics"). These legends included *König Rothar* (*King Rothar,* ca. 1160), *Herzog Ernst* (ca. 1180), *Der Münchener Oswald* (fifteenth century), *Orendel* (late twelfth century), and *Salman und Moralf* (late twelfth century). In the 1830s, the folklorist Elias Lönnrot organized Finnish runo-songs (*runolauluja*) to create the *Kalevala,* a Balto-Finnish epic. In the 1860s, the folklorist F. Reinhold Kreutzwald followed suit and used Estonian runo-songs to compose Estonia's national epic, *Kalevipoeg.*

There are two main types of European songs that tell stories: epics and ballads. Whereas the ballad is a short strophic form that focuses on a primary event, the epic song is a long non-strophic form that focuses on a variety of events. But the genres sometimes blur and there is considerable thematic overlap, often dramatic, between the longer ballads and the shorter epic songs that have been collected in a wide range of cultures.

The Serbs, Croatians, Montenegrins, Bulgarians, and Albanians all have epic songs, which are performed by *guslari* (the *gusle* or *gusla* is a single-stringed instrument). The *guslari* have specialized in *junačke pesme* ("men's songs"), heroic narratives chanted or sung on aggressively masculine themes, like war. They also perform *narodne pesme* ("people's songs") — the word *pesma* also means "poem." There are nine epic cycles of these popular narrative poems based on historical events. The *guslari* provided the models for Milman Parry and Albert Lord's theories of an oral-formulaic method that stretches back to the Homeric bards.

The slow-moving, unrhymed, and typically unaccompanied Russian epic songs are called *byliny*. The Ukrainian version of the epic is a body of songs called *dumy*, which were traditionally performed by itinerant Cossack bards called *kobzani*. The Tibetan *Epic of King Gesar* (ca. twelfth century) is performed both by amateurs and professional epic bards. A typical episode of the story contains five to ten thousand lines of verse (fifty to one hundred songs) linked by a spoken narration. The West African Mande epic of Son-Jara is recited by professional *finah* ("poet-historians") and runs to more than three thousand lines. The Kyrgyz national epic, *Manas* (ca. eighteenth century), can approach close to half a million lines and take up to three weeks to recite.

Sïrat Banï Hiläl (ca. eleventh century) is the epic history of the Banï Hiläl Bedouin tribe. It has been told and retold throughout the Arab world, from the Indian Ocean to the Atlantic coast, for almost a thousand years. Dwight Fletcher Reynolds points out that "in different regions and over different historical periods the epic has been performed as a complex tale cycle narrated entirely in prose, as a prose narrative embellished with lengthy poems, as a narrative recited in rhymed verse, and as a narrative sung to the accompaniment of various musical instruments." Al-Bakātūsh, a village in northern Egypt, is known as the "village of the poets" because of its large community of hereditary epic singers who recite and perform the poem.

Ezra Pound called the epic "a poem including history." Literary or secondary epics — Virgil's *Aeneid* (29–19 B.C.E.), Dante's *Divine Comedy* (ca. 1308–21), Ariosto's *Orlando furioso* (1516), Camões's *Lusiads* (1572), Spenser's *Faerie Queene* (1590–96), Tasso's *Jerusalem Delivered* (1581), Milton's *Paradise Lost* (1667) — adopted many of the conventions and strategies of the traditional epic, even though they are written poems meant to be read rather than oral ones intended to be told and sung. "Homer makes us hearers," Alexander Pope said, "and Virgil leaves us readers." The editors of *Epic Traditions in the Contemporary World* argue that "epic conceived as a poetic narrative of length and complexity that centers around deeds of significance to the community transcends the oral and literary divide that has long marked the approach to the genre."

Byron playfully satirizes the epic apparatus he employs in this stanza from *Don Juan* (1819–24):

My poem's epic, and is meant to be
    Divided in twelve books; each book containing,
With Love, and War, a heavy gale at sea,
    A list of ships, and captains, and kings reigning,
New characters; the episodes are three:
    A panoramic view of Hell's in training,
After the style of Virgil and of Homer,
    So that my name of Epic's no misnomer.

The epic also generated several types of revisionary epics and even anti-epics, such as the epic with a recent action (Lucan's *Pharsalia,* ca. 61–65 C.E.) or Christian "brief epics" (Abraham Cowley's *Davideis: A Sacred Poem of the Troubles of David,* 1656, or John Milton's *Paradise Regained,* 1671), which they claimed were modeled on the Book of Job but more closely followed the classical epic. "All the types of Biblical epic developed during the Divine Poetry movement [in sixteenth-century England] answered the pagan epic repertoire feature by feature," Alastair Fowler explains. The pagan Muse was replaced by the Holy Spirit, or a prayer to God, and the national or legendary action became the redemptive history of scripture.

Pound's *Cantos* (1915–69) were a bid to revive the epic as a modernist form. Nikos Kazantzakis's Greek poem *The Odyssey: A Modern Sequel* (1924–38), David Jones's Welsh poem *Anathemata* (1952), and Derek Walcott's West Indian *Omeros* (1990) all make epic bids. From a Turkish prison cell, Nazim Hikmet wrote a five-volume epic novel in verse, *Human Landscapes from My Country* (1963), which he regarded as a historical synthesis of oral poetry, designed to be sung, and the printed novel, designed to be read silently in private. An epic apparatus has been employed by American poets from Anne Bradstreet's *Exact Epitome of the Four Monarchies* (1650), which could be called the first North American epic, to William Carlos Williams's *Paterson* (1940–61), Hilda Doolittle's (H. D.) *Helen in Egypt* (1974), Louis Zukofsky's *"A"* (1928–68), Charles Olson's *The Maximus Poems* (1950–70), and James Merrill's *Changing Light at Sandover* (1976–82).

All in all, as Jorge Luis Borges wrote, "the epic is one of the necessities of the human mind."

SEE ALSO *aoidos, ballad, bard, epic question, epic simile, epithet, in medias res, invocation, mock epic, oral-formulaic method, oral poetry.*

epicedium The Latin spelling of the Greek word for "funeral song" (plural *epicedia*). A funeral ode or hymn, a mourning song in praise of the dead. The *epicedium* was sung in the presence of the dead, which gave it a raw, ritualistic feeling and made it a functional form, like the wedding song. This differentiates it from the dirge, which isn't limited to time or place. The elegiac statements over the bodies of Hector and Achilles are *epicedia*.

My anthology of Latin *epicedia* would include "Catullus 101" (57 B.C.E.), Catullus's grief-stricken elegy for his brother, as well as examples by Virgil (*Eclogue 5*, lines 20–44, 42–39 B.C.E.; and *Aeneid*, book 6, lines 860–86, 29–19 B.C.E.), Horace (*Odes*, book 1, number 24, 23–13 B.C.E.), Propertius (book 3, elegy 7, line 18, 18–23 B.C.E.), Ovid (*Amores*, book 3, elegy 9, 16 B.C.E.; and *Epistulae ex ponto [Letters from the Black Sea]*, book 1, part 9, 9–12 C.E.), Martial (*Epigrams*, book 5, number 37, 89 C.E., and book 6, numbers 28, 29, and 85, 90 C.E.), and Statius (*Silvae*, book 2, part 1, 90 C.E.; book 3, part 3, 93 C.E.; and book 5, parts 1, 3, and 5, in or after 96 C.E.).

SEE ALSO *dirge, elegy.*

epic question The traditional epic often begins in media res. The singer of tales invokes the Muse, states the theme, and raises a question about the nature and cause of the conflict. The answer initiates the narrative. "What god drove them to fight with such a fury?" the Homeric singer wonders at the beginning of the *Iliad* (ca. eighth century B.C.E.). Milton raises an epic question at the outset of *Paradise Lost* (1667): "What cause / Mov'd our Grand Parents, in that happy state / Favour'd of Heaven so highly to fall off / From their Creator?"

SEE ALSO *epic.*

epic simile An extended verbal comparison. This epic-scale or fully developed analogy (usually using *like* or *as*) is also called a Homeric simile, since it is a minor convention of the epic and plays a prominent role in Homer's poems. The epic simile is lingering and digressive — it can extend for twenty or more lines — and tends to suspend the action. It often shifts perspective. Thus Homer compares a battle to a snowstorm and Virgil compares the ghosts of the dead on the shores of Lethe to a swarm of bees.

SEE ALSO *epic, simile.*

epigram From the Greek word *epigramma,* "to write upon." An epigram is a short, witty poem or pointed saying. Ambrose Bierce defined it in *The Devil's Dictionary* (1881–1911) as "a short, sharp saying in prose and verse." In Hellenistic Greece (third century B.C.E.), the epigram developed from an inscription carved in a stone monument or onto an object, such as a vase, into a literary genre in its own right. It may have developed out of the proverb. *The Greek Anthology* (tenth century) is filled with more than fifteen hundred epigrams of all sorts, including pungent lyrics on the pleasures of wine, women, boys, and song.

Ernst Robert Curtius writes, in *European Literature and the Latin Middle Ages* (1953), "No poetic form is so favorable to playing with pointed and surprising ideas as epigram — for which reason seventeenth- and eighteenth-century Germany called it 'Sinngedicht.' This development of the epigram necessarily resulted after the genre ceased to be bound by its original definition (an inscription for the dead, for sacrificial offerings, etc.)." Curtius relates the interest in epigrams to the development of the "conceit" as an aesthetic concept.

Samuel Taylor Coleridge defined the epigram in epigrammatic form (1802):

> What is an epigram? A dwarfish whole;
> Its body brevity and wit its soul.

The pithiness, wit, irony, and sometimes harsh tone of the English epigram derive from the Roman poets, especially Martial, known for his caustic short poems, such as book 1, epigram 32 (85–86 B.C.E.): "Sabinus, I don't like you. You know why? / Sabinus, I don't like you. That is why."

The epigram has no particular form, though it often employs a rhymed couplet or quatrain, which can stand alone or serve as part of a longer work. Here is Alexander Pope's "Epigram from the French" (1732):

> Sir, I admit your general rule,
> That every poet is a fool:
> But you yourself may serve to show it,
> That every fool is not a poet.

Geoffrey Hartman points to two diverging traditions of the epigram. These were classified by J. C. Scaliger as *mel* and *fel* (*Poetices libri septem,*

1561), which have been interpreted as *sweet* and *sour, sugar* and *salt, naive* and *pointed*. Thus Robert Hayman, echoing Horace's idea that poetry should be both "*dulce et utile*," sweet and useful, writes in *Quodlibets* (1628), "Short epigrams relish both sweet and sour, / Like fritters of sour apples and sweet flour."

The "vinegar" of the epigram was often contrasted with the "honey" of the sonnet, especially the Petrarchan sonnet, though the Shakespearean sonnet, with its pointed final couplet, also combined the sweet with the sour. "By a natural development," Hartman writes, "since epigram and sonnet were not all that distinct, the pointed style often became the honeyed style raised to a higher power, to preciousness. A new opposition is frequently found, not between sugared and salty, but between pointed (precious, overwritten) and plain." The sometimes sweet, sometimes sour, and sometimes sweet-and-sour epigram has been employed by contemporary American formalists, such as Howard Nemerov, X. J. Kennedy, and J. V. Cunningham.

SEE ALSO *conceit, epitaph, proverb, sonnet, wit.*

epinicion   (plural *epinicia*) Victory songs. The Greek *epinicion* odes were commissioned victory poems (named for epi-Niké-an, the goddess of victory) about sports. Stories of gods and heroes were woven into them. Each ode focused on a triumphant athlete who had a symbolic connection to a god, and thus incorporates a mythology. The poems have their roots in religious rites, and each one called for an ecstatic performance that communally reenacted the ritual of participation in the divine. Albin Lesky explains that "the epinicion elevates the significant event of victory into the realm of values, the world from which the poet's creation flows. This world of values is displayed and exemplified in its various spheres: in the divine itself, in the tales of the heroes, in the rules of conduct and not least in the poet's own creative activity as an artistic realm in its own right."

The tradition of celebrating athletic achievement begins with Pindar, whose choral odes to commemorate athletic victories from the fifth century B.C.E. are the first truly written narrative texts of any length in the Western tradition. Greeks simultaneously sang the poems and danced to them at shrines or theaters, though now the words are all that remains of the complete Pindaric experience. The movement of the verse, which mirrors a musical dance pattern, tends to be emotionally intense and highly exalted. Horace (65–8 B.C.E.) compared Pindar (ca. 522–443 B.C.E.) to a great swan conquering the air by long, rapturous flights. He claimed that the athletes were given more glory by Pindar's voice "than by a hundred statues standing mute / Around the applauding city."

Simonides also wrote *epinicion* odes. C. M. Bowra explains that the *epinicion* ode became something "serious and stately; it assumed characteristics which had hitherto belonged to the hymn; it told instructive and illuminating stories; it contained aphorisms on man's relations with the gods. All these can be found in Pindar's *Odes,* and we cannot doubt that Simonides did something to prepare the way for them." A special place should also be reserved for the *epinicion* odes of Bacchylides, who was known after antiquity by a mere 107 nonsequential lines (in 69 fragments) until 1896, when a papyrus containing his work was discovered in Egypt. The papyrus was cut up into sections, smuggled from Egypt, and delivered to the British Museum. There a papyrologist reassembled 1,382 lines, including fifteen *epinicion* odes.

SEE ALSO *ode.*

epistle, see *letter poem.*

epitaph From the Greek: "on a tomb." An epitaph can be either a commemorative short poem inscribed on a gravestone or a poem that imitates one. The imitative type creates the fiction of a memorial site. The epitaph generally refers to the dead in the third person (think of Keats's poignant line "Here lies one whose name was writ in water") and serves as an abbreviated elegy. The inscribed poem addresses itself to the stranger passing by. Roman tombs were placed along the highways near Rome and thus a typical Roman epigraph began, "Read, passing friend . . ." The earliest epitaphs are Egyptian pieces carved on sarcophagi and coffins. The classical epitaphs found in book 4 of *The Greek Anthology* (tenth century) have influenced writers of epitaphs ever since — from the Latin poets to the English and American ones — from Ben Jonson to William Wordsworth to Edgar Lee Masters, who employed the fictive epitaph to create the voices of an entire village in *Spoon River Anthology* (1916). The most famous Greek epitaph memorializes the dead at Thermopylae:

> Go, tell the Lacedaimonians, passer-by,
> That here obedient to their laws we lie.

Jonathan Swift imitated the Roman tradition of addressing passing strangers in his epitaph, written in Latin, which appears above his tomb in Saint Patrick's Cathedral, Dublin. Translated by John Middleton Murry, it reads, "The body of Jonathan Swift, Dean of this Cathedral Church, is buried here, where fierce indignation can lacerate his heart no more. Go, traveler, and imitate if you can one who strove his utmost to champion liberty."

SEE ALSO *elegy.*

epithalamium From the Greek: "at the bridal chamber"; Latin form: epithalamium, Greek form: epithalamion. A poem or song celebrating a marriage, the epithalamium was intended to be recited or sung outside the bridal chamber on the wedding night. Traditional marriage songs exist in most cultures (the biblical Song of Songs is a notable example), though Sappho (late seventh century B.C.E.) is credited with first using it as a distinct literary form. Most of her epithalamiums are lost. In the *Iliad* (ca. eighth century B.C.E.), Homer describes wedding processions accompanied by torches, music, dancing, and song. The epithalamium reached classical peaks with Theocritus in Greek (*Idyll 18,* on the marriage of Helen and Menelaus) and Catullus in Latin (*Carmina,* poems 61 and 62). Philip Sidney imported the wedding song into English in the 1580s ("A Ditty"); Edmund Spenser influentially marked the form with his *Epithalamion* (1595), which was written for his own wedding and consists of twenty-four stanzas that progress from first awakening until late at night. In 1595, he invented a new title, "Prothalamion" (i.e., before, in time or place, the bridal chamber), for his poem commemorating a betrothal ceremony, thus perhaps suggesting a separate genre. The epithalamium, a ceremonial poem with no specific formal requirements, marks an occasion.

epithet A fixed formula, usually an adjective or adjectival phrase, used to characterize a person or thing. The Homeric epithet refers to Homer's way of conjoining adjectives and nouns to make stock phrases, as in "wine-dark sea" and "rosy-fingered dawn," and praise names, such as "divine Odysseus" and "swift-footed Achilles." In the 1930s, Milman Parry analyzed these Homeric epithets and demonstrated that Homer's language was a structure built up from fixed formulas. He considered the formula "a group of words regularly employed under the same metrical conditions to express a given essential idea." These prefabricated phrases and repetitions were part of the formulaic method, particularly important because they satisfied the needs of the Homeric meter, dactylic hexameter. They were a rhythmic device for oral poets, who were sewing things together from memory (*rhapsode* means "one who sews songs"). The Homeric epithet was thus essential to the oral-formulaic compositional method. It was also a way of capturing something essential about a person or thing.

The spelling out of a hero's special praise name is not exclusively an epic device. In many places in Africa and elsewhere, praise names lie at the heart of public life. Praise singers elaborate upon these names during heightened public events such as rituals and ceremonies. A person's praise name often includes references to past deeds as well as ancestors.

SEE ALSO *epic, oral-formulaic method, oral poetry, oríki, panegyric, praise poems, rhapsode.*

epode From the Greek: "after-song." The third section of a classical ode is called an epode; it differs in meter from the first two sections, the strophe and the antistrophe. The epode suggests a coming together, a unified and completed movement. Horace titled his fifth book of odes *Epodon libor* (*The Book of Epodes,* ca. 29 B.C.E.).

SEE ALSO *antistrophe, ode, strophe.*

erasure A form of found poetry that operates by selectively erasing words from a text that already exists. Using appropriation as a poetic tool, writers have found many ways in recent years to cut away at precursor works. They have deleted, crossed out, blacked out, redacted, and drawn over the words. The idea, spurred by similar gestures in the visual arts, is to give a precursor work a decisive new set of questions and meanings. It is a poetics of reduction and removal, of meaningful fragmentation. "If you have ever read the work of Sappho or Aeschylus then you are already intimately familiar with the foundation of erasure poetics," Travis Macdonald writes. Ronald Johnson's *Radi os* (1977), for example, revised the first four books of Milton's *Paradise Lost* by excising words, discovering a modern poem within the seventeenth-century one.

SEE ALSO *found poetry, fragment.*

euphony From the Greek: "good sound." A pleasing or sweet sound, euphony is the opposite of cacophony. Vowel sounds are usually considered more euphonious than consonants. The liquids and semi-vowels (*l, m, n, r, y, w*) are generally deemed the most euphonic of the consonants. This is a matter of taste. Since the ancients, emphasis on beautiful sounds has been an essential part of poetry, but harmonic sounds are a means to an end, not an end in themselves. Some poets prefer a more dissonant music. Poetry in English is a river fed by two streams: the more euphonic Latinate words and the more cacophonous Anglo-Saxon ones.

Listen for how John Keats grasps and modulates the pitch of a nightingale across several lines in "Ode to a Nightingale" (1819), how suggestively he invokes "a light-winged Dryad of the trees" who

> In some melodious plot
> Of beechen green, and shadows numberless,
> Singest of summer in full-throated ease.

And how he captures the sound of the wind (listen for the light *i* sounds as well as the consonants *f* and *w*) in a famous line from "To Autumn," one of the most euphonic poems in the English language: "Thy hair soft-lifted by the winnowing wind."

SEE ALSO *assonance, cacophony.*

euphuism An affected, highly elaborated and ornate style. John Lyly popularized the name and the artificial style in his prose works *Euphues: The Anatomy of Wyt* (1578) and *Euphues and his England* (1580). Lyly's high-flown style, which provided a model for many of the courtiers and wits at the court of Queen Elizabeth, depended on balanced phrasing, excessive alliteration, far-fetched figures of speech:

> Though the chamomile the more it is trodden and pressed down, the more it spreadeth, yet the violet the oftener it is handled and touched, the sooner it withereth and decayeth.

"Though we cannot say that euphuism is verse," John Dover Wilson writes in his 1905 book on Lyly, "we can say that it partakes of the nature of verse."

Lyly's influential style dated rapidly. Shakespeare notably parodies Lyly's euphuistic manner in *Henry IV* (1598). Falstaff, taking on the persona of the king, sounds comically bombastic in lecturing Prince Harry:

> For though the chamomile, the more it is trodden on, the faster it grows, yet youth, the more it is wasted, the sooner it wears. That thou art my son I have partly thy mother's word, partly my own opinion, but chiefly a villainous trick of thine eye, and a foolish hanging of thy nether lip, that doth warrant me. If then thou be son to me, here lies the point. Why, being son to me, art thou so pointed at? Shall the blessed son of heaven prove a micher, and eat blackberries? — A question not to be asked. Shall the son of England prove a thief, and take purses? — A question to be asked.

exemplum   (plural *exempla*) A short narrative that makes a moral point. The term is primarily applied to illustrative stories within longer prose works, such as medieval sermons, though there are examples in poetry. John Gower's thirty-thousand-line poem, *Confessio Amantis* (ca. 1385), employs exempla to illustrate sins against Love.

eye rhyme, see *rhyme.*

F

fable A short allegorical narrative, in verse or prose, that makes a moral point. The fable is a didactic genre, and the fabulist, whether an oral storyteller or a writer, traditionally anthropomorphizes animals, plants, and inanimate objects to dramatize human weakness. Many great fables employ speaking animals. The first collection is attributed to Aesop (sixth century B.C.E.); *Aesop's Fables* is known throughout the world. The Roman Phaedus employed iambic trimeters to imitate Aesop in the first century; Babrius wrote a series of Aesop-like fables in the second century. Jean de La Fontaine's *Fables,* which began to appear in the 1660s, combined a sense of childlike openness with literary sophistication, a quality captured in nineteenth-century Russian by Ivan Andreyevich Krylov and in twentieth-century American English by Marianne Moore (*The Fables of La Fontaine,* 1965). The definition of the fable has sometimes been widened to include other kinds of pointed narratives, as in John Dryden's *Fables, Ancient and Modern* (1700). John Crowe Ransom suggested that Thomas Hardy's poems were best described as fables: "They offer natural images of the gods in action or, sometimes unfortunately, in inaction." Most people think of fables as animal stories to educate children.

fabliau A short, comic, often bawdy tale in verse. This literary genre, which was performed by jongleurs — part farce, part dirty story — was especially popular in medieval France. The vogue spread to Italy and England, where Chaucer re-created the genre in "The Miller's Tale" and "The Reeve's Tale" in *The Canterbury Tales* (ca. 1387–1400). The French *fabliau* was gradually replaced by the short story, but its influence lived on in the works of Boccaccio and Molière.

SEE ALSO *dit, jongleur.*

falling rhythm, descending rhythm   Rhythm in which the stress comes first. Trochaic (/ u) and dactylic (/ u u) meters are falling rhythms and thus give a sense of "falling" or "descending" from a stressed syllable to an unstressed one. Here is a trochaic line and thus a falling rhythm from Henry Wadsworth Longfellow's "Song of Hiawatha" (1855):

Shóuld yŏu | ásk mĕ, | whénce thĕse | stóriĕs?

The first three feet are dactylic, and thus a descending rhythm, in Robert Browning's "Lost Leader":

Júst fŏr ă | hándfŭl ŏf | sílvĕr hĕ | léft ŭs

The term *falling rhythm* can be misleading because it seems to suggest something about the emotional movement or impact of the verse, but it is merely a technical term.

SEE ALSO *dactyl, rising rhythm, trochee.*

feminine rhyme   A rhyme of two syllables, the first stressed and the second unstressed (*trances/glances*). It is also called double rhyme and has often been employed for light verse, as when Lewis Carroll playfully riffs through the opening stanza of "Rules and Regulations":

A short direction
To avoid dejection,
By variations
In occupations,
And prolongation
Of relaxation,
And combinations
Of recreations,
And disputation
On the state of the nation
In adaptation
To your station,
By invitations
To friends and relations,
By evitation
Of amputation,

By permutation
In conversation,
And deep reflection
You'll avoid dejection.

SEE ALSO *masculine rhyme, rhyme.*

figures of speech   The various rhetorical uses of language are considered figures of speech. These nonliteral expressions employ words in imaginative or "figurative" ways. Think of John Donne addressing the sun as a "busy old fool" ("The Sun Rising," 1633) or Christopher Smart treating his cat's daily activities as a form of devotion to God in *Jubilate Agno* (*Rejoice in the Lamb,* 1759–63). The study of figurative speech and thought was originally a branch of rhetoric, but gradually became part of poetics. Henry Peacham delights in them in *The Garden of Eloquence* (1593):

> The most excellent Ornaments, Exornations, Lightes, Flowers, and Formes of Speech, commonly called the Figures of Rhetorike. By which the singular Partes of Man's Mind, are most aptly expressed, and the sundrie Affections of his Heart most effectualie uttered.

George Puttenham defines and illustrates 121 figures of speech in "Of Ornament" (*The Arte of English Poesie,* 1589). Figures of speech were once considered "ornaments" of poetry, something added on, but they are actually at its core, the quintessence of poetic thinking, a way of knowing through language.

SEE ALSO *metaphor, metonymy, poetics, rhetoric, trope.*

fili   (plural *filidh*) The *filidh* were a professional caste of poets in early Ireland who were often credited with the supernatural power of prophecy. The words *fili* and *filidh* are etymologically connected to "seer." These poets, who were the successors of the druids and could practice divination, were magicians and lawgivers. They were the highest-ranking members of a group called the *áes dána* (literally, "the people of skill, craft"). In English, the word *bard* usually denotes a Celtic poet, but the *filidh* were more aristocratic and enjoyed greater privileges than the bards. Their poetry is nonetheless called bardic, since they were entrusted with an oral tradition that predated Christianity. Their education was daunting; they spent years at a dedicated school where poetry was studied as a craft. There were seven orders of *filídh;* the highest grade, the *ollamh,* studied for twelve years. The *filídh* practiced an elaborate form of syllabic poetry and mastered complex metrical forms, which employed both internal rhymes and end-rhymes, consonance, alliteration, and other devices of sound. They learned by heart at least 300 poetic meters, 250 primary stories, and 100 secondary stories. They recited traditional tales and topographical lore. They also served as crucial advisors and historical chroniclers, who remembered the genealogies of their patrons. They were so bound by tradition that there is little change in their work from 1250 to 1650. In the thirteenth century, the poet Giolla Bríghde Mac Con Midhe explained,

> If poetry were to be suppressed, my people,
> if we were without history, without ancient lays,
> forever, but the father of each man,
> everyone will pass unheralded.

Ted Hughes characterized the *fili* as "the curator and re-animator of the inner life which held the people together and made them what they were."

SEE ALSO *bard, oral poetry.*

flyting From the Scots: "scolding." A contest of insults; cursing matches in verse. The flyting is a formal exchange of taunts, a form of rhetorical one-upmanship in which poets alternately blast and assail each other. In early heroic narratives, there is often an exchange of boasts and insults between two warrior-heroes in a public setting, which often ends in a trial of arms, as in the quarrel between Beowulf and Unferth in *Beowulf.* These heroic flytings became the model for "ludic flytings," a more playful version. The finest example of the ludic flyting in Scottish literature is the early sixteenth-century poem "The Flyting of Dunbar and Kennedy," which pitted William Dunbar against his rival, Walter Kennedy. The flyting is crucial to Scottish poetry, but cursing matches in verse are also found in a startling range of poetries.

SEE ALSO *poetic contest.*

folio From the Latin word *folium,* "leaf." A folio is a large book that consists of sheets folded once only, into halves. During the early modern era, the folio format was prestigious, used for the work of leading theologians, historians, and philosophers. A quarto is much smaller and consists of sheets folded twice, into quarters. An octavo, even smaller, is folded three times. During his lifetime, many of Shakespeare's plays were issued as quartos, which were less prized than the more expensive folios. The First Folio appeared in 1623, seven years after his death. This was the first time that a folio was devoted entirely to plays. Three subsequent folios appeared in 1632, 1663, and 1685.

folk song   A traditional song. The essential trait of folk song, a large part of the repertoire of folk verse, is that it is sung aloud. Folk songs are composed by individuals, usually untrained, nonprofessional musicians, and passed on by word of mouth, which is why there are so many variants of a given song. There are also many types of folk song, such as children's songs and lullabies, ballads and carols, spirituals and work songs. The folk song is composed by an individual and perpetuated by oral tradition, honed and changed by usage, which is how it becomes the expression of a group of people. There is often a strong connection between written songs and oral ones, as in the interchange between ballads and broadside ballads. Some nineteenth-century scholars believed that folk songs were created by people improvising in groups, which is untrue, though many people make changes to these songs over time in a process known as "communal re-creation."

Folk songs were traditionally considered rural, but they can thrive both in the country, as in the rural blues, and in the city, as in the urban blues. They are both preindustrial and postindustrial. Individual singers continually modify the songs, which tend to be in a relatively simple style. The lyrics are memorized and carried along by the music. Folk songs often have highly formalized structures. The meters are frequently short, the verses fluent and melodic, the stanzas regular, reinforced by refrains. There is a specialized form, the cumulative song, or *randonnée,* in which the content as well as the length of each stanza expands by the introduction of new elements, which are then repeated. Many songs revolve around rites of passage, such as births, weddings, and deaths, which give them a functional dimension, recognized and understood by a wide swatch of a community. The cultural idea of folk song significantly changed in the mid-twentieth century because of the widespread folk-song movement. The rubric "folk song" widened to include new compositions and performances, some recorded, others adapted orally, by artists working in the mode of traditional folk songs. Here the line blurs between folk songs and popular songs.

SEE ALSO *ballad, blues, carol, lullaby, oral poetry, refrain, romances, sea shanties, song, spirituals, work song.*

foot A group of syllables forming a metrical unit. The poetic foot is a measurable, conventional unit of rhythm. The term derives from Greek meter, which is quantitative — a syllable unit is measured not by its loudness or stress, but by the time taken to speak it. The word *foot* relates to dance, and it seems likely that individual "feet" were based on dancing steps, on the balance and difference between short and long movements. The steps were matched by music. Later, written poetry was severed from dance (and music), but the notion of the foot was retained as a conventional unit of measurement. Quantitative meter depends on the relation of long (—) and short (u) syllables in each line. Every two- or three-syllable unit constituted the equivalent of a foot, which was called a *metron*. The main feet, or *metra*, were the iamb (u —), the trochee or choree (— u), the anapest (u u —), the dactyl (— u u), the pyrrhic (u u), the spondee (— —), and the tribach (u u u).

Though few pure examples of any of the standard feet can be found in English verse, the concept of the foot may be a useful abstraction. As Hugh Kenner contends, "you will never encounter a round face, though the term is helpful . . . The term 'iambic foot' has the same sort of status as the term 'round face.'" Yet there is also some controversy over the usefulness of classical scansion in English.

These are the most common feet in English versification:

> *iamb:* a pair of syllables with the stress on the second one, as in the word ădóre.
> *trochee:* a pair of syllables with the stress on the first one, as in the word árdŏr.
> *dactyl:* a triad consisting of one stressed syllable followed by two unstressed ones, as in the word rádiănt.
> *anapest:* a triad consisting of two unstressed syllables followed by one stressed one, as in the words ĭn ă bláze.

spondee: two equally stressed syllables, as in the word *ámén*. It is the
most common syllabic variation or substitution.

Here is Coleridge's witty illustrative poem "Metrical Feet" (ca. 1806):

Trochee trips from long to short;
From long to long in solemn sort
Slow Spondee stalks; strong foot! yet ill able
Ever to come up with Dactyl trisyllable.
Iambics march from short to long; —
With a leap and a bound the swift Anapests throng.

Here are some classical feet. First, the three-syllable ones:

amphibrach u — u
amphimacher, cretic — u —
antibacchius, palimbacchius — — u
bacchius, bacchiac — — u
molossus — — —

And the four-syllable feet:

antispast u — — u
choreus (by resolution) u u u u
choriamb — u u —
di-iamb u — u —
dispondee — — — —
ditrochee — u — u
epitrite u — — — (known as the first, second, third, or fourth, according
    to the position of the short or unstressed syllable)
ionic majore — — u u
ionic minore u u — —
paeon (known as the first, second, third, or fourth, according to the
    position of the long or stressed syllable) — u u u
proceleusmatic u u u u

The dochmiac is a five-syllable foot: u — — u —.
I have not included separate entries for feet that generally can't be ap-

plied to English-language poetry, such as the antispast ("pulling against"), a four-syllable foot (u — — u), which in English resolves into an iamb (u /) and a trochee (/ u), or the molossus, a unit of three long syllables (— — —), which, as George Saintsbury points out, is "practically impossible in English verse."

SEE ALSO *amphibrach, anapest, choriamb, cretic, dactyl, iamb, ionic, meter, paeon, pyrrhic, spondee, trochee;* also "accentual-syllabic meter" in *meter.*

form From the Latin: "shape." A poetic form refers to the shape and structure of a literary work, the manner in which it is made, which is different than its subject matter. The formal shape and underlying structure of a poem are the way it unfolds, its mode of being and method of understanding. Written poetic forms have their origins in oral musical forms. As John Hollander explains, "Poetic form, as we know it, is an abstraction from, or residue of, musical form, from which it came to be divorced when writing replaced memory as a way of preserving poetic utterance in narrative, prayer, spell, and the like."

Critics often use the word *form* to designate the genre or type of a work (lyric form, epic form) or the pattern of metrical lines and rhymes. A prescribed or fixed form is thus a poetic form with a set of rules, such as the sonnet or villanelle, but it is not simply a container. The poet plays with the traditional structure, which creates a series of expectations that are fulfilled or defied in various ways. An organic form is an individual form that grows from within a poem, taking shape as it develops, like a plant. A larger critical sense of form treats it as the underlying principle of a work, the concept or idea that determines its organization.

SEE ALSO *genre, organic form.*

formes fixes From the French: "fixed forms." Three structural *formes fixes* — the ballade, the rondeau, and the virelay — characterized secular French poetry in the fourteenth and fifteenth centuries. The *bergerette,* a related form, was popular in the late fifteenth century. Each of the traditional *formes fixes* has a complex pattern of repetitions and a refrain. The lyrics were translated into musical forms until the end of the fifteenth century. After that, they were written but no longer sung. The medieval poet and composer Guillaume de Machaut compiled the first comprehensive repertory of these forms.

SEE ALSO *ballade, rondeau, virelay.*

found poem   A borrowed text; a piece of writing that takes an existing text and presents it as a poem. Something that was never intended to be a poem — a newspaper article, a street sign, a letter, a scrap of conversation — is refashioned as a poem, often through lineation. The found poem works by changing the concept in a piece of writing, by distorting and appropriating its original intent. "Art must not look like art," Marcel Duchamp said, and the found poem is similar to his ready-mades and the found objects that appear in Pop Art, such as Andy Warhol's soup cans. "The original meaning remains intact, but now it swings between two poles," as Annie Dillard puts it. Without calling what they are doing found poetry, many modern poets have taken portions of previous texts and incorporated them into longer poems. The found poem suggests that something was hidden or lost that has now been discovered or "found." In French, found poetry is called *poésie d'emprunt,* which translates as "borrowed poetry" or "expropriated poetry." George Hitchcock put together the first anthology of found poetry in *Losers Weepers: Poems Found Practically Everywhere* (1969).

SEE ALSO *collage, erasure.*

fragment   A part broken off, something detached from the whole, something imperfect. Much of the work of the ancients comes down to us in fragments and tatters, cut pieces. As W. R. Johnson explains in *The Idea of Lyric* (1982),

> No experience in reading, perhaps, is more depressing and more frustrating than to open a volume of Sappho's fragments and to recognize, yet again — one always hopes that somehow this time it will be different — that this poetry is all but lost to us . . . Even though we know that Greek lyric is mere fragments, indeed, *because* we know that Greek lyric is mere fragments, we act, speak, and write as if the unthinkable had not happened, as if pious bishops, careless monks, and hungry mice had not consigned Sappho and her lyrical colleagues to irremediable oblivion.

In the medieval and Renaissance eras, fragments were often allegorical, suggesting something broken off from a divine whole. They were survivals from an earlier era. Readers had become so accustomed to reading unfinished texts by the early nineteenth century that it became acceptable and even fashionable to publish poems that were intentionally fragmentary. The passion for ruins as well as the taste for poetic relics and antiquities contributed to the acceptance of the Romantic fragment, a genre in its own right and a prototype of Romantic poetry in general. One of Friedrich Schlegel's fragments defines the genre: "A Fragment must as a miniature work of art be entirely isolated from the surrounding world and perfect in itself, like a hedgehog." Coleridge's "Kubla Khan: or a Vision in a Dream. A Fragment" (1816), Keats's "Hyperion. A Fragment" (1818–19), and Byron's "The Giaour. A Fragment of a Turkish Tale" (1813) all were presented as lyrics with a purposeful partialness. Anne Janowitz characterizes the Romantic fragment as "a *partial whole* — either a remnant of something once complete and now broken or decayed, or the beginning of something that remains unaccomplished." It becomes a radiant moment out of time.

The modernist poets reinvented the fragment as an acutely self-conscious mode of writing that breaks the flow of time, leaving gaps and tears, lacunae. They created discontinuous texts, collages and mosaics, fragmentary epics such as Ezra Pound's *Cantos* (1915–69), Louis Zukofsky's *"A"* (1927–78), and T. S. Eliot's "Waste Land" (1922), which he summarizes as "These fragments I have shored against my ruins." There is even greater vertigo in the destabilizing fragments of contemporary poetry, sometimes coolly giddy, as in John Ashbery, sometimes desperate for insight, as in Jorie Graham. In general, postmodernism is less regretful and nostalgic than modernism — it no longer yearns for wholeness — and postmodern poets typically view the fragment as a kind of emancipation that breaks the omnipotence of totalizing systems. As a genre of disruption, the postmodern fragment revels in its own incompleteness, since all texts are incomplete and all poetic language insufficient. "The interruption of the incessant," Maurice Blanchot writes, "that is the distinguishing characteristic of fragmentary writing."

SEE ALSO *allegory, collage, modernism, postmodernism, Romanticism.*

free verse   A poetry of organic rhythms, deliberate irregularity, improvisatory delight. Free verse is a form of nonmetrical writing that takes pleasure in an emergent verbal music. "As regarding rhythm," Ezra Pound declared in "A Retrospect" (1918), "to compose in the sequence of the musical phrase, not in sequence of a metronome." Free verse is often inspired by the cadence — the natural rhythm, the inner tune — of spoken language. It possesses visual form and uses the graphic line to differentiate itself from prose. "The words are more *poised* than in prose," Louis MacNeice notes in *Modern Poetry* (1938); "they are not only, like the words in typical prose, contributory to the total effect, but are to be attended to, in passing, for their own sake." The dream of free verse: an originary verbal music for every poem. Jorge Luis Borges explains that "beyond its rhythm, the typographical appearance of free verse informs the reader that what lies in store for him is not information or reasoning but emotion."

The term *free verse* is a literal translation of *vers libre,* which was employed by French symbolist poets seeking freedom from the strictures of the alexandrine. It has antecedents in medieval alliterative verse, in highly rhythmic and rhymed prose, in Milton's liberated blank-verse lines and verse paragraphs. The greatest antecedent is the King James translation of the Psalms and the Song of Songs. The rhetorical parallelism and expansive repetitions of the Hebrew Bible inspired Christopher Smart, who created his own canticles of praise in *Jubilate Agno* (*Rejoice in the Lamb,* 1759–63); William Blake, whose long-lined visionary poems have the power of prophetic utterance; and Walt Whitman, the progenitor of American free verse, who hungered for a line large enough to express the totality of life:

> My voice goes after what my eyes cannot reach,
> With the twirl of my tongue I encompass worlds and volumes of worlds.
> Speech is the twin of my vision, it is unequal to measure itself . . .

Whitman's rhythms influenced Gerard Manley Hopkins's long-lined metrical experiments and William Carlos Williams's exercises in a new measure. They are an influence, mostly repressed, on T. S. Eliot, who initiated modern poetry with the iambic-based free-verse rhythms of "The Love Song of J. Alfred Prufrock" (1920), and Ezra Pound, whose poem "The Return"

(1912) W. B. Yeats praised as the "most beautiful poem that has been written in the free form, one of the few in which I find real organic rhythms." Some of Whitman's international progeny: Apollinaire (France), Pessoa (Portugal), Lorca (Spain), Vallejo (Peru), Neruda (Chile), Paz (Mexico), Borges (Argentina), Martí (Cuba), Darío (Nicaragua). Whitman leads a long line of visionary poets, such as Hart Crane and D. H. Lawrence, Galway Kinnell, Gerald Stern, and Muriel Rukeyser. Formally, Whitman is the progenitor of C. K. Williams's rangy inclusive cadences and Charles Wright's use of a two-part dropped line. So too Whitman stands behind the improvisatory free-verse rhythms of such poets as Langston Hughes, Philip Levine, and Michael Harper, all influenced by jazz, and such New York poets as Frank O'Hara, John Ashbery, and James Schuyler, all influenced by abstract expressionism. Jazz and action painting provide American analogues for modern free verse.

"If one thinks of the literal root of the word verse, 'a line, furrow, turning — *vertere*, to turn . . . ,' he will come to a sense of 'free verse' as that instance of writing in poetry which 'turns' upon an occasion intimate with, in fact, the issue of its own nature," Robert Creeley explains. Free verse also turns in the space of short-lined poems. The short line often gives a feeling that something has been taken away, which has proved suitable for poems of loss. It can also give the feeling of clearing away the clutter and has thus proved useful for the imagist poems of T. E. Hulme, F. S. Flint, and H. D., and the objectivist works of George Oppen, Charles Reznikoff, and Louis Zukofsky. The free-verse poem has no preexistent pattern. The reader supplies the verbal speeds, intonations, emphasis.

SEE ALSO *blank verse, cadence, jazz poetry, line, prose poem, variable foot, vers libre.*

fu From the Chinese: "rhyme-prose." This narrative form — a mixed genre of prose and verse — often started with a narrative or expository passage, and then shifted into long descriptions in verse. It sometimes concluded with a short poem called a *tz'u* or *fan tz'u*. Some early examples, such as "Rhapsody on Mount Kao-t'ang," which is attributed to Sung Yü (ca. 290–222 B.C.E.), suggest that the form may have originated in the magical incantations of shamanism. Over time, the *fu* became regularized into a style of parallelism, which created balanced units, as in Yü Hsin's sixth-century "Lament for the South." The masterwork of the poet and critic Lu Chi (261–303) is his "Wen-fu" ("The Art of Writing"), a poetic treatise on the nature of the creative process, which begins, "The poet stands at the center of the universe."

SEE ALSO *parallelism, rhymed prose, shaman.*

futurism Filippo Tommaso Marinetti (1876–1944) launched the futurist movement in 1909 with his "violently upsetting, incendiary manifesto" called "The Founding and Manifesto of Futurism." He bombarded Europe with proclamations. The word *futurism* had a startling success and the movement spread rapidly through Italy, France, Spain, England, and Russia. The hyperkinetic Marinetti, "the caffeine of Europe," was the driving force of futurism. The manifesto was his weapon, and he used it to praise danger and revolt, aggressive action, "the beauty of speed" (he famously proclaimed that "A racing car . . . is more beautiful than the *Victory of Samothrace*"), "the metallization of man," the violent joys of crowds and cities. He also showed appalling innocence about war, which he glorified as "the world's only hygiene."

The Italian futurists include the poets Paolo Buzzi and Corrado Govani. Even in Italy, there were a variety of futurisms, including Noisism or Bruitism, which wanted to join experiences and senses to each other, Tactilism (the futurism of touch), and a Futurism of Woman (Valentine de Saint-Point, "Manifesto of Futurist Woman," 1912). As Apollinaire noted in his parody manifesto "L'antitradition futuriste" (1913), futurism was the first collective effort to suppress history in the name of art. Walter Benjamin gives the movement a damning summary judgment at the end of "The Work of Art in the Age of Mechanical Reproduction" (1936).

Russian futurism was an offshoot of futurism that was so various and contradictory that it became its own movement. There were four distinct Russian futurist groups: Cubo-futurism, ego-futurism, the Mezzanine of Poetry, and Centrifuge. What these groups shared was a dedication to modernism and a determination to denounce one another.

SEE ALSO *avant-garde, collage, Cubist poetry, Dadaism, modernism, sound poetry, zaum.*

G

genre From the Latin word *genus,* meaning "kind" or "sort." A genre is a class or species of texts, a subgroup of literature. We move from the particular work (*King Lear,* 1608) to the general literary category (tragedy). The works within a genre are marked by conventions and norms, resemblances and differences, which suggest possibilities of meaning. A genre provides a mode of discourse. It exists in relationship to other genres. Each genre creates a set of expectations, an implicit agreement between an oral performer and an audience, or a writer and a reader. Genres are time-bound and continually change. Modulation is the norm. The conventions that determine a genre are often fulfilled and expanded, sometimes thwarted, frequently violated. Genre criticism has traditionally been concerned with both the development of literary forms and the classification and description of literary texts. Literary theory brought the account of genres to the forefront of literary studies.

SEE ALSO *kind.*

georgic From the Latin word *georgicus,* "agricultural," which derives from *gê,* the Greek word for "earth." The georgic is a didactic poem that gives instructions about some skill, art, or science. In "Essay on the Georgics" (1697), Joseph Addison points out that this "class of Poetry ... consists in giving plain and direct instructions," which is what distinguishes it from other types of pastoral poem. Its subject is nature. Its practical strategy is to instruct readers on rural occupations, such as farming, shearing, etc. It puts physical labor into poetry.

Hesiod inaugurated the tradition in *Works and Days* (eighth century B.C.E.), which consists of agricultural advice, with frequent digressions for mythological lore and philosophical considerations. The poem is directed toward a second person and broods on the inevitability of work: *labor omnia vincit.* Virgil's *Georgics* (37–30 B.C.E.), which John Dryden called "the best poem of the best poet," is the centerpiece of the genre. Virgil's four long poems take up plowing and the weather, the cultivation of trees and vines, the rearing of cattle, and the care of bees. Virgil makes the farmer's hard work a basis for living.

Virgil's influence was far-reaching, especially in eighteenth-century Britain, where the country tradition was developed by James Thomson ("the English Vergil") in *The Seasons* (1730) and William Cowper in *The Task* (1785), his spiritual autobiography: "God made the country, and man made the town." Andrés Bello, who was born in Venezuela and later became a Chilean citizen, inaugurated a tradition of American georgics in his two-volume epic poem *América* (1823, 1826). The tradition includes Gregorio Gutiérrez González's *Memoir on the Cultivation of Maize in Antioquia* (1881) and Leopoldo Lugones's *Secular Odes* (1910). Robert Frost, like Henry David Thoreau, had georgic tendencies. Both writers emphasize rural labor and the hard knowledge born of it. The Kentucky poet and farmer Wendell Berry forcefully brings the georgic into contemporary poetry.

SEE ALSO *didactic poetry, eclogue, ecopoetry, pastoral.*

ghazal   A lyric form of Eastern poetry, which dates to seventh-century Arabia and has flourished in Arabic, Persian, Turkish, Urdu, and Pashto. It developed as an offshoot of the praise poem. One meaning of the word *ghazal* is "the talk of boys and girls"; in other words, sweet talk or verbal love-making. Another meaning of *ghazal* is the cry of the gazelle when it is cornered in a hunt and knows it must die. This explains, as Ahmed Ali puts it, "the atmosphere of sadness and grief that pervades the ghazal" as well as its "dedication to love and the beloved." The ghazal tends to blur the distinction between erotic and divine love. So too wine-drinking is one of the most common metaphors for spiritual intoxication.

The form consists of five named parts:

1. *Sher:* Five or more autonomous couplets. Each two-line unit is independent, disjunctive. This is the most consistent — and sometimes the only — rule followed by English-language ghazals.
2. *Beher:* Metric consistency, counted syllables. There are nineteen *beher* in Urdu, which can be classified as short, medium, and long.

The key formality is that the lines of each couplet should be of equal *beher,* or length.

3. *Radif:* The second end word of each couplet should repeat: *aa, ba, ca, da,* etc. The two-line stanzas thus set up a kind of echo chamber.

4. *Qafia:* The poem contains internal rhyme in each line of the first couplet and in the last line of each couplet.

5. *Mahkta:* The poet often signs his name in the final couplet.

The early ghazals were short and easy to sing. Later, the form began to take on mystical and philosophical themes. The Farsi master is Hafez (1325–1389), the Urdu master Ghalib (1797–1869). The Pakistani poet Faiz Ahmad Faiz (1911–1984), who wrote in both Urdu and Panjabi, used the ghazal to address secular and political themes. Since the eighteenth century, the ghazal has played a central role in the literature and music of many cultures, from the Middle East to Malaysia. The ghazal came to India via Persian Muslims, and the Indian ghazal tends to be more songlike than its Urdu counterpart, which is often performed at poetry gatherings.

The ghazal was introduced into Western poetry by the German Romantics: Schlegel, Rückert, and von Platten. It became widely known through Goethe's imitations of the Persian in *West-East Divan* (1819). Over the past few decades, the form, loosely constructed, has had a particular vogue among American poets, such as Robert Bly and Adrienne Rich. Agha Shahid Ali called ghazals "ravishing disunities."

SEE ALSO *praise poems.*

gleeman In Anglo-Saxon England, the gleeman was a singer of songs and a teller of tales. He had something of the status of the Teutonic scop. The gleeman reemerged as a figure in the fourteenth century a bit lower on the social scale, as an itinerant minstrel, a juggler and performer. John Davidson romanticized the figure in his poem "The Gleeman" (1891). In *The Celtic Twilight* (1893), W. B. Yeats called the blind Irish minstrel Michael Moran (ca. 1794–1846) "the last gleeman."

SEE ALSO *minstrel, scop.*

gnome (plural *gnomai*); **gnomic verse** A proverbial expression, a brief reflection or maxim that expresses a general truth or fundamental principle. The gnome is a form of wisdom literature. Aristotle defines it as "a statement not relating to particulars … but to universals." More than twelve hundred gnomai, which were originally part of a living oral tradition, have been identified in the works of the archaic Greek poets.

Gnomai are among the oldest literary expressions in the world and can be found in ancient Sumerian and Egyptian literature. In *The Growth of Literature* (1932), H. Munro Chadwick and Nora Chadwick divide gnomai from around the world into three categories: (1) those that urge moral behavior by listing human virtues, (2) those that observe human activities or the workings of destiny or fate but do not pass judgment, and (3) all other gnomai, which observe natural processes. Gnomai have a proverbial quality, but some scholars distinguish them from proverbs and precepts.

The primary Old English gnomai, *Maxims I* and *II*, are found in *The Exeter Book* (ca. 960–90) and the eleventh-century *Cotton Psalter*. They tend to be generalizations about the natural or human world, such as "Frost shall freeze, fire eat wood" or "A king shall win a queen with goods." A gnomic strain runs through all of Old English poetry as well as through early Icelandic, Irish, and Welsh poetry.

SEE ALSO *proverb, wisdom literature.*

goliardic verse A type of medieval lyric poetry. Goliardic verse probably derives its name from the tribe of Golias, or the Philistine giant Goliath, who was slain by David. The goliardic poets were the wandering scholars of the twelfth and thirteenth centuries, academic drifters who composed secular songs in rhymed and accented Latin verse. Their boisterous youthful poems strike a pose, parodying religious hymns, mocking institutions, reveling in gambling, and celebrating physical love and excessive drinking. The foundational examples of goliardic verse (*Vagantenlider*) are found in the *Carmina Burana,* a thirteenth-century compendium of Latin and German poems, which was discovered in Munich in the nineteenth century. The greatest poet of the tradition is the shadowy figure known as the Archpoet. Ten of his poems have survived, including a scathing mock confession, "Estuans intrinsecus / ira vehementi" ("Burning inside / with violent rage"), the most famous poem of the Middle Ages.

griot (feminine *griotte*) The West African griot, or *jeli,* is a praise singer, a poet-historian who preserves the genealogies, historical narratives, and oral traditions of a people. The griots are members of a hereditary caste who hold the memory of West Africa by maintaining an oral tradition that is more than six centuries old (the first portrait of a griot dates to the fourteenth century). Until the late nineteenth century, griots were attached to the courts of local kings. We have no equivalent for the complex social role of these oral storytellers and official chroniclers who also serve as trusted advisors, messengers, mediators, teachers, and ambassadors. The griots are skilled musicians who often play a wooden xylophone called a *balafon,* a plucked lute called a *koni,* or *ngoni,* and a twenty-one-stringed instrument called a *kora,* a cross between a lute and a harp. They specialize in reciting the epic of Son-Jara (also known as Sunjata or Sundiata). The griots have a formidable knowledge of local history, a gift for extemporizing on current events, and the capacity to cut their enemies with devastating wit. Licensed to sing and dance alone, to behave outlandishly, these singers of praise and scandal at the center of the artistic universe of most sub-Saharan African societies are commonly considered outcasts, scorned and feared, called on at times of ritual elevation to represent power.

The most common view of the controversial term *griot* is that the word derives from the French *guiriot* and thus smacks of colonialism. Others maintain that it has a Portuguese, Spanish, Catalan, or Arabic origin. Yet others suggest that it has an African origin. In *Griots and Griottes,* Thomas Hale posits that the term goes as far back as the Ghana Empire and moved by way of the slave trade through Berber to Spanish and then French: *Ghana-agenaou-guineo-guiriot-griot.* He calls the griot a time-binder, "a person who links past to present and serves as a witness to events in the present, which he or she may convey to persons living in the future."

SEE ALSO *oral poetry, praise poems, song.*

H

haibun A work that combines haiku and prose. Matsuo Bashō's *Hut of the Phantom Dwelling* (1690), closely modeled on Kamo no Chōmei's extended prose essay *Ten Foot Square Hut* (1212), is the first outstanding example of *haibun* literature. Bashō's subsequent travel journal, or *nikki, The Narrow Road to the Deep North* (1694), established the *haibun* as a major form that connects individual haiku with a surrounding prose narrative. The prose of the travel diaries is written in the same spirit as the poems, which has the aesthetic of *haikai*. The link between each prose passage and each subsequent poem is implicit. Some of the Japanese poets best known for *haibun* are Yosa Buson (1716–1783), the samurai Yokoi Yayū (1702–1783), and Kobayashi Issa (1763–1827).

The *haibun* has sometimes provided a model for the crossing of genres in contemporary poetry, from poetic diaries by Gary Snyder and lyrical prose works by Jack Kerouac, who saw much of his work as prose written by a haiku poet, to the six *haibun* in John Ashbery's *A Wave* (1984) and the mixture of poetic plays and photo-documentary poems in Mark Nowak's *Shut Up Shut Down* (2004). Sam Hamill's *Bashō's Ghost* (1989) is structured as a series of *haibun* around his visit to Japan.

SEE ALSO *haikai, haiku.*

haikai A Japanese term, the *haikai no renga,* abbreviated to *haikai,* is an inclusive type of *renga,* a form of Japanese poetry that flourished in the fourteenth and fifteenth centuries. *Renga* literally means "linked poetry." The *renga* began as a courtly form written by a team of poets with a circumscribed subject matter and a strict set of rules. The *haikai* (the word means "playful style") was a lighthearted type of linked poetry. Aesthetically relaxed, it democratized poetry by embracing the language and the emotions of common people.

Matsuo Bashō (1644–1694) was the first major poet of *haikai,* combining spiritual depth with comic playfulness. *Haikai* more generally refers to all types of literature derived from *haikai no renga,* such as *hokku* (the opening verse of a *renga* sequence), haiku (an independent verse form), *haiga* (a form of painting that combines a *hokku* and a visual image), and *haibun* (a genre that links haiku and narrative prose). Bashō believed that all these genres embodied the "*haikai* spirit" (*haii*). Bashō's school cherished *sabi* ("lonely beauty"), a kind of impersonal sadness or melancholy latent in nature, a recognition in humble scenes, such as the light of dusk in autumn or the solitary voice of a cuckoo in the trees.

SEE ALSO *haibun, haiku, renga, yūgen.*

haiku   A Japanese poetic form usually consisting, in English versions, of three unrhymed lines of 5, 7, and 5 syllables. The Japanese haiku is divided into seventeen phonic units, which are the equivalent of syllables. It is written as a single vertical line that is broken into three metrical units or phrases. The English spacing tries to replicate the aural effects of the Japanese. The haiku has its roots in the Middle Ages, or earlier, in the classic poetic form of the tanka and the *renga.* The *hokku,* or opening verse of the *renga* sequence, consists of seventeen syllables, which include a season word. At some point during the late Edo period (1600–1868), the *hokku* came to be appreciated in its own right. Matsuo Bashō was the first poet to elevate the *hokku* to a major form. Bashō was followed by Yosa Buson and Kobayashi Issa. In the late nineteenth century, Masaoka Shiki distinguished more clearly between the *hokku* as the initial verse of a larger sequence and the *hokku* as a self-contained poem. He named the autonomous seventeen-syllable poem a haiku. The syllable pattern of 5–7–5 may be ancient, but the word *haiku* is a modern invention. *Haijin* is an honorific name for a person who writes *haikai* or haiku.

The haiku, invariably written in the present tense, almost always refers to a time of day or season (the *kigo* is a season word), focuses on a natural image, and captures the essence of a moment. Its goal: a sudden insight or spiritual illumination. R. H. Blyth's four-volume *Haiku* (1949–52), the first work in English based on the *saijiki,* is a dictionary of haiku in which the poems are arranged by seasons. He states, "It is not merely the brevity by which the haiku isolates a particular group of phenomena from all the rest; nor is it suggestiveness, through which it reveals a whole world of experience. It is not only in its remarkable use of the season word, by which it gives us a feeling of a quarter of the year; not its faint all-pervading humor. Its peculiar quality is its self-effacing, self-annihilative nature, by which it enables us, more than any other form of literature, to grasp the thing-in-itself."

Haiga is a style of Japanese painting that combines a haiku and a visual image, as in Buson's poetry-paintings.

The *senryū* (the word means "river willow" in Japanese) has the same structure as the haiku. But whereas the haiku deals with nature, the *senryū* deals with human nature. It is often satiric and treats human foibles. The haiku, on the other hand, seeks the momentary and eternal.

SEE ALSO *renga, tanka.*

hemistich   A half-line of verse. A hemistich can stand as an unfinished line, usually for emphasis, or form half of a complete line, which is divided by a caesura. Virgil isolated half-lines in the *Aeneid* (29–19 B.C.E.) to great effect, but the strategy troubled his neoclassical translator John Dryden, who called his hemistiches "the imperfect products of a hasty Muse." The principal line of medieval Arabic and Hebrew poetry was divided into two symmetrical hemistiches. In Hebrew, this was known as the *delet* ("door") and the *sogair* ("latch" or "lock"). In Arabic, it was known as the *sadr* ("chest, front") and the *'ajouz* ("backside" or "rump"). So too the hemistich was used as the fundamental metrical structural unit in Old English, Old High German, Old Saxon, and Old Norse. Think of the two halves of the Old English four-beat line, which divides near the middle. It has two metrical stresses on either side of the divide (caesura). "Caedmon's Hymn," probably the earliest extant Old English poem, begins,

> Nu we sculan herian   heofonrices Weard,
> Metodes mihte   and his modgeþonc,
> weorc Wuldorfæder;   swa he wundra gehwæs,
> ece Dryhten,   ord onstealde.

SEE ALSO *caesura, verset.*

hendecasyllabics   Lines of eleven syllables. The term *hendecasyllable* usually refers to the precise metrical line used by the ancient Greek poets, which consists of an opening pair of syllables (u u, u —, — u, or — —) followed by a dactyl (— u u) and three trochees (— u). It was perfected by the Roman poet Catullus (84–54 B.C.E.) and later became the standard verse line of Italian poetry, exploited by Dante in *The Divine Comedy* (ca. 1304–21) and by Petrarch in his sonnets. Popularized by Garcilaso de la Vega (ca. 1501–1536), it is also one of the primary verse forms in Spanish poetry since the Renaissance; it is customarily accentuated on the sixth and tenth syllables, or else on the fourth, eighth, and tenth syllables. Hendecasyllabics are relatively rare in English, though Tennyson experimented with them in "Hendecasyllabics" (1863). Swinburne followed with his own "Hendecasyllabics" (1866) and Robert Frost employs them in his poem "For Once, Then, Something" (1920). James Wright referred to it as "the difficult, the dazzling / Hendecasyllabic" ("The Offense," 1972).

SEE ALSO *meter, silvae*.

heptameter, see "accentual-syllabic meter" in *meter*.

heptastich, see *septet*.

heroic couplet, see *couplet*.

heroic quatrain   Four iambic pentameter lines rhyming alternately (*abab*). The heroic quatrain, also known as the elegiac stanza and Hammond's meter, is used in Thomas Gray's "Elegy Written in a Country Churchyard" (1751) and James Hammond's *Love Elegies* (1732), which contains this exemplary stanza:

> Beauty and worth in her alike contend
> To charm the fancy and to fix the mind:
> In her, my wife, my mistress, and my friend,
> I taste the joys of sense and reason join'd.

SEE ALSO *quatrain*.

heterometric stanza   A stanza that consists of lines of varying length. The Pindaric ode, the Sapphic stanza, and the medieval bob and wheel are all heterometric. John Donne's early poem "Song" (1635), for example, pushed the limits of heterometric verse in English. The first stanza establishes the pattern. Notice especially the short seventh and eighth lines.

> Go and catch a falling star,
>> Get with child a mandrake root,
> Tell me where all past years are,
>> Or who cleft the Devil's foot,
> Teach me to hear mermaids singing,
>> Or to keep off envy's stinging,
>>> And find
>>> What wind
> Serves to advance an honest mind.

SEE ALSO *bob and wheel, isometric stanza, ode, Sapphic stanza, stanza.*

hexameter A six-foot metrical line. Shelley uses an iambic hexameter line in "To a Skylark" (1820): "Ĭn pró | fŭse stráins | ŏf ún- | prĕméd- | ĭtát- | ĕd árt." The Homeric hexameter is the oldest type of Greek verse. The classical dactylic hexameter also reached its pinnacle in Greek and Latin epic poetry (the *Iliad* and the *Odyssey,* ca. eighth century B.C.E.; the *Aeneid,* 29–19 B.C.E.). It was adapted to German and Russian poetry by Goethe and Pushkin, among others. Despite many experiments, such as Longfellow's epic poem *Evangeline* (1847), it has never found a natural place in French, English, or American poetry. In "Notes upon English Verse" (1842), Edgar Allan Poe prints a line that he describes as "an unintentional instance of a perfect English hexameter upon the model of the Greek." He seems to have made it up himself: "Man is a | complex, | compound, | compost, | yet is he | God-born." The dactylic hexameter is to classical verse what iambic pentameter is to English-language poetry. Coleridge wittily discriminates between them in "The Ovidian Elegiac Metre" (1799): "In the hexameter rises the fountain's silvery column; / In the pentameter aye falling in melody back."

SEE ALSO *alexandrine, dactyl, foot, iambic pentameter, meter.*

hexastich, see *sestet.*

hip-hop poetry, rap poetry   Rap is the rhythmic vocal style of rap or hip-hop music. A rapping (emceeing) performer speaks rhythmically, and in rhyme, generally to a strong beat. The lyrics fit a metrical pattern. As Jerry Quickley puts it in "Hip Hop Poetry" (2003), "Hip hop incorporates many of the technical devices of other forms, including slant rhymes, enjambment, A-B rhyme schemes, and other techniques, usually parsed in sixteen-bar stanzas, and generally followed by four-to-eight-bar hooks."

Rap is poetry, Adam Bradley notes, "but its popularity relies in part on people not recognizing it as such." He points out that rappers prefer similes to metaphors because similes "shine the spotlight on their subject more directly than do metaphors." Sometimes rappers perform pieces they have already written; other times they improvise and freestyle new poems in front of an audience. Their public art is pitched to their listeners. Kanye West is boasting about his flow when he raps, in "Get Em High" (2004), "my rhyme's in the pocket like wallets / I got the bounce like hydraulics." The synergy of beats and rhyme is what Bradley calls "rap's greatest contribution to the rhythm of poetry: the *dual rhythmic relationship.*"

Hip-hop, which arose in the 1970s, has its roots in African American and West African music. It started with Jamaican DJ music, in which DJs spin dub versions of rhythm tracks with MCs, who are part singers, part rappers, "chatting" over them. Hip-hop connects to other types of contemporary oral poetry, such as slam and performance poetry, which also provide voices for the disenfranchised.

SEE ALSO *oral poetry, performance poetry, rhythm, slam poetry.*

Hudibrastic verse   A type of comic narrative poetry, Hudibrastic verse (Hudibrastics) consists of jangling eight-syllable rhyming couplets. It is named after Samuel Butler's satirical long poem *Hudibras* (1663–80), which uses deliberately absurd iambic tetrameter couplets to ridicule and attack the Puritans. Here is an example from Canto III:

> He would an elegy compose
> On maggots squeez'd out of his nose;
> In lyric numbers write an ode on
> His mistress, eating a black-pudden;

And, when imprison'd air escap'd her,
It puft him with poetic rapture.

Jonathan Swift used the octosyllabic rhyming couplet with greater variety, as in these lines from "Vanbrugh's House" (1703):

So, Modern Rhymers strive to blast
The Poetry of Ages past,
Which having wisely overthrown,
They from it's Ruins build their own.

Swift's use of Hudibrastics provided a model for contemporaries, such as Oliver Goldsmith ("New Simile, in the Manner of Swift," 1765) and Alexander Pope ("The Seventh Epistle of the First Book of Horace, Imitated in the Manner of Dr. Swift," 1739), and pointed the way to the use of modern Hudibrastics, such as W. H. Auden's 1940 "New Year Letter." John Barth, who based his novel *The Sot-Weed Factor* (1960) on a poem in Hudibrastics by Ebenezer Cook (ca. 1672–1732), declared, "The Hudibrastic couplet, like Herpes simplex, is a contagion more easily caught than cured."

SEE ALSO *burlesque, couplet, doggerel, mock epic, octosyllabic verse.*

hunting chants, hunting songs Wherever there are hunters in traditional societies, there is also a tradition of hunting chants or songs. From the Ammassalik Inuit of Greenland to the Navajo and the Zuni of the American Southwest, Native peoples have had a tradition of offerings to deceased hunters, of words to summon game and prayers before killing animals ("Prayer Before Killing an Eagle," "Before Butchering the Deer"). These poems incarnate a belief that everything is holy.

Hunting chants are found throughout Africa. "Like a poet," Judith Gleason writes in *Leaf and Bone: African Praise-Poems* (1994), "the African hunter is a mediator between the unknown and the familiar." The hunter moves away from the cultivated world of the village into the uncultivated, spirit-saturated natural world of the forest.

The Yoruba have an especially powerful tradition of hunting chants called *ijala*. The poetry of hunters is customarily recited during festivals of Ogun, the god of iron. The chanter recites the *oríkì,* or praise names, of important hunters as well as of Ogun, who is worshiped by all those who use iron. Inspiration comes from a divine source and the poet taps Ogun's power to create and transmit the poem.

SEE ALSO *oríkì.*

hymn From the Greek word *hymnos,* "song in praise of a god or hero." In the classical world, odes were composed in honor of gods and heroes and chanted or sung at religious festivals and other ceremonial occasions. One thinks of the ringing hexameters of the Homeric hymns, which provided models for the hymns of Callimachus (ca. 305–ca. 240 B.C.E.), and the Orphic hymns chanted by initiates in the Orphic mysteries. Hymns were also a major genre in ancient Egyptian literature, where they served as poems worshiping a deity or a divine king, or, more occasionally, praising a city, such as Thebes, or one or more objects, such as the Red Crowns of Egypt. Charles Boer explains that the word *hymn* derives from the East. The Greek *hymnos* is connected to the word *woven* or *spun:* "in its primal sense, a hymn was thought of as what results when you intertwine speech with rhythm and song." Bacchylides refers to "weaving a hymn."

With the coming of Christianity, "praise of God in song" took the place of praise of gods and heroes. Hymns as scriptural texts came into the church in the fourth century (early examples include the nativity song "Gloria in excelsis" and the three Gospel canticles) and have been part of devotional services ever since. Latin hymns were written throughout the Middle Ages. Isaac Watts (1674–1748) wrote modern hymns that take joy in God's created world. He envisioned the Promised Land as on a clear day, and dramatically adapted the Psalms to his own purposes, as when he "translated the scene of this psalm — 67 — to Great Britain":

> Sing to the Lord, ye distant lands,
>> Sing loud with solemn voice;
> While British tongues exalt his praise,
>> And British hearts rejoice.

Charles Wesley (1707–1788) brought a stately grace to the hymnal stanza, also known as common measure. Similar to the ballad stanza, it has the stricter rhythms and rhymes found in the hymnal. The hymn has accrued liturgical importance as a source of communal devotion. Think, then, of what it meant for Emily Dickinson to fracture the common measure, thus invoking the hymn tradition and responding to its communal nature with her own radical individuality.

SEE ALSO *ballad, long meter, ode, psalm, short meter.*

hyperbole From the Greek: "overshooting" or "excess." A rhetorical figure of deliberate exaggeration. George Puttenham called it a "loud liar" and claimed it is used "to advance or . . . abase the reputation of any thing or person" (1589). Hyperbole can be rhetorically marshaled to great effect, for, as Oliver Goldsmith put it, "Poetry is animated by the passions; and all the passions exaggerate. Passion itself is a magnifying medium" ("On the Use of Hyperbole," 1837). Hyperbole is crucial for panegyrics and other forms of praise poetry. The poetry of the Hebrew Bible is filled with prophetic hyperboles. So too Jesus was fond of hyperbole as a strategy: "it is easier for a camel to go through the eye of a needle than for a rich man to enter the kingdom of God" (Mark 10:25, Luke 18:25). Hyperbole is a central device of love poetry from the Song of Songs onward.

SEE ALSO *panegyric, praise poems, rhetoric.*

iamb A two-syllable metrical foot, the first unstressed, the second stressed, as in the word *ŭnknówn*. It is an upbeat followed by a downbeat. In classical poetry, the iamb, or iambus, consisted of a short and a long syllable. Two iambs in a row constituted a di-iamb. Iambic rhythm was considered close to ordinary speech in ancient Greek and Latin verse. Aristotle argues that "the iambic is, of all measures, the most colloquial: we see it in the fact that conversational speech runs into iambic lines more frequently than any other kind of verse." Michael Schmidt points out that iambic poetry "described at first a genre as much as a metre. The genre presumed that humour would be an ingredient, but humour of a specific kind, humour at someone's expense ... The term 'iambic' may derive from the name of the maidservant Iambe, whose tart wit, expressed perhaps in metrical form, brought laughter back to the heart of bereaved and grieving Demeter." Archilochus, Semonides, and Hipponax are the three classical writers of iambics (*iambopoioi*).

Despite similarities, the English iamb is not precisely equivalent to the Greek one. The iamb is by far the most typical foot in English because it fits the natural stress pattern of English words and phrases. Shakespeare understood this and employed it in many of his greatest dramatic speeches. The iamb functions, as Alexander Pope puts it, "Tŏ wáke | thĕ sóul | bў tén- | dĕr strókes | ŏf árt" ("Prologue to Mr. Addison's 'Cato,'" 1713).

SEE ALSO *foot, iambic pentameter, meter.*

iambic pentameter A five-stress, roughly decasyllabic line. This fundamental line, established by Chaucer (ca. 1340–1400) for English poetry, was energized when English attained a condition of relative stability in the late fifteenth and early sixteenth centuries. It may be the traditional formal line closest to the form of our speech. It has been favored by dramatists ever since Christopher Marlowe, whose play *Tamburlaine* (1587) inaugurated the greatest Elizabethan drama, and William Shakespeare, who used it with astonishing virtuosity and freedom. John Milton showed the supple dignity of the pentameter line in *Paradise Lost* (1667):

> Of man's first disobedience, and the fruit
> Of that forbidden tree, whose mortal taste
> Brought death into the world, and all our woe,
> With loss of Eden, till one greater Man
> Restore us, and regain the blissful seat,
> Sing, Heav'nly Muse . . .

The iambic pentameter line was strategically employed by most of the great nineteenth-century English poets, from William Wordsworth and Samuel Taylor Coleridge to Robert Browning and Alfred, Lord Tennyson. It was given a distinctly American stamp in the cadences of Robert Frost, Wallace Stevens, and Hart Crane.

SEE ALSO *blank verse, decasyllable, meter.*

ictus, see *beat.*

identifical rhyme, see *rhyme.*

idyll   A short poem (or prose piece) that deals with rustic life. There are no formal requirements for this poem of innocent tranquility, but the description of a picturesque rural scene is quintessential. The term derives from the Greek word *eidyllion,* meaning "little picture," and the idyll is indeed a framed picture, a portrait fantasy of rural life. The ten pastoral poems of the Greek poet Theocritus (third century B.C.E.) defined the genre. Theocritus assembled shepherds and goatherds who are either musicians playing on the syrinx or poets singing of their feelings in pastureland beyond cultivated fields, in hills where there are flowering trees and flowing streams. His idylls established the conventions that would be imitated in Virgil's *Eclogues* (42–39 B.C.E.), Dante's Latin idylls, Spenser's *Shepheardes Calender* (1579), Milton's "Lycidas" (1638), and other poems of the Italian, French, and English Renaissance.

In the seventeenth century, there was a critical attempt to apply the term *eclogue* to pastoral poems in dialogue, and reserve the term *idyll* for pastoral poems in narrative, though the words are now mostly interchangeable. Since the Renaissance, there have been many idyllic moments in poetry, but very few idylls per se. In the nineteenth century, Robert Browning widened the term for his poems of psychological crisis, *Dramatic Idylls* (1879–80), and Alfred, Lord Tennyson, applied the word to his Arthurian verse romance, *Idylls of the King* (1856–85).

SEE ALSO *eclogue, ecopoetry, nature poetry, pastoral.*

image, imagery The image, which Wyndham Lewis calls the "primary pigment" of poetry, relates to the visual content of language. Cleanth Brooks and Robert Penn Warren define it, in *Understanding Poetry* (1938), as "the representation in poetry of any sense experience," whereas another handbook characterizes it as "a mental picture evoked by the use of metaphors, similes, and other figures of speech." These are, then, the two bases for its definition: the image is sensuous ("I give you my sprig of lilac"); the image is figurative ("The star my departing comrade holds and detains me"). The literal literally bubbles over into the symbolic in Walt Whitman's "When Lilacs Last in the Dooryard Bloom'd" (1865): "All over bouquets of roses, / O death, I cover you over with roses and early lilies."

The poetic image is delivered through words. Poetry engages our capacity to make mental pictures, but also taps a place in our minds that has little to do with direct physical perceptions. There are poetic images that give us hindsight (Shakespeare's "When to the sessions of sweet silent thought / I summon up remembrance of things past") or that summon up the memory of the dead, as in the opening of W. B. Yeats's "In Memory of Major Robert Gregory" (1918), where he broods about his lost friends ("All, all are in my thoughts to-night being dead"). There are images that have the character of daydreams, and images that have the hallucinatory power of fevers and dreams. The term *imagination* originally meant the image-making faculty of the mind, and the sense of an image is thus buried in the very concept of imagination.

The imagist movement (1912–17) placed the image at the center of modern poetry. Ezra Pound, F. S. Flint, and other imagists treated the image as something directly apprehended in a flash of perception. In the 1960s, Robert Bly, James Wright, and others rejected the pictorial image and replaced it with the deep image, that is, an image saturated with psyche, welling up out of the unconscious and thus uniting the inner and outer worlds. In *The Poetics of Space* (1958), the French phenomenological critic Gaston Bachelard recognizes the poetic image as "a sudden salience on the surface of the psyche," something free of causality and thus escaped from time, something with its own ontology, which places us "at the origin of the speaking being." The reader enters into the "dreaming consciousness" and functions in a state of receptivity to language "in a state of emergence." In *Reading the Written Image* (1991), Christopher Collins contends that since every literary image is also a mental image and since every mental image is a representation of an absent entity, then the imagination itself is a poiesis, a making-up, an act of free play for both the writer and the reader.

SEE ALSO *archetype, deep image, imagination, imagism, metaphor, simile, symbol, trope.*

imagination   The term *imagination* originally meant the faculty that forms mental images. For Aristotle, the word translated as *imagination* meant "how the object appears." It referred both to objects present and sensed as well as to those absent and merely thought about. *Imagination* was thus a practical term for picturing things, a mode of visualization, though the term evolved during the Renaissance to suggest a greater creative faculty, a deeper power of mind. Shakespeare brings together these two senses of imagination in a passage in *A Midsummer Night's Dream* (1590–96):

> The poet's eye, in a fine frenzy rolling,
> Doth glance from heaven to earth, from earth to heaven,
> And as imagination bodies forth
> The forms of things unknown, the poet's pen
> Turns them to shapes, and gives to airy nothing
> A local habitation and a name.

The imagination looks beyond the immediate and enables us to make fictions. David Hume treated ideas as images and recognized the crucial place the imagination plays in thinking. Immanuel Kant's word for the imagination, *Einbildungskraft,* suggested forming a picture in the mind, the power of making images, representing things. Taken together, Hume and Kant developed an account of the imagination, as Mary Warnock explains, "as that which functions both in the presence of an object of perception in the world, and in its absence, when we turn to it in our thoughts. Imagination both presents and re-presents things to us." How we account for the world is dependent upon this faculty, which is also engaged, provoked, and accompanied by the emotions. The Romantic poets especially made the imagination the hallmark of their poetics. For Byron, the imagination was a psychological release: "Poetry is the lava of the imagination, whose eruption prevents an earthquake." For Keats, "the Imagination may be compared to Adam's dream — he awoke and found it truth." For Wordsworth, it was "but another name for absolute strength / And clearest insight, amplitude of mind / And reason in her most exalted mood" (*The Prelude*, 1805, 1850). For Blake, imagination's greatest apostle, it was by contrast the absolute enemy of reason, a sign of inspiration, and an entrance into the larger world of truth, a vision of the infinite. In *Biographia Literaria* (1817), Coleridge distinguished between two kinds of imagining, which he deemed fancy and imagination. He describes the imagination as a power that "dissolves, diffuses, dissipates, in order to recreate or where the process is rendered impossible, yet still at all events it struggles to idealize and to unify." The fancy, however, merely "receive[s] all its materials ready made from the law of association." Coleridge also distinguishes between primary imagination ("the living power and prime agent of all human perception") and secondary imagination ("an echo of the former, co-existing with the conscious will").

For many poets, the imagination takes something from life — a remote scene, a distant detail — and creates a full-blown vision out of it. Memory is the spark; imagination the process of enlargement. The power of the imagination is to work from the known to the unknown, and then from the unknown back to the known, incorporating the world.

SEE ALSO *image, invention, negative capability, organic form, Romanticism.*

imagism   The movement (and doctrine) of a small group of British and American poets who called themselves imagists or *Imagistes* between 1912 and 1917. T. S. Eliot said, "The *point de repère* usually and conveniently taken as the starting-point of modern poetry is the group denominated 'imagists' in London about 1910." The group included Ezra Pound, who edited the first anthology, *Des Imagistes: An Anthology* (1914), Richard Aldington, H. D. (Hilda Doolittle), F. S. Flint, and others. Amy Lowell became a strong advocate for the movement and edited three anthologies, all of which were called *Some Imagist Poets* (1915–17). Pound, who had defected to a new movement called vorticism, sneeringly called it Amygism.

The image was the prevailing aesthetic device of the movement. Pound offered a one-sentence definition of an image as "that which presents an intellectual and emotional complex in an instant of time." He added, "It is the presentation of such a 'complex' instantaneously which gives the sense of sudden liberation; that sense of freedom from time limits and space limits; that sense of sudden growth, which we experience in the presence of the greatest works of art."

The imagists practiced directness and concision. They focused on concrete language and avoided abstractions, seeking "direct treatment of the thing." The one-image poem of the imagists owes a strong debt to the Greek lyricists and to the Japanese haiku poets. The imagists were against fixed meters, vague language, and moral reflections. Their precise free-verse poems were meant to extricate poetry from the nineteenth century. Imagism died as a movement, but its values influenced the poetry not only of Pound and H. D., but also of such poets as Wallace Stevens and William Carlos Williams. The question for poets after imagism was how to maintain imagist precision while introducing larger poetic structures. The movement purged the lyric of discourse, which then had to be reintroduced into modern poetry.

SEE ALSO *discursive, objectivism, vorticism.*

imitation The Latin word *imitatio* is a translation of the Greek *mimesis*. The concept of imitation began its long history in aesthetics with Plato's critique of poetry and other "mimetic arts," which he considered dangerous and inferior to philosophy. In book 10 of *The Republic* (ca. 380 B.C.E.), Plato characterizes mimesis — counterfeit "creations" — as the method of all poetry. He condemns the poet as a "creator of phantoms" who knows "only how to imitate." For him, the world of appearances imitates the real world of ideal forms, and since poetry imitates the appearance of the world of objects, it is the imitation of an imitation and thus "three removes from reality" or "at the third remove from truth." Plato never revised or withdrew his attack on poetry, though the later Neo-Platonists affirmed the value of poetry as imitation by arguing that it is a sensuous embodiment of the ideal realm. Plotinus argues in *The Enneads* (ca. 270) that poetry imitates "the Ideas from which Nature itself derives." This notion would become important to German Romantics, such as F.W.J. Schelling, who considered poetry a representation of the Absolute.

Aristotle accepted the assumption that art is representational and defined poetry as imitation, but rejected Plato's transcendental world of ideas and widened the scope of the notion of mimesis beyond mere "copying." In the *Poetics* (350 B.C.E.), he calls imitation "one instinct of our nature" and considered human beings "the most imitative of living creatures," relishing the pleasures of imitation or representation. He redefined mimesis as no mere counterfeiting of the sensible world, but a representation of "universals." Aristotle characterized all poetry as imitating general truths, an idea revived in the eighteenth century by Samuel Johnson, who argued, "The business of a poet is to examine, not the individual, but the species; to remark general properties and large appearances: he does not number the streaks of the tulip." For Aristotle, poetry essentially imitated human beings in action. The literary work itself represents a preexistent reality, though it is not a mere copy but an object in its own right.

This Aristotelian stress on formal harmony links to a second idea of imitation: the classical and neoclassical notion of formal models, the imitation of the classics. John Dryden developed the idea of imitation as a mode of translation, and here imitation comes to mean adaptation or re-creation. The Romantic poets replaced the idea of poetry as imitation with a notion of poetry as spontaneous creation, and imitation fell into disrepute as a critical term. Edward Young sneered at "that meddling ape imitation," and declared, "We read imitation with somewhat of his languor who listens to twice-told tales: our spirits rouse at an original." Modern and contemporary poets have almost exclusively used the word *imitation* to refer to a freer mode of translation, the adaptation of an existing poem. In modern criticism, especially post-Aristotelian criticism, *imitation* has been used as synonymous with *mimesis* and roughly means "representation."

SEE ALSO *comedy, epic, mimesis, originality, Romanticism, tragedy, translation.*

impersonality   T. S. Eliot brought this term into modern poetry criticism in "Tradition and the Individual Talent" (1919). Eliot argued for "an impersonal theory of poetry." He suggested that the poet must develop and procure a full consciousness of the past: "What happens is a continual surrender of himself as he is at the moment to something which is more valuable. The progress of an artist is a continual self-sacrifice, a continual extinction of personality." The artist surrenders his own personality to the tradition. Eliot's classical position sought to sever poetry from the personality and subjectivity of the poet. He devalued the emotionalism of Romantic poetry. "Poetry is not a turning loose of emotion, but an escape from emotion; it is not the expression of personality, but an escape from personality." This formulation was so powerful for New Critics and others who valued objectivity and the scientific method that it was forty years before anyone really noticed the next sentence: "But, of course, only those who have personality and emotions know what it means to want to escape from these things." Impersonality is an ideal that never can be realized.

SEE ALSO *confessional poetry, objective correlative, tradition.*

incantation   A formulaic use of words to create magical effects. *Incantation* derives from a Latin word meaning "to consecrate with charms or spells," and, indeed, charms, spells, chants, and conjurations all employ the apparatus of sympathetic magic. Incantations, whether spoken or chanted, are characteristic of archaic poetries everywhere, which have always employed the rudimentary power of repetition to create enchantment. Oracular and prophetic poets rely on what Roman Jakobson calls "the magic, incantatory function" of language to raise words beyond speech, to create dream states and invoke apocalyptic forces. The Orphic poets and Hebrew prophets, as well as those vatic figures who identify with them (Christopher Smart, William Blake, Walt Whitman, Robert Desnos), deliver incantations formally, not haphazardly, and harness the rhythmic power of repetition through parallel structures and catalogs.

SEE ALSO *anaphora, catalog poem, charm, parallelism, repetition, rune, spell, vatic.*

incremental repetition   This term, coined by Francis Gummere in *The Popular Ballad* (1907), describes one of the key rhetorical devices of the ballad form. It refers to the repetition of succeeding stanzas that also incorporates small substitutions or changes. The refrain, modified each time it is repeated, takes on added power through changes to crucial words, which build, develop, and heighten the suspenseful dramatic situation, as in the traditional Scottish ballad "Lord Randal":

> "What d'ye leave to your mother, Lord Randal, my son?
> What d'ye leave to your mother, my handsome young man?"
> "Four and twenty milk kye: mother, mak my bed soon,
> For I'm sick at the heart, and I fain wad lie down."
>
> "What d'ye leave to your sister, Lord Randal, my son?
> What d'ye leave to your sister, my handsome young man?"
> "My gold and my silver; mother, mak my bed soon,
> For I'm sick at the heart, and I fain wad lie down."

The poetry of the Hebrew Bible commonly relies on a type of incremental repetition. As Robert Alter puts it in *The Art of Biblical Poetry* (1985), "Something is stated; then it is restated verbatim with an added element." Here is an example from the Song of Deborah (Judges 5:23):

> Curse Meroz, says the Lord's angel.
> Curse, O curse *its inhabitants.*
>
> For they came not to the aid of the Lord,
> to the aid of the Lord *among the warriors.*

SEE ALSO *ballad, refrain.*

in medias res   From the Latin: "into the middle of things." Horace coined this phrase in *Ars poetica* (ca. 19–18 B.C.E.) to describe a way of commencing a story at a crucial point in the action. It is opposed to *ab ovo,* or starting a story at the beginning. Homer provides the model for leaping into the midst of things. In medias res is a formulaic prescription for the epic poem, a license to enter a tale at a peak moment. It is as if the story is already familiar to the audience — "the epic is indifferent to formal beginnings," as Mikhail Bakhtin puts it in "Epic and Novel" (1941) — and thus the poet has greater narrative freedom to tell it out of chronological order, shuttling back and forth in time, linking events. The epic poet can also end at any time.

SEE ALSO *epic.*

In Memoriam stanza   This stanza — a quatrain in iambic tetrameter (ta TUM | ta TUM | ta TUM | ta TUM) with an envelope rhyme scheme of *abba* — is named for the pattern Alfred, Lord Tennyson, used in his poem *In Memoriam* (1849). Tennyson did not invent the stanza, as he had thought — Ben Jonson uses it in "An Elegy" (1640), as does Lord Herbert of Cherbury in "Ode upon a Question Moved, whether Love Should Continue for ever" (1665) — but he did reserve it for all his poems dealing with the death of his friend Arthur Hallam, and turned it into one of the most ingenious elegiac devices of nineteenth-century poetry.

inspiration   In-breathing, indwelling. Inspiration is connected to enthusiasm, which derives from the Greek word *enthousiasmos,* or "inspiration," which in turn derives from *enthousiazein,* which means "to be inspired by a god." Shelley's "Defence of Poetry" (1819) makes clear that he considered poetic composition both an uncontrollable force beyond the dispensation of the poet's conscious intellect ("Poetry is not like reasoning, a power to be exerted according to the determination of the will. A man cannot say, 'I will compose poetry'") and an internal phenomenon of the deeper mind: "for the mind in creation is as a fading coal which some invisible influence, like an inconstant wind, awakens to transitory brightness; this power arises from within, like the color of a flower which fades and changes as it is developed, and the conscious portions of our natures are unprophetic either of its approach or its departure."

There is a long lineage for the idea that, as Cicero put it, "I have heard that — as they say Democritus and Plato have left on record — no man can be a good poet who is not on fire with passion and inspired by something like frenzy" (*On the Orator,* 55 B.C.E.). There is a point in creation when voluntary effort merges with something involuntary and some unknown force takes over. "Henceforward, in using the word *Poetry,*" Robert Graves writes in *On English Poetry* (1922), "I mean both the controlled and the uncontrollable parts of the art taken together, because each is helpless without the other."

There are two views of inspiration — that it comes as a force from beyond the poet; that it comes as a power from within the poet — but these views keep intertwining. In *The Greeks and the Irrational* (1951), E. R. Dodds suggests that Democritus was the first writer to hold that the finest poems were composed "with inspiration and a holy breath." Dodds points to the belief that minstrels derive their creative power from a supreme source: "It was a god who implanted all sorts of lays in my mind" (the *Odyssey,* ca. eighth century B.C.E.). So too Pindar begged the Muse to grant him "an abundant flow of song welling from my own thought" ("Nemean III," 475 B.C.E.). These poets characterize inspiration as a power from without that is a source within.

Poets have invoked something that can't be controlled. This is the touch of madness that Plato made so much of, the freedom that terrified him. Here is Socrates (ca. 470–399 B.C.E.) in the dialogue *Phaedrus* (ca. 370 B.C.E.):

> There is a third form of possession or madness, of which the Muses are the source. This seizes a tender, virgin soul and stimulates it to rapt passionate expression, especially in lyric poetry, glorifying the countless mighty deeds of ancient times for the instruction of posterity. But if any man comes to the gates of poetry without the madness of the Muses, persuaded that skill alone will make him a good poet, then shall he and his works of sanity with him be brought to nought by the poetry of madness, and behold, their place is nowhere to be found.

Dodds notes that for Plato, "the Muse is actually *inside* the poet." The Neo-Platonic Shelley spoke of "the visitations of the divinity in man."

No one entirely understands the relationship between trance and craft in making poetry. On one side, we have the idea of poetry as something entirely inspired by an outside force. Hesiod claimed that he heard the Muses singing on Mount Helicon, and they gave him a poet's staff and told him what to sing. English poetry begins with just such a vision, since it commences with the holy trance of a seventh-century figure called Caedmon, an illiterate herdsman, who now stands at the top of the English literary tradition as the initial Anglo-Saxon or Old English poet of record, the first to compose Christian poetry in his own language. So too in tribal societies, poets are considered the instruments of a power, an external source, which speaks through them.

Longinus added a crucial dimension to the idea of inspiration by considering the way the sublime affects not the speaker but the listener. Poetry also instills a sense of inspiration in the listener or reader. Paul Valéry goes so far as to claim that this is the function or purpose of a poet's work. Thus he writes, in "Poetry and Abstract Thought" (1954), "A poet's function — do not be startled by this remark — is not to experience the poetic state: that is a private affair. His function is to create it in others. The poet is recognized — or at least everyone recognizes his own poet — by the simple fact that he causes his reader to become 'inspired.'"

SEE ALSO *the sublime.*

intentional fallacy Equating the meaning of a poem with the author's intention. W. K. Wimsatt and Monroe Beardsley used this phrase to describe what they considered a common critical mistake: "The Intentional Fallacy is a confusion between the poem and its origins, a special case of what is known to philosophers as the Genetic Fallacy. It begins by trying to derive the standard of criticism from the psychological *causes* of the poem and ends in biography and relativism" (*The Verbal Icon,* 1954). The Wimsatt-Beardsley hypothesis was a corrective to reductive criticism, usefully focusing on the poem itself as a work of art, but it ignores the reality that a whole range of contextual formation, including an author's so-called intentions, can help us better understand a literary work. Intentions are complicated and can refer to something more than what is locked up in the private mind of a writer.

interlaced rhyme An interlaced rhyme is a medial rhyme that occurs in long rhyming couplets, especially the hexameter. Words in the middle of each line rhyme at the caesura. Swinburne employs the device in "Hymn to Proserpine" (1866):

Thou art more than the day or the *morrow,* the seasons that laugh or that
weep;
For these give joy and *sorrow;* but thou, Proserpina, sleep.

SEE ALSO *hexameter, rhyme.*

invention   The word *invention* began its long critical life in classical
rhetoric, where *inventio* was listed as the first of five parts of oratory, con-
cerned with the discovery and deployment of arguments. The noun *inven-
tio* corresponds to the verb *invenire,* meaning "to find, to discover, to come
upon." One of the ancient criticisms of rhetoric is that it is an art without
a proper subject matter and can be manipulated at will. This charge, which
Plato launched against the sophist philosophers, such as Gorgias, whom he
accused of empty words, is the source of *inventio* as a term of abuse. Aristotle
countered that *inventio* is a term for how rhetoric discovers truth. In *De
inventione* (ca. 87 B.C.E.), Cicero, who views rhetoric as the source of civi-
lization, hedges the argument when he defines *inventio* as "the discovery
of valid or seemingly valid arguments that render one's thoughts plausible."
The idea of finding valid or true arguments was always dogged in classi-
cal rhetoric by its evil twin, arguments that only seem valid, which suggests
duplicity. This was a charge of philosophy against poetry.

Invention migrated from rhetoric to poetics and at first referred to the
discovery of subjects for poems. Leonardo da Vinci stated that "the poet
says that his science consists of invention and measure, and this is the main
substance of poetry—invention of the subject-matter and measurement in
metre." Invention was contrasted with the "imitation" of prior literary mod-
els, and thus came to signal new and original discoveries. It has had a bewil-
dering variety of uses. It was equated with wit and applied to the fanciful and
the incredible. It was associated with the imagination and thus came to refer
to "creating" rather than "finding" new truths. It was used to describe fic-
tional, i.e., "invented," rather than historical truths—or the combination of
them. It was characterized as an originating power and thus contrasted with
judgment. It was used in opposition to convention. In his *Life of Pope* (1781),
Samuel Johnson defined invention as the faculty "by which new trains of
events are formed and new scenes of imagery displayed ... and by which
extrinsic and adventitious embellishments and illustrations are connected

with a known subject." In modern times, invention tends to suggest innovation in either content or form — or both. There remains a sliding ambiguity in the concept that dates to its origins in rhetoric. The invention that poetry undertakes suggests either the discovery of something previously overlooked or unknown, or else the creation of something fresh and original.

SEE ALSO *convention, imagination, imitation, inspiration, originality.*

inversion   In rhetoric, inversion is the turning of an opponent's argument against him. In poetry, it refers to a grammatical reversal of normal word order, sometimes for the sake of rhyme or meter. It is a notorious device in bad poetry, where words are often wrenched to fit a rhyme scheme, but can also be used for rhetorical and metrical effect. In her poem beginning "There's a certain Slant of light, / Winter Afternoons—" (1861), Emily Dickinson places a direct object before a subject and verb and thus writes, "Heavenly Hurt, it gives us." In book 2 of *Paradise Lost* (1667), John Milton purposely inverts the word order in identifying with prophetic poets of the past: "Blind *Thamyris* and blind *Maeonides,* / And *Tiresias* and *Phineas* prophets old."

SEE ALSO *rhetoric.*

invocation   An apostrophe asking a god or goddess, asking the Muse, for inspiration, especially at the beginning of an epic, as when John Milton calls out at the beginning of *Paradise Lost* (1667), "Sing, Heavenly Muse." The invocation — a prayer to initiate a story — recognizes that a poet has a complex indebtedness to tradition. The invocation also acknowledges the uncontrollable aspect of art. Poetry is helpless without an element of mania, of the irrational or unconscious. Thus the invocation becomes a plea for creativity.

SEE ALSO *apostrophe, epic, inspiration, muse, tradition.*

ionic   The Ionians of Asia Minor seem to have used ionic verses for the orgiastic worship of Dionysus and Cybele. The greater ionic foot (*Ionicus a maiore*) was composed of two long syllables followed by two short ones. The lesser ionic foot (*Ionicus a minore*) reversed the order; two short syllables preceded two long ones. Anacreon employed ionics in lyric poetry, Euripides (ca. 480–406 B.C.E.) in tragedy.

SEE ALSO *Anacreontic, foot, tragedy;* also "quantitative meters" in *meter.*

irony From the Greek: "dissimulation." *Irony* is a notoriously slippery term. Eric Heller noted in 1958 that "every attempt to define irony unambiguously is in itself ironical. It is wiser to speak about it ironically." Nonetheless, there are some traditional ways of looking at this shifty concept. Until the eighteenth century, irony referred to the rhetorical mode of dissembling ignorance, saying something less or different than one means. In Greek comedy, the *eirön* was the underdog, a weak but clever dissembler, who pretended to be less intelligent than he was and ultimately triumphed over his adversary. In Plato's dialogues (fourth century B.C.E.), the philosopher Socrates (ca. 470–399 B.C.E.) takes up the role of the *eirön* ("dissembler"). He asks seemingly innocuous questions that gradually undermine the arguments of his interlocutor, thus trapping him into discovering the truth. This became known as Socratic irony. John Thirwall named this dialogue form "Dialectical Irony" (*On the Irony of Sophocles,* 1833). The sense of dissembling still clings to the word *irony.*

Verbal irony. A speaker states one thing, but means something else, often the opposite of what one thinks. Samuel Johnson defined irony in verbal terms as "a mode of speech in which the meaning is contrary to the words: as, *Bolinbroke was a pious man."* Some rhetorical terms may be placed under the rubric of irony, such as *hyperbole* (overstatement), *litotes* (understatement), *antiphrasis* (contrast), *chleuasm* (mockery), *mycterism* (the sneer), and *mimesis* (imitation). We can also add *pastiche, puns, parody,* and *conscious naiveté.*

Dramatic irony. A situation turns out to be different than it seems. As a plot device, dramatic irony operates in a number of established ways: (1) the spectators know more than the protagonist; (2) the character acts in an unwise or inappropriate way; (3) characters or situations are compared; or (4) there is a marked difference between what the character recognizes and understands and what the play suggests.

Cosmic irony is the irony of fate. A deity, a destiny, the universe itself, leads a character to a sense of false hope, which is duly frustrated and mocked. This characteristic plot device works so well for Thomas Hardy because it reflects his worldview.

Friedrich Schlegel and other late eighteenth- and early nineteenth-century German writers introduced the notion of Romantic irony. The author builds the illusion of representing external reality, but shatters it by revealing that the author himself is self-consciously manipulating the scene. Lord Byron's narrative poem *Don Juan* (1819–24) repeatedly draws attention to itself in this way.

The New Critics enlarged and generalized irony into a criterion of value. Thus I. A. Richards defined irony in poetry as the equilibrium of opposed attitudes and evaluations. As he writes in *Principles of Literary Criticism* (1924), "Irony in this sense consists in the bringing in of the opposite, the complementary impulses; that is why poetry which is exposed to it is not of the highest order, and why irony itself is so constantly a characteristic of poetry which is." Robert Penn Warren ("Pure and Impure Poetry," 1942), Cleanth Brooks ("Irony as a Principle of Structure," 1949), and other New Critics developed the idea that weaker poems are vulnerable to a reader's skepticism, but that greater poems are invulnerable because they incorporate into their very being the poet's ironic awareness of opposite or complementary attitudes.

In *On the Concept of Irony with Constant Reference to Socrates* (1841), the philosopher Søren Kierkegaard considers irony, especially Socratic irony, a mode of seeing things, a way of viewing life. To be ironic is to be double-minded.

SEE ALSO *ambiguity, hyperbole, imitation, parody, pun, rhetoric, satire.*

isometric stanza   A stanza using lines of the same length. Verse forms and stanzas that employ a single kind of metrical line — all the traditional fixed forms, for example, or poems in blank verse, heroic couplets, or terza rima — are isometric. "It is a simple fact," T.V.F. Brogan states, "that most of the poems written in English from Chaucer to Tennyson and Browning are isometric."

SEE ALSO *blank verse, couplet, formes fixes, heterometric stanza, stanza, terza rima.*

J

jazz poetry   Jazz is an art of improvisation (the performance of music without following a prearranged score), which is also the core value in jazz poetry, a verbal music that brings the lyric "into the moment," whether it is composed spontaneously with music in the background, or deliberately by the poet in solitude. Jazz has provided a particular beat for American poetry from the 1920s to the present. Hart Crane declared, "Let us invent an idiom for the proper transposition of jazz into words! Something clean, sparkling, elusive!" The transposition of jazz into words takes place in the work of the poets of the Harlem Renaissance, the Beat movement, and the Black Arts movement. The music of jazz and blues has been central to the emerging aesthetics of African American poetry, but it has also had a reach throughout modern and contemporary poetry, whether black or white.

Langston Hughes was the first poet devoted to jazz. He used its syncopated rhythms and repetitive phrases as a way to address the struggles of African American life, especially in such early short poems as "Jazzonia" and "The Weary Blues" (1923). His later jazz poems relate to jazz more directly, especially *Ask Your Mama: Twelve Moods for Jazz* (1961) and *Montage of a Dream Deferred* (1951), which he said was "like be-bop, marked by conflicting changes, sudden nuances, sharp and impudent interjections, broken rhythms, and passages sometimes in the manner of the jam session, sometimes the popular song, punctuated by the riffs, runs, breaks, and distortions of the music of a community in transition." Hughes, Kenneth Rexroth, and Maxwell Bodenheim all started reciting poetry with jazz bands. Rexroth defined jazz poetry in 1958 as "the reciting of suitable poetry with the music of a jazz band, usually small and comparatively quiet. Most emphatically, it is not recitation with 'background' music. The voice is integrally wedded to the music and, although it does not sing notes, is treated as another instrument, with its own solos and ensemble passages."

Kenneth Patchen and Jack Spicer both read their poems with jazz accompaniments. During the Beat era, reading poetry to jazz became part of the San Francisco club scene. Jack Kerouac called his work "spontaneous bop poetry." Kerouac was a jazz aficionado, like Ted Joans, who was also a musician, and LeRoi Jones, later Amiri Baraka, who collaborated with musicians and helped pioneer jazz studies with his book *Blues People* (1963).

Jazz also operates as a metaphor and subject matter in poems such as Frank O'Hara's "The Day Lady Died" (1964), Paul Blackburn's "Listening to Sonny Rollins at the Five-Spot" (1967), and Michael Harper's "Dear John, Dear Coltrane" (1970). My shortlist of other poets in the jazz tradition includes Sterling Brown, Hayden Carruth, Joy Harjo, Garrett Hongo, T. R. Hummer, Yusef Komunyakaa, Philip Levine, Mina Loy, William Matthews, Robert Pinsky, Sonia Sanchez, Charles Simic, Lorenzo Thomas, and Al Young.

SEE ALSO *blues, sound poetry.*

jeli, see *griot.*

jeremiad   A lamentation, a doleful complaint, a sustained invective. The jeremiad, named after the prophet Jeremiah, is a long literary work, usually in prose, sometimes in poetry. The Lamentations of Jeremiah is a series of poems mourning the desolation of Jerusalem and the sufferings of its people after the siege and destruction of the city and the burning of the temple by the Babylonians. In *The New England Mind: From Colony to Province* (1953), Perry Miller first identified the jeremiad as a New England specialty, formalized in Puritan sermons as a response to a tragedy and a warning of greater tribulations to come. It also holds out hope for a brighter future. The sermon comes as a verse jeremiad in Michael Wigglesworth's "God's Controversy with New England," which he composed during the drought of 1662. Emory Elliot explains the conventions of the Puritan jeremiad: "Taking their texts from Jeremiah and Isaiah, these orations followed — and re-inscribed — a rhetorical formula that included recalling the courage and piety of the founders, lamenting recent and present ills, and crying out to return to the original conduct and zeal." In current scholarship, the term *jeremiad* has expanded to include not only sermons but also other like-minded texts, such as captivity narratives, letters, and covenant renewals, as well as some histories and biographies. The Puritan poet Edward Taylor took Samuel Hooker's death as an occasion to preach a verse jeremiad in "An Elegy upon the Death of that Holy and Reverend Man of God, Mr. Samuel Hooker" (1697).

jingle   Any catchy little verse. The jingle, marked by repetitive rhythms and emphatic rhymes, strikes a light chord and sticks in the mind, a memorable piece of nonsense. In "A Literary Nightmare" (1876), later retitled "Punch, Brothers, Punch!," Mark Twain tells the story of catching a viruslike jingle in the morning paper, which he can't dislodge from his mind until he "infects" someone else ("Punch brothers! Punch with care! / Punch in the presence of the passenjare!"), who continues the cycle. The term is sometimes used to deprecate poetry that is too tinkling. William Dean Howells reported that Ralph Waldo Emerson dismissed Edgar Allan Poe as "*the jingle man.*"

SEE ALSO *doggerel, light verse, nonsense poetry, nursery rhymes.*

jongleur   A wandering minstrel and entertainer of the Middle Ages. Jongleurs existed in France from the fifth to the fifteenth century. The name first applied to all entertainers, including actors and acrobats — they considered themselves "jugglers" — but from the tenth century on it referred exclusively to musicians and performers of verse. "A jongleur is a being of multiple personalities," Edmond Faral declared. The terms *jongleur* and *troubadour* were at one time used interchangeably, but later *jongleur* came to refer to entertainers who presented material composed by others, such as the chansons de geste. The gulf had widened between creative and performing artists. Troubadours composed but did not perform their own work. Yet some troubadours fell on hard times and became jongleurs, and some inventive jongleurs became troubadours. The jongleurs were outsiders, frequently treated as madcaps and fools, but there was a lordship of jongleurs in Arras. In 1221, a member of the *carité de nostre dame des ardents,* which was known in the late Middle Ages as the "confraternity of the jongleurs and the townspeople of Arras," declared that

> this Carité was founded by jongleurs, and the jongleurs are the lords of it [*li iogleor en sont signor*]. And those whom they put in, are in. And whoever they keep outside cannot be in, unless they say so. Because there is no lordship with us, save that of jongleurs [*Car sor iogleors ni a nus signorie*].

The jongleurs played a crucial role in transmitting poetry from one country to another. Marius Barbeau points out that "the New World settlers brought the songs to North America as part of their French heritage two or three hundred years ago" (*Jongleur Songs of Old Quebec,* 1962).

SEE ALSO *chansons de geste, juglar, troubadour.*

juglar (plural *juglares*) The Spanish word for "wandering minstrels" and "entertainers." The French term *jongleur* and the Spanish term *juglar* — they are equivalent — derive from the Latin word *ioculari,* "jokes," or *ioculator,* "a clown or joker, someone who entertains." According to one theory, their style of performance and way of life reach back to the wandering street entertainers of Rome. *Juglares* are known to have existed by the seventh century in Spain, but emerged only in the twelfth century as creators and performers of epic *cantares,* sung poems. The *mester de juglaria* ("art of the minstrel") refers to the oral and epic narrative poetry of the twelfth, thirteenth, and fourteenth centuries.

SEE ALSO *jongleur, romances.*

K

keening The Irish form of lamenting over the dead, "Raising the Keen" was primarily a form of women's oral poetry, a public display of grieving, sometimes sung by relatives and neighbors of the deceased, sometimes by professional mourners. It was once common, both in Europe and in Africa, to hire professional mourners to keen one's relatives. In the *Aeneid* (29–19 B.C.E.), Virgil notes the ancient practice among the Phoenicians: "Lamentations, keening, and shrieks of women / sound through the houses." The Ossian poems may be made up of keenings for a dead warrior king in Ireland. Keening, which derives from the Irish word *caoineadh,* is a more verbally articulated expression of grief than the high-pitched moaning of the death wail, the *ullagone.* Seán Ó Súilleabháin explains that "many of the lamentations about the corpse at wakes and funerals were in the form of extempore poetry in Irish." It was common for a relative of the dead to recite mournful poetry in praise of the deceased.

Gaelic keening — atonal, primitive — has informed the elegies and dirges that make up an essential part of Irish poetry and drama. Keening is expressed in traditional folk ballads, such as "The Keening of the Three Marys," which Douglas Hyde collected and translated in *The Religious Songs of Connacht* (1906). John Synge describes the rhythmic power of keening among a group of neighbors in *The Aran Islands* (1907): "While the grave was being opened the women sat down among the flat tombstones, bordered with a pale fringe of early bracken, and began the wild keen, or crying for the dead. Each old woman, as she took her turn in the leading recitative, seemed possessed for the moment with a profound ecstasy of grief, swaying to and fro, and bending her forehead to the stone before her, while she called out to the dead with a perpetually recurring chant of sobs."

W. B. Yeats evokes the keening tradition in the song "Do Not Make a Great Keening" in his play *Cathleen ni Houlihan* (1902), and so does Pádraic Pearse in his lyric "A Woman of the Mountain Keens Her Son" (*Songs of Sleep and Sorrow,* 1914). Traditional keening has mostly died out in Ireland, and contemporary Irish poets continue to lament its loss, which is associated with ritual grief. In Scots Gaelic the term *coronach,* and the practices of lament, have not been completely lost.

SEE ALSO *dirge, elegy, oral poetry.*

kenning   A standard phrase or metaphoric compound used in Old Norse and Old English poetry as a poetic circumlocution for a more familiar noun. In *Beowulf* (ca. eighth to eleventh century), for example, the human body is called *banhus* ("bone house"), a ship is termed *saewudu* ("sea wood"), and the sea is named *swanrud* ("swan road"). There is a riddling element to the kenning, which is a way of renaming and thus reenvisioning an object. It is a miniature riddle. This idea can be illustrated by turning the declaration into a question. "What is the sky's candle [*rodores candel*]"? *The sun.* "What is the home of the winds [*windgeard*]?" *The sea.*

SEE ALSO *metaphor, riddle.*

kind   In the seventeenth and eighteenth centuries, the term *kind* was used to suggest a literary genre, such as the epic. The notion of kind implies that formal genres are characterized both by their intrinsic values and their particular social usefulness. As Susan Stewart explains, "The notion of poetic *kinds* is tied to the specificity of their use and occasion: the epithalamion, the elegy, the aubade are at once works of art independent of their particular contexts of production and use and social acts tied to specific rules of decorum. Poems are in this sense acts of social intent and consequence and not things in a world of things." Literary kinds also have histories, and new kinds are continually made out of old ones.

SEE ALSO *decorum, genre.*

kitsch   A term that originally applied to cheap, trashy, ephemeral works of art: sentimental illustrations, paintings, poems, and novels. Kitsch is art in bad taste, what in Yiddish goes by the terms *schlock* (stuff of low quality) and *schmaltz* (sentimental exaggerations). The art critic Clement Greenberg explained, in "Avant-Garde and Kitsch" (1939), that where there is an avant-garde, generally we also find a rear-guard. True enough — simultaneously with the entrance of the avant-garde, a second new cultural phenomenon appeared in the industrial West: the thing to which the Germans gave the wonderful name of *Kitsch* . . . Kitsch is vicarious experience and faked sensations. Kitsch changes according to style, but remains always the same. Kitsch pretends to demand nothing of its customers except their money — not even their time.

Kitsch was first used in Munich in the 1860s and '70s among painters and art dealers to characterize cheap artistic stuff. It became an international term in the first decades of the twentieth century. *Kitsch* is such a derogatory word that, perhaps inevitably, it began to reappear in the modern domain of high art. Matei Călinescu notes that "from Rimbaud's praise of 'poetic crap' and 'stupid paintings' through Dada and Surrealism, the rebellious avant-garde has made use of a variety of techniques and elements directly borrowed from kitsch for their ironically disruptive purposes."

SEE ALSO *avant-garde, modernism.*

Knittelvers, Knütttelvers, Knüppelvers, Klippelvers　A German form of rhyming couplets, using four stressed syllables. In its earliest incarnation, the line contained any number of unstressed syllables. It was later regularized by Hans Sachs (1494–1576) and others to eight or nine syllables. *Knittelvers* was the most popular meter in German poetry in the fifteenth and sixteenth centuries. The German classical poets of the seventeenth century gave it its derogatory name (*Knittelvers* means "badly knit verse" or "cudgel-verse") and considered it doggerel. It was revived by Gottsched in the eighteenth century, who used it for comedy, and then by Schiller (*Wallensteins Lager,* 1798), and especially Goethe ("The Poetical Mission of Hans Sachs," 1776, and the older parts of *Faust,* 1808–32), who discovered the literary potential of doggerel and other forms of popular entertainment. On a bumpy local train in June 1774, Goethe declaimed to a drowsy friend the *Knittelvers* from his epic fragment *The Wandering Jew.*

SEE ALSO *doggerel, Meistersingers, octosyllabic verse.*

kyrielle　This French form is composed of any number of four-line stanzas, usually rhymed. The last line of the first stanza repeats, sometimes with meaningful variations, as the final line of each quatrain. Repeated lines in any style of poetry are sometimes called *rime en kyrielle*. The name *kyrielle* is a foreshortened form of the response "Kyrie eleison" ("Lord, have mercy upon us") from the Roman liturgy. A number of Anglican hymns preserve the form. Thomas Campion's "With broken heart and contrite sigh" (1613) fits the letter and law of *kyrielle*. It repeats the plea "God, be merciful to me" for four stanzas and concludes with the recognition "God has been merciful to me." William Dunbar's "Lament for the Makers" (ca. 1508) is a secular *kyrielle* that concludes with the Latin phrase "Timor mortis conturbat me" ("The fear of death disturbs me"). Theodore Roethke takes a different tack with the *kyrielle* in his comic poem "Dinky" (1973), which concludes, "*You* may be dirty dinky."

SEE ALSO *quatrain.*

L

lai (French), **lay** (English) The term *lay* is now virtually synonymous with *song*. In Old French poetry, a *lai* was a short lyrical or narrative poem. Gautier de Dargies wrote the earliest lyrical *lais* in the thirteenth century. Marie de France's short romantic tales (*contes*), usually written in octosyllabic verse, are the oldest narrative *lais* and date to the twelfth century. Later, the term became synonymous with *contes*. In Provençal poetry, the *lai* was a love song set to a popular tune. In fourteenth-century Britain, the term *Breton lay* applied to poems set in Brittany, which echoed Marie de France's poems. Two examples: the anonymous Middle English poem *Sir Orfeo* (late thirteenth or early fourteenth century) and Chaucer's "Franklin's Tale" in *The Canterbury Tales* (written between 1387 and 1400 but not published until the 1470s).

In the nineteenth century, the term *lay* was often used for a short historical ballad, as in Sir Walter Scott's *The Lay of the Last Minstrel* (1805). The term invoked antiquity, and Scott associated the minstrel with the French trouvère.

> The way was long, the wind was cold,
> The Minstrel was infirm and old;
> His withered cheek, and tresses gray,
> Seemed to have known a better day;
> The harp, his sole remaining joy,
> Was carried by an orphan boy.
> The last of all the Bards was he,
> Who sung of Border chivalry . . .

SEE ALSO *dit, octosyllabic verse, trouvère.*

laisse The basic lyric, dramatic, and narrative unit of Old French poetry. The medieval French epics (chansons de geste), such as *La chanson de Roland*

(*Song of Roland,* ca. 1090), are written in *laisses* or *tirades,* which are stanzas of varying length. The early works were assonanced and thus used the same vowel sound in the last accented syllable of each line. The later ones were monorhymed (all the lines rhyme with one another). Old French poetry was highly formulaic, and strong repetitions carried material from one *laisse* to the next. The scholar Jean Rychner first named the use of block repetitions — stanzaic correspondences — *laisses similaires.*

SEE ALSO *chansons de geste, oral-formulaic method.*

lament   A poem or song expressing grief. The lament is powered by a personal sense of loss. The poetry of lamentation, which arose in oral literature alongside heroic poetry, seems to exist in all languages and poetries. One finds it in ancient Egyptian, in Hebrew, in Chinese, in Sanskrit, in Zulu. A profound grief is formalized as mourning, as in Lamentations 2:10:

> The elders of the daughter of Zion sit upon the ground, *and* keep silence: they have cast up dust upon their heads; they have girded themselves with sackcloth: the virgins of Jerusalem hang down their heads to the ground.

The poetry of intense grief and mourning, such as the Lamentations of Jeremiah or David's lament for Saul and Jonathan, has its roots in religious feeling and ritual. The Hebrew Bible is filled with both individual laments (a worshiper cries out to Yahweh in times of need) and communal laments, which mourn a larger national calamity.

Laments may have developed from magic spells to call back what was lost — a destroyed temple, a dead god. "Lament for the Destruction of Ur" (early second millennium B.C.E.) memorialized the destruction of the Third Dynasty of Ur (2112–2004 B.C.E.) and turned out to be the last great masterwork of Sumerian civilization. It is one of five known Mesopotamian "city laments" (along with "The Lament for Sumer and Ur," "The Lament for Nippur," "The Lament for Eridu," and "The Lament for Uruk"), which were the province of elegists called *gala.* Thorkild Jacobsen points out that "the great laments for destroyed temples and cities usually divide into a part called *balağ* 'harp,' which was to be sung to the strains of the harp, and a following *ershemma,* a lament to be accompanied by a tambourine-like drum called *shem.*" The laments served ritual purposes. The ones for dead gods were performed during annual mourning processions of weeping; the ones for destroyed temples were "originally performed in the ruins to induce the gods to rebuild the destroyed structure."

A few other early examples: The minstrel in the Anglo-Saxon poem "Deor's Lament" (ninth or tenth century) is a poet who is no longer favored and consoles himself by reciting the misfortunes of others. Yosef Ibn Avitor's "Lament for the Jews of Zion" (eleventh century) is a mournful Spanish-Hebrew poem written after Jews were attacked by Bedouins from the tribe of Bnei Jaraakh in Palestine in 1024; Avraham Ibn Ezra's "Lament for Andalusian Jewry" (mid-twelfth century) is an elegy for the Jewish communities of Spain and North Africa destroyed in 1146 by the invading Almohads.

The late eighteenth-century poet Eibhlín Dubh Ní Chonaill, or Dark Eileen, mourns the death of her husband in "Lament for Art O'Leary" (1773). "The Hag of Beare" (ninth century), the greatest of all early Irish poems written by a woman, is a lament not just for one but for many loves, an outcry against aging. The Polish poet Jan Kochanowski's *Laments* (1580) consists of nineteen poems that wrestle with his grief over the death of his two-and-a-half-year-old daughter ("Wisdom for me was castles in the air; / I'm hurled, like all the rest, from the topmost stair").

SEE ALSO *dirge, elegy, keening.*

lampoon   A harsh, personal, and often scurrilous type of satire. The term came into use in the mid-seventeenth century as a cross between the French *lampons* ("let us drink") and the slang *lamper* ("to guzzle"). But the satiric attack on an individual goes back to ancient Greek drama, when Aristophanes lampooned Euripides in *The Frogs* (405 B.C.E.) and Socrates in *The Clouds* (423 B.C.E.). The lampoon was also one of the modes of classical Arabic poetry known as *hija* ("invective, satire"). The Scottish flyting was a contest of insults. Similar cursing matches have been found in a wide variety of poetries.

In English poetry, the lampoon took on life in Restoration and eighteenth-century England. Samuel Johnson defined it as "a personal satire; ridicule; abuse." Johnson considered the lampoon a lesser form of satire because of the particularity of its reflections. John Dryden declared that the lampoon "is a dangerous sort of weapon and for the most part unlawful. We have no moral right on the reputation of other men" (*Discourse Concerning the Origin and Progress of Satire,* 1693). He was nonetheless a terrific lampooner, which he demonstrates in *Absalom and Achitophel* (1681–82).

SEE ALSO *flyting, panegyric, poetic contest, satire.*

leonine rhyme In English poetry, a leonine rhyme occurs when a word near the middle of the line rhymes with a word at the end. Thus Alfred, Lord Tennyson, writes in *The Princess* (1847),

> The splendor *falls* on castle *walls*
>   And snowy summits old in story:
> The long light *shakes* across the *lakes,*
>   And the wild cataract leaps in glory.

Leonine rhyme dates to the classical age (Ovid uses it in *The Art of Love,* 2 C.E.), but was especially favored in the Latin poetry of the European Middle Ages. It was referred to as *rime leonine* in the anonymous twelfth-century romance *Guillaume d'Angleterre.* The name has been fancifully attributed both to Pope Leo I (ca. 400–461) and to Leonius, a twelfth-century Parisian canon and Latin poet who was fond of the device. In Latin and French poetry, it is called a leonine rhyme when the last word in the line rhymes with the word before the caesura, as in the ecclesiastical "Stabat mater."

SEE ALSO *rhyme.*

letter poem, epistle The verse epistle, as it was once called, is a poem specifically addressed to a friend, a lover, or a patron. In his *Epistles* (20–14 B.C.E.), Horace established the type of letter poem that reflects on moral and philosophical subjects. In his *Heroides* (ca. 25–16 B.C.E.), Ovid established the type of epistle poem that reflects on romantic subjects. Horace's letters on the art of poetry, known since Quintilian as the *Ars poetica* (ca. 19–18 B.C.E.), are also verse epistles, and so are Ovid's poems of exile, *Tristia* (9–12 C.E.).

Ovid's *Heroides* particularly influenced the troubadours and their poems of courtly love. The Horatian epistle had impact throughout the Renaissance and the eighteenth century. There are Petrarch's *Epistulae metricae* (1331–61) in Latin, Ariosto's *Satires* (1517–25) in vernacular Italian, Garcilaso's *Epístola a Boscán* (1543) in Spanish, and Boileau's *À mes vers* (1695) and *Sur l'amour de Dieu* (1698) in French. Ivan Funikov's ironic verse epistle, "Message of a Nobleman to a Nobleman" (1608), is the oldest Russian work in verse that can be accurately dated. Epistolary poetry was also the most popular literary genre in fourteenth-century Uzbekistan. Elif Batuman explains that "poems during this period took the form of love letters between nightingales and sheep, between opium and wine, between red and green. One poet wrote to a girl that he had tried to drink a lake so he could swallow her reflection: this girl was cleaner than water."

Samuel Daniel introduced the verse epistle into English in *Letter from Octavia to Marcus Antonius* (1599) and in *Certain Epistles* (1601–3). Ben Jonson employed the Horatian mode in *The Forest* (1616), which was also taken up by John Dryden in his epistles to Congreve (1694) and to the Duchess of Ormond (1700). Alexander Pope modeled "Eloisa to Abelard" (1717) on Ovid's *Heroides,* and adapted the Horatian epistle in his *Moral Essays* (1731–35) and *Epistle to Dr. Arbuthnot* (1735). The epistle fell into disuse in the Romantic era. Since then, it has been occasionally revived and renamed as a letter, as in W. H. Auden and Louis MacNeice's *Letters from Iceland* (1937). Richard Hugo brings the form closer to a real letter in *31 Letters and 13 Dreams* (1977).

The letter poem is addressed to a specific person and written from a specific place, which locates it in time and space. It imitates the colloquial familiarity of a letter, though sometimes in elaborate forms. Some create fictive speakers, as in Ezra Pound's adaptation of Li Po, "The River-Merchant's Wife: A Letter" (1915). Some are addressed to those long dead, as in Auden's "Letter to Lord Byron" (1937), others to contemporaries. But unlike an actual letter, the letter poem is never addressed exclusively to its recipient; it is meant to be overheard by a third person, a future reader.

light verse   Light verse, which is both lightfooted and lighthearted, sets out to amuse and entertain. It seems to imply an opposite, "heavy verse," and is sometimes taken less seriously than "serious poetry," which it makes light of and often takes to account. It measures itself against the pretensions of its own era. Its power lies in its irreverent spirit and technical skill, its witty derring-do, the way it turns things upside-down. Its strategy is laughter rather than tears.

Light verse is a broad category that includes a variety of poetic types, from the clerihew, the double dactyl, the limerick, and *vers de société* to burlesques and mock heroics, nonsense poetry and occasional verse, pointed epigrams, ironic epitaphs, parodies. Its subject can be trivial or carry deep poetic significance, as in, say, Petrarchan love poems and Cavalier lyrics. A. A. Milne accounts for light verse in *Year In, Year Out* (1952):

> Light Verse obeys Coleridge's definition of poetry, the best words in the best order; it demands Carlyle's definition of genius, transcendent capacity for taking pains; and it is the supreme exhibition of somebody's definition of art, the concealment of art. In the result it observes the most exact laws of rhythm and metre as if by a happy accident, and in a sort of nonchalant spirit of mockery at the real poets who do it on purpose.

One characterization of light verse is "poets at play."

SEE ALSO *clerihew, comedy, doggerel, double dactyl, epigram, limerick, nonsense poetry, parody.*

limerick The only English stanzaic form used exclusively for light verse, the limerick is a five-line verse that rhymes *aabba*. The first, second, and fifth lines have three beats, the third and fourth lines two beats. The dominant rhythm is anapestic. It is sometimes written in four lines. One theory of its origins is that it was brought to the Irish town of Limerick in 1700 by veterans returning from the French War; another is that it originated in the nursery rhymes published in *Mother Goose's Melody* (ca. 1765); a third is that it stems from a refrain in the nonsense verse "Will you come up to Limerick?" The most convincing theory is that it was used by the poetic school Fili na Maighe in County Limerick in the mid-eighteenth century; the form is undoubtedly much older. The limericks collected in the *History of Sixteen Wonderful Old Women* (1820) include this one:

> There was an old woman of Lynn,
> Whose nose very near reach'd her chin;

> You may easy suppose
> She had plenty of beaux,
> This charming old woman of Lynn.

There are also limericks in *Anecdotes and Adventures of Fifteen Gentlemen* (1822). Edward Lear mastered and popularized the form in his *Book of Nonsense* (1846), though he never used the word *limerick* himself. A friend introduced him to the limerick "as a form of verse lending itself to limitless variety for Rhymes and Pictures," and he started composing verses and drawings for children. M. Russel, SJ, coined the term *learic* for this type of nonsense:

> There was an old Person of Sparta,
> Who had twenty-five sons and one "darta";
> He fed them on Snails, and weighed them in scales,
> That wonderful Person of Sparta.

One of the charms of the limerick is that it taps the odd magic of place. Eudora Welty points out that "there's something unutterably convincing about that Old Person of Sparta who had twenty-five sons and one darta, and it is surely beyond question that he fed them on snails and weighed them in scales, because we know where that Old Person is *from* — Sparta!"

Alfred, Lord Tennyson (1850–1892), Algernon Charles Swinburne (1837–1909), Rudyard Kipling (1865–1936), Robert Louis Stevenson (1850–1894), Dante Gabriel Rossetti (1828–1882), Mark Twain (1835–1910), W. S. Gilbert (1836–1911), Morris Bishop (1893–1973), and Edward Gorey (1925–2000) are just some of the poets who have continued to experiment with the limerick form over the past two centuries, adding new twists and surprises.

The limerick is a popular oral form, invariably bawdy and off-color. The scholar Gershon Legman maintained that the folk limerick is always obscene. An anonymous lyric makes his point:

> A limerick packs laughs anatomical
> Into space that is quite economical.
> But the good ones I've seen
> So seldom are clean,
> And the clean ones so seldom are comical.

SEE ALSO *double dactyl, light verse, nonsense verse, quintet.*

line   A unit of meaning, a measure of attention, a way of framing poetry. All verse is measured by lines. On its own, the poetic line immediately announces its difference from everyday speech and prose. It creates its own visual and verbal impact. Paul Claudel called the fundamental line "an idea isolated by blank space." I would call it "words isolated by blank space."

"Poetry is the sound of language organized in lines," James Longenbach asserts in *The Art of the Poetic Line* (2008). "More than meter, more than rhyme, more than images or alliteration or figurative language, line is what distinguishes our experience of poetry as poetry, rather than some other kind of writing." There are one-line poems called monostiches, which are timed to deliver a single poignancy. An autonomous line in a poem makes sense on its own, even if it is a fragment, an incomplete sentence. It is end-stopped and completes a thought. An enjambed line carries the meaning over from one line to the next. Whether end-stopped or enjambed, however, the line in a poem moves horizontally, but the rhythm and sense also drive it vertically, and the meaning continues to accrue as the poem develops and unfolds.

In "Summa Lyrica" (1992), Allen Grossman proposes a theory of the three modular versions of the line in English:

1. Less than ten syllables more or less.
2. Ten syllables more or less.
3. More than ten syllables more or less.

The ten-syllable or blank-verse line provides a norm in English poetry. Wordsworth (1771–1850) and Frost (1874–1963) both perceived that the blank-verse line could be used to give the sensation of actual speech. "The topic of the line of ten is conflict," Grossman says, which is why it has been so useful in drama, where other speakers are always nearby. In the line of less than ten syllables, then, there is a sense that something has been taken away or subtracted, attenuated or missing. There is a greater silence that surrounds it, a feeling of going under speech, which is why it has worked well for poems of loss. It has also proved useful for the stripped-down presentation of objects. The line of more than ten syllables consequently gives a feeling of going above or beyond the parameters of oral utterance, or over them, beyond speech itself. The long lines widen the space for reverie. "The speaker in the poem bleeds outward as in trance or sleep toward other states of himself," Grossman says. This line, which has a dreamlike associativeness, also radiates an oracular feeling, which is why it has so often been the line of prophetic texts, visionary poetry.

SEE ALSO *blank verse, end-stopped line, enjambment, free verse, imagism, monostich, verse.*

lineation The organization of a poem into lines. Lineation specifies that we are in the presence of a poem, which requires a special act of attention.

list poem, see *catalog poem.*

litany From the Greek: "prayer" or "supplication." In Christian worship, the litany is a type of liturgical prayer used in services and processions. It is chanted between the clergy and the congregation and consists of a series of supplications and fixed responses. The frequent repetition of the prayer Kyrie eleison was probably the original form of the litany in the early church. The Litany of the Saints continues to be widely used as a sacred prayer. Seventeenth-century religious poets mined the formal possibilities of the litany, hence John Donne's "A Litany" (1608–9) and Robert Herrick's "His Litany, to the Holy Spirit" (1647), which mimics a sense of call and response:

> In the hour of my distress,
> When temptations me oppress,
> And when I my sins confess,
>   Sweet Spirit, comfort me!

In contemporary usage, the litany suggests any long, syntactically repetitive work, such as the Book of Psalms, Walt Whitman's "Song of Myself" (1855), or Allen Ginsberg's "Kaddish" (1961). The litany has in essence become a catalog poem. John Ashbery takes the original idea of the litany and turns it into an experimental form in his sixty-eight-page "Litany" (1978), a poem in two columns "meant to be read as simultaneous but independent monologues."

SEE ALSO *anaphora, catalog poem, parallelism, praise poems.*

logopoeia   The linguistic qualities of a poem, particularly as they pertain to intelligence. In *How to Read* (1929), Ezra Pound uses this term for one of three "kinds of poetry":

> LOGOPOEIA, "the dance of intellect among words," that is to say, it employs words not for their direct meaning, but it takes count in a special way of habits of usage, of the context we *expect* to find with the word, its usual concomitants, of its known acceptances, and of ironical play.

Pound points to the rhythmical progression of ideas, the capacity of poetry to estrange language, to charge words and phrases with new meanings. He found an elegant use of *logopoeia* in the Latin of Propertius (ca. 50–ca. 15 B.C.E.) and the French of Jules Laforgue (1860–1887). Richard Sieburth characterizes *logopoeia* as "language commenting upon its own possibilities and limitations as language."

SEE ALSO *melopoeia, phanopoeia.*

long meter   The long meter of the hymn books is a variant of the ballad stanza. The four lines of the ballad follow a pattern of alternating stresses: 4, 3, 4, 3. The long meter lengthens the trimeters and equalizes the stresses: 4, 4, 4, 4. The meter is usually iambic. Instead of the *abcb* rhyme scheme, long meter usually rhymes *abab* or *aabb*. In 1707 Isaac Watts employed long meter in a hymn, which begins,

> When I survey the wondrous cross
> On which the Prince of Glory died,
> My richest gain I count but loss,
> And pour contempt on all my pride.

SEE ALSO *ballad, hymn, short meter.*

lullaby   A bedtime song or chant to put a child to sleep. Lullabies typically begin "Hush-a-bye, baby, on the tree top," or "Rock-a-bye, baby," or "Sleep, my child," or "Hush, little baby, don't say a word." The English term *lullaby* may derive from the sounds *lu lu* or *la la,* a sound that mothers and nurses make to calm babies, and *by by* or *bye bye,* another lulling sound and also a way to say good night. The oldest lullaby to survive may be that of Roman nurses recorded in a scholium on the poet Persius: "Lalla, Lalla, Lalla, / aut dormi, aut lacte" ("Lullaby, Lullaby, Lullaby, / either go to sleep or suckle"). As ancient folk poems, lullabies range from meaningless jingles to semi-ballads. They are closely related to nursery rhymes. Rodrigo Caro called these sooth- ing melodies, which are found all over the world, the "reverend mothers of all songs."

SEE ALSO *carol, nursery rhyme.*

lyric   The short poem has been practiced for at least forty-five hundred years. It is one of the necessary forms of human speech, one of the ways we invent and know ourselves. It is as ancient as recorded literature. It precedes prose in all languages, all civilizations, and it will last as long as human beings take pleasure in playing with words, in combining the sounds of words in unexpected and illuminating ways, in using words to convey deep feeling and perhaps something even deeper than feeling. The lyric poem immerses us in the original waters of consciousness, in the aboriginal nature of being itself.

The Greeks defined the lyric as a poem to be chanted or sung to the accompaniment of a lyre (*lyra*), the instrument of Apollo and Orpheus, and thus a symbol of poetic and musical inspiration. The Greek lyric has its origins, like Egyptian and Hebrew poetry, in religious feeling and practice. The first songs were most likely written to accompany occasions of celebra- tion and mourning. Prayer, praise, and lamentation are three of the oldest impulses in poetry. Aristotle (384–322 B.C.E.) distinguished three generic categories of poetry: epic, drama, and lyric. This categorization evolved into the traditional division of literature into three generic types or classes, based on who is supposedly speaking in a literary work:

> *epic* or *narrative:* the narrator speaks in the first person, then lets the
> characters speak for themselves.
> *drama:* the characters do all the talking.
> *lyric:* a first-person speaker utters the words.

The lyric, which offers us a supposed speaker, a person to whom we often assign the name of the author, shades off into the dramatic utterance ("All poetry is of the nature of soliloquy," John Stuart Mill writes) but has always been counterposed to the epic. Whereas the speaker of the epic serves as the deputy of a public voice, a singer of tales narrating the larger tale of the tribe, the lyric offers us a solitary singer or speaker singing or speaking on his or her own behalf. Ever since Sappho (late seventh century B.C.E.), the lyric poem has created a space for personal feeling. It has introduced a subjectivity and explored our capacity for human inwardness. The intimacy of lyric — and the lyric poem is the most intimate and personally volatile form of literary discourse — stands against the grandeur of epic. It asserts the value and primacy of the solitary voice, the individual feeling.

The definition of the lyric as a poem to be sung held until the Renaissance, when poets began to write their poems for readers rather than composing them for musical presentation. The words and the music separated. Thereafter, lyric poetry retained an associational relationship to music. Its cadences and sound patterns, its tonal variations and rhythms, all show its melodic origins (hence Yeats's title *Words for Music Perhaps*). But writing offers a different space for poetry. It inscribes it in print and thus allows it to be read and reread. Writing fixes the evanescence of sound and holds it against death. It also gives the poem a fixed visual as well as auditory life. With the advent of a text, the performer and the audience are physically separated. Hence John Stuart Mill's idea that "eloquence is *heard;* poetry is *overheard*," and Northrop Frye's notion that the lyric is "a literary genre characterized by the assumed concealment of the audience from the poet." Thereafter, the lyric becomes a different kind of intimate communiqué, a highly concentrated and passionate form of communication between strangers. It delivers on our spiritual lives precisely because it gives us the gift of intimacy and interiority, of privacy and participation. Perhaps the asocial nature of the deepest feeling, the "too muchness" of human emotion, is what creates the space for the lyric, which is a way of beating time, of experiencing duration, of verging on infinity.

SEE ALSO *dramatic monologue, epic, poetry.*

M

macaronic verse   Poetry in which two or more languages are mixed together. Strictly speaking, macaronic verse incorporates words from the poet's native language into another language and subjects them to its rules, thus creating a comic effect. It was first used in the late fifteenth century by interspersing vernacular Italian with Latin. Teofilo Folengo made the form famous in his mock epic *Macaroneae* (1517–21). The humor came in bending the vernacular to literary language, as in doggerel. Later, the term came to be applied to any poem, humorous or serious, in which languages are intermingled. We could extend the term to include the work of Chicano and other English-language poets who incorporate vernacular Spanish into their poems and thus create a new idiomatic American poetry. The fusion of languages speaks to complex modern identities.

SEE ALSO *doggerel, mock epic.*

madrigal   From the Medieval Latin word *matricale,* "country song." A verse to be sung to music; a secular vocal composition for two or more voices. The madrigal originated as a pastoral song in northern Italy in the fourteenth century. The simple rustic song consisted of two or three three-line tercets followed by one or two rhyming couplets. The lines were either seven or eleven syllables long. The madrigal was revived by European composers in the sixteenth century. Freed of traditional formal strictures, all that remained of the original form was the final rhyming couplet, which has also been abandoned in most modern madrigals. The English madrigal flourished from the 1580s to the 1620s. Thomas Morley (1557–1602), Thomas Weelkes (1576–1623), and John Wilbye (1574–1638) were great English composers of the madrigal.

SEE ALSO *lyric, pastoral.*

mannerism   When capitalized, the term specifically refers to the artistic period of the "Late" Renaissance, basically the years between Michelangelo (1475–1564) and Rubens (1577–1640). Vasari (1511–1574) used the word *maniera* to refer to the impressive or distinctive quality in a work of art, the way it fuses particular characteristics into a beautiful whole. In the seventeenth century, the term *mannerism* came to suggest a highly affected or exaggerated literary style. Ernst Robert Curtius broadens the concept of mannerism to represent "the common denominator for all literary tendencies which are opposed to Classicism, whether they be pre-classical, post-classical, or contemporary with any Classicism," and thus mannerism becomes a complementary phenomenon to classicism in all periods, "a constant in European literature." Whereas classicism values clarity and restraint, mannerism looks for ingeniousness and ornamentation. It embraces complex forms and moves on the wings of high rhetoric, piling up words, preferring circumlocution to straightforwardness, elaboration to plainness.

SEE ALSO *baroque, classic, metaphysical poets.*

martial verse   War verses, battle poems, marching songs. There has sometimes been poetic accompaniment to military campaigning, and that poetry sounds a drumbeat of fury. According to Plutarch, the Athenian statesman and elegiac poet Solon (ca. 638–558 B.C.E.) was given leadership for the Athenian war against Megara on the basis of a poem he wrote about Salamis Island. He used martial verse ("Let us march to Salamis") to inspire his men to take Salamis from the Megarians. So too the Spartan poet and general Tyrtaeus (seventh century B.C.E.) used his poems to rally his men to quell the Messenian revolt. According to the Athenian orator Lycurgus, Tyrtaeus's exhortations were recited to men in front of the king's tent. There are also less martial settings for military exhortations to fight bravely.

Martial verse is prevalent in pre-Islamic poetry, as in the eighth-century *Romance of Antar.* There is a category of martial verse in most tribal poetries. All wars inspire patriotic poems. One conventional kind of martial verse is the military elegy, which extols the heroic valor of the fallen warrior. Martial verse, which shows a patriotic and even warmongering spirit, should be distinguished from the poetry of war, which frequently dramatizes its horrors.

"Despite these ancient connections, war and poetry are fundamentally different activities," James Anderson Winn explains in *The Poetry of War* (2008). "War dismembers bodies, scattering limb from limb. Poetry re-members those bodies and the people who lived in them, making whole in verse what was destroyed on the battlefield."

SEE ALSO *epic.*

masculine rhyme   A rhyme on a terminal syllable (*Pan/man*). The commonest kind of rhyme, masculine or single-syllable rhyme, is contrasted to feminine or multisyllabic rhyme. The gendering of the terms is arbitrary. The one-syllable rhyme makes emphatic connections, creating a force field of relation — as when an anonymous sixteenth-century poet declares, in "To Her Sea-Faring Lover," "Alas! say nay! say nay! and be no more so dumb, / But open thou thy manly mouth and say that thou wilt come."

SEE ALSO *feminine rhyme, rhyme.*

masque   A Renaissance form, the masque was a brief and festive poetic entertainment usually performed at court, a lavish spectacle that incorporated poetic drama with singing and dancing to ornate music. The masked performers wore sumptuous costumes and extravagant jewelry. Professional actors and musicians performed the speaking and singing parts, while masked courtiers assumed the other roles. The masque may derive from a folk tradition in which masked players would call on a nobleman, dancing and bringing gifts to commemorate a special occasion, as in the rustic presentation of "Pyramus and Thisbe" as a wedding entertainment in Shakespeare's *Midsummer Night's Dream* (1590–96). Many traditions contributed to its development, such as morris dancing, "disguisings" (also called "mummings" — the disguised performers say nothing that betrays their identity), and mummers' plays, age-old dramas performed by English ritual maskers on Christmas Day. From these folk forms, with their roots in archaic religious rites, the masque evolved into an elaborate court spectacle that reached its zenith in the first half of the seventeenth century in the courts of the English monarchs James I, who ruled from 1603 to 1625, and Charles I, who ruled from 1625 to 1649. The masque was a complimentary offering to a patron, and the image of an idealized feudal court was at the heart of the entertainment. The masque celebrates the audience, and the figure of the monarch is the center of the universe.

The structure of the masque was simple, the action ritualized. A prologue introduced a group of actors to a social gathering. The masked revelers then entered. The procession introduced a sequence of vices or figures of topical interest. The more elaborate masques presented a short drama with a theme that was mythological, allegorical, or symbolic. The moralizing was evident: good defeats evil, light triumphs over darkness. In the concluding dance, the masquers removed their masks and danced with partners from the audience.

Ben Jonson transformed the masque into a significant poetic form. From 1605 to 1631, he collaborated with the set designer Inigo Jones, who brought a new architectural style to English theater. Jonson considered the words the key feature of the masque and quarreled with his collaborator, who believed the spectacle was of primary importance. Jonson also invented the anti-masque — an antic, unruly revelry, which presented grotesque or comic figures to contrast with the main mythological figures of the masque itself. The masque died as a primary form with the outbreak of the English Civil War and the closing of the theaters by the Puritans. Over the centuries, the form has occasionally been adapted into a different kind of entertainment, as in Robert Frost's *A Masque of Reason* (1945) and *A Masque of Mercy* (1947).

SEE ALSO *allegory, drama.*

measure "Verse has always been associated in men's minds with 'measure,' i.e., with mathematics," William Carlos Williams declared. The word *measure,* which is linked to counting, is often used interchangeably with *meter,* which derives from the Greek word *metron,* meaning "measure." A single measure is a rhythmic unit that refers to a foot in English-language prosody, or to two feet, dipody, in classical Greek prosody. In contemporary poetry, it refers to the rhythmic cadence of a line or a group of lines. "Poetry began with measure," Williams asserted, "it began with the dance, whose divisions we have all but forgotten but are still known as measures. Measures they were and we still speak of their minuter elements as feet."

SEE ALSO *cadence, meter, rhythm.*

Meistersingers The German burgher poets of the fourteenth through sixteenth centuries formed guilds, which were governed by town councils, to perpetuate and emulate the art of the minnesingers, the lyric poets of the twelfth and thirteenth centuries. They established hierarchical categories for the study and performance of *Meistergesang,* poetry for singing to melodies. One began as an apprentice (*Schüler*), became a journeyman or school friend (*Schulfreund*), progressed through the positions of singer and poet (*Dichter*), and, hopefully, reached the summit as a master (*Meister*). These middle-class artists worked with regularized *Töne,* certain set metrical patterns and tunes, and held singing contests during religious festivals at Easter, Whitsuntide, and Christmas. Three of the most well-known Meistersingers: the Swabian weaver Michel Beheim (1416–ca. 1472), the master barber-poet Hans Folz (ca. 1437–1513), and the Nuremberg shoemaker-poet Hans Sachs (1494–1576), the hero of Wagner's opera *Die Meistersinger von Nürnberg.* Adam Puschman's songbook (1571) is the richest collection of Meistersinger tunes.

SEE ALSO *Knittelvers, minnesingers, poetic contest.*

melic poetry From the Greek word *melos,* meaning "song." Melic poetry is the root of melody and means "connected with music." The Greeks applied the name to all forms of lyric poetry. Melic poetry flourished in the hands of the Aeolians and the Dorians between the seventh and fifth centuries B.C.E. It was divided into the solo or monodic lyric, which was sung by a single voice and expressed the emotions of an individual (its poets include Sappho, Alcaeus, and Anacreon), and the choral lyric, which was sung by a chorus and expressed the emotions of the group (Alcman, Stesichorus, Simonides, Pindar, and Bacchylides wrote choral lyrics). Melic poetry became the lyric.

SEE ALSO *lyric, melopoeia, ode.*

melopoeia From the Greek: "song making." *Melopoeia* refers to the aural qualities of a poem, the making of music. In *How to Read* (1929), Ezra Pound employed this term for one of three "kinds of poetry": "MELOPOEIA, wherein the words are charged, over and above their plain meaning, with some musical property, which directs the bearing or trend of that meaning." In Greek, the infinitive form of *melopoeia* is the verb for composing lyric poems, or composing music, or composing lyric poems set to music. Pound, who may have discovered the term *Melopoiia* in Aristotle's *Poetics* (350 B.C.E.) or Longinus's treatise on the sublime, argued that there are three kinds of *melo-poeia,* or poetry on the borders of music: "(1) that made to be sung to a tune; (2) that made to be intoned or sung to a sort of chant; and (3) that made to be spoken." Pound might also have known the Irish poet Thomas MacDonagh's distinctions between song-verse, chant-verse, and speech-verse. The no-tion of *melopoeia* is what Samuel Taylor Coleridge called "poetry of the ear."

SEE ALSO *logopoeia, melic poetry, phanopoeia.*

Menippean satire, see *satire.*

metaphor   A figure of speech in which one thing is described in terms of another — as when Whitman characterizes the grass as "the beautiful uncut hair of graves." The term *metaphor* derives from the Greek *metaphora,* which means "carrying from one place to another," and a metaphor transfers the connotations of one thing (or idea) to another. It says *A* equals *B* ("Life is a dream"). It is a transfer of energies, a mode of energetic relation, a matter of identity and difference in the identification of unlike things. There is some-thing dreamlike in its associative thinking. Kenneth Burke calls this "perspec-tive by incongruity." Robert Frost states, "There are many other things I have found myself saying about poetry, but the chiefest of these is that it is meta-phor, saying one thing and meaning another, saying one thing in terms of another, the pleasure of ulteriority."

In *The Philosophy of Rhetoric* (1936), I. A. Richards distinguished the two parts of a metaphor by the terms *tenor* and *vehicle.* The tenor, the subject, stands for what is being talked about. The vehicle stands for the way it is being talked about and carries the weight of the comparison. When Mac-beth says that "life is but a walking shadow," "life" is the tenor and "walking shadow" is the vehicle.

One philosophical tradition maintains that there is no logical difference between metaphors and similes. Metaphors are considered literal compari-sons with the explicit "like" or "as" suppressed. Another tradition, the one to which I belong, holds that there is a radical difference (or should be) between saying that A is *the same as* B and saying that A is *like* B. Metaphor operates by condensation and compression, simile by discursiveness and digression. Metaphor works by a process of interaction. It draws attention to the categories of language by crossing them. The language of poetry, Shelley writes in "A Defence of Poetry" (1821), is "vitally metaphorical; that is, it marks the before unapprehended relations of things and perpetuates their apprehension." Shelley suggests that the poet creates relations between things unrecognized before, and that new relations create new thoughts and revitalize language.

Readers actively participate in making meaning through metaphor, in thinking through the conjoining of unlike things. The philosopher Ted Cohen argues that one of the main points of metaphor is "the achievement of intimacy" because the maker and the appreciator of a metaphor are brought into deeper relationship. The speaker issues a concealed invitation through metaphor that the listener makes a special effort to accept and interpret. Such "a transaction constitutes the acknowledgment of a community."

SEE ALSO *figures of speech, metonymy, rhetoric, simile, trope.*

metaphysical poets A group of early seventeenth-century poets, including John Donne, George Herbert, Abraham Cowley, Henry Vaughan, Andrew Marvell, Thomas Carew, and Richard Crashaw. They did not form a school or a movement, but their work shares some common characteristics: a bold wit, a clever sense of inventiveness, a love of intellectual elaboration. They like to construct arguments and find analogies, discovering likeness in unlike things, exploring metaphysical concerns.

The Scottish writer William Drummond seems to have been first to apply the term *metaphysical poets* to particular poets. Around 1630, he objected to his contemporaries who attempted to "abstract poetry to metaphysical Ideas and Scholastic Quiddities." In 1693, John Dryden remarked that Donne "affects the Metaphysics . . . not only in his satires, but in his amorous verses, where only nature should reign." In his *Life of Cowley* (1779), Samuel Johnson expanded the term to name a "school" of poets: "about the beginning of the seventeenth century appeared a race of writers that may be termed the metaphysical poets." He added that "the metaphysical poets were men of learning, and to show their learning was their whole endeavor." Johnson characterized their work by "a kind of *discordia concors;* a combination of dissimilar images, or discovery of occult resemblances in things apparently unlike," and described their method of wit as "the most heterogeneous ideas . . . yoked by violence together."

Johnson's negative evaluation of the metaphysical poets held sway until the 1890s and the early part of the twentieth century. T. S. Eliot helped elevate John Donne and bring the metaphysical poets into favor. In "The Metaphysical Poets" (1921), Eliot argued that these poets embodied a fusion of thought and feeling that was unavailable to later generations because of a "dissociation of sensibility." Donne could "feel [his] thought as immediately as the odour of a rose. A thought to Donne was an experience; it modified his sensibility." He found in the metaphysical "a direct sensuous apprehension of thought, or a recreation of thought in feeling." Donne and the other metaphysical poets became the central objects of study for the New Critics of the 1940s and '50s.

SEE ALSO *wit*.

meter From the Greek word *metron*, meaning "measure." Meter is a way of describing rhythmic patterning in poetry, of keeping time, of measuring poetic language. Meter is one quality that marks a poem as verse. Barbara Herrnstein Smith writes in *Poetic Closure* (1968) that "meter serves . . . as a frame for the poem, separating it from a 'ground' of less highly structured speech and sound . . . Meter is the stage of the theater in which the poem, the representation of an act of speech, is performed. It is the arena of art, the curtain that rises and falls as well as the music that accompanies the entire performance."

The first pleasures of meter are physical and connected to bodily experience — to the heartbeat and the pulse, to breathing, walking, running, dancing, working, and lovemaking. The meter of a poem can slow us down or speed us up; it can focus our attention; it can hypnotize us. Imagine you have gone down to the ocean in the early morning. You stand in the water and feel the waves breaking against the shore. You watch them coming in and going out. You feel the push and pull, the ebb and flow, of the tide. The waves repeat each other, but no two waves are exactly the same. Think of those waves as the flow of words washing across the lines and sentences of a poem. To measure the rhythmic pattern of those waves is to establish its meter. It is something you observe, but also something you experience. As I. A. Richards states in *Principles of Literary Criticism* (1952), the effect of meter "is not due to our perceiving a pattern in something outside us, but to our becoming patterned ourselves. With every beat of the metre a tide of anticipation in us turns and swings, setting up as it does extraordinarily extensive reverberations." Meter has to do with beating out time, with counting and naming. Syllables are temporal and meters restructure time.

The terminology of metrics is borrowed from classical languages and applies imperfectly to English. Still, there are readers who find metrical analysis an important constitutive feature of poetic meaning, and it is useful for all readers of poetry to know the four generally distinguishable metrical systems.

- *pure accentual meter:* This system, which we recognize from nursery rhymes, measures only the number of stressed or accented syllables in each line. Accentual meter — the four-stress line with a caesura after the second stress — is common to all Germanic poetries. English poetry began in a pure accentual meter (*Piers Plowman, Beowulf*). The standard line throughout the Old and Middle English periods consists of four accents with a strong medial pause (caesura) and a pattern of repetitive consonants (alliteration, consonance), as in this line from Ezra Pound's version of the tenth-century poem "The Seafarer": "Wáneth the wátch, | but the wórld hóldeth." Robert Graves speculated that the rhythm of accentual meter was based on the synchronized rowing of oars across rough northern seas. The fifteenth-century poet John Skelton came up with a version of accentual meter called Skeltonics, Coleridge experimented with pure accentual verse in "Christabel" (1797–1800), and Gerard Manley Hopkins developed a creative form that he called "sprung rhythm."
- *pure syllabic meter:* This system measures only the number of syllables in each line. It ignores accentuation. Some languages, such as German and English, are accent-timed; other languages, such as Japanese, are syllable-timed. Japanese court poetry, Toda songs, Balinese poetry, Malay verse, and a good deal of Chinese, Korean, and Mongolian

poetry are syllabic. In Arabic poetry, the meter (*wazn*) is based on the length of syllables. Pure syllabic verse frustrates what Paul Fussell calls "our own Anglo-Saxon lust for stress."

Both Robert Bridges (1844–1930) and his daughter Elizabeth Daryush (1887–1977) experimented with syllabics. Marianne Moore (1887–1972) is the great twentieth-century practitioner of syllabics.

- *quantitative meter:* This system measures duration — the time it takes to pronounce a syllable — rather than contrasting stresses or accents, or counting syllables. Sanskrit, Greek, and Latin meters were quantitative. Greek verse was connected to the ecstatic beat of dancers moving around a sacred altar. The foot in classical prosody was something like a musical measure. Syllables were long or short, and one long syllable took the same length of time it took to utter two short ones. Every unit of two or three syllables constituted a foot. A verse was two to six feet. The Homeric hexameter is a meter based on quantity. "Scarcely any facet of the culture of the ancient world is so alien to us as its quantitative metric," Paul Maas writes in *Greek Metre* (1923). We don't know how Greek poetry sounded, and applying durational values to English verse has generally failed because English is such a heavily accented language. Only when classical feet were replaced with pairs or triads of stressed and unstressed syllables could classical meter contribute to the evolution of English poetry.

- *accentual-syllabic meter:* This system counts both the number of accents and the number of syllables in each line. Rhythm results from the interplay between them. Accentual-syllabic meter, sometimes called syllable-stress meter or foot verse, comprises the main tradition of English poetry from the late sixteenth century to the early twentieth century. It is traditionally discussed as a sequence of feet. Each foot usually consists of a nucleus of one stressed syllable and one or two unstressed syllables. The main feet in English versification are the iamb (a pair of syllables with the stress on the second one), the trochee (a pair of syllables with the stress on the first one), the dactyl (a triad of one stressed syllable followed by two unstressed ones), and the anapest (a triad of two unstressed syllables followed by a single stressed one).

A meter is determined by the prevailing accentual pattern (iambic, trochaic, dactylic, anapestic) plus the number of feet per line. The monometer is one foot, as in Robert Herrick's "Upon His Departure Hence" (1648). The dimeter is two feet, as in Tennyson's "Charge of the Light Brigade" (1854). The trimeter is three feet, as in Theodore Roethke's "My Papa's Waltz" (1942). The tetrameter is four feet, as in Andrew Marvell's "To His Coy Mistress" (ca. 1650s). The pentameter is five feet, as in William Shakespeare's sonnets. The hexameter is six feet, as in the first sonnet of Sir Philip Sidney's *Astrophil and Stella* (1591). The heptameter or septenary is seven feet, as in Rudyard Kipling's "Tommy" (1890). The octometer is eight feet, as in Robert Browning's "Toccata of Galuppi's" (1855). The most common meters in English verse are iambic ∪ /; trochaic / ∪; anapestic ∪ ∪ /; dactylic / ∪ ∪; spondaic / /; and paeonic / ∪ ∪ ∪ (first paeon). A line of verse in which one or more extra syllables are added to the first and/or last lines is called hypermetric.

The native four-beat rhythm, which is rooted in the Old English line, has an inescapable feeling of symmetry. It establishes the rhythm of ballads and hymns, of most folk, rock-and-roll, and rap songs. The reason that iambic pentameter (five beats) became the preferred meter in our language is that, as Derek Attridge observes in *The Rhythms of English Poetry* (1982), "it is the only simple metrical form of manageable length which escapes the elementary four-beat rhythm, with its insistence, its hierarchical structures, and its close relationship with the world of ballad and song." It has been estimated that three-fourths of English poetry from Chaucer (ca. 1340–1400) to Frost (1874–1963) has been written in rhymed or unrhymed iambic pentameter. The Irish tradition developed a technique of craftsmanship based on the hammer and anvil. "When two hammers answer each other five times on the anvil — *ti-tum, ti-tum, ti-tum, ti-tum, ti-tum* — five in honour of the five stations of the Celtic year," Graves suggests, "there you have Chaucer's familiar hendecasyllabic line."

> A knight there was, and that a worthy man
> That fro the time that he first began
> To ryden out, he loved chivalry . . .

Iambic pentameter was the modal line in English for over three hundred years — the meter that Chaucer used for most of *The Canterbury Tales* (ca.

1387–1400), Spenser employed for *The Faerie Queene* (1590–96), Shake-speare utilized in most of his plays, Milton employed for his epics, Pope used judiciously for most of his verse, Wordsworth used with great flexibility in *The Prelude* (1805, 1850), Robert Browning carried through *The Ring and the Book* (1868–69), and Yeats, Frost, Stevens, and Crane re-created for many of their greatest poems.

Every meter has accrued a history that haunts later usages. It becomes part of its conscious and unconscious associations, its meanings and memories.

SEE ALSO *alliteration, ballad, blank verse, caesura, consonance, foot, hymn, iambic pentameter, measure, rhythm, Skeltonics, sprung rhythm,* and the entries for individual feet: *anapest, dactyl, iamb, spondee, trochee.*

metonymy From the Greek: "change of name." A figure of speech that replaces or substitutes the name of one thing with something else closely associated with it. We say, "The pen is mightier than the sword" (and mean that writing is more powerful than warfare). We state, "Homer says," rather than "In the *Iliad* it is written" (and thus substitute the name of an author for his work). Metonymy strategically employs concrete, tangible, or corporeal terms to convey abstract, intangible, or incorporeal states, as when we speak of "the heart" and mean "the emotions." It's a way of embodying emotive and spiritual experiences. "If you trail language back far enough," Kenneth Burke explains, "you'll find all our terms for 'spiritual' states were metonymic in origin."

Synecdoche, the most crucial kind of metonymy, substitutes the name of a part for that of a whole (e.g., "hired hand" for "worker"). Burke argues that "all such conversions imply an integral relationship, a relationship of convertibility between the two terms." In "The Four Master Tropes" (1941), Burke goes on to argue for the synecdochic nature of ancient metaphysical doctrines:

> The "noblest synecdoche," the perfect paradigm or prototype for all lesser usages, is found in metaphysical doctrines proclaiming the identity of "microcosm" and "macrocosm." In such doctrines, where the individual is treated as a replica of the universe, and vice versa, we have the ideal synecdoche, since microcosm is related to macrocosm as part to whole, and either the whole can represent the part or the part can represent the whole.

The metonym and the metaphor are complementary figures. Whereas a metaphor establishes a likeness between two different things, a metonym establishes a contiguous relationship between them. It is a form of associative or representational thinking. The linguist Roman Jakobson (1896–1982) extended the field of complementary figures, metaphor and metonym, to encompass dreams, myths, psychoanalysis, types of aphasia, and other things.

SEE ALSO *figures of speech, metaphor, rhetoric, trope.*

metrical variation   Any number of techniques, such as swapping one foot for another ("substitution") to vary a basic metrical pattern. For example, John Milton substitutes a trochee (/ u) for an iamb (u /) in the second foot of this iambic pentameter line in *Paradise Lost* (1667): "Ă mínd | nót tŏ | bĕ chánged | bў pláce | ŏr time."

SEE ALSO *counterpoint, foot, meter.*

metrics   The study of meter. It implies measurement. A metrist is a practitioner or student of meter. Paul Maas explains, in *Greek Metre* (1923), that "the art of metric is the means by which a regular rhythm is imposed upon the natural rhythm of language in a work of literature."

SEE ALSO *measure, meter, prosody, rhythm.*

metron   (plural *metra*) The unit of measurement in classical prosody. A metron is composed of long (—) and short (u) syllables, which roughly corresponds to a foot in English poetry.

SEE ALSO *foot, measure;* also "quantitative meter" in *meter.*

mimesis   A transliteration of the Greek word for "imitation" and a key term in aesthetics since Aristotle asserted in the *Poetics* (350 B.C.E.) that tragedy is the imitation of an action. *Mimesis* has come to mean "representation," especially in terms of verisimilitude. We call a work "mimetic" or "realistic" when it gives the semblance of truth, the sense of fidelity to an external reality. Philip Sidney argues, in *Apology for Poetry* (1583), that "poesy . . . is an art of imitation, for so Aristotle termeth it in the word mimesis — that is to say, a representing, counterfeiting, or figuring forth — to speak metaphorically, a speaking picture." Poetry is not reality itself, Sidney suggests, but a representation modeled closely on reality. We may think of imitation as something static, but mimesis — the act of responding to the outside world — is a dynamic process, a convention with its own evolving aesthetic properties. It responds to reality by redefining it, challenging received notions of what is real.

SEE ALSO *imitation.*

minnesingers (German *Minnesänger*) German lyric poets and singers of the twelfth and thirteenth centuries. They were mostly knights of the lower nobility who carried on the tradition of the Provençal troubadours and sang of courtly love, hence the name, which derives from the word *Minne* ("love"). The term *Minnesang* first referred to the courtly love poem, sung in open court, but later expanded to include the entire corpus of *Sprüche* — political, social, and religious songs.

The oldest songs consisted of a strophe with three movements. The tripartite structure developed into a poem with three stanzas. The first two formally identical sections, or "doorposts," which were called *Stollen* individually and *Aufgesang* collectively, stated and developed the argument. The third section, called *Abgesang,* concluded it. The terms derive from the later *Meistersingers* ("mastersingers"), musical guilds that carried on the minnesinger tradition from the fourteenth to the seventeenth century. Some of the well-known minnesingers: Dietmar von Aist, Friedrich von Hausen, Heinrich von Morungen, Reinmar, Walther von der Vogelweide, and Tannhaüser, the legendary figure in Wagner's opera *Tannhaüser and the Singers' Contest at Wartburg* (1845).

SEE ALSO *Meistersingers, troubadour.*

minstrel A musician or poet. Professional entertainers of the Middle Ages were generically termed *minstrels.* The Middle English *minestral* derived from the Latin *minister* ("servant") and especially referred to a singer of verses accompanied on the harp. The minstrel lived by song. The troubadours were the poet-musicians of Provence or the South of France, the trouvères were the poet-musicians of Northern France, and the minnesingers were the poet-musicians of Germany. Minstrels also were a class of acrobat-musicians who were called jongleurs in France, *Gauklerin* in Germany, and gleemen in Britain.

From the eleventh to the fourteenth century, minstrels tramped across Europe, alone or in company, carrying musical instruments and providing enter-tainment to local audiences. At the top of the profession and the hierarchy, there were accomplished poet-musicians permanently attached to royal or noble households. One rung below were itinerant bands of players who had a repertory of short dramas, songs, and debates, such as the *dit* and *fabliaux* of France. On the lowest rung, there were anonymous jugglers, rope-walkers, ac-robats, conjurors, animal trainers, and others, the forerunners of performers in the circus and the music hall.

The minstrel became a romantic emblem for the itinerant poet endan-gered by changing times. Today the word *minstrel* is a generic term for all types of popular entertainers.

SEE ALSO *dit, fabliau, gleeman, jongleur, minnesingers, troubadour, trouvère.*

mock epic, mock heroic   A fake epic, a satiric poem that takes the low and trivial and elevates it to absurd heights. The mock epic ludicrously imi-tates the tone, content, and/or formal requirements of heroic narratives. The anonymous burlesque of Homer, the *Batrachomyomachia* (*War Between the Mice and the Frogs,* first century B.C.E.), is possibly the earliest manifesta-tion of a parody epic. "This is an *image of the Homeric style*," M. M. Bakhtin writes. "It is precisely style that is the true hero of the work." This is also true of the seven books of Paul Scarron's *Virgil travesti* (1638–53). The mock epic flourished in the late seventeenth and early eighteenth centuries, when it was used to observe how far the contemporary world had fallen from the classi-cal age. For example, Alexander Pope's *Rape of the Lock* (1712–14) treats the theft of a lock of hair as if it were comparable to the events that sparked the Trojan War.

The term *mock epic* is sometimes used in a modern context for a long poem that is not a full-fledged or classical epic, such as Ezra Pound's *Cantos* (1915–69) or Ted Hughes's *Crow* (1970). These serious and self-conscious poems imply that a fragmented or parody epic is more suitable for the mod-ern age.

SEE ALSO *burlesque, epic, parody, satire.*

modernism   The modernism that we still recognize originated in the mid-dle of the nineteenth century as a movement against conventional taste. It was fresh, convulsive, and transgressive. But the idea of the modern as a break with the past, something forward-looking, has a much longer history and dates to medieval times. Christianity's eschatological understanding of history raises the question of linear progress, the either-or of *modernus* versus *antiquus*. For much of the past millennium, the idea of the modern was a negative one associated with the degradation of past achievements. During the Enlightenment, however, modernism began to take on more positive connotations. The emphasis on the capacity of human reason and the renewed belief in the possibility of human progress made the future seem like a promising alternative to antiquity.

Charles Baudelaire (1821–1867) is the first hero of modernism, a key figure in the transformation of modernity as a concept, which he vaunted as "the ephemeral, the fugitive, the contingent, the half of art whose other half is the eternal and the immutable." Baudelaire inaugurated our modernity by emphasizing what is current, unadorned, and uninhibited by the shackles of the past. Arthur Rimbaud turned the Baudelairean premise into an injunction in *A Season in Hell* (1873) with his anarchic motto: "One must be absolutely modern."

Matei Călinescu identifies a radical division within modernity. At some point in the first half of the nineteenth century, he argues, a split occurred between "modernity as a stage in the history of Western civilization — a product of scientific and technological progress, of the industrial revolution ... and modernity as an aesthetic concept." On the one side, you have the "bourgeois idea of modernity ... the doctrine of progress, the confidence in the beneficial possibilities of science and technology." On the other side, you have an alternative anti-bourgeois modernity, "the one that was to bring into being the avant-gardes." Since then the relations between the two modernities have been hostile.

Some of the major cultural precursors to modernism as a literature of crisis: Friedrich Nietzsche (1844–1900), Karl Marx (1818–1883), Sigmund Freud (1856–1939), and James Frazer (1854–1941). Albert Einstein (1879–1955) transformed our perception of the universe. Some date modernism to 1890, some to the pivotal years around the turn of the century, some to 1910. The period of high modernism is generally thought of as 1910–30. The fifty-two slaughterous months of World War I called all values and certainties into question. In the 1920s, the term *modernism* underwent a sea change — it moved from a general sense of sympathy with modern things to a particular association with experimentation in the arts. The rallying cry was Ezra Pound's slogan, "Make It New!"

Modernism in poetry is a laceration within language. One of the recurring strategies of modern poetry is to break up traditional ways of making meaning, to use asyntactical, nonlinear language to create new semantic relationships. The American modernist poets also begin with a sense of what Pound called "a botched civilization" ("Hugh Selwyn Mauberley," 1920). T. S. Eliot's "The Waste Land" (1922) was unquestionably the central summary text of generational despair over the decline of the West. The technique was collagist.

SEE ALSO *collage, Dadaism, modernismo, Romanticism, Surrealism, symbolism.*

modernismo   The Nicaraguan poet Rubén Darío (1867–1916) coined the term *modernismo* for Hispanic modernism. He fused Continental symbolism with Latin American themes and subjects, affecting a fresh musical synthesis in Spanish-language poetry. Darío believed in the urgent need for change, in freedom, passion, and the renewal of beauty. The movement began in Latin America in the late nineteenth century and spread to Spain early in the twentieth century. The Cuban poet José Martí was the great forerunner of Darío, who in turn modernized the language and created a link between two hemispheres.

SEE ALSO *modernism, symbolism.*

Monk's Tale stanza   Geoffrey Chaucer employed this stanza in "An A.B.C." (ca. 1370) and in "The Monk's Tale" (*The Canterbury Tales,* ca. 1387–1400), hence its name. It consists of eight iambic pentameter lines that rhyme *ababbcbc*. It looks backward to the French ballade and forward to the Spenserian stanza, which keeps the pattern and adds an alexandrine, a conclusive ninth line. The first letter in Chaucer's acrostic "A.B.C." sets the pattern:

> ALMIGHTY and al merciable quene,
> To whom that al this world fleeth for socour,
> To have relees of sinne, sorwe and tene [affliction],

Glorious virgine, of alle floures flour,
To thee I flee, confounded in errour!
Help and releve, thou mighty debonaire,
Have mercy on my perilus languor!
Venquisshed m'hath my cruel adversaire.

SEE ALSO *ballade, iambic pentameter, octave, Spenserian stanza.*

monody, see *elegy.*

monologue   A single person speaking alone — either with an audience, as in a play, or without an audience, as in a prayer or a lament. It is a solo voice. "But a monologue is not the same as talking to oneself," Paul Goodman warns, in *Speaking and Language* (1972); "it is more like a daydream." It is the sort of daydream intended to be overheard.

SEE ALSO *dramatic monologue.*

monometer, see "accentual-syllabic meter" in *meter.*

monostich   A one-line poem. An example is the Japanese haiku, which is written in a single vertical line. As *The Greek Anthology* (tenth century) illustrates, the monostich can be a proverb, an aphorism, an enigma, a fragment, an image, or an inscription. It is so short that it often has the feeling of a cryptic piece of wisdom literature. A. R. Ammons (1926–2001) wrote monostiches in which the title is so integral to the poem that it becomes a kind of couplet. The Scottish poet and artist Ian Hamilton Finlay (1925–2006) reduced the monostich to a one-word poem; he painted some on tortoise shells and some on wooden circles, which he floated on ponds. An exhibit of his neon works was titled "The Sonnet Is a Sewing-Machine for the Monostich." A monostich can also be a single or independent line of verse, as in the first verse of Psalm 23: "The Lord is my shepherd; I shall not want."

SEE ALSO *fragment, image, line, proverb, stanza, stich, tanka, wisdom literature.*

mourning songs, see *dirge, elegy, keening.*

muse, Muses   A source of poetic inspiration. Each of the nine Greek goddesses, daughters of Zeus and Mnemosyne (or Memory), traditionally presided over an activity or art: Calliope (epic poetry), Clio (history), Erato (love poetry), Euterpe (lyric poetry), Melpomene (tragedy), Polyhymnia (songs of praise to the gods), Terpsichore (dancing), Thalia (comedy), Urania (astronomy, i.e., cosmological poetry). Homer calls out to them in the *Iliad* (ca. eighth century B.C.E.):

> Sing to me now, you Muses who hold the halls of Olympus!
> You are goddesses, you are everywhere, you know all things —
> all we hear is the distant ring of glory, we know nothing —

Hesiod's *Theogony* (ca. 700 B.C.E.) opens with a hymn to the Muses; while he was keeping his sheep on Helicon, they gave him a staff of bay and then inspired and commanded him to sing "of the race of immortals, blessed Gods." The invocation to the Muse ("Sing, goddess . . .") acknowledges the need for an inspiring spirit. "Prophesy [*manteueo*], Muse," Pindar sings, "and I will be your interpreter" (fragment 150, early fifth century B.C.E.). Poetry is never entirely at the dispensation of the poet's conscious will or intellect, and whoever calls out "Help me, O Heavenly Muse" advertises a dependency on a force beyond the intellective powers. Hence this invocation of the chorus at the beginning of Shakespeare's *Henry V* (1600): "O! for a Muse of fire, that would ascend / The brightest heaven of invention . . ."

The sacred muse (the phrase is Spenser's) is the spirit of creativity, and thus inspires reverence or awe. Wallace Stevens invokes her as "*Inexplicable sister of the Minotaur, enigma and mask*" ("The Figure of the Youth as Virile Poet," 1944); Robert Graves exalted her as the resplendent White Goddess. Louis MacNeice remembers that "the Muse will never / Conform to type" ("Autumn Sequel," 1954). In "Envoi" (1983), Eavan Boland calls on the muse to do something different than the mythical figures invented by male poets. She seeks a muse who will "bless the ordinary" and "sanctify the common."

SEE ALSO *inspiration, invocation.*

muwashshah   An Andalusian Arabic strophic poem that regularly alternates sections with separate rhymes and others with common rhymes (e.g., *aa bbaa ccaa,* etc.). The form thus weaves together two rhyme schemes (and sometimes two complex metrical patterns as well). The *muwashshah* first appeared in Arabic in Muslim Spain during the ninth century. It was apparently a formal inheritance from romance folk poetry. Possibly used for choral recitals, it is closely related to the Arabic form *zéjel*. Whereas the *zéjel* is written in vernacular Spanish, the *muwashshah* is composed in classical Arabic, though it typically closes with an envoi, or closing couplet, in Arabic or Spanish vernacular (*kharja*), the Mozarab dialect, which is why it is sometimes known as the Mozarabic lyric. The word *kharja* means "exit," and the closing couplet was often drawn from folk tradition and spoken by a young woman or a part of nature that has been feminized, like a bird or the wind. Both the *zéjel* and the *muwashshah* are closely associated with music. The poems were sensuous celebrations of love and drink. These types of poems reached their peak between the eleventh and thirteenth centuries in Muslim Spain as well as in various other parts of the Arabic-speaking world.

The Jewish poets of Andalusia adopted the *muwashshah* in the fourteenth century. The term is often translated as "girdle poems." The Arabic verb *washshaha* means "to dress or adorn," and the noun *wushshaah* is "an ornamented sash or belt—in older times a doubled band with embedded gems worn sash-like over the shoulder." Peter Cole notes that it helps to think of the *muwashshah* "as a poem in which the rhyming chorus winds about the various strophes of the poem as a gem-studded sash cuts across the body." The secular *muwashshah* was considered a "nonclassical" form in Arabic tradition, but it was adapted for the liturgical Hebrew poems called *piyyut*. Some of the most moving medieval liturgical lyrics were written as belted poems.

SEE ALSO *piyyut, zéjel.*

naked poetry A term for the modern impulse to strip poetry down to bare essentials. Lafcadio Hearn coined the phrase *naked poetry* for a lecture at the Imperial University in Tokyo (1896–1903). He said, "I want to make a little discourse about what we might call Naked Poetry ... that is, poetry without any dress, without any ornament, the very essence or body of poetry unveiled by artifice of any kind." The sparseness and classical restraint of Japanese poetry helped lead Hearn to the concept.

The Spanish poet Juan Ramón Jiménez also invented the term *poesia desnuda* ("naked poetry") in *Eternidades* (1916–17). The impulse to a pure and exposed poetry has had many modern articulations. Charles Baudelaire took the title for his intimate journals, *My Heart Laid Bare* (1887), from Edgar Allan Poe, who said that if any man dared to write such a book with complete frankness it would be a masterpiece. "But to write it — *there* is the rub," Poe said. "No man dare write it. No man ever will dare write it. No man *could* write it, even if he dared. The paper would shrivel and blaze at every touch of the fiery pen" (1848).

In 1921, the Yiddish poet Peretz Ravitch published a collection titled *Nakete Lider* (*Naked Songs*). The Greek poet Pantelis Prevalakis borrowed Jiménez's phrase and called his second and third books *The Naked Poetry* (1939) and *The Most Naked Poetry* (1941). In 1969, Stephen Berg and Robert Mezey borrowed Jiménez's phrase for the title of their anthology, *Naked Poetry*, which they followed with *The New Naked Poetry* (1976).

SEE ALSO *free verse, projective verse.*

narrative poetry A poem that tells a story. It has a plot and employs many of the devices of prose fiction, such as character and setting. Narrative poems may be short, as in ballads, or long, as in epics, which are the two basic early types of narrative poetry. Both ballads and epics originated as forms of oral poetry. They were sung aloud, created and re-created by individuals performing with a participating audience. Ballads may originally have been danced and sung by a group of people participating in a ritual action. The epic singer narrated the story of gods and heroes. Heroic poetry secularized the epic by making it the story of a mortal hero, as in the *Epic of Gilgamesh* (ca. 1600–1000 B.C.E.), the *Iliad* and the *Odyssey* (ca. eighth century B.C.E.), *La chanson de Roland* (*The Song of Roland,* ca. 1090) and *Beowulf* (ca. eighth to eleventh century).

The first narrative poems were recorded around 2000 B.C.E. in Sumer, Egypt, and generally in the Middle and Near East. This epoch yielded the Creation epic and the *Epic of Gilgamesh,* which were most fully preserved in Akkadian texts. The second major period of narrative poems was the era of about 1000–400 B.C.E. in Babylon, Greece, and Palestine. This gave us parts of the Hebrew Bible, the Homeric poems, the Cyclic epics, and the works of Hesiod. Pindar's choral odes (fifth century B.C.E.) are the first written narrative poems. Callimachus's *Aetia* (*Causes,* ca. 270 B.C.E.), a series of narrative poems about the origins of legends and customs, is the precursor to Ovid's *Metamorphoses* (8 C.E.). Virgil's *Aeneid* (29–19 B.C.E.) is a monument from the Augustan period. The Icelandic and early Irish sagas tell stories about legendary heroes. French literature began in the eleventh century with religious narrative poems, such as the "Song of St. Alexis" (ca. 1050). *The Vision of Piers Plowman* (ca. 1360–87) is an allegorical narrative that stands near the top of English poetry. Chaucer's *Canterbury Tales* (ca. 1387–1400) turned narrative into a central strategy of English poetry.

Each era of English poetry has had major narratives. Think of John Lydgate's *Fall of Princes* (ca. 1431–38), a nine-book adaptation of Boccaccio's *De casibus virorum illustrium* (*The Fall of Princes,* 1355–60), and Spenser's allegorical *Faerie Queene* (1590–96), of Michel Drayton's *England's Heroical Epistles* (1597), of the broadsides of *Robin Hood* and *Chevy Chase,* which circulated in England in the sixteenth century, of Christopher Marlowe's "Hero and Leander" (1593), which George Chapman completed (1598), of Milton's *Paradise Lost* (1667), of John Dryden's imitations of Ovid, Virgil, Chaucer, and Boccaccio, and Alexander Pope's translations of Homer, of James Macpherson's Ossian poems (1760, 1761, 1763, 1765) and Thomas Percy's *Reliques of Ancient English Poetry* (1765), of Byron's satirical narrative *Beppo: A Venetian Story* (1818) and Keats's "The Eve of Saint Agnes" and "Lamia" (1819), of Tennyson's *Idylls of the King* (1856–85) and William Morris's *Earthly Paradise* (1868–70), of Rudyard Kipling's ballads and John Masefield's *Everlasting Mercy* (1911).

"The secret subject, or subtext, of narrative is time," Stanley Plumly writes. "The subtext of time is mortality, mutability; the subtext of mortality is emotion. Loss is our parent, poetry a parental form." A wide variety of lyric poems takes on narrative values. They focus on the feelings of a character, but they also tell or imply a foreshortened story. They have an inferred or compacted plot, which is often signaled by a change in tenses, a suggestion of movement over time. Thus Wordsworth and Coleridge named some of their short poems *Lyrical Ballads* (1798). Rather than lyricizing narrative, the verse novel, a legacy of the nineteenth century, narrativizes verse. It is a novel-length narrative told through poetry. Alexander Pushkin's *Eugene Onegin* (1833) is the classic case of a poem conscious of the novel as a form.

Narrative poetry was sidelined in the modernist era. Poets employed collage and fractured continuous narratives. Imagism, for example, sought to purge modern poetry of narrative altogether. But such poets as Edwin Arlington Robinson, Robert Frost, and Robinson Jeffers continued to write narrative poems of a high order in the early part of the twentieth century.

SEE ALSO *ballad, epic, imagism, mock epic, oral poetry, saga, verse novel.*

nature poetry, nature in poetry   The natural world has been one of the recurring subjects of poetry, frequently the primary one, in every age and country. Yet we cannot easily define nature, which, as Gary Snyder points out in *No Nature* (1992), "will not fulfill our conceptions or assumptions" and "will dodge our expectations and theoretical models." Yet the urge to describe the natural world — its various landscapes, its changing seasons, its surrounding phenomena — has been an inescapable part of the history of poetry. Wendell Berry defines nature poetry as poetry that "considers nature as subject matter and inspiration."

Our concepts of nature are relative, historically determined. The nature poem is affected by ideology, by literary conventions as well as social and cultural ideas. Raymond Williams contends that "*nature* is perhaps the most complex word in the language." The term *nature* is itself contested now because it seems to assume an oversimplified relationship between the human and the environment. "Nature" has been the site of so many different naive symbolisms, such as purity, escape, and savagery. That's why poets and critics often prefer the concept of ecopoetry, which presupposes a complicated interconnection between nature and humankind.

The idea that the seasons structure the actual rhythms or symbolic passages of life goes back to antiquity. The Canaanite mythical *Poem of Aqhat* (fifteenth century B.C.E.) rotates around seasonal change. Hesiod's *Works and Days* (eighth century B.C.E.) takes special interest in agricultural practices. There is a long tradition of the pastoral, stemming from Theocritus's *Idylls* (third century B.C.E.), which honor the simplicities of rural life and create such memorable figures as Lycidas, the archetypal poet-shepherd who inspired John Milton's pastoral elegy "Lycidas" (1638). Virgil's *Eclogues* (37–30 B.C.E.) define the tradition by characterizing the serenity of shepherds living in idealized natural settings. The Chinese *Book of Songs* (tenth to fifth century B.C.E.) is rife with seasonal poetry, as is the Japanese haiku, which began as a short associative meditation on the natural world. Think of the Old English "Seafarer" and the Middle English "Cuckoo's Song," of the passage of seasons in *Sir Gawain and the Green Knight* (late fourteenth century). In the Renaissance, urbane poets apprenticed themselves to poetry by writing pastoral soliloquies or dialogues, which construct and imagine rural life. The tradition is exemplified by Sir Philip Sidney's *Arcadia* (1580) and Edmund Spenser's *Shepheardes Calender* (1579). Rural poetry flourished in seventeenth-century retirement and garden poems, in landscape poems that delivered formal and structured descriptions of topography, such as John Denham's "Cooper's Hill" (1642).

James Thomson, the first important eighteenth-century nature poet, infused his descriptions in *The Seasons* (1730) with his age's sense of God's sustaining presence in nature. Alexander Pope leads "Essay on Criticism" (1711) with the rule "First follow Nature." For him, "following nature" means honoring classical precedent: "Learn hence for Ancient *Rules* a just Esteem; / To copy *Nature* is to copy *Them*." Pope describes these rules as "*Nature Methodiz'd*." Writing at a time when English society was being transformed from an agricultural society to an industrial one, the Romantic poets treated nature in a groundbreaking way, dwelling in its localities, praising its nurturing powers, spiritualizing it. John Clare was inspired by Thomson's *The Seasons* to become a poet with a rural muse. "Poets love nature and themselves are love," he wrote in a late sonnet. His poetry intimately chronicles a world that was rapidly disappearing. Each of the English Romantics had a particular view of that world, a singular way of describing it — they were sometimes solaced, sometimes frightened by its alienating majesty and inhuman force — and yet Romantic poetry as a whole inaugurated a new ecological consciousness, a fresh way of treating human beings and nature as interdependent.

Henry David Thoreau is the guiding spirit of American nature writing in general and American nature poetry in particular. "Shall I not have intelligence with the earth? Am I not partly leaves and vegetable mould myself?" he asks in *Walden* (1854). Ralph Waldo Emerson's *Nature* (1836) is foundational, but *Walden* is a forerunner to and a reference point for green thinking. It would take a volume in itself to track the ways that American poets have envisioned the environment — in *Democratic Vistas* (1871) Walt Whitman calls nature "the only complete, actual poem" — but I would pause over Emily Dickinson's garden poems and Whitman's "Out of the Cradle Endlessly Rocking" (1860), over William Cullen Bryant's celebration of the prairie and Robert Frost's terrifying notion of "design," over Robinson Jeffers's California poems and Theodore Roethke's horticultural reminiscences, over A. R. Ammons's ecological lyrics, Wendell Berry's agricultural ideals, and Gary Snyder's grounded lyrics. W. S. Merwin also invokes native peoples for a reaffirmation of our connection to the natural world. I wish I had time to compare North American nature poems, which are often sympathetic to natural forces, with those of Canadian poets, who often manifest, as Northrop Frye points out, "a tone of deep terror in regard to nature." There is an ecofeminist pastoralism in Susan Griffin's *Women and Nature: The Roaring Inside Her* (1978) and a recent anthology, *Black Nature* (2010), celebrates the overlooked tradition of African American nature poetry over four centuries. We are not yet done envisioning the natural world.

SEE ALSO *Arcadia, descriptive poetry, eclogue, ecopoetry, georgic, idyll, neoclassicism, pastoral, Romanticism, shan-shui, topographical poetry.*

near rhyme   A form of close rhyme. The final consonants of stressed syllables agree but the preceding vowel sounds do not match, as when Emily Dickinson rhymes *room* with *firm* and *storm* (poem number 465, 1862). It is also called approximate, half, imperfect, oblique, partial, or slant rhyme. Dickinson, W. B. Yeats, Wilfred Owen, W. H. Auden, and Dylan Thomas were all masters of half rhyme. Some critics use *pararhyme* as a synonym for *near rhyme;* others reserve it for a type of double consonance, near rhymes in which the consonants are identical but the vowels differ, as when Owen rhymes *hall* and *Hell, grained* and *ground,* and *moan* and *mourn* in three consecutive couplets in "Strange Meeting" (1918). Near rhyme, which offers more possibilities in a rhyme-poor language like English, often feels modern to us, perhaps because of its slight sense of dissonance, but in fact, it was used in medieval Icelandic, Irish, and Welsh verse. It was probably brought into English poetry in the mid-seventeenth century by Henry Vaughan, who was influenced by Welsh models. Slant rhyme offers the pleasures of novelty and imperfection, of affinity and difference, without the sonic closure of full rhyme.

SEE ALSO *rhyme.*

negative capability   John Keats coined this term in a letter to his brothers George and Thomas (December 21, 1817):

> several things dove tailed in my mind, and at once it struck me what quality went to form a Man of Achievement, especially in Literature, and which Shakespeare possessed so enormously — I mean *Negative Capability,* that is when man is capable of being in uncertainties, Mysteries, doubts, without any irritable reaching after fact and reason.

The displacement of the poet's protean self into another existence was for Keats a key feature of the artistic imagination. He attended William Hazlitt's Lectures on the English Poets (1818) and was spurred further to his own thinking by Hazlitt's notion that Shakespeare was "the least of an egotist that it was possible to be" and "nothing in himself," that he embodied "all that others were, or that they could become," that he "had in himself the germs of every faculty and feeling," and he "had only to think of anything in order to become that thing, with all the circumstances belonging to it." Keats took to heart the ideal of "disinterestedness," of Shakespeare's essential selflessness, his capacity for shape-shifting.

neoclassicism   A new or revived classicism. The term summarizes the turn back toward ancient Greek and Latin models for guidance. In English literature, neoclassicism refers to the period 1660–1785, which is sometimes divided into three sub-periods: the Restoration Age (1660–1700), presided over by John Milton, John Bunyan, and John Dryden; the Augustan Age (1700–1745), with Alexander Pope as the central figure; and the Age of Johnson (1745–1785), which was stamped by Samuel Johnson's sensibility. The movement had a precedent in contemporary French models; neoclassicism in France reached its height in the period 1660–1700. An example of French neoclassic doctrine: The critics of drama adhered to the precept of the Three Unities. They believed a play should be a unified whole, the scene should be confined to a single place, and the action should unfold over a single day.

Neoclassicism is a retrospective label applied by critics. The term was first recorded in 1877. The neoclassical poets believed in returning to first principles, to the work of the ancients, and turned this into one of the great eras of classical translation. They sought a pragmatic reformation in English language and literature. They placed their faith in reason, which is why the period has frequently been designated the age of reason. This faith suggests to me a shadowy fear of unreason or the irrational, of madness. Whoever loves wit, balance, and decorum, whoever values artistic symmetry and proportion, whoever favors conscious craftsmanship and bracing intellect, will turn to this fundamentally social poetry. The revival of classical values, the call for a return to prescribed forms and rules of composition, has been part of the ongoing dialogue in poetry between tradition and innovation.

SEE ALSO *classic.*

nonce forms   Poetic forms invented for a single purpose or occasion, i.e., "for the nonce," meaning "for the occasion." Nonce forms have a discernible pattern, which is seldom (or never) repeated in other poems. They do their work once only. It is a mystery why certain patterns, which began as nonce forms, become fixed for generations, while others do not recur. The old spelling of *nonce* is *nones*. Many of the poems in W. H. Auden's book *Nones* (1951) are nonce poems.

nonsense poetry, nonsense verse *The Oxford English Dictionary* defines *nonsense* as "that which is not sense; spoken or written words which make no sense or convey absurd ideas; also, absurd or senseless action." The earliest use of the word occurs in Ben Jonson's *Bartholomew Fair* (1614): "Here they continue their game of Vapours, which is Nonsense." Nonsense has a prehistory in oral tradition, in children's nursery rhymes and games, in ancient Greek writing, such as the Old Comedy of Aristophanes in which humans behave like birds and birds behave like humans (*The Birds*, 414 B.C.E.). Nonsense upends the way we normally view things; it disrupts, disorganizes, and then reorganizes common sense. "In every case, nonsense depends upon an assumption of sense. Without sense there is no nonsense," Susan Stewart writes in her definitive study, *Nonsense* (1979). "Nonsense stands in contrast to the reasonable, positive, contextualized, and 'natural' world of sense as the arbitrary, the random, the inconsequential, the merely cultural. While sense is sensory, tangible, real, nonsense is 'a game of vapours,' unrealizable, a temporary illusion." Nonsense operates by turning everyday things inside-out, by inversions and reversals, by negations.

Nonsense verse rejects ordinary logic and creates an autonomous world, as in Lewis Carroll's famous opening from "Jabberwocky" (1872):

> 'Twas brillig, and the slithy toves
>   Did gyre and gimble in the wabe:
> All mimsy were the borogoves
>   And the mome raths outgrabe.

Edward Lear (1812–1888) considered nonsense a response to "this ludicrously whirligig life which one suffers from first & laughs at afterwards." He said, "Nonsense is the breath of my nostrils." He began *A Book of Nonsense* (1846) with this dedication:

> There was an old Derry down Derry,
> Who loved to see little folks merry;
>   So he made them a Book,

And with laughter they shook,
At the fun of that Derry down Derry!

Lear published his first nonsense collections — he called his limericks "Nonsenses" or "Old Persons" — under the pseudonym "Derry down Derry," one of the fools of the traditional English mummers' plays. He sometimes employed what he called his "long nonsense name." Vivien Noakes gives one example in her edition of *The Complete Verse and Other Nonsense* (2001), which he got from *Aldiborontiphoskyphorniostikos: A Round Game, for Merry Parties* by R. Stennett (ca. 1812): "Mr. Abebika Kratoponoko Prizzikalo Kattefello Ablegorabalus Ableborintophashyph or Chakonoton the Cozovex Dossi Fossi Sini Tomentilla Coronilla Polentilla Battledore & Shuttlecock Derry down Derry Dumps, otherwise Edward Lear."

number, numbers   The old term for metrical units, as in Alexander Pope's line "I lisped in numbers, for the numbers came." In "An Essay on Criticism" (1711), he declared, "But most by numbers judge a poet's song: / And smooth or rough, with them, is right or wrong . . ." *Numbers* was also a Renaissance term for poems or poetry in general. It refers to the mathematic harmonies of classical poetry, a way of ordering the universe. George Santayana wrote, in "The Elements and Function of Poetry" (1900), "Although a poem be not made by counting of syllables upon the fingers, yet 'numbers' is the most poetical synonym we have for verse, and 'measure' the most significant equivalent for beauty, for goodness, and perhaps even for truth. Those early and profound philosophers, the followers of Pythagoras, saw the essence of all things in number, and it was by weight, measure, and number, as we read in the Bible, that the Creator first brought Nature out of the void."

SEE ALSO *measure, verse.*

nursery rhymes   Traditional rhymes and songs passed on to young children. Nursery rhymes initiate us into verbal rhythms and rhymes. These catchy verses, also called "Mother Goose Rhymes," are hundreds of years old and have surprising persistence. Most adults have a basic repertoire ("Baa Baa Black Sheep," "Little Bo Peep," "Little Jack Horner," "Jack and Jill," "Mary Had a Little Lamb," "Hickory Dickory Dock," etc.) that returns with renewed force when they become parents. Many nursery rhymes derive from street cries and songs, proverbs and riddles. Their origins are obscure. Most nursery rhymes were not written down until the late eighteenth century. The term *nursery rhyme* came into vogue in the nineteenth century. The earliest known collection of nursery rhymes is *Tommy Thumb's (Pretty) Song Book* (1744), which includes "Little Tom Tucker," "Sing a Song of Sixpence," and "Who Killed Cock Robin?" The most influential collection was *Mother Goose's Melody* (1781), which included "Jack and Jill," "Ding Dong Bell," and "Hush-a-bye, Baby, on the Tree Top."

O

objective correlative   An external equivalent for an internal state. The term *objective correlative* was coined by the American poet and painter Washington Allston in *Lectures on Art* (1850). T. S. Eliot employed it in his essay "Hamlet and His Problems" (1919): "The only way of expressing emotion is by finding an 'objective correlative'; in other words, a set of objects, a situation, a chain of events which shall be the formula of the *particular* emotion." Eliot's argument that Shakespeare's *Hamlet* (1603) was an artistic failure because the character's emotion does not match the facts of the action was dubious, but the term had a great vogue among the New Critics. The idea of the objective correlative coincided with the critical values of concreteness, impersonality, and objectivity. It was deployed as the staging or manifestation of an emotion embodied in action. Eliot himself later considered it one of "those notorious phrases" that "have had a truly embarrassing success in the world."

SEE ALSO *impersonality.*

occasional poem, occasional verse   (French *pièce d'occasion,* German *Gelegenheitsgedichte*) A poem written to memorialize a particular occasion, such as a wedding (Edmund Spenser's "Epithalamion," 1595), a death (John Milton's "Lycidas," 1638), or other rites of passage. The poet laureates of Britain have been obliged to write lyrics to celebrate coronations and royal weddings, to dedicate buildings, etc. They add a ceremonial dimension to the occasion. Some occasional poems are endorsed by political power, others come unsponsored. The tone of an occasional poem can be light or serious, respectful or ironic, the event revered or satirized. In periods of national crisis, such poems sometimes take up the ideological intentions of the epic. Goethe called occasional poems "the first and most genuine of all kinds of poetry." The great occasional poem represents its specific occasion in time and yet speaks beyond it, as in Andrew Marvell's "Horatian Ode upon Cromwell's Return from Ireland" (1650). The genre represents the public side of poetry and flourished in the Victorian era. It can sometimes feel rhetorical, as if the voice is declaimed over a loudspeaker. Robert Frost wrote a weak poem ("Dedication") for the inauguration of John F. Kennedy in 1961, but the glare of the sun blinded him on inauguration day and so he recited a splendid poem that he had written in 1942 ("The Gift Outright"). It was not an occasional poem but a poem that suited the occasion.

SEE ALSO *elegy, epithalamium, silvae, skald.*

octameter   A line of eight measures or feet. This long line is rare in English poetry, though Edgar Allan Poe made a claim for using octameters in "The Raven" ("Once upon a midnight dreary, while I pondered weak and weary," 1845) and Algernon Charles Swinburne managed them in "March: An Ode" ("Ere frost flower and snow-blossom faded and fell, and the splendour of winter had passed out of sight," 1887).

SEE ALSO *octave;* also "accentual-syllabic meter" in *meter.*

octastich, see *octave.*

octave, octet   The first eight lines of an Italian or Petrarchan sonnet, the octave, or octet, is followed by the last six lines, the sestet. The octave rhymes *abbaabba.* English-language poets have often loosened the Italian rhyme scheme to *abbaacca.* The octave tends to raise an issue, suggest a problem, create a conflict. The first four lines establish the subject; the second four complicate it. The octave can also refer to any eight-line poem or stanza (a brace octave), as in W. B. Yeats's "Among School Children" (1928), in which he employs ottava rima, an eight-line stanza in iambic pentameter rhyming *abababcc.* A stanza of eight lines can also be called an octastich. The French huitain is an octave — well balanced, symmetrical, a poem in itself.

SEE ALSO *ottava rima, sestet, sonnet, stanza.*

octavo, see *folio.*

octosyllabic verse   Verse in eight-syllable lines. Each tetrameter line (a line with four metrical feet) uses iambs (each one consisting of an unstressed syllable followed by a stressed one) or trochees (each one consisting of a stressed syllable followed by an unstressed one). The most common type of octosyllabic verse is the octosyllabic couplet, which probably derives from late medieval French poetry, in which it was first used for chronicles and romances and then for *lais* and *dits*. The Provençal troubadours brought it to Spain, where it became the primary form of courtly love poetry. It migrated to England via the Anglo-Norman poets and became firmly established by the fourteenth century, when it was employed in longer poems by John Gower (*Confessio Amantis [The Lover's Confession]*, ca. 1385) and Geoffrey Chaucer ("The Book of the Duchess" and "The House of Fame"). It was used for satirical verse, such as Samuel Butler's Hudibrastics, and for philosophical short poems, such as John Milton's "Il Penseroso" (1645). It worked well for both light and serious lyrical narratives by William Wordsworth ("She was a phantom of delight"), Samuel Taylor Coleridge ("Christabel," 1797–1800), Robert Burns (*Tam o' Shanter,* 1791), and Lord Byron ("The Corsair," 1814), who warned of "the fatal facility of the octo-syllabic meter."

SEE ALSO *dit, Hudibrastic verse, iamb, In Memoriam stanza, lai, romances, tetrameter, trochee.*

ode   A celebratory poem in elevated language on an occasion of public importance or on a lofty common theme. Think of Tennyson's ceremonial "Ode on the Death of the Duke of Wellington" (1852) and of Keats's partly rhapsodic, partly forlorn "Ode to a Nightingale" (1819). The word *ode* derives from the Greek *ōidē*, a poem intended to be sung, and thus was virtually synonymous with *lyric.* It comes to us through its Latin form, *oda.* Johann Gottfried von Herder called the ode "the firstborn child of feeling, the origin of poetry, the germ of life" (1765). The modern ode, which freely intermingles Greek and Latin elements, represents the claiming of an obligation, some inner feeling rising up in urgent response to an outer occasion, something owed.

Greek lyrics took the form of monodies, sung by single persons, or choral odes, sung by groups. Alcaeus ("Ode to Castor and Polydeuces") and

Sappho ("Ode to Aphrodite") were unsurpassed monodists, Pindar the key exponent of the choral form. Simultaneously sung and danced, the Pindaric ode consists of three stanzas that mirror a musical dance pattern: strophe, antistrophe, and epode. The strophe and antistrophe share the same metrical pattern and structure (the chorus in movement and countermovement); the epode has a different pattern (the chorus at rest). The Pindaric ode called for ecstatic performance and communally reenacted the ritual of participation in the divine.

Horace (65–8 B.C.E.) adapted the meters of Greek monodists to Latin verse, and replaced the irregular stanzas of the Pindaric ode with symmetrical arrangements. Horace's odes tend to be personal rather than public, general rather than occasional, contemplative rather than frenzied. The English ode begins with Ben Jonson's "To the Imortall Memorie and Friendship of That Noble Paire, Sir Lucius Cary and Sir H. Morison" (1629), a self-conscious attempt to create an exact equivalent for Pindar's complicated stanzaic form. Andrew Marvell represented the Horatian model in his outstanding political poem "An Horatian Ode upon Cromwell's Return from Ireland" (1681). In both English and Continental poetry the ode developed a life of its own, with deep roots as a poem on a theme of acknowledged importance. There are odes of speculation, odes *on* (Milton's "On the Morning of Christ's Nativity," 1629; Gray's mock ode "Ode on the Death of a Favourite Cat, Drowned in a Tub of Gold Fishes," 1748) and odes of address, odes *to* (Dryden's "To the Pious Memory of the Accomplished Young Lady, Mrs. Anne Killigrew," 1686; Shelley's "Ode to the West Wind," 1819; and Schiller's "Ode to Joy," 1785). The idea of a formal poem of considerable length written in elevated language has had less currency in modern times, but has sometimes been revitalized, as in Friedrich Hölderlin's mystical odes or in Pablo Neruda's odes on daily subjects, which praise the dignity and strangeness of ordinary things.

SEE ALSO *antistrophe, epode, lyric, strophe.*

Omar Khayyám quatrain, see *rubaiyat stanza.*

onomatopoeia From the Greek: "name making." The formation and use of words that imitate sound, such as *arf, blare, crash, dip, flare, growl, hum,* *jeer, knock, lick, murmur, nip, purr, quack, rustle, swish, thud, veer, wallop, yell,* and *zoom.* Shakespeare imitates animal sounds in this exchange from *The Tempest* (ca. 1611):

> Hark, hark!
>   Bow-wow!
> The watch-dogs bark.
>   Bow-wow!
> Hark, hark, I hear
> The strain of strutting Chanticleer
>   Cry, "cock-a-diddle-dow!"

Onomatopoeia is a form of name making, a device that creates verbal texture by weaving sounds through lines. It differs according to language and operates by convention. It turns the arbitrariness of each language into an intentionality and physicalizes Pope's dictum that "the sound must seem an echo to the sense." Actually, the sound becomes the sense.

SEE ALSO *sound poetry.*

oral-formulaic method Milman Parry (1902–1935) and his student Albert Lord (1912–1991) discovered and studied what they called the oral-formulaic method of oral epic singers in the Balkans. Their method has been variously referred to as "oral-traditional theory," "the theory of Oral-Formulaic Composition," and the "Parry-Lord theory." Parry used his study of Balkan singers to address what was then called the "Homeric Question": Who was Homer, and what are the Homeric poems? Parry's most critical insight was his recognition of the "formula," which he initially defined as "*a group of words which is regularly employed under the same metrical conditions to express a given essential idea.*" The formula revised the standard ideas of "stock epithets," "epic clichés," and "stereotyped phrases." Such often-repeated Homeric phrases as "rosy-fingered dawn" and "wine-dark sea" were mnemonic devices that fitted a certain metrical pattern and aided the epic singer in extemporaneous composition. Such phrases could be substituted and adapted, serving as placeholders, as a response to the needs of both grammar and narrative. These formulas were not particular to individual artists, but a shared traditional inheritance of many singers. Parry's work revolutionized the study of the Homeric poems by treating them as essentially oral texts.

Parry and Lord discovered that the epic form was well suited to the singer's need for fluency and flexibility, for composition as well as memorization. The singers composed poems orally by calling upon a storehouse of ready-made building blocks. Singers could call upon this stock of lines and formulas for describing places, portraying different characters, and narrating action — and thus perform epics of ten thousand lines or more with uninterrupted fluency. Parry and Lord provided a generative model of epic performance.

The oral-formulaic method has subsequently been applied to a wide variety of texts and genres, such as Babylonian, Hittite, and Anglo-Saxon epic poetry, medieval romances, Russian *byliny,* the corpus of pre-Islamic poetry, Toda ritual songs, Coorg dance songs, English and Spanish ballads, and even African American revivalist sermons. Oral formulas also clearly influenced written poetry. It is now possible, for example, to view Old English poems as transitional texts, written poems that embody oral formulas.

SEE ALSO *aoidos, epic, oral poetry.*

oral poetry Verbal art presented orally. A mode of communication that is usually transmitted by word of mouth and performed in face-to-face interaction. It is a language-based art characterized by a heightened awareness of the act of expression — how it says what it says — and it is marked, framed, and identified by the community as poetry. Historically, oral poetry ranges across the ancient world and includes the Greek Homeric poems the *Iliad* and the *Odyssey* (ca. eighth century B.C.E.), the Sumerian *Epic of Gilgamesh* (ca. 1600–1000 B.C.E.), and the Sanskrit epic of India *Mahabharata* (ninth to eighth century B.C.E.). Yet it is not a fossilized survival from the past or the exclusive property of nonliterate peoples. It includes Serbo-Croatian epics and Anglo-American ballads, but also Gond love songs, Malay *pantuns,* Nigerian election songs, South African praise poems, Inuit meditative poems, Siberian shaman songs, Australian song cycles, West Indian calypso, blues songs, Native American chants and spells, children's rhymes and riddles, and different varieties of work songs (sea shanties, the songs of chain gangs), which are timed to physical labor all over the world.

Oral and written poetry are two branches of the same river, repeatedly intertwining. Influence flows in both directions. Oral poetry may be composed and transmitted orally. It may be written and then circulated orally, or composed orally and then transmitted by written means. Once thought to be entirely spontaneous, oral poetry is often highly self-conscious and regulated by social conventions. One thinks of how praise poems reinforce authority and protest songs upset it, how riddles disturb cognitive categories and proverbs reinforce morays, how wedding songs celebrate joy and mourning songs assuage grief, marking a rite of passage, keeping celebrants and mourners in the social fabric. It was once thought that all oral poetry was composed anonymously, instinctively, but many communities have poets who are studied professionals, such as the Irish School of Bards, or the Maori School of Learning. The role and position of oral poets vary from community to community.

Oral poetry is an art that unfolds in performance. There is usually no fixed text or correct version; each performance is original. Oral poetry still thrives among rural peoples. Drum poetry, which exists in tonal languages, is the most remarkable kind of instrumental poetry. Drummers convey the words of the poem through the sounds of the drum. As Ruth Finnegan explains in *Oral Poetry* (1980),

> The same principle of transmission can be used by other instruments: so long as an instrument can conventionally represent different tones it can "speak" the words of a tonal language; even a mono-tone instrument like a gong can convey messages by use of stress and rhythm. Other instruments too are used to convey verbal utterances, such as whistles, horns, bells and flutes. This instrumental mode must be included in any list of the media of poetry.

Poetry changes based on its function, whether it is meant primarily to be spoken or written, heard or read. Oral poetry can't be paused or returned to, and its effectiveness therefore depends on immediate response, how it affects a live audience.

SEE ALSO *amoebean verses, aoidos, ballad, the dozens, epic, epithet, flyting, keening, narrative poetry, oral-formulaic method, oríkì, performance poetry, picong, poetic contest, praise poems, qasida, shaman, slam poetry, song, sound poetry, spoken word poetry, voice.*

organic form   Since the development of natural history and biology in the eighteenth century, the word *organic* has primarily referred to things living and growing. Machines took on new significance during the industrial revolution, and Romantic thinkers began to reject eighteenth-century mechanical philosophies of mind, differentiating between organic and inorganic systems, natural and mechanical bodies. Taking a lead from the German critic A. W. Schlegel, Samuel Taylor Coleridge distinguished between mechanic form and organic form in an essay on Shakespeare:

> The form is mechanic when on any given material we impress a pre-determined form, not necessarily arising out of the properties of the material — as when to a mass of wet clay we give whatever shape we wish it to retain when hardened. The organic form on the other hand is innate, it shapes as it develops itself from within, and the fullness of its development is one and the same with the perfection of its outward Form. Such is the Life, such is the form. Nature, the prime genial artist, inexhaustible in diverse powers, is equally inexhaustible in forms.

Coleridge distinguished between the mechanical fancy and the living imagination, suggesting that the work of art is like a living organism, especially a plant.

The metaphor of the organic has been critical to the development of Romantic and certain crucial strands of American poetry. The idea that art derives from nature rather than from other art has fueled American ideas of originality. Ralph Waldo Emerson created a credo for American poetry when he adapted Coleridge's botanical metaphor for poetic form and declared, in "The Poet" (1844), "For it is not metres, but a metre-making argument, that makes a poem, — a thought so passionate and alive, that, like the spirit of a plant or an animal, it has an architecture of its own, and adorns nature with a new thing." The premise of all theories of organic form is that form should not be prescribed or fixed but should emerge from the subject matter at hand. Ezra Pound formulated an imagist version when he wrote, "I think there is a 'fluid' as well as a 'solid' content, that some poems may have form as a tree has form, some as water poured into a vase" (1918). In the 1960s, Denise Levertov and Robert Duncan developed a more broadly theological concept of organic form. They believed that the form of the individual poem intuits the divine.

In literary criticism and aesthetics, the word *organic* is commonly used to indicate the interrelationship between the parts of a work. We employ a metaphor from nature when we say that things have an organic relation or organic connection, meaning that they seem to occur "naturally" rather than being imposed "artificially."

SEE ALSO *form, free verse, imagination, originality, Romanticism.*

originality   Something new and unexpected, novel, unprecedented. The word *original* referred in Medieval Latin to a document composed firsthand, the source from which copies were made. An original was distinguished from a replica, translation, or imitation. The meaning migrated toward modern usage mainly in the seventeenth century. "In the case of works of art," as Raymond Williams explains, "there was a transfer from the retrospective sense of original (the first work and not the copy) to what was really a sense close to *new* (not like other works)." Originality became a value and a term of praise in the second half of the eighteenth century. It was proposed in opposition to the neoclassical idea that poetry should imitate the ancients. "An *Original* may be said to be of a *vegetable* nature; it rises spontaneously from the vital root of Genius; it *grows,* it is not *made: Imitations* are often a sort of *Manufacture* wrought up by those *Mechanics, Art* and *Labour,* out of pre-existent materials not their own," Edward Young wrote in *Conjectures on Original Composition* (1759), thus helping to inaugurate the Romantic idea of originality as something natural and organic rather than mechanical. There has ever after been an ongoing debate about the rival claims of tradition and innovation.

The Romantic concept of originality has been especially charged in American poetry, where it seems almost to define the American character. "Why should not we also enjoy an original relation to the universe?" Emerson asked in "Nature" (1836). "Why should not we have a poetry and philosophy of insight and not of tradition, and a religion by revelation to us, and not the history of theirs?" Here the New World is opposed to the old one, the freshness of insight contrasted to the staleness of tradition. The question of what constitutes originality has often been worked out at the level of form, the difference between a new poetics of free verse (Whitman) and a fresh remaking of traditional forms (Poe). There is a subsequent dialogue in modern poetry between Ezra Pound's dictum to "Make It New" and T. S. Eliot's idea that the individual poet's originality exists in relationship to those who have come before.

SEE ALSO *imitation, inspiration, invention, organic form, tradition.*

oríkì   The oral praise poetry of the indigenous Yoruba communities of West Africa. Similar praise poems turn up throughout much of Africa (Zulu *izibongo,* Basuto *lithoko,* etc.). The invocation or praise poem starts out as the stringing together of praise names that describe the qualities of a particular person, animal, plant, place, or god. These praise names are handed down from the past and invented by relatives or neighbors or often drummers. The *akewi* are praise-singers at a king's court. The *oríkì* of a plant or an animal is sung by hunters, the *oríkì* of a god is sung by worshipers. As Olatunde Olatunji explains, "Oríkì is the most popular of Yórùbá poetic forms. Every Yórùbá poet therefore strives to know the oríkì of important people in his locality as well as lineage oríkì because every person, common or noble, has his own body of utterances by which he can be addressed." In Yoruba culture, a person's name relates to his or her spiritual essence and each individual has a series of praise names. The use of one's praise name is part of daily life as well as traditional performance. *Oríkì Esu* are the narrative praise poems or panegyrics to the divine trickster of Yoruba mythology.

SEE ALSO *epic, epithet, oral poetry, panegyric, praise poems.*

ottava rima   An eight-line stanza in iambic pentameter, rhyming *abab abcc.* The pattern unfolds as six interlocking lines followed by a climactic couplet. The three insistent alternating rhymes propel the narrative forward while encouraging meditation and commentary. The couplet, on the other hand, is a stopping point, a turn or summation. The Italian poets of the early modern period (Boccaccio, Pulci, Tasso) favored this aristocratic and symmetrical stanza, cast in eleven-syllable lines, for narrative and epic verse; Ariosto showed that it could be simultaneously lyrical, contemplative, and narrative (*Orlando furioso,* 1516). The ottava rima form was imported to England by Thomas Wyatt (1503–1542), who used it for epigrams; it flourished during the Renaissance; and Lord Byron deployed it in *Don Juan* (1819–24), a poem "meant to be a little quietly facetious upon everything." Here Byron uses the stanza to send up some classic ancestors:

> Ovid's a rake, as half his verses show him,
>> Anacreon's morals are a still worse sample,
> Catullus scarcely has a decent poem,
>> I don't think Sappho's Ode a good example,
> Although Longinus tells us there is no hymn
>> Where the Sublime soars forth on wings more ample;
> But Virgil's songs are pure, except that horrid one
> Beginning with *"Formosum pastor Corydon."*

For W. B. Yeats, ottava rima suggested an aristocratic poise and decorum, and he memorably employed the form in a score of meditative lyrics, such as "Sailing to Byzantium" (1927), "Among School Children" (1928), "Coole Park and Ballylee, 1931" (1931), and "The Circus Animals' Desertion" (1939). In central Italy, however, the medieval tradition of ottava rima is a folk way of singing, sometimes called the chant of the *poeti contadini* ("peasant poets"). The songs are sometimes based on texts by Dante (1265–1321) and Ariosto (1474–1533), sometimes improvised in competition. Each singer begins a new eight-line stanza with the last rhyme of the previous singer. This is the style of the *Contrasto* ("contrast"), or improvised, poetry in the Tuscan dialect. The oral poets use the verbal art of ottava rima for heated debate.

SEE ALSO *octave, poetic contest.*

oxymoron From the Greek: "pointedly foolish." A figure of speech that combines two seemingly contradictory elements, as when Charles Lamb said, "I like a smuggler. He is the only honest thief." As an apparent contradiction in terms, a condensed paradox, the oxymoron turns on a phrase and seeks a hidden unity of opposites. It draws attention to its way of fusing disparate elements. Thus John Milton describes hell as "darkness visible" (*Paradise Lost,* 1667) and T. S. Eliot hears "soundless wailing" ("The Dry Salvages," 1941). The oxymoron has a long history in poetry, but was an especially strong device for the baroque and metaphysical poets, who created elaborate figures to evoke sacred mysteries.

Modern poets often employed very compact oxymorons. Thus Dylan Thomas writes of "Grave men, near death, who see with blinding sight" ("Do Not Go Gentle into That Good Night," 1951) and Theodore Roethke declares, "I wake to sleep, and take my waking slow" ("The Waking," 1953). In "Oxymorons" (1998), William Matthews lists as further examples *"friendly fire, famous poet, common sense."* Anne Stevenson suggests that "poetic language is essentially oxymoronic, a coinage stamped on two sides with logically irreconcilable messages."

SEE ALSO *paradox.*

P

paean A song of joyful praise. In ancient Greece, a paean was originally a hymn to worship Apollo, who was invoked as Paian ("Healer"). These hymns were later expanded to be sung to other gods and eventually to human beings, thus evolving into choral odes of thanksgiving, which were frequently sung by troops before battles and after victories. The great paeans of antiquity were written by Bacchylides and Pindar. Paeans were Apollonian, dithyrambs Dionysian. The term *paean* can now be used to describe any song of joy or triumph. Thus in *Helen in Egypt*, H. D. calls for chanting "new paeans to the new Sun" (1961).

SEE ALSO *dithyramb.*

paeon In classical Greek prosody, a foot of one long and three short syllables. Depending on the position of the long syllable, it is known as the first (— u u u), second (u — u u), third (u u — u), or fourth (u u u —) paeon. This quadruple quantitative measure is generally too long for English-language poetry, though Gerard Manley Hopkins loosely managed to adapt it to accentual use in "The Windhover" (1918) and other poems. Each long line in Alfred, Lord Tennyson's "The Making of Man" (1892) consists of an anapest (u u /) and three paeons, which create a rhythm of great rapidity. Here is the representative last line: "Hăllĕlú- | jăh tŏ thĕ Má- | kĕr. 'Ĭt ĭs fín- | shĕd. Măn ĭs máde.'"

SEE ALSO *foot;* also "quantitative meter" in *meter.*

palindrome A word (like "eye") or phrase (like "Able was I ere I saw Elba") that can be read the same way forward or backward. It is a word game, a mirroring device, which invites us to read in a contrary direction, and thus draws attention to our pattern of visual perception. A verse that reads both ways is called a *cancrine* (from the Latin: "crab-wise"). In Latin, a verse that has the same meter when the order of words is reversed was called *reciprocus versus*. In the fifth century, Sidonius Apollinaris referred to *versus recurrentes* ("recurrent verses"), lines that have the same meter and order of letters when they are read forward and backward. As an example of perhaps misplaced ingenuity, in 1802 an author who called himself Ambrose Hieromonachus Pamperes published a 416-line Greek poem in which every line was a palindrome.

SEE ALSO *acrostic, anagram.*

palinode   A poem or song of retraction. The palinode (*palin-ode;* literally, "singing back or over again") formally retracts a view from a previous poem. The term was first given to a poem by Stesichorus (seventh century B.C.E.), who retracted his attack upon Helen as the cause of the Trojan War. As Plato recorded it in *Phaedrus* (ca. 370 B.C.E.), "The story is not true, / She never went in the well-decked ships, / She didn't travel to the towers of Troy." Ovid created a common theme in love poetry when he wrote *Remedia amoris* (ca. 2 C.E.) supposedly to retract *Ars amatoria* (ca. 1 C.E.). In "The Legend of Good Women" (1386), Chaucer repudiates his defamatory view of women in *Troilus and Criseyde* (ca. 1380s).

panegyric   A public speech or poem in praise of an individual, a group of people, or a public body. Pindar's odes have been loosely characterized as panegyrics. After the third century B.C.E., the panegyric was generally recognized as a specific poetic type (a formal eulogistic composition intended as a public compliment), which persisted until the Renaissance. In English poetry, the panegyric began with the Stuart succession to the throne and suggested "praise of great persons," which gives it a political dimension, as in Samuel Daniel and Ben Jonson's panegyrics to James I, or John Dryden's panegyrics for the restoration of Charles II in 1660. Exaggeration is predictably built into the occasion. The panegyric may have led to a form of public flattery about which we are now rightly skeptical since it colludes with power, but it most likely has its roots in religious practice, in the Greek and Latin cult hymns. Behind it persists one of the most long-standing ceremonial impulses in poetry: to praise.

SEE ALSO *epithet, oríki, praise poems, qasida.*

pantoum, pantun   The Western pantoum adapts a long-standing form of oral Malayan poetry (*pantun*) that entered written literature in the fifteenth century. The most basic form of the *pantun* is a quatrain with an *abab* rhyme scheme. Each line contains between eight and twelve syllables. Like the ghazal, it is a disjunctive form, since the sentence that makes up the first pair of lines (*ab*) has no immediate logical or narrative connection with the second pair of lines (*ab*). The prefatory couplet is called the *pembayang* and the closing couplet the *maksud.* The rhymes and other verbal associations, such as puns and repeating sounds (assonance, consonance), connect them. But there is also an oblique but necessary relationship, and the first statement often turns out to be a metaphor for the second one. The most famous *pantuns* are learned by heart and interconnected by refrains, which serve as an aid to memory for both the oral poet and the audience. The *pantun* is sung very slowly according to a fixed rhythm.

The Malayan *pantun berkait* is what we know as the pantoum. It is a repetitive form of indefinite length that unfolds in interweaving quatrains and often rhymes *abab.* Lines 2 and 4 of each stanza repeat as lines 1 and 3 of the following stanza. The reader always takes four steps forward and two back:

> Line 1: A
> Line 2: B
> Line 3: C
> Line 4: D
>
> Line 5: B
> Line 6: E
> Line 7: D
> Line 8: F
>
> Line 9: E
> Line 10: G
> Line 11: F
> Line 12: H

It is customary for the second and fourth lines in the last stanza of the poem to repeat the first and third lines of the initial stanza, so that the whole poem circles back to the beginning, like a snake eating its tail. This slow and highly balanced repetitive form was introduced to Western poetry in the nineteenth century by the French Orientalist Ernest Fouinet (who called it the *malais pantun*) and popularized by Victor Hugo in *Les orientales* (1829). It was a recognizable form in nineteenth-century French poetry (by Théodore de Banville, Louisa Siefert, Leconte de Lisle, Charles Baudelaire) and entered English poetry through the vogue for songlike French forms, such as the villanelle and the ballade. As a form, the pantoum is always looking back over its shoulder, and thus is well suited to evoke a sense of times past. It works well for poems of loss, such as Donald Justice's "Pantoum of the Great Depression" (1995), and departure, such as Louis MacNeice's "Leaving Barra" (1937).

SEE ALSO *ghazal*.

paradox From the Greek: "beyond belief." A literary paradox is beyond belief because it brings together two seemingly incongruous or contradictory ideas that turn out to be well founded or true, as when Oscar Wilde announces, "I can resist anything except temptation." The witty exploration and testing of outrageous paradoxes was one of the strategic devices of seventeenth-century poets such as John Donne ("The Paradox," 1633), George Herbert ("A Paradox: that the sicke are in a *better case,* then the Whole," first printed 1835), and Andrew Marvell, who writes in "Upon Appleton House" (ca. 1650),

> Let others tell the *Paradox,*
> How Eels now bellow in the Ox;
> How Horses at their Tails do kick,
> Turn'd as they hang to Leeches quick;
> How boats can over Bridges sail;
> And fishes do the Stables scale.
> How *Salmons* trespassing are found
> And Pikes are taken in the Pound.

In twentieth-century literary criticism, paradox was a key concept for the New Critics. Cleanth Brooks argues that "the language of poetry is the language of paradox."

SEE ALSO *ambiguity, analogy, irony, metaphysical poets, oxymoron, tension.*

parallelism From the Greek: "side by side." The correspondence between two parts of an utterance (a phrase, a line, a verse) through syntactic and rhythmic repetition. One thinks of the oral-formulaic strategies of the early epics, of chants, charms, and spells, of incantatory prayers. It is the central device of biblical Hebrew poetry, as in these lines from Psalm 96:

> Let the heavens rejoice, and let the earth be glad;
> let the sea roar, and the fulness thereof.
> Let the field be joyful, and all that *is* therein: then
> shall all the trees of the wood rejoice.

The buildup of parallel lines often creates a feeling of intense emotion. The Russian formalist Viktor Shklofsky notes, in "Art as Technique" (1917), that "the perception of disharmony in a harmonious context is important in parallelism. The purpose of parallelism, like the general purpose of imagery, is to transfer the usual perceptions of an object into the sphere of a new perception — that is, to make a unique semantic modification." This device of synthesis and accumulation animates the visionary poetry of Christopher Smart (1722–1771) and William Blake (1757–1827). It is at the heart of Walt Whitman's ecstasies and the work of his free-verse progeny, D. H. Lawrence (1885–1930), Theodore Roethke (1908–1963), and Allen Ginsberg (1926–1997).

SEE ALSO *anaphora, catalog poem, chant, charm, incantation, litany, spell.*

paraphrase From the Greek: "tell in other words." To paraphrase a passage or text is to render it in different language. In particular, to paraphrase a poem is to render it in prose, which raises inevitable problems, since the way a thing is said in poetry cannot be separated from what is being said. Paraphrase becomes a mode of translation. We tend to think of paraphrase as a problem taken up by modern literary criticism — the New Critics spoke of "the heresy of paraphrase" — but the issue has a long history in rhetorical studies. Turning poetry into prose became an exercise in the schools of rhetoric around the first century. Quintilian recommended it as a model for orators. Ernst Robert Curtius points out that a significant portion of early Christian poetry continues the practice of paraphrase. The Bible was recast into hexameters. "The Spaniard Juvencus (ca. 330) applies this procedure to the Gospels, the Egyptian Nomus (fifth century) to the Gospel of John (in Greek), the Ligurian Arator to the Acts of the Apostles." The lives of the saints were also versified and then freshly turned back into prose. Caedmon inherits this tradition with his metrical paraphrase of parts of the Holy Scriptures in Anglo-Saxon.

SEE ALSO *translation.*

pararhyme, see *near rhyme.*

Parnassus A mythological home for poetry and music, Parnassus was a mountain in Greece with two peaks, one sacred to Apollo, the other to Dionysus. It represents the two poles of poetry: the cool, rational, and classical as well as the heated, irrational, and romantic. Its Castilian spring was sacred to the Muses.

SEE ALSO *muse.*

parody The exaggerated imitation of a work of art. It distorts for comic effect. *The Oxford English Dictionary* defines parody as "a composition . . . in which characteristic turns of an author . . . are imitated in such a way as to make them appear ridiculous, especially by applying them to ludicrously inappropriate subjects." Parody is close to burlesque, which ridicules a style by exaggerating it, as well as to travesty ("a grotesque or debased imitation or likeness"). Dwight Macdonald proposes the following hierarchy in "Some Notes on Parody" (1960):

> *Travesty* (literally "changing clothes," as in "transvestite") is the most primitive form. It raises laughs from the belly rather than the head, by putting high, classic characters into prosaic situations, with a corresponding stepping-down of the language . . . *Burlesque* (from Italian *burla,* "ridicule") is a more advanced form since it at least imitates the style of the original. It differs from parody in that the writer is concerned with the original not in itself but merely as a device for topical humor . . . *Parody,* from the Greek *parodia* (a beside- or

against-song), concentrates on the style and thought of the original. If burlesque is pouring new wine into old bottles, parody is making a new wine that tastes like the old but has a slightly lethal effect.

Parody tends to be socially motivated. In Greek literature, Aristophanes (ca. 450–ca. 388 B.C.E.) first made the leap from burlesque to parody. His satirical imitations of Aeschylus (525–456 B.C.E.), Euripides (ca. 480–406 B.C.E.), and Socrates (ca. 470–399 B.C.E.) turned parody into a genuine art. Parody is by its nature a late, self-conscious, responsive form. Its mockery feeds off something prior. It captures something of an originating spirit while distancing itself from the original, which it shows up by pointing to its artificiality.

SEE ALSO *burlesque, satire.*

partimen, see *tenson.*

pastoral From the Latin word *pastor,* meaning "shepherd." In the third century B.C.E., the Greek poet Theocritus originated the pastoral in ten poems (idylls) representing the life of Sicilian shepherds. Virgil imitated Theocritus in his *Eclogues* (42–39 B.C.E.) and created the enduring literary model of the pastoral: a conventional poem that expresses an urban poet's nostalgic image of the simple, peaceful life of shepherds living in idealized natural settings. The term *bucolic,* introduced by Theocritus in *Idyll 1* and taken from the Greek word for "herdsman," is used as a synonym for *pastoral.* Virgil's ten pastoral poems, which he refers to as *pastorem carmen* (*Georgic 4*), were labeled "bucolics" by grammarians. Virgil believed that a young poet should learn the craft by writing pastorals before proceeding to the grander form of the epic.

The forms of the pastoral lyric include the complaint, the singing match, the elegy, the blazon, and the palinode. Many bucolic poems end with the setting of the sun, which befits an outdoor conversation. This became one of the conventions of the pastoral. Alexander Pope defined the pastoral as "an imitation of the action of a shepherd; the form of the imitation is dramatic or narrative, or mixed of both, the fable simple, the manners not too polite nor too rustic" ("A Discourse on Pastoral Poetry," 1704). In the eighteenth century, poets began to critique the formulas of the pastoral by contrasting them to actual rural life. George Crabbe wrote in *The Village* (1783), "By such examples taught, to paint the Cot, / As Truth will paint it, and as Bards will not." Crabbe proposed a counter-pastoral:

> Fled are those times, when in harmonious strains
> The rustic poet praised his native plains:
> No shepherds now, in smooth alternate verse,
> The country's beauty or the nymphs' rehearse.

In *Some Versions of Pastoral* (1936), William Empson expanded the concept of the pastoral to include any work that contrasts the simple and the complicated life. The simple life can be represented by a shepherd, a child, a working man, and Empson applies the term to works ranging from Andrew Marvell's seventeenth-century poem "The Garden" to the modern proletarian novel. Writing in the middle of the Depression, Empson considered pastoral a "puzzling form" in which educated poets from the city idealized the lives of poor people close to the land. It implies "a beautiful relation between the rich and the poor" by making "simple people express strong feelings . . . in learned and fashionable language." After Empson, no one could read pastorals without awareness of the complex ambiguities and class tensions between cultivated urban authors and lowborn rural subjects. Raymond Williams demonstrates that the pastoral is based on a rhetorical contrast between the country and the city. The United States doesn't have shepherds or shepherdesses, but versions of pastoral have flourished in the cult of the Noble Red Man and the heroizing of cowboys, farmers, and miners.

SEE ALSO *amoebean verse, blazon, complaint, eclogue, ecopoetry, elegy, nature poetry, palinode, poetic contest.*

pathetic fallacy In *Modern Painters* (1856), John Ruskin invented the term *pathetic fallacy* to describe the attribution of human characteristics to the natural world, or to inanimate objects. To illustrate, he quoted from Charles Kingsley's "The Sands of Dee" (1849):

> They rowed her in across the rolling foam —
> The cruel, crawling foam.

"The foam is not cruel, neither does it crawl," Ruskin wrote. "The state of mind which attributes to it these characters of a living creature is one in which the reason is unhinged by grief. All violent feelings . . . produce in us a falseness in all our impressions of external things, which I would characterize as the 'pathetic fallacy.'"

What was for Ruskin a derogatory term has been a central poetic device of archaic and tribal poetries everywhere, which view the natural world as alive in all its parts. One might alternately think of the pathetic fallacy as empathic feeling for the overlooked world. George Santayana pointed out that "the pathetic fallacy is a return to that early habit of thought by which our ancestors peopled the world with benevolent and malevolent spirits; what they felt in the presence of objects they took to be part of the objects themselves." This projection of feeling has also flourished as a strain in epic poetry from Homer onward, as a feature of visionary poetry from the prophets of the Hebrew Bible to Smart and Blake, Coleridge and Shelley, Whitman and Crane. It emerges whenever poets testify to, or dream of, a natural world saturated with psyche.

SEE ALSO *personification.*

pathos From the Greek: "suffering," "passion." The quality in a work of literature that evokes feelings of pity, tenderness, sympathy, or sorrow. Aristotle defines *pathos* in the *Poetics* (350 B.C.E.): "The pathos is a destructive or painful action, for example, deaths in full view, and great pain, and wounds, and things of this kind." It persuades by appealing to the emotions of an audience. "The root idea of pathos is the exclusion of an individual on our own level from a social group to which he is trying to belong," Northrop Frye explains. "Hence the central tradition of sophisticated pathos is the study of the isolated mind, the story of how someone recognizably like ourselves is broken by a conflict between the inner and outer world, between imaginative reality and the sort of reality which is established by a social consensus."

SEE ALSO *tragedy.*

pattern poetry A form of spatial prosody, pattern poetry (*technopaignia*) offers verses as visual arrangements on the page. The impulse to display poetry in concrete shapes is ancient, and pattern poems have been found in

Greek, Latin (*carmen figuratum,* "shaped poem"), Hebrew, Chinese, Sanskrit, ancient Persian, and German (*Bildergedicht,* "picture poem") and most of the other modern European languages. The pattern poem (for example, the poem shaped like an egg or a pair of wings) promotes itself as a combination of verbal and visual art. It concretizes the relationship between content and form, and challenges the reader to perceive the relationship between the shape and the theme.

SEE ALSO *concrete poetry, emblem.*

Pegasus The winged horse of Greek mythology. Hesiod (eighth century B.C.E.) thought that Pegasus, a favorite of the Muses, was named for the springs (*pegai*) of Oceanus, and Ovid (43 B.C.E.–18 C.E.) tells how the winged horse produced the spring on Mount Helicon by striking the ground with his hoof. In post-classical times, Pegasus became a symbol of poetic inspiration.

pentastich A stanza or poem of five lines.

SEE ALSO *quintet.*

perfect rhyme, see *rhyme.*

performance poetry Oral poetry is actualized in performance. Poetry itself originated as a performing art. In languages that are not written, all poetry is by its very nature performance poetry, since it can be experienced only through live performance. The term *performance poetry* specifically came into vogue in the 1980s to refer to a type of poetry composed either for or during a performance before an audience. It is closely akin to performance art (live artistic events) and part of the spoken word movement. The idea of performance highlights poetry as something emergent. The poet takes responsibility for the event before an audience. In written poetry, words also perform, but on the page, for the reader. "I look upon a poem as a performance," Robert Frost told an interviewer in 1960. "The whole thing is performance and prowess and feats of association."

SEE ALSO *ballad, epic, oral poetry, proverb, riddle, slam poetry, sound poetry, spoken word poetry.*

persona From the Latin: "mask" (a false face of clay or bark worn by actors in the ancient classical theater). The character or voice created by the speaker or narrator in a literary work. The term *dramatis personae,* which refers to the characters in a play, derives from *persona,* as does the word *person.* The concept of persona originates in magical thinking, in archaic rituals during which masks function as independent beings that possess the ones who assume them. The poetic move into personae has a quality of animism; it embodies the displacement of the poet's self into a second self.

In "A General Introduction for My Work" (1937), W. B. Yeats said that the poet "never speaks directly as to someone at the breakfast table, there is always a phantasmagoria." The term *personae* refers to all forms of this phantasmagoria, from the narrators in Chaucer's *Canterbury Tales* (ca. 1387–1400) to the unidentified autobiographical speakers in Emily Dickinson's lyrics and Stevie Smith's poems, to the characters in Robert Browning's dramatic monologues. Writing to Thomas Wentworth Higginson in 1862, Dickinson warned, "When I state myself, as the Representative of the Verse — it does not mean — me — but a supposed person." Creating a persona is a way of staging an utterance. There is always a difference between the writer who sits down to work and the author who emerges in the text.

SEE ALSO *dramatic monologue.*

personification The attribution of human qualities to inanimate objects, to animals or ideas, as when Sylvia Plath genders the moon as female ("The Moon and the Yew Tree," 1961) or when Sir Philip Sidney apostrophizes it: "With how sad steps, O moon, thou climb'st the skies! / How silently, and with how wan a face!" Personification is a prominent feature of most tribal poetries. Sometimes thought of as a marginal poetic activity, it may be central to the Orphic function of the poet, who, as Emerson said, "puts eyes and tongues into every dumb and inanimate object."

Prosopopoeia is a form of personification in which an inanimate object gains the capacity to speak. For example, in the Old English poem "The Dream of the Rood" (early eighth century) the wooden cross describes the death of Christ from its own point of view.

Personification has special purpose as the basis for allegory. Think of those medieval morality plays in which characters are named "Lust" or "Hope," thus indicating that general ideas, not individual people, are being drama-tized.

SEE ALSO *allegory, pathetic fallacy, praise poems.*

Petrarchism   Petrarch's *Rerum vulgarium fragmenta* (*Fragments of Vernacular Matters*), more commonly known as *Rime sparse* (*Scattered Rhymes*) or *Il canzoniere* (*Songbook*), consists of 366 lyrics composed between 1336 and 1374. It comprises what Michael Spiller calls "the single greatest influence on the love poetry of Renaissance Europe until well into the seventeenth century." Petrarchism is the widespread imitation of the conventions of Petrarch's poetry, its themes, motifs, and meters, its conflicts and values, its repertoire of situations, its modes of praise, its idealizations. Some of the topoi, or commonplaces, of Petrarchism: unrequited love; the lover addicted to love even though he is burning in his own passion; love as pain; love as a passion beyond the will; love as an invisible chain; the lover eternally faithful to his idealized lady. Petrarch created a stylized language of love that became an international Esperanto in Renaissance and baroque poetry. This also gave rise to a demythologizing anti-Petrarchism. William Shakespeare's early "Sonnet 18," "Shall I compare thee to a summer's day?" (1609), develops a Petrarchist conceit. His later "Sonnet 130," "My mistress' eyes are nothing like the sun" (1609), rejects what had by then become the convention of flat-tering a typecast mistress in clichéd language. It is anti-Petrarchan.

SEE ALSO *baroque, complaint, conceit, courtly love, rhyme royal, songbook, sonnet, topos.*

phanopoeia   The imagistic qualities of poetry. In *ABC of Reading* (1934), Ezra Pound described *phanopoeia* as "the throwing of an image on the mind's retina." In *How to Read* (1929), he utilized the term to characterize one of three "kinds of poetry": "PHANOPOEIA, which is a casting of images upon the visual imagination." Pound emphasized that "in *Phanopoeia* we find the greatest drive toward utter precision of word." He noted that the pictorial or revelatory image is the one part of poetry that survives translation. What Pound termed *phanopoeia*, Samuel Taylor Coleridge called "poetry of the eye" ("On the Principles of Genial Criticism," 1814).

SEE ALSO *imagism, logopoeia, melopoeia.*

picong   In the West Indies, a series of sustained taunts is called *picong*. The word may derive from the Spanish adjective *picón*, meaning "mocking" or "huffing," or the French *piquant* (literally, "prickling"), which now means "appealingly provocative," but once also carried the meaning of "stinging" or "causing hurt feelings." Roger Abrahams notes in *Singing the Master* (1992) that this kind of verbal play is found in many places in the West Indies and other parts of the black New World, where it is also called 'busin', cursing, *manguyu,* and rhyming. It can tip over into what Trinidadians call *mamaguy,* putting someone on, deceiving them with flattery. The earliest Trinidadian calypsonians were called chantwells, and in the Francophonic areas the chantwell or praise poet is empowered to aim songs at specific politicians and groups. The name for their songs is *chant pwen* ("pointed song").

Picong originated as a verbal duel in song. At calypso festivals in Trinidad, *picong* takes the form of a spontaneous, highly competitive verbal contest between two or more performers (calypsonians). The singers are pitiless in pillorying each other.

SEE ALSO *poetic contest, praise poems.*

picturesque   The word *picturesque* was used as early as 1703 to mean "in the manner of a picture; fit to be made into a picture." It came into vogue in the early eighteenth century as an Anglicization of the Italian *pittoresco* or the French *pittoresque.* William Gilpin defined *picturesque* as "a term expressive of that peculiar kind of beauty, which is agreeable in a picture" (*Essay on Prints,* 1768) and introduced it as an English aesthetic ideal.

The picturesque is part of the history of travel and tourism. It reflects an eighteenth-century taste for natural scenery and scenic touring. Picturesque poetry aspired to the condition of painting. It inscribes a tension between the spatial dimension of pictorial art and the temporal nature of poetry. Aesthetically, it situated itself between the counter ideals of the beautiful and the sublime. As Angus Fletcher explains in *Allegory* (1964), "Picturesque might best be defined as inverse, or microscopic, sublimity: where the sublime aims at great size and grandeur, the picturesque aims at littleness and a sort of modesty; where the sublime is austere, the picturesque is intricate; where the sublime produces 'terror,' or rather, awed anxiety, the picturesque produces an almost excessive feeling of comfort." The strength of the picturesque is in the landscape poetry of the late eighteenth and early nineteenth centuries. The problem of the picturesque is that it is also a mode of veiling whatever doesn't suit the prettiness of the picture. It turns people into figures in a landscape or painting.

SEE ALSO *Romanticism, the sublime, ut pictura poesis.*

piyyut   A Jewish liturgical poem. The medieval *piyyut* was a formal poem, written in Hebrew or Aramaic, intended to be recited, chanted, or sung during religious services. The form developed in Palestine between the second and sixth centuries. The *piyyut* was a poetic supplement to the fixed prayers of the traditional liturgy. The major forms followed a strict strophic structure and a rhythm based on a fixed number of words per line. They rhymed in different ways. Many poems were structured around an acrostic that employed all (or some) of the twenty-two letters of the Hebrew alphabet. Often the poet signed the poem with an acrostic of his name. *Paytan* is the term for the liturgical poet who composes *piyyutim.* Both words derive from the Greek *poietes* ("maker").

SEE ALSO *acrostic, parallelism.*

the plain style   The plain style originated as an informal rhetorical term to characterize speech or writing that is simple, direct, and unambiguous. Richard Lanham characterizes its three central values as "Clarity, Brevity, and Simplicity." Dating to the Latin Stoics, it was associated with a "low style" as opposed to a "high style." In "The Sixteenth-Century Lyric in England" (1939), Yvor Winters demonstrated the presence of two styles of poetry in the English Renaissance lyric: one plain, the other ornate and decorative. According to Winters, the plain-style poem has "a theme usually broad, simple, and obvious, even tending toward the proverbial, but usually a theme of some importance, humanly speaking; a feeling restrained to the minimum required by the subject; a rhetoric restrained to a similar minimum, the poet being interested in his rhetoric as a means of stating his matter as economically as possible, and not, as are the Petrarchans, in the pleasures of rhetoric for its own sake."

The two Renaissance types of poetry grew out of different traditions, one the "popular" or "vulgar" style, the other the eloquent style. The plain style originated in the idiom of common people whereas the eloquent style developed out of court traditions. The plain style registered as anti-courtly and classically minded. Ben Jonson's classicism has been identified as a model of the plain style. The Puritans developed a plain style, which was simple, spare, and straightforward. It defined their sermons and informed their poems.

SEE ALSO *ballad, madrigal, pastoral, Petrarchism, psalms.*

planh A funeral lament in Provençal poetry. This specialized type of the *sirventes* typically mourns the loss of a lover, a friend, or a grand personage. Forty or so *planhs* have survived from the years 1137 to 1343. Most of them conventionally bewail the death of a noble, usually the patron or patroness of the poet. These are official poems. The most famous poem of the Italian troubadour Sordello (ca. 1180–1269) was his *planh* "Serventes" on the death of his patron. Ezra Pound borrowed the tone for his "Planh for the Young English King" (1909), which was a translation of a poem written by Bertran de Born on the death of Prince Henry, the "Young King." Pound called the poem "one of the noblest laments or 'planh' in the Provençal" (*The Spirit of Romance*, 1910). W. S. Merwin's "Planh for the Death of Ted Hughes" (1999) imparts the contemporary with a sense of poetic lineage.

SEE ALSO *elegy, lament, sirventes, troubadour.*

poem From the Greek word *poiesis,* meaning "making." A made thing, a verbal construct, an event in language. As Plato explains in the *Symposium* (ca. 385–380 B.C.E.), "All production of things is *poiesis.* Producing poetry stands to the general domain of production as part to the whole." The medieval and Renaissance poets used the word *makers,* as in "courtly makers," as a precise equivalent for *poets,* hence William Dunbar's "Lament for the Makers" (1508). The word *poem* came into English in the sixteenth century and has been with us ever since to denote a form of fabrication, a verbal composition.

Poems are made out of sounds. William Carlos Williams defined the poem as "a small (or large) machine made of words." In "What Is Poetry?" (1933–34), the linguist Roman Jakobson declared, "Poeticity is present when the word is felt as a word and not a mere representation of the object being named or an outburst of emotion, when words and their composition, their meaning, their external and internal form, acquire a weight and value of their own instead of referring indifferently to reality."

The old Irish word *cerd,* meaning "people of the craft," was a designation for artisans, including poets. It is cognate with the Greek *kerdos,* meaning "craft, craftiness." In many oral cultures, poets are considered artisans as well as prophets. "Whatever else it may be," W. H. Auden said, "a poem is a verbal artifact which must be as skillfully and solidly constructed as a table or a motorcycle." The true poem has been crafted into a living entity. There is always something inexplicable in a poem. It is an act beyond paraphrase because what is said is inseparable from the way it is being said. A poem creates an experience in the reader that cannot be reduced to anything else. Perhaps it exists in order to create that aesthetic experience.

SEE ALSO *poetry.*

poète maudit From the French: "accursed poet." A term for the poet as outsider, rejected by bourgeois society, damned. Poets criminally inclined or socially off-kilter, prone to alcohol or drugs, crazy or suicidal, are often labeled *poètes maudits.* Alfred de Vigny coined the term in 1832 in his philosophical narrative *Stello,* in which he argues that poets such as André Chénier (1762–1794) and Thomas Chatterton (1752–1770) come to unhappy ends because they belong to "a race always cursed by the powerful of the earth." Paul Verlaine subsequently took *Les poètes maudits* as the title of his 1884 homage to six symbolist poets: Tristan Corbière, Arthur Rimbaud, Stéphane Mallarmé, Marceline Desbordes-Valmore, Auguste Villiers de l'Isle-Adam, and Pauvre Lélian (an anagram for Paul Verlaine himself). Pierre Seghers redeploys the term in his 1972 anthology, *Poètes maudits d'aujourd'hui* (*The Accursed Poets of Today*). The curse can be a description, a cliché, a mode of praise, or all three at once.

poetic contest The verbal duel is common worldwide. It has been documented in a large number of poetries as a stylized form of male aggression, a model of ritual combat, a release through abuse. It provides a socially acceptable form of rivalry and battle, a forum for insults with a built-in safety valve — humor and exaggeration. It is a competitive venue for those who are not physically strong but enterprising and quick-witted.

The poetic contest has an ancient origin. There are instances in Aristophanes's plays *The Clouds* (423 B.C.E.) and *The Frogs* (405 B.C.E.). The experience of two speakers going back and forth against each other played a crucial role in the development of drama. The Greek rhapsodes contended for prizes at religious festivals. Indeed, the Greeks created contests out of nearly every form of poetry, from wine songs to high tragedy. The Homeric *Hymn to Apollo,* usually dated to the seventh century B.C.E., depicts competitive singing, which is also mentioned in the *Hymns to Aphrodite* (from the same period). Hesiod claimed that he won a prize for performing a song at funeral games in Euboea. Singing competitions in local peasant communities stand behind the literary pastoral, and there are contests of wit in the idylls of Theocritus and the eclogues of Virgil (amoebean verses, "responsive verses"). In antiquity, the memorization of poetry was frequently turned into a contest to enliven festive gatherings. "In pre-romantic, rhetorical culture," Walter Ong declares, "the poet is essentially a contestant."

The first professional competition for Welsh bards, an *eisteddfod* ("session") was held in the twelfth century. The *Sängerkrieg* ("minstrel's contest") or *Wartburgkrieg* ("Wartburg contest") was a legendary competition among the German *Minnesänger* at Thuringia in 1207. The French *débat,* especially popular in the twelfth and thirteenth centuries, sets up a contest, a quarrel or debate. The *tenson* (*tenzone, tencon*) was a type of debate poem developed by the troubadours in the twelfth century. From the twelfth to the seventeenth century, musical and literary societies in northern France competed against each other in poetic contests (*puys*). Among the heirs of the French debate poem are the Brazilian improvised verse dialogues or contests called *desafios* or *pelejas*. The *pregunta-respuesta* was a form of poetic debate in fourteenth- and fifteenth-century Castilian *cancionero* court poetry. One poet asks a question (the *pregunta* or *requesta*) or a series of questions, the other replies in matching form (the *respuesta*). There is verbal dueling in fifteenth-century Spanish plays. In this type of poetic contest, known as *echarse pullas,* as J. P. Wickersham Crawford explained in 1915, "one person wished all sorts of misfortunes, for the most part obscene, upon another, who replied in a similar strain." Rodrigo Caro labeled these contests *darse grita* ("shouting at one another") and traces Hispanic verbal dueling back to Horace, who in the *Epistolae* (*Epistles,* book 2, epistle 1, lines 145–46) speaks of the ritual, invented by the Fescennians, of hurling alternate verses, *opprobria rustica* ("rustic taunts"), at each other (*Días geniales o lúdicos,* ca. 1618).

Hija, or the poetry of invective, was one of the main modes of classical Arabic verse. It was insulting and frequently obscene. Abū al-Faraj al-Isfahānī's *Kitab al-Aghānī* (*Book of Songs,* tenth century) is filled with anecdotes of pre-Islamic and medieval poets dueling and debating. The *Aghānī* refers to the poetry competitions at Sūq ʿUkāz, where the seventh-century female poet al-Kansā gained fame for her elegies for her brothers and dueled with famous male poets. When the judge suggested that she was the best of poets with a uterus, she responded, "And of those with testicles as well!"

The spontaneously composed verbal duel in colloquial Hispano-Arabic dates to the tenth century, which makes it the oldest extant poetry composed in the Hispano-Arabic dialect. In 1161, the poets of the Levantine flocked to Gibraltar for a poetic contest presided over by ʿAbd al-Muʾmin to celebrate his conquest of al-Andalus. In Japan, from 1087 through 1199, approximately two hundred formal poetry competitions were held in the imperial palace as well as in temples and shrines. *Utaawase* is the equivalent Japanese form of the poetry match. A *danjo utaawase* pitted men against women in a tanka contest. The topics were handed out in advance for major competitions such as the Poetry Contest in 600 Rounds (1193) and the Poetry Contest in 1,500 Rounds (1201). The fifteenth- and sixteenth-century Scottish flyting consisted of two bards excoriating each other and the chieftains with whom they were associated. Verbal contests are called *scolding* in Scandinavia.

The West Indian *picong* is a series of sustained insults. Among the hill-dwelling peoples of Nepal, such as the Tamangs, pairs of men and women duel against each other in improvised duets. The risk is great, especially for women, since a woman who loses is sometimes offered in marriage to the victor. Oral poetry duels are still an integral part of rural Palestinian weddings in the Galilee. The individual poetic duel, or "wedding *didong,*" was once the dominant verbal performance form of the Gayo, who live in northern Sumatra, Indonesia. Group poetic combats (*didong klub*) also emerged in the town of Takèngen in the late 1940s; these competitions involved two teams, each consisting of ten to thirty men and boys representing their respective villages.

In the late nineteenth century, folk poets along the Texas-Mexico border competed to improvise ten-verse *décimas,* a tradition still alive in the Canary Islands. The Argentine *payada* was a poetic contest of questions and answers among gauchos. In Panama, poetic duels and competitions take place in formal public settings. In Madagascar, *hain-teny* ("the knowledge of words") is structured as a competitive verbal exchange between two "opponents" on the subject of love. The Chamula of Southern Mexico have a genre of verbal dueling they call "truly frivolous talk." The African American verbal game of playing the dozens continues to thrive in American cities. The poetry contest has been given a sociopolitical slant in contemporary slam poetry. The beat goes on — fiery, social, engaged, competitive.

SEE ALSO *amoebean verses, débat, the dozens, flyting, oral poetry, picong, rhapsode, slam poetry, tenson, utaawase.*

poetic diction   Language employed in a manner that sets poetry apart from other kinds of speech or writing. It involves the vocabulary, the phrasing, and the grammar considered appropriate and inappropriate to poetry at different times. In *Poetic Diction* (1928), Owen Barfield writes, "When words are selected and arranged in such a way that their meaning either arouses, or is obviously intended to arouse, aesthetic imagination, the result may be described as *poetic diction.*"

Aristotle established poetic diction as a subject in the *Poetics* (350 B.C.E.). "Every word is either current, or strange, or metaphorical, or ornamental, or newly-coined, or lengthened, or contracted, or altered," he declared, and he then considered each type of word in turn. His overall concern was "how poetry combines elevation of language with perspicuity." Changes in poetic fashion often have to do with the effectiveness of poetic diction. "The weightiest theoretical legacy which antiquity and the Renaissance passed on to neoclassicism was the ornamental conception of poetic style," Emerson Marks writes. "Till the dawn of Romanticism, writers continued to regard the characteristics of verse as raiment adorning the 'body' of a poet's thought." In *The Life of Dryden* (1779–81), Samuel Johnson argued that before the time of Dryden, there was simply "no poetical diction: no system of words at once refined from the grossness of domestic use and free from the harshness of terms appropriated to particular arts. Words too familiar, or too remote, defeat the purposes of a poet."

In the preface to *Lyrical Ballads* (1802), William Wordsworth argued against the ornate effects of his predecessors and insisted on the essential identity of poetic and nonpoetic language. He argued that poetry should employ "the real language of men in *any situation.*" Wordsworth revolutionized the idea of poetic diction by connecting it to speech. Poetry may be linked to the way that people talk at any given time, but it is framed and marked differently.

poetic justice   A literary device in which virtue is rewarded and vice punished. Thomas Rymer coined the term in *The Tragedies of the Last Age Considered* (1678) to suggest that a work of art should uphold moral principles by rewarding the good and punishing the wicked. It persists as an idea, though it is at odds with reality and was out of fashion by the late seventeenth century.

poetic license   Poetry frees words and disturbs our ordinary usage of language. Sometimes it departs from agreed-upon rules of pronunciation, diction, or syntax, even from common sense. "This poeticall license is a shrewde fellow," George Gascoigne wrote in 1575; "it maketh words longer, shorter, of mo sillables, of fewer, newer, older, truer, falser, and, to conclude, it turkeneth [alters] all things at pleasure." John Dryden (1631–1700) defined poetic license as "the liberty which poets have assumed to themselves, in all ages, of speaking things in verse which are beyond the severity of prose."

poetics   The systematic doctrine or theory of poetry. The term derives from Aristotle's *Poetics* (350 B.C.E.), where he defined it as dealing with "poetry itself and its kinds and the specific power of each." Poetics investigates the distinguishing features of poetry — its branches, its governing principles, its technical resources, the nature of its forms, etc. The study of the nature of poetry has broadened in modern usage to refer to the general theory of literature, of literariness, the sum of features distinguishing literary texts from nonliterary ones. Thus it becomes possible to speak of *The*

Poetics of Space (Gaston Bachelard, 1958), *Structuralist Poetics* (Jonathan Culler, 1975), *The Poetics of Prose* (Tsvetan Todorov, 1971), or *Everyday Life: A Poetics of Vernacular Practices* (Roger Abrahams, 2005). In *Language as Symbolic Action* (1966), Kenneth Burke concludes that the desire behind his poetics was to solve this equation: "poem is to poet as Poetics is to critic." Poetics is his testament to the human love of symbols.

poetry   An inexplicable (though not incomprehensible) event in language; an experience through words. Jorge Luis Borges believed that "poetry is something that cannot be defined without oversimplifying it. It would be like attempting to define the color yellow, love, the fall of leaves in autumn." Even Samuel Johnson maintained that "to circumscribe poetry by a definition will only show the narrowness of the definer."

Poetry is a human fundamental, like music. It predates literacy and precedes prose in all literatures. There has probably never been a culture without it, yet no one knows precisely what it is. The word *poesie* entered the English language in the fourteenth century and begat *poesy* (as in Sir Philip Sidney's "Defence of Poesy," ca. 1582) and *posy*, a motto in verse. *Poetrie* (from the Latin *poetria*) entered fourteenth-century English vocabulary and evolved into *poetry*. The Greek word *poiesis* means "making." A poem is a construction.

Poets (and others) have made many attempts over the centuries to account for this necessary instrument of our humanity:

In his treatise on vernacular poetry, *De vulgari eloquentia,* Dante Alighieri (1265–1321) suggests that around 1300, poetry was typically conceived of as a species of eloquence.

Sir Philip Sidney (1554–1586) said that poetry is "a representing, counterfetting, a figuring foorth: to speak metaphorically: a speaking picture: with this end, to teach and delight."

Ben Jonson (1572–1637) referred to the art of poetry as "the craft of making."

The baroque Jesuit poet Tommaso Ceva (1649–1737) stated, "Poetry is a dream dreamed in the presence of reason."

Samuel Taylor Coleridge (1772–1834) claimed that poetry equals "the *best* words in the best order." He characterized it as "that synthetic and magical power, to which we have exclusively appropriated the name of imagination."

William Wordsworth (1771–1850) famously called poetry "the spontaneous overflow of powerful feelings . . . recollected in tranquility." John Stuart Mill (1806–1873) followed up Wordsworth's emphasis when he wrote that poetry is "feeling confessing itself to itself in moments of solitude."

Percy Bysshe Shelley (1792–1822) joyfully called poetry "the record of the best and happiest moments of the happiest and best minds."

Matthew Arnold (1822–1888) narrowed the definition to "a criticism of life." Ezra Pound (1885–1972) later countered, "Poetry is about as much a 'criticism of life' as red-hot iron is a criticism of fire."

Gerard Manley Hopkins (1844–1889) characterized it as "speech framed . . . to be heard for its own sake and interest even over and above its interest of meaning."

W. B. Yeats (1865–1939) loved Gavin Douglas's 1553 definition of poetry as "pleasance and half wonder."

George Santayana (1863–1952) said that "poetry is speech in which the instrument counts as well as the meaning." But he also thought of it as something beyond "verbal expression," as "that subtle fire and inward light which seems at times to shine through the world and to touch the images in our minds with ineffable beauty."

Wallace Stevens (1879–1955) characterized it as "a revelation of words by means of the words."

Leo Tolstoy (1828–1910) noted in his diary, "Poetry is verse: prose is not verse. Or else poetry is everything with the exception of business documents and school books." The response of Marianne Moore (1887–1972), years later: "nor is it valid / to discriminate against 'business documents and // school books.'" She called poems "imaginary gardens with real toads in them."

Gertrude Stein (1874–1946) decided that "poetry is doing nothing but using losing refusing and pleasing and betraying and caressing nouns."

Robert Frost (1874–1963) said wryly, "Poetry provides the one permissible way of saying one thing and meaning another."

Robert Graves (1895–1985) thought of it as a form of "stored magic," André Breton (1896–1966) as a "room of marvels."

Howard Nemerov (1920–1991) said that poetry is simply "getting something right in language."

Joseph Brodsky (1940–1996) described poetry as "accelerated thinking"; Seamus Heaney (1939–2013) called it "language in orbit."

Poetry seems at core a verbal transaction. In oral form, it establishes a relationship between a speaker and a listener; in written form, a relationship between a writer and a reader. Yet at times that relationship seems to go beyond words. John Keats (1795–1821) felt that "Poetry should . . . strike the Reader as a wording of his own highest thoughts, and appear almost a Remembrance." The Australian poet Les Murray (b. 1938) argues that "poetry exists to provide the poetic experience." That experience is "a temporary possession."

Emily Dickinson (1830–1886) wrote in an 1870 letter, "If I read a book [and] it makes my whole body so cold no fire can ever warm me I know *that* is poetry. If I feel physically as if the top of my head were taken off, I know *that* is poetry. These are the only ways I know it. Is there any other way?"

political poetry Poetry of social concern and conscience. The partisan feeling runs high in the social poetry of engagement. Poets write on both sides of any given war, defend the State or attack it. The Greek writer Strabo came up with the term *stasiotika* ("stasis-poems") for Alcaeus's partisan songs, which are propagandistic poems of civil war and exile. All patriotic and nationalistic poetry is political. Political poetry, ancient and modern, good and bad, frequently responds vehemently to social injustice. The Lamentations of Jeremiah, a series of poems mourning the desolation of Jerusalem and the sufferings of its people after the siege and destruction of the city and the burning of the temple by the Babylonians, is a political poem.

The premise of political poetry is to carry "news" or information crucial to the populace. Political poetry is self-consciously written inside of history and responds to external events. The madness of any country's brutality has often wounded its poets into a political response. Behind the poem in quest of justice, these lines from Shakespeare's *Antony and Cleopatra* (1623) resonate: "our size of sorrow, / Proportion'd to our cause, must be as great / As that which makes it."

There is an ephemeral quality to most political poetry, but a political poem need not be didactic. It can be a poem of testimony and memory. There is a strong tradition in England of political poems, such as Edmund Spenser's *Complaints* (1591) and John Milton's pro-Cromwellian short poems in the 1640s and '50s. Some of John Dryden's greatest poetry was written in response to events, such as his two-part political satire *Absalom and Achitophel* (1681, 1682). William Wordsworth's political poems, such as his sonnet "To Toussaint L'Ouverture" (1803), are among his best, though a few of his late patriotic poems are also among his worst. Percy Bysshe Shelley's *The Mask of Anarchy* (1819), which was "Written on the Occasion of the Massacre at Manchester," is a chilling political poem. During her Italian sojourn, Elizabeth Barrett Browning published two books of political poetry, *Casa Guidi Windows* (1850) and *Poems Before Congress* (1860). The most popular Victorian poet, Alfred, Lord Tennyson, never distinguished between the personal and the political, the private and the public.

Political poetry has often seemed suspect in American literary history, though the poetry of engagement has sustained a strong underground tradition. It runs from Walt Whitman's political poems of the 1850s and John Greenleaf Whittier's *Anti-Slavery Poems* (1832–87), to the leftist poets of the 1930s (Kenneth Fearing, Edwin Rolfe, Muriel Rukeyser). The civil rights movement and the Vietnam War enraged poets, and some of the most inward poets, such as Robert Duncan, Denise Levertov, and Galway Kinnell, wrote some of the best poems against the Vietnam War. Most poetry of the 1940s and '50s shunned politics, but Thomas McGrath ("Ode for the American Dead in Korea," retitled in the early 1970s "Ode for the American Dead in Asia") and Kenneth Rexroth ("A Christmas Note for Geraldine Udell," 1949) bucked the trend. "No true political poetry can be written with propaganda as an aim, to persuade others 'out there' of some atrocity or injustice," Adrienne Rich writes. "*As poetry,* it can come only from the poet's need to identify her relationship to atrocities and injustice, the sources of her pain, fear, and anger, the meaning of her resistance."

SEE ALSO *didactic poetry, protest poetry.*

polyrhythmic From the Greek: "of many rhythms." Any poem that combines two or more rhythmic patterns. Over the centuries poets have energized their poems by varying and crossing rhythms, by bringing in different patterned energies. Léopold Sédar Senghor states that polyrhythms establish "unity within diversity." Jazz poetry is just one of the kinds of cross, or polyrhythmic, poetry. According to Adrienne Rich, "What poetry is made of is so old, so familiar, that it's easy to forget that it's not just the words, but polyrhythmic sounds, speech in its first endeavor (every poem breaks a silence that had to be overcome), prismatic meanings lit by each others' light, each others' shadows."

SEE ALSO *counterpoint, free verse, jazz poetry, ode.*

postmodernism   Postmodernism is a reaction to modernism, a reappraisal. This wide-ranging term applies to poetry and fiction, art and architecture, literary and cultural criticism, philosophy, and other fields. *The Oxford English Dictionary* calls it "a style and concept in the arts characterized by distrust of theories and ideologies and by the drawing of attention to conventions." Postmodernism follows many of the ideas of modernism, but takes a more ironic attitude toward them. It rejects the boundaries between high and low forms of art, shows a decided preference for pastiche, and combines genres and tropes from different historical periods. The postmodernist position: Language is the actual author of any work of art; all narratives can be taken apart and deconstructed; what seems determined by nature is actually determined by culture. Reality is a construction; everything is interpreted. Postmodernism is ultimately a skeptical position that denies the existence of all ultimate principles and truths.

Randall Jarrell was perhaps the first American poet to speak of postmodernity when he characterized Robert Lowell's poetry in 1946 as "post- or anti-modernist." Around the same time, the British historian Arnold Toynbee declared that there was a new "Post-Modern" age of Western history. This was possibly the last phase of Western history, Toynbee suggested. As Matei Călinescu puts it, "Such an optimistic-apocalyptic interpretation of the term postmodern made it fit to receive a prominent place in the revolutionary rhetoric of the 1960s."

In midcentury American poetry, the term *postmodernism* was taken up by innovative American poets. *Postmodernism* is an umbrella term that refers to such groups as the Black Mountain poets (Charles Olson, Robert Duncan, Robert Creeley, Denise Levertov), the Beats (Allen Ginsberg, Jack Kerouac,

Lawrence Ferlinghetti, Gregory Corso), the San Francisco renaissance poets (Kenneth Rexroth, William Everson, Gary Snyder, Jack Spicer, Robin Blaser), and the New York school (Frank O'Hara, John Ashbery, Kenneth Koch, James Schuyler). Marjorie Perloff considers indeterminacy or undecidability the chief feature of postmodern work. Umberto Eco points out that postmodernism "consists of recognizing that the past, since it cannot really be destroyed, because its destruction leads to silence, must be revisited: but with irony, not innocently."

SEE ALSO *avant-garde, fragment, modernism.*

poulter's measure   Rhyming couplets that alternate iambic hexameter (twelve-syllable) and iambic heptameter (fourteen-syllable) lines. George Gascoigne coined the term *poulter's measure* based on the poultryman's traditional practice of giving twelve eggs for the first dozen and fourteen for the second (*Certain Notes of Instruction*, 1575). The meter was frequently used by Wyatt (1503–1542), Surrey (1517–1547), and Sidney (1554–1586), among others, but seldom thereafter. It has seemed monotonous and heavy to later practitioners. But if you divide the six-beat and seven-beat couplets into rhyming iambic quatrains, you get the "short meter" or "common time" of the English hymns.

SEE ALSO *hymn, meter, short meter.*

praise poems   The tradition of praise-singing is cross-cultural. The praise poem is one of the most developed poetic genres in the oral poetry of Oceania and especially of Africa, where it has a long history and goes by a variety of overlapping terms, many linked to the word *jamu.* For the Soninké-speaking people, one meaning of *jamu* is "praise song"; in Barnana it is a verb meaning "to praise someone, to express recognition." The Fulbe variant is *jammude.* The Hausa-speaking people use the terms *kirari* ("praise-epithets") and *take* ("short vocal or drummed praises"). The Yoruba have a form of praise poetry called *oríkì.* The Zulu term for praise poems is *izibongo,* the Basurto is *lithoko,* and the Kirundi is *amazina,* which literally means "names."

The praise poem is a way of naming. The format of praising—the art of assemblage—also implies that everything is interconnected. There are praise poems for a wide variety of things (animals, clans, hunters, spirits, etc.), but the most significant are the poems directly addressed to people, living or dead, who are celebrated and praised. The praise poem in the second person is part epic, part ode, and it exalts power when it is addressed to the king or chief. It solidifies authority, unlike the protest poem, which questions it.

SEE ALSO *encomium, epithet, griot, oríki, panegyric.*

proem From the Greek: "prelude." A proem is a preface or preamble; an introductory passage, either in poetry or prose, to a longer work. One fine early example is the 104-line proem to Hesiod's *Theogony* (late eighth to early seventh century B.C.E.). Hesiod's proem praises the Muses — it is sometimes called "Hymn to the Muses" — but it also enables him to praise and name himself. The poet can commence by using "I" or the royal "we," a liberty not allowed in the epic proper. The proem takes on a different function outside the Greek epic tradition. In his proem to *The Prelude* (1805, 1850), Wordsworth uses the prefatory lines to describe the origins of the work itself; in his "Proem" to *In Memoriam* (1849), Tennyson summarizes his feelings about the mysteries of grief. The proem has seldom been used in modern poetry, though Hart Crane's "Proem: To Brooklyn Bridge" serves as a prelude to *The Bridge* (1930).

SEE ALSO *invocation.*

projective verse Charles Olson coined this term for an organic composition process, a type of free verse that he also called "composition by field." His essay "Projective Verse" (1950) treated the composition of poetry as a kinetic process, "a high-energy construct." He opposed projective verse to so-called closed or nonprojective verse ("inherited line, stanza, over-all form"), praised immediacy and spontaneity, emphasized the importance of breath in the creative process, argued that "one perception must immediately and directly lead to a further perception," and quoted Robert Creeley to the effect that "form is never more than an extension of content." Projective verse emphasizes process over product and inspires a quick, high-octane, idiomatic poetry.

SEE ALSO *free verse.*

prose poem A composition printed as prose that names itself poetry. The prose poem takes advantage of its hybrid nature — it avails itself of the elements of prose (what Dryden called "the other harmony of prose") while foregrounding the devices of poetry. The French writer Aloysius Bertrand established the prose poem as a minor genre in *Gaspard de la nuit* (1842), a book that influenced Baudelaire's *Petits poèmes en prose* (1869). Baudelaire used prose poems to rebel against the straitjacket of classical French versification. He dreamed of creating "a poetic prose, musical without rhyme or rhythm, supple and jerky enough to adapt to the lyric movements of the soul, to the undulations of reverie, to the somersaults of conscience." Baudelaire's prose poems — along with Rimbaud's *Les illuminations* (1886) and Mallarmé's *Divagations* (1897) — created a mixed musical form widely practiced in the twentieth century. "The prose poem is the result of two contradictory impulses, prose and poetry, and therefore cannot exist," Charles Simic explains. "This is the sole instance we have of squaring the circle."

SEE ALSO *alexandrine, free verse, vers libre.*

prosody Anglicized from the Latin word *prosodia,* meaning "accent of a syllable," which derives from the Greek word *prosōidia,* "song sung to instrumental music." Prosody is the systematic art or study of versification — its notation, principles, and theory. It especially refers to aspects of musicality, such as rhythm and sound (alliteration, assonance, euphony, onomatopoeia, and so forth), but can also include the study of structure and rhetoric. Linguistic prosody is the study of these elements as they appear in ordinary language. Literary prosody, which is also known as metrics, focuses on their use in the literary arts.

SEE ALSO *meter, scansion, verse, versification.*

protest poetry Poetry of dissent and social criticism. It protests the status quo and tries to undermine established values and ideals. The protest poet is a rebellious citizen, speaking out, expressing disapproval of a political policy or social action. Protest poetry, the most earnest of genres, is timely, oppositional, reactive, urgent. It is an activist type of political poetry born from outrage and linked to social action. It turns poetry into a medium for polemics.

The reprehensible policy of apartheid in South Africa, which legalized racism, also stimulated a powerful tradition of protest poetry. The Zulu poet Herbert I. E. Dhlomo's long poem *Valley of a Thousand Hills* (1941) is the most extended work of South African protest poetry. The New Black poetry of the 1970s, or Soweto poetry, was a protest poetry of black consciousness. In the United States, a strong tradition of African American poetry protests racism. It extends from the Harlem Renaissance to the Black Arts movement.

Most antiwar poetry is protest poetry. The antiwar poetry of Wilfred Owen (1893–1918) and Siegfried Sassoon (1886–1967), both of them soldiers, protested the technological horrors of modern warfare. The Spanish Civil War generated both local and global protest poetry. The Vietnam War galvanized protest poetry, written by such poets as Robert Lowell, Allen Ginsberg, Adrienne Rich, and Robert Bly. Much of the feminist poetry of the 1960s and '70s is protest poetry. "A patriot is not a weapon," Adrienne Rich writes in her long poem *An Atlas of the Difficult World* (1981). "A patriot is one who wrestles for the soul of her country / as she wrestles for her own being." Sam Hamill's anthology *Poets Against the War* (2003) was a hastily gathered book of protest poems against the war in Iraq.

The strength of protest poetry is its sense of furious immediacy. Most of these politically motivated poems, often made in response to a specific outrage, don't outlive their historical moment.

SEE ALSO *didactic poetry.*

prothalamion, see *epithalamium.*

proverb A terse didactic statement that embodies a general truth, the proverb is short and pithy, akin to the aphorism and the maxim, and draws attention to itself as a formal artistic entity. Folk and traditional proverbs are well-known expressions, usually the length of a simple sentence, that function in conversation. They are part of daily discourse and also operate in educational situations and judicial proceedings. Proverbs take personal circumstances and embody them in impersonal form. Their meanings seem fixed, but they depend on context; the texts are adapted to different situations.

Proverbs are normative, consensual. The proverb simplifies a problem by naming and solving it with a traditional solution.

The linguist Roman Jakobson called the proverb "the largest coded unit occurring in our speech and at the same time the shortest poetic composition." Proverbs frequently employ traditional devices of poetry, such as balanced phrasing ("Out of sight, out of mind") and binary construction ("A stitch in time / saves nine"), rhyme ("Haste makes waste"), alliteration ("Live and learn"), and repetition ("Live and let live"). They often apply a metaphor to a situation ("Don't change horses in midstream"). By definition, proverbs must be memorable. Expressions become proverbial through repeated use. In "Literature as Equipment for Living" (1938), Kenneth Burke pointed out that "social structures give rise to 'type' situations . . . many proverbs seek to chart, in more or less homey and picturesque ways, these 'type' situations." Through proverbs, literature provides fundamental "equipment for living." Burke extended the analysis of proverbs to the whole field of literature in *Philosophy of Literary Forms: Studies in Symbolic Action* (1941): "Could the most complex and sophisticated works of art legitimately be considered somewhat as 'proverbs writ large'?"

The humble proverb has an ancient literary provenance. Proverbs are among the oldest works in Sanskrit. They animated early Germanic, Scandinavian, and especially Hebrew literature, as in the Book of Proverbs, a form of wisdom literature whose principle is encapsulated in the following example: "Treasures of wickedness profit nothing: / but righteousness delivereth from death" (10:2).

The binary proverb is the literary foundation of wisdom poetry. It consists of two units brought together in a type of parallelism:

Pride goeth before destruction,
    and an haughty spirit before a fall. (16:18)

A soft answer turneth away wrath:
    but grievous words stir up anger. (15:1)

Proverbs entered European literature through the Bible, the church fathers, and classical Greek writers such as Aristophanes (ca. 450–ca. 388 B.C.E.), Plautus (ca. 254–184 B.C.E.), and Lucian (ca. 125–after 180). Erasmus's enormously popular *Adagia* (1500) was crucial in spreading classical proverbs into vernacular European languages. John Heywood's *A Dialogue contening . . . all the proverbs in the English tongue* (1546) was the first English collection. An intermittent tradition of creating poems and songs from proverbs extends from François Villon's "Ballade des proverbes" (1458) to works by Gilbert and Sullivan, such as the *Pinafore* duet (1878), which includes sixteen identifiable proverbs. The proverb contributed to the development of the epigram, a short occasional verse with a moral point. Proverbs are employed in face-to-face situations, and the literary epigram compensates by pointing to the situation, either as a title or within the poem itself. The proverb also had a direct influence on the heroic couplet, which in turn provided proverbs that became part of conventional wisdom, such as Alexander Pope's "To err is human, to forgive divine." Proverbs are embedded in poems by writers from Geoffrey Chaucer, especially in *Troilus and Criseyde* (ca. 1380s), to Carl Sandburg ("Good Morning, America") and Robert Frost ("Good fences make good neighbors"). William Blake's provocative "Proverbs of Hell" (1790–93) teach us that "Exuberance is Beauty."

SEE ALSO *epigram, gnome, parallelism, riddle.*

psalm   A sacred song or hymn. The term *psalm* generally refers to the Hebrew poems in the biblical Book of Psalms, which *The Oxford Companion to Music* (2002) calls "the oldest and the greatest book of songs now in use anywhere in the world." The psalms have been traditionally ascribed to King David, but this David seems to be a composite author ensuring the formal integrity of poems composed over a period of more than five hundred years. The earliest manuscripts date from the ninth century B.C.E. in Hebrew, from the fourth century B.C.E. in Latin, and from the second century B.C.E. in Greek, when the Book of Psalms, spliced together from at least four previous collections, took final form. The Hebrew heading of the complete psalter (collection of psalms) found in several early manuscripts is a word meaning "the book of praises," and the psalms are ancient liturgical praise poems with terrific performative power.

> MAKE a joyful noise unto the LORD, all ye lands.
> Serve the LORD with gladness: come before his presence with singing.

Know ye that the LORD he *is* God: *it is* he *that* hath made us, and not we
ourselves; *we are* his people, and the sheep of his pasture. (Psalm 100:1–3)

The psalms have been a sourcebook for Western poets. As Donald Davie
writes in *The Psalms in English* (1966), "Through four centuries there is
hardly a poet of even modest ambition who does not feel the need to try his
hand at paraphrasing some part of Scripture, most often the psalms." One
legacy of the psalms is what Coburn Freer calls "joyful religious play."

All people that on earth do dwell,
　　Sing to the Lord with cheerful voice:
Him serve with mirth, his praise forth tell,
　　Come ye before him, and rejoice.
(a rendering of Psalm 100, by William Kethe, 1561)

pun　A form of wordplay, the pun is a figure of speech that depends upon
words that have a similar sound or spelling yet disparate meanings. Joseph
Addison called the pun "A Sound, and nothing but a Sound." Charles Lamb
pointed out that a pun "is a pistol let off at the ear." It has, he said, "an ear-kiss-
ing smack with it." Since the early eighteenth century, the pun has sometimes
been condescended to as a "low species of wit" (Noah Webster), but the de-
vice has appeared in all literatures and seems to be as old as language itself. A
good pun releases the multiple energies in words. The punning used as a lit-
erary device in the Hebrew Bible is called *paronomasia*.

The homographic pun consists of words that are spelled the same but
have different meanings. In *Romeo and Juliet* (1597), the dying Mercutio
declares, "Ask for me to-morrow, you shall find me a grave man." He thus
combines two meanings of the word *grave* ("somber or reflective" and "a
place of burial"). A homophonic pun consists of words that sound alike but
have different meanings. In this stanza from "A Hymn to God the Father"
(1633), John Donne puns both on his own name (done, Donne) and on
the word *Son* (meaning both "Christ" and "the sun"):

I have a sin of fear, that when I have spun
　　My last thread, I shall perish on the shore;
Swear by Thyself that at my death Thy Son

Shall shine as he shines now, and heretofore;
 And, having done that, Thou hast done,
  I have no more.

pyrrhic From the Greek: "war dance." Also called *dibrach*. A metrical foot of two unstressed beats (u u), the pyrrhic is the shortest foot in classical poetry. But in English, an accentual-syllabic language, the pyrrhic is a hypothetical metrical unit. The unstressed syllables are usually treated as a substitution or associated with adjacent feet. In "The Rationale of Verse" (1848), Edgar Allan Poe contemptuously dismissed the pyrrhic in English: "Its existence in either ancient or modern rhythm is purely chimerical, and the insisting on so perplexing a nonentity as a foot of *two short* syllables, affords, perhaps, the best evidence of the gross irrationality and subservience to authority which characterize our Prosody."

SEE ALSO *foot, meter.*

Q

qasida From the Arabic: "to aim for, to intend." The term *qasida* was at times employed in early Arabic poetry for any poem, though more commonly for a poem with a minimum length — sometimes ten, sometimes sixty, sometimes one hundred or more lines, depending on the particular era and place. It began as a form of oral poetry, an ode with varied themes (eulogy, panegyric, satire), some of which was improvised, some inherited. The meters vary. The poem establishes a rhyme word at the end of the first hemistich (half-line). This becomes the single end-rhyme that carries through the entire composition. The earliest specimens date to the fifth century. It was a primary genre of pre-Islamic Bedouin poetry and continues to be crucial to Bedouin poetry. It was also employed by Persian, Turkish, and Urdu poets.

In the ninth century, the Arabic writer Ibn Qutaybah (d. 889) codified a tripartite structure for the *qasida* (in his *Book of Poetry and Poets*), which scholars divide into "remembrance poems," "message poems," and "laudatory poems." The medieval *qasida* begins with a prelude, usually erotic and nostalgic — the poet rediscovering a place and recalling his lost beloved (*nasib*). It then moves on to recount various journeys (*rahil*) and concludes with a summary, the poet praising himself, his patron, or his tribe (*fakhr*).

The *qasida* was traditionally revered as the highest form of poetry. Poets with a classical bent maintained it until the nineteenth century, when it began to lose its luster. The first Egyptian neoclassical poet, Mahmūd Sāmī al-Bārūdī (1839–1904), started the trend of the nineteenth- and twentieth-century traditional *qasida,* which conforms to the conventions established by classical Arabic poets and critics. This became known as the school of al-Bārūdī. The *qasida* form retains its advocates, but the pre-Islamic *qasidas* continue to shine.

quantity, see "quantitative meter" in *meter.*

quarto, see *folio.*

quatorzain From the French word *quatorze,* "fourteen." The quatorzain is a fourteen-line poem that deviates from the patterns of a sonnet. It has the feeling of a sonnet but eschews the ruling structure, usually by avoiding or missing the turn, or volta. The quatorzain especially flourished during the Elizabethan era. Spenser first translated the French poet Joachin du Bellay into quatorzains in blank verse ("The Visions of Bellay," 1591). Sir Thomas Wyatt wrote a quatorzain in octosyllabics, which was otherwise a sonnet, a form mimicked by Shakespeare in "Sonnet 20." Sidney wrote quatorzains in alexandrines, the twelve-syllable line of French poetry (*Astrophil and Stella,* sonnets 1, 76, 77, 102). Sir Walter Raleigh's "A Vision upon the Fairy Queen" (1590) is an expansive quatorzain of seven poulter's measures.

Thomas Campion railed against the fourteen-line poem in his polemic against rhymed verse, *Observations in the Arte of English Poesy* (1602): "in Quatorzens, methinks, the poet handles his subject as tyrannically as *Procustes* the thiefe his prisoners, whom, when he had taken, he used to cast upon a bed, which if they were too short to fill, he would stretch them longer, if too long, he would cut them shorter." He was not a sonneteer and considered fourteen lines too long to make a simple point and too short to develop an argument or tell a story. The history of the sonnet suggests otherwise. The term *quatorzain* now sounds old-fashioned, and most critics refer to most fourteen-line poems as sonnets.

SEE ALSO *poulter's measure, sonnet.*

quatrain A four-line stanza. The quatrain—used as a unit of composition in longer poems and as a complete utterance unto itself—is probably the most common stanzaic form in the world. It has the power of heavy stone, sturdy buildings, and rooted trees, the adaptability of workers everywhere. It has great antiquity and travels well between languages and countries. Thus it is the staple of the English ballad and the Latin hymn, the Malay *pantun,* the Russian *chastushka.* It exists in a variety of formal variations. One thinks of Alcaics and Sapphics (named after two of the greatest early Greek lyric poets), of the heroic quatrain (also known as the elegiac stanza and Hammond's meter because it is used in Thomas Gray's "Elegy Written in a Country Churchyard," 1751, and James Hammond's *Love Elegies,* 1732), of the In Memoriam stanza (so called for its adept use in Tennyson's *In Memoriam,* 1849), and the Omar Khayyám quatrain or rubaiyat stanza (from Edward FitzGerald's loose adaptation of the Persian original).

Each form of the quatrain has its own way of treating the stanza as a solid block of meaning, a rectangular place of indwelling. Here is a famous anonymous poem that was found in an early sixteenth-century manuscript:

> Western wind, when wilt thou blow,
>> That the small rain down can rain?
> Christ, if my love were in my arms
>> And I in my bed again!

SEE ALSO *Alcaic, ballad, heroic quatrain, hymn, In Memoriam stanza, pantoum, rubaiyat stanza, Sapphic stanza, stanza.*

quintain, see *quintet.*

quintet   A stanza of five lines. Also called a quintain, it appears in various forms, from the clever English limerick (which rhymes *aabba* and thus relies on a principle of return) and the classical Japanese tanka (each line contains a set number of syllables: 5, 7, 5, 7, 7). A mask of insanity energizes the conventional "mad song," as in this anonymous example from a sixteenth-century "Tom o' Bedlam" song:

> I know more than Apollo,
>> For, oft when he lies sleeping,
>>> I behold the stars
>>> At bloody wars
> And the wounded welkin weeping.

There seems to be something a little beyond reason and emotionally excessive in punching past the symmetrical quatrain. Thus the possibilities of five unfold: Edmund Waller joins a three-line stanza to a couplet (*ababb*) in "Song: Go, lovely Rose" (1645); Sir Philip Sidney employs the Sicilian quintet (an iambic pentameter stanza that rhymes *ababa*) in "Eleventh Song" (1591); Sir Thomas Wyatt utilizes an interlocking tetrameter pattern (*aabab*) in "The Lover Complaineth the Unkindness of His Love" (1557), the last stanza of which concludes,

> Now cease, my lute, this is the last
> Labour that thou and I shall waste,
> And ended is that we begun.
> Now is this song both sung and past,
> My lute, be still, for I have done.

SEE ALSO *cinquain, limerick, quatrain, stanza, tanka.*

R

rasa   This multidimensional Sanskrit word may mean "sap," "essence," "juice," "semen," "nectar," "intoxicating drink of Soma," "taste," "flavor," "mystic ecstasy." In the Rig-Veda (1700–1100 B.C.E.), it meant the ecstasy-producing taste of a drink. *Rasa* is the most important term in Sanskrit poetics. The legendary priest and theorist Bharata defined it as "a realization of one's own consciousness as colored by emotions" in the Sanskrit treatise *Nātyaśāstra*, which consists of six thousand *sutras* ("verse stanzas") and loosely translates as *A Manual of Dramatic Arts* (second century B.C.E.). The term *rasa* was first formulated for drama, but soon adapted to poetry. As René Daumal explains in *Rasa, or Knowledge of the Self* (1982), *rasa* "is neither an object, nor an emotion, nor a concept; it is an immediate experience, a gestation of life, a pure joy, which relishes its own essence as it communes with the 'other'—the actor or poet." *Rasa* can transport one to a transcendental level, a merging with the absolute. There is no Western equivalent for this widely discussed and debated Sanskrit term.

SEE ALSO *the sublime, sutra.*

refrain   A phrase, a line, or a group of lines recurring at intervals in a poem, often at the ends of stanzas. A refrain can be as short as a single word; it can appear irregularly or as a partial rather than a complete repetition (then it tends to be called a repetend); it can be as long as an entire stanza (then it is called a burden). The refrain is a universal device of archaic and tribal poetries. Reiterated words and phrases may stand at the origin of poetic practice. The refrain functionally accompanies communal labor, dance, and song (it is called a chorus because it allows everyone to join in) and perhaps evokes its distant ancestry in collective life. Refrains can be found in *The Egyptian*

Book of the Dead, some of which dates to 3000 B.C.E., in the Hebrew Bible, in Greek and Latin poetry, in Provençal and Renaissance verse, in English and Scottish ballads.

The refrain can build and accrue meaning, whether by exact repetitions that change meaning in each new context ("nevermore" in Poe's "The Raven," 1845) or by undergoing slight modulations in a process called incremental repetition (as in Trumbull Stickney's poem "Mnemosyne," 1902). As John Hollander puts it, in *Melodious Guile* (1990), "Refrains are, and have, memories — of their prior strophes or stretches of text, of their own preoccurrences, and of their own genealogies in earlier texts as well." Refrains are haunted by circularity, by turnings and recurrences.

SEE ALSO *burden, chorus, incremental repetition, work song.*

renga From the Japanese: "linked poem." This verse form, a collaborative venture, originated in Japan as a party game around a thousand years ago. Poets took turns composing alternate three-line and two-line stanzas. Each stanza links to the one before it. The *renga,* which follows the tanka's prescribed thirty-one syllables (5–7–5, 7–7), enabled poets to test their skills at creating images and linking dissimilar elements. The *hokku,* or opening verse of a *renga* sequence, consisted of seventeen syllables and included a season word. It was eventually singled out, especially during the late Edo period (1600–1868), and appreciated for its own beauty. Thus, the seventeen-syllable haiku (5, 7, 5) originated in the *renga.*

Renga started as a frivolous kind of poetry (an alternative to the rigors of creating tanka), but later evolved into playful (*mushin*) and serious (*ushin*) forms. One hundred stanzas was the standard length, though Matsuo Bashō (1644–1694) preferred a thirty-six-verse form that he called a *kasen,* a word that previously had referred to the thirty-six immortal poets of Japan. A fifty-link *renga* is called a *gojuin.* The traditional *renga* had highly elaborated rules of progression and association. The team leader, usually the honored guest, would write an opening verse (a *hokku*), which the host would follow with a *wakiku* ("accompanying verse") consisting of two phrases with seven syllables in each. This was followed by a third poet's three-phrase, seventeen-syllable verse, then by a fourth poet's two-phrase, fourteen-syllable verse, and so forth until the sequence reached its final thirty-sixth, or one-hundredth verse. The last stanza was called the "completing verse" (*ageku*), which summarized the work by referring back to the opening stanza.

The *haikai de renga* or *haikai* (literally "playful style") was a lighthearted kind of linked poetry that emerged from the traditional *renga* and gradually included people of all classes. The *haikai* democratized Japanese poetry. Bashō was the first poet to transform the *haikai* from an entertaining game into a serious poetic form.

SEE ALSO *haikai, haiku, tanka.*

repetition   The use of the same term several times. "Repetition in word and phrase and in idea is the very essence of poetry," Theodore Roethke writes in "Some Remarks on Rhythm" (1960). It is one of the most marked features of all poetry, oral and written. Repetition, as in rhyme, is a strong mnemonic device. Oral poets especially use it for remembering structures. The incantatory magic of poetry — think of spells and chants, of children's rhymes and lullabies — has something to do with recurrence, with things coming back to us in time, sometimes in the same way, sometimes differently. Repetition is the primary way of creating a pattern through rhythm. Meaning accrues through repetition. One of the deep fundamentals of poetry is the recurrence of sounds, syllables, words, phrases, lines, and stanzas. Repetition creates expectations, which can be fulfilled or frustrated. It can create a sense of boredom and complacency, but it can also incite enchantment and inspire bliss.

Many of the sound devices of poetry (alliteration, assonance, consonance) depend on recurrence. Metrical patterns are established by recurrences, and so are poetic forms (the canzone, the sestina), some with repetends and refrains. The repeating structure of the catalog is one of the Hebrew Bible's legacies to later poets, and some of the key devices of free verse (anaphora, parallelism) are structures of repetition. This glossary contains a wide repertoire of poetic modes of repetition in poetries around the world. One could be forgiven for thinking that our brains are hardwired for repetition. Peter Sacks writes, in *The English Elegy* (1987), "Repetition creates a sense of continuity, of an unbroken pattern such as one may oppose to the extreme discontinuity of death."

SEE ALSO *alliteration, assonance, catalog poem, consonance, incantation, incremental repetition, litany, meter, parallelism, refrain, rhythm.*

reverdie From the Old French: "regreening." A dance poem that celebrates the arrival of spring. The type originated in troubadour ballads of the Middle Ages, in which spring is often symbolized as a beautiful woman, as in other troubadour lyrics. The Middle English song "Sumer is icumen in, / Lhude sing cuccu!" is a *reverdie.* William Carlos Williams's poem "Spring and All" (1923) inherits and inverts the tradition of the *reverdie.* Set in New Jersey in March, it enacts the difficult struggle of everything to get born, to "enter the new world naked."

SEE ALSO *aisling, troubadour.*

rhapsode (or **rhapsodist**), **rhapsody** From the Greek: "stitch song." In ancient Greece a rhapsode was an itinerant minstrel who composed and recited epic poetry aloud, orally "stitching together" various strands of heroic material. Some was memorized, some improvised by these professional performers. The Homëridai (literally "children of Homer") were a group of rhapsodists who traced themselves back to an ancestor called Homëros. Rhapsodes competed at religious festivals, and Plato's dialogue *Ion* (ca. 399–ca. 387 B.C.E.) concerns a formal competition among rhapsodes. In ancient Mesopotamia, Sumerian myths and epics were probably recited by rhapsodes, who were called *nar* and played the lyre, *zag-mí,* which developed into a term for praise.

A rhapsody originally referred to the section of epic literature sung by a rhapsode, but later it came to mean an intensely emotional literary work, an ecstatic poetic utterance, as in Sir William Watson's "Hymn to the Sea" (1895):

> While, with throes, with raptures, with loosing of bonds, with unsealings,
> Arrowy pangs of delight, piercing the core of the world,
> Tremors and coy unfoldings, reluctances, sweet agitations,
> Youth, irrepressibly fair, wakes like a wondering rose.

SEE ALSO *aoidos, epic, minstrel, poetic contest.*

rhetoric   The art of speaking well or "the art of discourse." Plato refers to rhetoric as "the art or science [*technē*] of speech." Rhetoric has meant two things since the ancients: ornamental speech (the study of tropes and figures) and persuasive speech (the study of argumentation, eloquence in action). One frequently bleeds into the other, and rhetoric now generally refers to the technique of persuading an audience through the artful use of language. The words *rhetoric, oratory,* and *eloquence* all derive from the same root, meaning "to speak." The sophist Gorgias of Leontini (ca. 483–ca. 376 B.C.E.), the first great rhetorician, said, "I hold all poetry to be speech with metre, and that is how I use the word. Those who hear poetry feel the shudders of fear, the tears of pity, the longings of grief." The scholar Ernst Robert Curtius explains that "rhetoric signifies 'the craft of speech'; hence, according to its basic meaning, it teaches how to construct a discourse artistically. In the course of time, this seminal idea became a science, an art, an ideal of life, and indeed a pillar of antique culture."

Rhetoric was recognized in literature long before it was codified as an art in its own right. In antiquity Homer earned the epithet "the father of rhetoric." Rhetoric was first established as an art because of its practical utility in civic life. As Plato has Gorgias say, in the dialogue of that name, "[Rhetoric] is in truth the greatest boon, for it brings freedom to mankind in general and to each man dominion over others in his own country ... I mean the power to convince by your words the judges in court, the senators in Council, the people in the Assembly, or in any other gathering of a citizen body." A powerful orator, Gorgias appropriated for prose the symmetries of poetry, which became known as the Gorgianic figures, some of the first staples of rhetoric: antithesis ("setting opposite," a counter proposition, the juxtaposition of contrasting words or ideas), isocolon and parison ("equal list," a sequence of clauses or sentences of identical length), and homoeoteleuton (several words or utterances ending in a similar fashion). Plato shows a great animus toward rhetoric in his dialogue *Gorgias* (ca. 399–387 B.C.E.), in which Socrates argues against the moral relativism of rhetoric, which has no subject matter of its own and can be manipulated for evil ends. In his treatise *Rhetoric* (ca. 335–330 B.C.E.), Aristotle defines rhetoric as "the faculty of discovering all the available means of persuasion in any given situation" and counters Plato's arguments, establishing the universal scope of rhetoric as a tool:

And if it be objected that one who uses such power of speech unjustly might do great harm, *that* is a charge which may be made in common against all good things except virtue, and above all against all things that are most useful, as strength, health, wealth, generalship. A man can confer the greatest of benefits by a right use of these, and inflict the greatest of injuries by using them wrongly.

Aristotle also identified persuasion as a characteristic of rhetoric and imitation as a characteristic of poetry. Since Aristotle, rhetoric has been intertwined with poetics. Aristotle's treatise was followed by a long string of rhetorical textbooks in Greek and Latin, which focused on the means and devices that orators used to persuade audiences to think or act in certain ways. Cicero sharpened the precepts of rhetoric in seven Latin treatises, especially *De oratore* (55 B.C.E.) and *Orator* (46 B.C.E.), in which he argues that both oratory and poetry depend on the same five parts: *inventio* (invention), *dispositio* (arrangement), *elocutio* (style), *memoria* (memory), and *actio* (delivery); Quintilian's *Institutio oratorio* (ca. 95) refashioned the subject of rhetoric into a humanistic recognition of the importance of literature to life: "The love of literature and the reading of the poets are not confined to school days, but end only with life itself." In his first-century treatise *On the Sublime*, Longinus demonstrated how rhetoric served as a method of transport to deliver sublimity in poetry.

Curtius identifies Ovid (43 B.C.E.–18 C.E.) as the poet who first brought the principles of rhetoric into the service of a written poetry that revels in sound and sense. Horace's notion, in his *Ars poetica* (first century B.C.E.), that poetry should instruct or delight, or preferably both, opened the gateway to rhetorical criticism, which studies the means through which a work achieves its effect upon a listener or reader. George Puttenham applied rhetoric to the consideration of English poetry in *The Arte of English Poesie* (1589), which takes 107 figures adapted from classical sources and divides them into three categories, according to their appeal: the auricular (to the ear), the sensable (to the mind), and the sententious (to the mind and ear). Puttenham's telling descriptions, examples, and nicknames for the figures have their own pleasurable rhetoric: eliminate conjunctions (*I saw it, I said it, I will swear it*) and you have "*Asyndeton,* or the Loose Language"; put them in (*And I saw it, and I say it and I / Swear* *it to be true*) and you have "*Polysendeton,* or the Couple Clause"; deliberately understate a case and treat the more dignified in terms of the less dignified (*A great mountaine as bigge as a molehill, / A heavy burthen, perdy, as a pound of feathers*) and you have "*Meiosis,* or the Disabler"; deliberately overstate and exaggerate a case (*What should I go about to recite your Maiestees innumerable vertues, euen as much as I took vpon me to number the stares of the sky, or to tell the sands of the sea*) and you have "*Hiperbole,* or the Ouer reacher, otherwise called the loud lyer.*"

There is no speech or poetry without a rhetorical dimension, and yet ever since the Renaissance the relationship between poetry and rhetoric has been conflicted. Didactic poetry is intentionally rhetorical, but what about non-didactic poetry? Many of the Romantic objections to rhetoric are actually objections to a particular kind of rhetoric, to oratory and didactic literature. Rhetoric depends on the relationship established between (or among) the speaker, the oral text, and the audience, or the writer, the written text, and the reader. The relationship changes according to genre. An oral poet is not an orator but a poet. The speaker in a lyric bears a different relationship to the audience than the narrator of either an oral or a written epic, who in turn stands in a different relationship to a live audience than the actors who portray characters in a play, who speak differently than the characters in a short story or novel. There is a difference between the two primary senses of rhetoric as (1) didactic persuasive language, which can have negative connotations, and (2) the means of communicating anything, which is neutral. Every poet uses a sort of rhetoric to communicate — the relationship between the poet and reader always includes some sort of persuasion, even by means of ambiguity and open-endedness. Rhetorical criticism inevitably addresses the similarities and differences between poetry, a noninstrumental art, and rhetoric, a practical one. Poets themselves have frequently divided on the usefulness of rhetoric in thinking about poetry. On one hand, the young Wallace Stevens wrote in a journal, "The best poetry will be rhetorical criticism." On the other hand, W. B. Yeats asserted, "We make out of the quarrel with others, rhetoric, but out of the quarrel with ourselves, poetry."

SEE ALSO *didactic poetry, figures of speech, genre, imitation, inversion, metaphor, metonymy, simile, the sublime, trope.*

rhetorical question   A question that doesn't need an answer because its answer is so obvious that it doesn't need to be stated. In his treatise *On the Sublime* (100 C.E.), Longinus views the rhetorical question as a way to arrest a listener, and cleverly casts his remarks as rhetorical questions: "What are we to say of inquiries and questions? Should we not say that they increase the realism and vigour of the writing by the actual form of the figure?" Rhetorical questions are one of the recurrent devices in biblical poetry, where they often come in pairs or sequences. They have their origins in oral poetry and public oratory, in the wisdom literature that stands behind a work like the Book of Job, which uses rhetorical questions extensively. In Job 38, for example, the Lord speaks to Job out of the whirlwind almost entirely in rhetorical questions:

> (verse 28) Hath the rain a father? or who hath begotten the drops of dew?
> (verse 29) Out of whose womb came the ice? and the hoary frost of heaven,
>   who hath gendered it?

John Suckling begins his seventeenth-century song of unrequited love — "Why so pale and wan, fond lover?" — with two stanzas of rhetorical questions, and Percy Bysshe Shelley closes his nineteenth-century "Ode to the West Wind" with one of the most well-known rhetorical questions in English literature: "O, Wind, / If Winter comes, can Spring be far behind?" In modern poetry, W. B. Yeats was especially fond of this strategic device. The twelve-line poem "No Second Troy" (1910) consists mostly of rhetorical questions, and concludes with two: "Why, what could she have done, being what she is? / Was there another Troy for her to burn?"

SEE ALSO *didactic poetry, figures of speech, rhetoric, the sublime, trope.*

rhyme   Rainer Maria Rilke called rhyme "a goddess of secret and ancient coincidences." He said that "she comes as happiness comes, hands filled with an achievement that is already in flower." Rhyme has the joyousness of discovery, of hidden relations uncovered as if by accident. Rhyme occurs, Joseph Brodsky said, "when two things sound the same but their meanings diverge." It creates a partnership between words, lines of poetry, feelings, ideas. Gerard Manley Hopkins called rhyming words "rhyme fellows" and declared, "All beauty may by a metaphor be called rhyme" (1865).

The Oxford English Dictionary defines *rhyme* as "agreement in the terminal sounds of two or more words or metrical lines, such that (in English prosody) the last stressed vowel and any sounds following it are the same, while the sound or sounds preceding it are different." There is something charged and magnetic about a good rhyme, something unsuspected and inevitable, utterly surprising and unforeseen and yet binding and necessary. It is as if the poet had called up the inner yearning of words to find each other.

Rhyme foregrounds the sounds of words as words. It also functions as a marker signaling the end of a rhythmic unit. It is mnemonic: "Red sky at night, sailor's delight. / Red sky at morning, sailor's warning." Two different kinds of rhyme capture two different portents here: one about safety, the other about danger.

There was systematic rhyming in ancient Chinese, Sanskrit, Arabic, Norse, Provençal, and Celtic languages, but the origins of rhyme in English are mysterious since no one really knows quite how or why or when rhyme actually entered our language. The word *rhyme* was spelled *rime* until the seventeenth century.

Rhyme is a device based on the sound identities of words. It is repetition with a difference. It involves the inner correspondence of end-sounds in words or in lines of verse. W. N. Ewer writes, in "The Chosen People" (1924), "How odd / Of God / To choose / The Jews." This is an example of exact rhyme (also called complete, full, perfect, true, or whole rhyme), since the initial sounds are different, but all succeeding sounds are identical (How *odd* / of *God* / To *choose* / The *Jews*). It is called a near rhyme when the final consonants are identical but the preceding vowels or consonants differ (as when W. B. Yeats rhymes *houses* and *faces* at the opening of "Easter, 1916"). Near rhyme is also called approximate, half, imperfect, oblique, partial, or slant rhyme. A pararhyme is a form of near rhyme in which all the consonants are the same but the vowels are different (as when Wilfred Owen pairs *blade* with *blood, flash* with *flesh,* and *leads* with *lads* in "Arms and the Boy," 1918). A rhyme that concludes a line is called an end-rhyme. Rarer is the rhyme that starts a line, which is called an initial rhyme, a head rhyme, or a beginning rhyme, as when Thomas Hood writes, in "The Bridge of Sighs" (1844), "*Mad* for life's history, / *Glad* for death's mystery." A rhyme that occurs within a line is called an internal rhyme ("Red sky at *night,* sailor's de-

light"). An internal rhyme is considered a leonine rhyme when a word near the middle of the line rhymes with a word at the end, as when Edgar Allan Poe summarizes, in "Annabel Lee" (1849), "For the moon never *beams* without bringing me *dreams.*" An interlinear internal rhyme rhymes two words that are not in end positions, as in Shelley's "Stanzas Written in Dejection" (1818): "Till death like sleep might *steal* on me, / And I might *feel* in the warm air." An interlaced rhyme, also known as a cross-rhyme, is a more elaborate form of medial rhyme that occurs in long rhyming couplets, especially the hexameter. Words in the middle of each line rhyme with each other, as in Swinburne's "Hymn to Proserpine" (1866):

> Thou hast conquered, O pale *Galilean;* the world has grown grey from
>   Thy breath;
> We have drunken of things *Lethean,* and fed on the fullness of death.
> Laurel is green for a *season,* and love is sweet for a day;
> But love grows bitter with *treason,* and laurel outlives not May.

A one-syllable rhyme is called masculine (*Oh/no*), a two-syllable rhyme feminine, as when Stevie Smith rhymes *epileptic* and *skeptic.* (The rules regulating the alternation of masculine and feminine rhymes in French prosody are called *alternance des rimes.*) A three-syllable rhyme (*wittily/prettily*) is called triple rhyme (or *sdrucciola,* an Italian word meaning "sliding" or "slippery"), a four-syllable rhyme (*magically/tragically*) a quadruple rhyme. In mosaic rhyme, one of the rhymes is composed of more than one word, as when Robert Browning rhymes *failure* and *pale lure* and *soon hit* and *unit* ("A Grammarian's Funeral," ca. 1854). Rhymes based on a similarity of spelling rather than sound are called eye rhyme (*prove/love*). Homographs are spelled the same, as in *well,* an adverb meaning "doing excellently," and *well,* a noun meaning "a hole dug in the ground." Homophones are spelled differently but sound alike (*blue/blew*). When the same words line up as a rhyme two or more times, it is called identical rhyme:

> And when we lay naked among the books,
> the books enclosed a sacred garden
> for Adam and Eve safely restored to Eden,
> ourselves immersed in a paradise of books.

Rhyming every other line, as in the ballad, is called an intermittent rhyme. Rhyming *abba,* as Tennyson does in the In Memoriam stanza (from *In Memoriam,* 1849), is called an envelope rhyme. Rhyming that doesn't follow a fixed pattern is called an irregular rhyme, as in the pseudo-Pindaric, and rhyming that occurs in an otherwise unrhymed poem is called sporadic rhyme or occasional rhyme. A thorn line is a line that doesn't rhyme in an otherwise rhyming passage.

A few other types: Monorhyme, which is common in Arabic, Latin, and Welsh poetry, is a poem or section of a poem in which all the lines have the same end-rhyme. One poem in the Middle Ages rhymed forty-eight lines on the letter *a,* which was called tirade rhyme. Macaronic rhymes use more than one language, as in medieval lyrics with Latin refrains. Linked rhyme, which was employed in Welsh poetry, connects the last syllable of one line with the first syllable of the next one. An apocopated rhyme rhymes a line end with a penultimate syllable. A so-called backward rhyme, or amphisbaenic rhyme, is a reversed rhyme (*tort* and *trot*). It can consist of words that are spelled backward (*rail/liar*) or pronounced backward (*later/retail*). A synthetic rhyme deletes, adds, or otherwise wrenches letters, which is why it is also called wrenched rhyme, in order to create a false rhyme, often for comic effect, as in this couplet from Ogden Nash's "Kindly Unhitch That Star, Buddy" (1929):

> Some people think they will eventually wear diamonds instead of *rhinestones*
> Only by everlastingly keeping their noses to the *ghrinestones.*

Tail rhymes are rhymes that answer each other across intervening stanzas. A word split across the end of a line is called a broken rhyme (or rhyme-breaking), as when Alexander Pope rhymes "for*get*- / Ful" and *debt*" ("Fourth Satire of Dr. John Donne, Dean of St. Paul's, Versified," 1733) or when Marianne Moore rhymes "*ac* / ccident" and "*lack*" ("The Fish," 1918).

Rhyme creates for the reader a sense of interaction between words and lines. In "One Relation of Rhyme to Reason" (1954), W. K. Wimsatt suggests that every rhyme invites the reader to consider similarities in semantics as well as sound. The reader participates by feeling the weight of the rhyming words, by forging the meaning of their connections, by teasing out the

implications of words coming together and identifying one another as part-
ners.

SEE ALSO *assonance, consonance, feminine rhyme, interlaced rhyme, leonine
rhyme, masculine rhyme, near rhyme, tail rhyme.*

rhymed prose   Many cultures have a category of rhymed prose to desig-
nate nonmetrical speech, which is regulated by rhythm rather than the sys-
tem of meter that characterizes the culture's poetry. Rhymed prose adapts the
devices of poetry to rhythmical prose. Rhyme in this general sense is used
to mean repetition, not matching vowel or consonant sounds. It sometimes
consists of free and irregular rhythms, as in the divine offices of the medieval
church, which were gradually replaced by more regular rhythmical patterns
of speech. Thomas of Capua (ca. 1230) defined rhymed prose as "ordinary
prose, whose members or cola, as delimited by pauses in delivery, are rhymed
at the ends of the colon." Rhymed prose also may be characterized by well-
balanced, strongly cadenced rhythms.

In Arabic literature, *saj'* is an artificial, rhythmical form of rhymed prose, a
stylistic tool used both in sacred literature, such as the Koran, and in secular
literature, such as the *One Thousand and One Nights. Maqāma* is an elaborate
form of picaresque stories in rhymed prose. In Chinese poetry, *fu* (rhyme-
prose) is a hybrid genre that combines narrative passages with descriptions in
verse. Rhymed prose was common in early nineteenth-century Urdu/Hindi
literature, such as Lallu Lal's popular *Prem Sagar* (*Ocean of Love,* 1867).

SEE ALSO *cadence, free verse, fu, meter, prose poem, rhythm.*

rhyme royal, rime royal   A seven-line stanza, usually written in iambic
pentameter, rhyming *ababbcc.* The most regal of all seven-line stanzas, the
rhyme royal was introduced into English poetry by Geoffrey Chaucer in his
long poems *Parlement of Foules* (ca. 1381–82) and *Troilus and Criseyde* (ca.
1380s), which is why it is sometimes also called the Troilus stanza. Chaucer
also used it for four of *The Canterbury Tales* (ca. 1387–1400) and for a num-
ber of short poems, including "Fortune," "Truth," "Complaint unto Pity,"
"Complaint of Chaucer to His Purse," "Gentilesse," "Complaint to His Lady,"
"Lak of Steadfastness," and "Against Women Unconstant." It was thus some-
times referred to as the Chaucerian stanza. Chaucer's friend John Gower

also used the stanza effectively in both French and English for occasional poetry (*In Praise of Peace*) as well as for philosophical love poetry (*Cinkantes balades, Traités pour essampler les amantz marietz,* Aman's "supplicacioun" from *Confessio Amantis*).

Chaucer probably borrowed this favored stanza from Guillaume de Machaut (ca. 1300–1377), who either invented it or developed it from earlier Provençal or French models. He may have adapted it from the French ballade stanza or the Italian ottava rima, omitting the fifth line. This ambidextrous stanza can be balanced as a tercet and two couplets (*aba, bb, cc*) or as a quatrain and a tercet (*abab, bcc*). Some scholars think that the rhyme royal derives its name from the chant royal, while others believe that it comes from one of its disciples, James I of Scotland, who employed it in his fifteenth-century poem "The Kingis Quair." James himself refers to the stanza within the poem as "thir versis sevin." George Gascoigne justified the name "rithhme royall" because he found it "a royall kinde of verse" in his treatise *Certayn Notes of Instruction concerning the Making of Verse or Rime in English* (1575).

Some key examples: Sir Thomas Wyatt, "They Flee from Me" (1557); William Shakespeare, "The Rape of Lucrece" (1594); William Wordsworth, "Resolution and Independence" (1802); William Morris, *The Earthly Paradise* (1868); John Masefield, "The Widow in the Bye Street" (1912); Theodore Roethke, "I Knew a Woman" (1958); and W. H. Auden's extended "Letter to Lord Byron" (1936).

SEE ALSO *ballade, chant royal, ottava rima, septet.*

rhyme scheme　　A characteristic pattern of rhymes. As a shorthand for representing a rhyme scheme, each different rhyme is assigned a different letter. Thus a pair of couplets is designated *aabb,* and a quatrain with alternating rhymes is represented as *abab* and called alternate rhyme. The French use the term *rimes croisées* ("crossed rhyme") for an *abab* rhyme scheme that alternates masculine and feminine rhymes. A rhyme scheme with mirror symmetry, like *abba,* is called arch-rhyme.

The rhyme scheme, an abstraction blooded, is a way of advancing meaning in a poem. Think of the winding staircase of Dante's terza rima, which rhymes *aba, bcb, cdc,* etc., or the logical development of the Shakespearean sonnet, which rhymes *abab, cdcd, efef, gg.* Some rhyme schemes repeat the same end-words in complex arrangements, as in the sestina. The term *rhyme scheme* suggests that use of rhyme is one way to organize the structure of a poem. Robert Frost said that whenever he read a poem that rhymed, he scanned the right side of the page to decide who had won, the poet or the rhyme scheme.

SEE ALSO *couplet, quatrain, rhyme, sestina, sonnet, terza rima, villanelle.*

rhythm From the Greek word *rhythmos,* meaning "measured motion," which derives from a Greek verb meaning "to flow." Rhythm is sound in motion. It is related to the pulse, the heartbeat, the way we breathe. It rises and falls, taking us into ourselves, taking us out of ourselves. Rhythm is the combination in English of stressed and unstressed syllables that creates a feeling of fixity and flux, of surprise and inevitability. It creates a pattern of yearning and expectation, of recurrence and change. It is repetition with a difference. Renewal is "the pivot of lyricism," as Marina Tsvetaeva puts it, comparing the lyrical element to the waves of the sea: "The wave always returns, and always returns as a different wave," she writes in her essay "Poets with History and Poets Without History" (1934):

> The same water — a different wave.
> What matters is that it is a *wave.*
> What matters is that the wave *will return.*
> What matters is that it will *always* return *different.*
> What matters most of all: however different the returning wave, it will always
>   return as a wave of the *sea.*
> What is a wave? Composition and muscle. The same goes for lyric poetry.

I would say with Robert Graves that there is a rhythm of emotion in poetry that conditions the musical rhythm, the patterned energy, the mental bracing and relaxing that come to us through our sensuous impressions. Rhythm is poetry's way of charging the depths, hitting the fathomless.

Les Murray points out that "there is a trance-like pleasure bordering on epileptic seizure to be had from certain regular rhythms" ("Poems and the Mystery of Embodiment," 1988). So too "rhythm is not measure, or something that is outside us," Octavio Paz writes in *The Bow and the Lyre* (1956), "but we ourselves are the ones who flow in the rhythm and rush headlong toward 'something.'" That "something" is a place where we are always arriving, an immanent revelation. In "The Symbolism of Poetry" (1900), W. B. Yeats declares unequivocally that the "purpose of rhythm is to prolong the moment of contemplation, the moment when we are both asleep and awake, which is the one moment of creation."

SEE ALSO *meter.*

riddle "A mystifying, misleading, or puzzling question posed as a problem to be solved or guessed often as a game" (*Webster's Third New International Dictionary*). Though the dictionary definition focuses on the riddle as a question and describes it as a game, the riddle is more than a puzzle. It is an interrogative and expressive form, possibly the earliest form of oral literature — a formulation of thought, a mode of association, a metaphor.

The comparative work of folklorists suggests that riddle-making is virtually a universal activity, a root of the lyric, a contest of wit, a process of naming. The earliest riddles on record are preserved on a clay tablet from ancient Babylon. They are inscribed in Sumerian, along with Assyrian translations. The riddle, a short form with a long history, uses the sentence as its frame. It is often employed for educational purposes, but there are whole cultures in which the riddle is more than child's play. The oldest Sanskrit riddles (ca. 1000 B.C.E.) appear in the riddle hymn of Dirhatamas (Hymn 164) in book 1 of the Rig-Veda (1700–1100 B.C.E.). The Hebrew Bible refers to riddling and riddling contests. Thus the prophet Daniel was "known to have a notable spirit, with knowledge and understanding, and the gift of interpreting dreams, explaining riddles and unbinding spells" (Daniel 5:12). The judge Samson is known for the riddle he poses to the Philistines at his wedding reception (Judges 14:14): "Out of the eater came something to eat, / Out of the strong came something sweet?" In the desert, Samson had chanced upon a lion's carcass in which bees had made a hive. With the help of his bride, who tells the riddle to her countrymen, the Philistines answer the riddle with another riddle: "What is sweeter than honey? What is stronger than a lion?" Samson replies to them with a startling metaphor: "If you had not ploughed my heifer, / you would not have solved my riddle."

Pindar (ca. 522–443 B.C.E.) was the first Greek poet to use the term *rid-*

dle in a way that we still recognize. Everyone remembers the riddle at the heart of the narrative in Sophocles's *Oedipus tyrannus* (ca. 430 B.C.E.), which has also been found in various parts of the world: "What has four legs in the morning, two legs in the afternoon, and three legs in the evening?" This is the riddle of the Sphinx. Oedipus solved the riddle with the word "man" and thus proved his cleverness, a quality that led to his destruction. Plato refers to riddling in *The Republic* (ca. 380 B.C.E.) and quotes a variant of Panarces's riddle: "a man who is not a man [a eunuch] threw a stone that was not a stone [a pumice stone] at a bird that was not a bird [a bat] sitting on a twig that was not a twig [a reed]." Heraclitus's remarks about the universe were so cryptic that Cicero and Diogenes Laertius referred to him as "the Riddler" and "the Obscure."

A riddle is a way of describing one thing in terms of another, as in "Humpty Dumpty," which describes an egg in terms of a man. In *English Riddles from Oral Tradition* (1951), Archer Taylor classifies descriptive riddles according to whether the object — "the answer" — is compared to a person, to several persons, to animals, to several animals, to plants, to things, or to a generalized living creature. As Aristotle pointed out in the *Rhetoric* (335–330 B.C.E.), "Good riddles do, in general, provide us with satisfactory metaphors: for metaphors imply riddles, and therefore a good riddle can furnish a good metaphor."

True riddles, as they are sometimes called, are enigmatic questions in descriptive form. They are meant to confuse or test the wits of those who don't know the answer. The riddle arrests our attention by establishing some paradox or internal contradiction, an opposition or blocking element, which makes it hard to solve. The folk riddle is staged, fundamentally aggressive, antisocial. It is vexing and socially disruptive, unlike, say, the proverb, which is reassuring and reinforces social wisdom.

Opposition is the most salient of four techniques by which the image (or *Gestalt*) of the riddle-question is impaired, making it indecipherable. The techniques of impairment establish the conventions by which riddles are recognized and remembered. Modes of impairment also provide literary strategies. The medieval Hebrew and Arabic poets of Spain, for example, wrote deliberately misleading riddles in verse. There are forty-nine such riddles in the work of the master of Hebrew poetry Yehuda Halevi (ca. 1075–1141).

So too the Arabic poet Al-Harari (1054–1122) filled his masterpiece known as the *Maqamat* (*Assemblies*) with a wealth of riddles. In western Europe, the literary riddle begins with the hundred Latin riddles of Symposius (fifth century). The oldest European vernacular riddles are the poetic riddles of the Old English *Exeter Book* (eighth century). In *Enigmas and Riddles in Literature* (2006), Eleanor Cook suggests that "riddling illuminates the greatest mysteries through the smallest things."

SEE ALSO *metaphor, oral poetry, proverb.*

rimas dissolutas A Provençal syllabic form. Each line in an unrhymed stanza rhymes with its corresponding line in a subsequent stanza. For example, James Merrill's two-stanza poem "A Renewal" (1959) rhymes *abcd abcd*. The *rimas dissolutas* provides a way of isolating rhyme and welding stanzas together. The form was employed by Provençal poets, such as Arnaut Daniel (ca. 1150–ca. 1200), who treated it as kin to the canzone and the sestina. My shortlist of American poems that use *rimas dissolutas* includes Frank O'Hara's "To the Poem" (ca. 1952), Sylvia Plath's "Black Rook in Rainy Weather" (1956), Mona Van Duyn's "Causes" (1970), David Wagoner's "Staying Alive" (1966), and Jon Anderson's "The Blue Animals" (1968).

SEE ALSO *canzone, sestina.*

rising rhythm, ascending rhythm Rhythm that moves from an unstressed syllable to a stressed syllable. Iambic and anapestic meters, which constitute most meters in English, are rising rhythms. This technical term can be misleading — it doesn't imply anything about the emotional movement or impact of the verse.

SEE ALSO *anapest, iamb.*

romance From the Old French word *romanz,* meaning "literature written in the vernacular," the Romance language of French. In Old French, the *roman,* or *romant,* was a "courtly romance in verse," a "popular book." The chivalric romance developed as a literary genre in the twelfth century. The stories of legendary knights celebrating an ideal code of behavior established the romance as an adventure story, which is why it has historically been so well suited to long verse narratives and prose fictions. The pursuit of love was one of the specialties of the early romances, though the genre was so diverse in the Middle Ages that it is nearly impossible to define. Certain recurrent motifs characterize what Corinne Saunders identifies as the backbone of romance: "exile and return, love, quest and adventure, family, name and identity, the opposition between pagan and Christian." Romances require handsome heroes and beautiful heroines, such as Tristan and Isolde, who stand above the ordinary, though they are human and not divine, as in mythological stories. In *Memesis* (1946), Erich Auerbach identified the archetypal pattern of medieval romance as the movement from court to forest, "setting forth" in search of adventure. The quest romance, the story of a hero's progressive journey — his tests, his struggle to the death with a supernatural enemy, his ultimate triumph — is the most complete and thus satisfactory form of literary romance.

Romance literature was originally written in Old French, Anglo-Norman, and Occitan (the language of the troubadours), and later in English and German. Northrop Frye argues, in *The Anatomy of Criticism* (1957), that romance is both a historical mode and a mythos, or generic narrative form, which reflects a "tendency ... to displace myth in a human direction and yet, in contrast to 'realism,' to conventionalize content in an ideal direction." The literature that stems from this romance impulse suggests "implicit mythical patterns in a world more closely associated with human experience." Romance, then, is not a genre but a generic plot, a dramatic structure found in poetry, drama, and fiction. As a mythos of summer, romance leads from a state of order through winter, darkness, and death, to rebirth, a fresh order, full maturity. Romance literature has many forerunners in biblical narratives, such as the story of Joseph in Genesis, and in classical Greek epics, such as Homer's *Odyssey* (ca. eighth century B.C.E.). It develops into a wide variety of genres with different formats and functions, such as Shakespeare's plays, pastoral romances, Gothic novels, Romantic poetry, modern fantasy, and science fiction movies.

SEE ALSO *archetype, chivalric romance, courtly love, pastoral, Romanticism, troubadour, trouvère, universality.*

romances   The *romances,* or Spanish ballads, are an essential part of Hispanic culture and heritage. These short episodic poems are concise and dramatic. Many of the early medieval *romances* adapted episodes and lines from the *cantares de gesta* ("heroic epic poems") or epic cycles, and they sound like fragments of lost epics. The *romances* were shaped by hundreds and even thousands of different voices and imaginations, and have had an incalculable influence on Spanish poets and prose writers. The poets of the Spanish golden age knew and loved the *romances,* as did the author of *Don Quixote* (1605, 1615).

The epic poems were sung at court, but the *romances* were ideal for the *juglares,* popular entertainers who performed in marketplaces. The early *romances* consist of long sixteen-syllable lines (written down, the verses are divided into two eight-syllable lines). The even-numbered lines rhyme. The heavy caesura, or pause, in the middle of the sixteen-syllable line grew fainter as the *romances* moved further and further from their origins in epic, but it has never been entirely lost. It is still there in the *romances* collected in Spain and South America in the twentieth century. As W. S. Merwin puts it in his translation, *Spanish Ballads* (1961), "This unbroken connection with the indigenous popular epics of the Middle Ages is one thing which makes the Spanish *romances* unique among the ballad literatures of the rest of Europe."

SEE ALSO *ballad, epic, juglar, octosyllabic verse.*

Romanticism   Romanticism describes both an ongoing sensibility and a particular historical period, the age of wonder, which spanned the sixty years from 1770 to 1830. A widespread cultural movement, Romanticism was characterized by new modes of thinking and feeling. The term *romantic* originally referred to the characteristics of the romances of the Middle Ages, i.e., something "that could happen in a romance," and suggested something fanciful, an extravagant idealization of reality. In the early nineteenth century, the German critic Karl Wilhelm Friedrich von Schlegel used the term *Romantic literature* to designate a new school opposed to classic literature. In 1798, he defined Romantic poetry as "a progressive universal poetry." The idea spread to France and England, as did the polar opposition. The controversy over Romanticism and classicism fuels the battle between the moderns and the ancients.

Romanticism is a retrospective label for a diverse group of poets. David

Perkins identifies Hippolyte Taine, in 1863, as the first critic to describe the early nineteenth-century English poets, especially the Lake poets, as a "romantic school." We now recognize three major English poets at the start of the era — William Blake, William Wordsworth, and Samuel Taylor Coleridge — and three others at the end of it — George Gordon, Lord Byron, Percy Bysshe Shelley, and John Keats. The first generation outlived the second one. The Romantic poets are darker and wilder than the classical poets of the Augustan Age who preceded them (John Dryden, Alexander Pope) and the Victorian poets who followed (Alfred, Lord Tennyson; Robert Browning). The period was a counter-Enlightenment shaped by the historical experience of the French Revolution, which opened new possibilities. "Old things seemed passing away, and nothing was dreamt of but the regeneration of the human race," Robert Southey said. Socially, as Jacques Barzun puts it, "romanticism has to do with creating a new society different from its immediate predecessor."

One of the fundamentals of the Romantic era is faith in the goodness of human beings, who are naturally pure but hindered by urban life, civilization itself. "Man is born free and everywhere he is in chains," Jean-Jacques Rousseau claimed in *The Social Contract* (1762). A constellation of ideas came together around the greatness of the "Noble Savage," the sacred innocence of childhood, and the sublimity of the natural world. Nature was for Romantic thinkers not just a place of inviolable physical beauty, local and concrete, but also the manifestation of a spiritual force that operated in, to use Wordsworth's phrase, "the Mind of Man" ("The Recluse," 1800). The passion for nature and "natural man" was accompanied by a vogue for "primitive" poetry, hence the popularity of Thomas Percy's *Reliques of Ancient English Poetry* (1765) and Charlotte Brooke's *Reliques of Irish Poetry* (1789). In general, the Romantic poets emphasized the primacy of feeling over reason and sought new means of artistic expression. They had an unhampered faith in the imagination.

The Romantic poets demonstrated a commitment to locale, a poetics of process, and skepticism toward closure, wholeness, and totalizing forms, which is why the greater Romantic lyric, a descriptive-meditative poem, and the Romantic fragment are two of the prototypes of Romantic poetry. The Romantic poets opposed placing any kind of inhibition upon the imagination. They were subjective idealists with what Lascelles Abercrombie called "*a tendency away from actuality*," and yet their belief in freedom extended to politics, and they demonstrated a strong commitment to political liberty. Romanticism continues to refer to a time-bound era, a particular achievement, and a permanent human impulse toward the limitless or infinite. "When I say I'm a romantic poet," Philip Levine once said, "it seems to me that I feel the human is boundless, and that seems to me the essential fact of Romanticism."

SEE ALSO *chivalric romance, classic, conversation poems, fragment, imagination, nature poetry, picturesque, romance, romances, the sublime.*

rondeau From the French word *rond,* meaning "round." The rondeau is a form that turns round and round. It originated in Provençal poetry of the thirteenth and fourteenth centuries. The term originally included various short poetic forms. The current form was fixed toward the end of the fifteenth century and became especially popular in French poetry. Théodore de Banville codified it in *Petit traité de poesie française* (*Little Treatise on French Poetry,* 1872). The whole poem consists of fifteen lines, which divide into three groups: (1) lines 1–5, (2) lines 6–9, and (3) lines 10–15. It is common but not necessary to place a stanza break after the first five lines. The refrain, which is the first half of the opening line, repeats at the ends of the second and third groups. It is a half-line, a tail. The whole poem turns on two rhymes. The meter of the thirteen longer lines usually consists of four or five iambic feet.

Sir Thomas Wyatt introduced the rondeau into English poetry in the first half of the sixteenth century. Here is his illustrative use of the form:

Helpe me to seke for I lost it there,	R (refrain) A
And if that ye have founde it ye that be here,	A
And seke to convaye it secretely,	B
Handell it soft and trete it tenderly,	B
Or els it will plain and then appere.	A
But rather restore it mannerly,	B
Syns that I do aske it thus honestly;	B
For to lese it, it sitteth me to nere	A
Helpe me to seke.	R

Alas, and is there no remedy,   B
But have I thus lost it wilfully?   B
I wis it was a thing all to dere   A
To be bestowed and wist not where.   A
It was myn hert: I pray you hertely   B
Helpe me to seke.   R

The most iconic twentieth-century rondeau is the Canadian John McCrae's war poem "In Flanders Field" (1915). The most well-known American rondeau is Paul Laurence Dunbar's "We Wear the Mask" (1896). W. H. Auden's "The Hidden Law" (1940) may be the high point of the form in English.

rondeau redoublé   This rare and twisted poetic form consists of twenty-four lines plus a coda line, a refrain comprised of the first half of the first line. It has five quatrains and one quintet. The whole poem turns on two rhymes, as do the rondeau and the rondel, and has five refrains modeled on the lines of the first stanza. The entire first line reappears as line 8 in the second stanza, the third line as line 16 in the fourth stanza, and the fourth line as line 20 in the fifth stanza. Jean de La Fontaine (1621–1695), who may have devised it, and Théodore de Banville (1823–1891) both experimented with this complex form. It has been used for light verse by such poets as Dorothy Parker (1893–1967) and Louis Untermeyer (1885–1977). Wendy Cope provides a witty contemporary example, "Rondeau Redoublé," in *Making Cocoa for Kingsley Amis* (1986).

SEE ALSO *rondeau, rondel.*

rondel   This French form consists of thirteen lines turning on two rhymes. It has three stanzas of four, four, and five lines, which rhyme *abba, abab, abbaa.* Lines 7 and 13 repeat the first line. Line 8 repeats line 2. The rondel is often confused with the rondeau. For example, Charles d'Orléans titled his fifteenth-century rondel "Rondeau." The Italian poet Eugenio Montale used *rondel* to refer to a series of short songlike lyrics and called the title section of his first book "my rondels."

SEE ALSO *rondeau.*

rondelet A shorter form of the rondeau, the rondelet consists of one seven-line stanza. The first line is a refrain that reappears as lines 3 and 7. The refrain is four syllables long. The rest of the lines have eight syllables each. The poem turns on two rhymes: *abaabba*. Here is a rondelet that the English Victorian poet May Probyn published in 1883:

> Say what you please,
> But know, I shall not change my mind!
> Say what you please,
> Even, if you wish it, on your knees —
> And, when you hear me next defined
> As something lighter than the wind,
> Say what you please!

SEE ALSO *rondeau, septet.*

roundel Algernon Charles Swinburne (1837–1909) invented this song-like variation of the French rondeau. Chaucer used the term *roundel* interchangeably with *rondel*, as in his poem "Merciles Beaute: A Triple Roundel" (late fourteenth century). Swinburne's refashioned roundel consists of eleven lines that employ two rhymes in three stanzas (of 4, 3, and 4 lines). There is an identical refrain after the third and tenth lines. The refrain, which can be a half-line, rhymes with the second line. The short refrain has only one or two stresses. The longer lines contain four or five stresses. Here is Swinburne's self-describing roundel from his collection *A Century of Roundels* (1883):

The Roundel

A roundel is wrought as a ring or a starbright sphere,	A
(refrain, first phrase)	
With craft of delight and with cunning of sound unsought,	B
That the heart of the hearer may smile if to pleasure his ear	A
A roundel is wrought.	B
(refrain)	
Its jewel of music is carven of all or of aught —	B
Love, laughter or mourning — remembrance of rapture or fear —	A
That fancy may fashion to hang in the ear of thought.	B

As a bird's quick song runs round, and the hearts in us hear	A
Pause answer to pause, and again the same strain caught,	B
So moves the device whence, round as a pearl or tear,	A
A roundel is wrought.	B
	(refrain)

SEE ALSO *rondeau, rondel.*

roundelay A simple song with a refrain. The term can also encompass the other highly repetitive fixed forms with refrains, such as the rondeau, the rondel, and the villanelle. In England, the Elizabethan poets used it for a wide range of songs without any fixed form. Thomas Chatterton's "Minstrel's Roundelay" (1770) begins,

O sing unto my roundelay,
    O drop the briny tear with me,
Dance no more at holy-day,
    Like a running river be.
        My love is dead,
        Gone to his death-bed,
        All under the willow-tree.

SEE ALSO *rondeau, rondel, villanelle.*

rubái, see *rubaiyat stanza.*

rubaiyat stanza, Omar Khayyám quatrain From the Persian word *rubái,* meaning "quatrain." The rubaiyat stanza consists of four ten-syllable lines that rhyme *aaba.* It occasionally rhymes *aaaa.* The rubaiyat stanza is also called the Omar stanza or Omar Khayyám quatrain. The rubaiyat, a collection of quatrains, was a particular strength of medieval Persian verse. The form was popularized in the English-speaking world by Edward FitzGerald's 1859 translation, a loose adaptation, of *The Rubaiyat* by the Persian astronomer-poet Omar Khayyám (1048–1131). FitzGerald arranged the iambic pentameter stanzas in a cohesive order, but each quatrain in a Persian rubaiyat is a distinct unit independent of its neighbors. Here is FitzGerald's beloved opening:

A book of Verses underneath the Bough,
A Jug of Wine, a Loaf of Bread — and Thou
   Beside me singing in the Wilderness —
Oh, Wilderness were Paradise enow!

It is called an interlocking rubaiyat when the unrhymed line of a stanza becomes the rhyme for the following stanza, as in Robert Frost's "Stopping by Woods on a Snowy Evening" (1923). Some excellent examples of the rubaiyat stanza in twentieth-century American poetry: Frost's "Desert Places" (1936), Ezra Pound's "Canto LXXX" (1946), a section of James Merrill's "Lost in Translation" (1976), Brad Leithauser's "Law Clerk, 1979" (1982), and Dick Davis's "A Letter to Omar" (1989). In 1945 and '46 the Turkish poet Nazim Hikmet managed to "put dialectical materialism into the rubaiyat form."

SEE ALSO *chain rhyme, quatrain.*

rune   A letter or character of the Old Germanic alphabet. The word *rune* meant "whisper, mystery, secret counsel," and from the earliest times runes were associated with magical incantations and practices. The Runic alphabets were eclipsed by the Latin alphabet during the spread of Christianity in the fourteenth century, but runes survived, often carved on coins, weapons, amulets, and memorial stones. The three extant "Rune Poems" (the "Anglo-Saxon Rune Poem," the "Norwegian Rune Poem," and the "Icelandic Rune Poem") list the letters of the Runic alphabets while presenting an explanatory stanza for each letter. Runes may have served as mnemonic devices that enabled speakers to remember and recite the order and names of each letter of the alphabet. They may also have been a way of transmitting secret or mystical knowledge. The Anglo-Saxon poet Cynewulf (ca. ninth century) signed his poems by weaving the runes for his name into his verses "to seek the prayers of others for the safety of his soul."

A rune now suggests a magical formula, incantation, or poem. Thus, Edgar Allan Poe hears the bells keeping "a sort of Runic rhyme" ("The Bells," 1849). And Robert Graves portrays an anonymous early Finnish poet hurling his "rough rune / at the wintry moon" ("Finland," 1918).

SEE ALSO *incantation, spell.*

S

saga From Old Norse and Icelandic: "narrative," "story," "history." The noun *saga* derives from the verb *sagja* ("to say") and means a tale or report. Saga was the goddess of poetry in Old Norse mythology, but the medieval sagas are tales in prose. They were written down between the twelfth and fourteenth centuries, but are based on older oral traditions. They tell stories, often legendary, about heroes and historical events. The Icelandic sagas and the early Irish sagas are the pinnacles of this narrative oral literature. Sometimes embedded with alliterative verses, the sagas prefigure the historical novel.

SEE ALSO *epic, narrative poetry.*

Sapphic stanza, Sapphics This stanza pattern is named after Sappho (late seventh century B.C.E.), the ancient Greek poet born on the isle of Lesbos, known in *The Palatine Anthology* (tenth century) as the Tenth Muse. The Sapphic stanza may have been invented by Sappho's contemporary Alcaeus of Mytilene, but it was favored by Sappho, who used it for a significant portion of her work. The Sapphic stanza consists of four lines. It was written in quantitative meter and later adapted into qualitative, or accentual-syllabic, meter. Each of the first three lines has eleven syllables (hendecasyllabics) and five verse feet (two trochees, a dactyl, two trochees). There are sometimes substitutions in the fourth and final syllables of each line. The final short line, an adonic, has five syllables and two verse feet (a dactyl and a trochee or spondee):

```
/ u | / u | / u u | / u | / u
/ u | / u | / u u | / u | / u
/ u | / u | / u u | / u | / u
/ u u | / u
```

Six centuries later, Catullus adapted Sappho's poem "Phanetai moi" ("He appears to me") into Latin in his poem number 51 ("Ille mi par . . ."). Horace transformed the form in his *Odes* (23–13 B.C.E.) — it was one of his two favorite meters — and provided a model for future poets. For example, William Cowper follows the Horatian model in "Lines Written During a Period of Insanity" (ca. 1774):

> Hatred and vengeance, my eternal portion,
> Scarce can endure delay of execution,
> Wait, with impatient readiness, to seize my
>   Soul in a moment.
>
> Damn'd below Judas: more adhorr'd than he was,
> Who for a few pence sold his holy Master.
> Twice betrayed Jesus me, the last delinquent,
>   Deems the profanest.
>
> Man disavows, and Deity disowns me:
> Hell might afford my miseries a shelter;
> Therefore hell keeps her ever-hungry mouths all
>   Bolted against me.
>
> Hard lot! encompass'd with a thousand dangers;
> Weary, faint, trembling with a thousand terrors;
> I'm call'd, if vanquish'd, to receive a sentence
>   Worse than Abiram's.
>
> *Him* the vindictive rod of angry justice
> Sent quick and howling to the centre headlong;
> *I,* fed with judgment, in a fleshly tomb, am
>   Buried above ground.

The Sapphic pattern has its own history in English. Some English Renaissance poets (Richard Stanyhurst; Mary Herbert, Countess of Pembroke) attempted to approximate syllable length as opposed to stress, but most adapted the form to accentual-syllabic meter, which is native to English; Thomas Campion did so in "Rose-Cheeked Laura" (1602), which he "offered as an example of the English Sapphick." In "Sapphics" (1866) Swinburne uses the pattern to depict Sappho herself. In 1919, William Faulkner adapted and condensed Swinburne's twenty-stanza poem into six stanzas of his own devising, an imitation that he also called "Sapphics." My anthology of Sapphics in English would include Isaac Watts, "The Day of Judgment" (1706); Fulke Greville, "Caelica 6" (ca. 1580); Thomas Hardy, "The Temporary the All" (1898); Louis MacNeice, "June Thunder" (1938); Louise Bogan, "Portrait" (1923); Hyam Plutzik, "I Am Disquieted When I See Many Hills" (1959); William Meredith, "Effort at Speech" (1970); James Merrill, "Farewell Performance" (1988); James Wright, "Erinna to Sappho" (1957); and Marilyn Hacker, "Cleis" (1991).

SEE ALSO *adonic, dactyl, foot, hendecasyllabics, quatrain, trochee.*

satire From the Latin term *satura lanx,* meaning "medley, dish of colorful fruits." A literary composition, either in poetry or prose, that scorns, derides, or ridicules human weakness, stupidity, or vice. Satire was the only literary form invented by the Roman poets — Quintilian boasted, "Satire is altogether ours" in the first century (*Institutio oratoria*) — though it has antecedents in Athenian Old Comedy, represented by Aristophanes (ca. 450–ca. 388 B.C.E.). Rich and various, satire consists of loosely related scenes that treat a wide range of issues. It is a sarcastic, sometimes scathing genre, not for the faint-hearted.

There were two main lines of Roman satire. The Syrian Cynic philosopher Menippus of Gadara (fl. 290 B.C.E.) invented the Menippean satire, a parody form that blended prose with short verse interludes, which he used to skewer those with a different philosophical viewpoint. His work is lost. The Menippean satire was brought into Latin by Varro (67–16 B.C.E.), whose work also did not survive. The only extant Menippean satire is *The Apocolocyntosis* (*Joke on the Death of Claudius,* or *Pumpkinification of Claudius*), attributed to Seneca (ca. 4 B.C.E.–65 C.E.), which parodies the deification of the drooling emperor.

The verse satirists, who represent the second line of Roman satire, specialized in invective against identifiable, often thinly disguised personalities. Gaius Lucilius (ca. 160s–103 B.C.E.) was the earliest Roman satirist, though his thirty books of satires survive in only about eleven hundred unconnected lines. Horace wrote that Lucilius "first had the courage / to write this kind of poetry and remove the glossy skin / in which people were parading before the world and concealing / their ugliness" (*Satires,* book 2, number 1). Lucilius and Horace called their satires *Sermones* (*Conversations*). As a term, *satire* was only later applied to their works. Horace's two-volume *Satires* are dedicated to his *pedestris* — a pedestrian muse, one who goes afoot rather than looking down from on high. *Satires,* book 1, which consists of ten poems, was completed near 35 B.C.E.; *Satires,* book 2, which comprises eight poems, toward 30 B.C.E. These conversational moral tales and preachy anecdotes are written in prosy hexameters. Nonetheless, Horace's humor was playful and urbane. His nature was more to laugh than to lacerate. The bitterly eloquent Juvenal (ca. 55–130) wrote sixteen poems in five books of satires: "It is hard not to write Satire. For who is so tolerant / of the monstrous city, so steeled, that he can restrain his wrath," he rhetorically asks, in his so-called Programmatic Satire (*Satire 1*). He said, "Indignation will drive me to verse," and understood that the satirist is interested in "all human endeavors."

The Romans bequeathed satire to other literatures. A satiric comedy became a poem or play that uses humor as its primary means of attack. The medieval Arab poets developed a genre of satirical poetry called *hija.* The Scottish flyting is a form of satirical name-calling. The French verse satirist Mathurin Régnier (1573–1613) boasted that satire had felt the tread of many poets, but was unvisited by French rhymers: "I enter it, following Horace close behind, / to trace the various humours of mankind" (*Satire 14*). He was followed by the strongest of all French satirists, Nicolas Boileau, called Despréaux (1636–1711).

The great era of satire in English literature was roughly from 1660 to 1800. One thinks especially of John Dryden, who provided the finest English version of Juvenal (1693) and created the mock epics *Absalom and Achitophel* (1681, 1682) and *Mac Flecknoe* (1682), as well as of Alexander Pope, who penned *The Rape of the Lock* (1712–14) and *The Dunciad* (1728, 1729, 1743). Jonathan Swift's enraged indignation often acts as a kind of experimental laboratory that, as Northrop Frye points out, "shows us man as a venomous rodent, man as a noisome and clumsy pachyderm, the mind of man as a bear-pit, and the body of man as a compound of filth and ferocity." Swift said, "Satire is a sort of glass, wherein beholders do generally discover everybody's face but their own." Lord Byron announced, "Fools are my theme, let satire be my song." In "An Essay on Comedy" (1877), George Meredith recognized that "the satirist is a moral agent, often a social scavenger, working on a storage of bile."

Satire is essentially moral. Its fundamental mode is earnest joking, improving society by attacking villains and fools. The editor of *The Oxford Book of Satirical Verse* (1980) notes, "One can say gravely that satire postulates an ideal condition of man or decency, and then despairs of it; and enjoys the despair, masochistically. But the joke must not be lost — the joke of statement, of sound, rhythm, form, vocabulary, rhyme, and surprise. Without the joke everything goes; and we may be left only with complaint, invective, or denunciation; all of which may be poetry, but of another kind."

SEE ALSO *flyting, irony, mock epic.*

scansion From the Latin word *scandere,* meaning "to climb" or "a climbing." Scansion, the study of metrical patterns, refers to the division of verse lines into feet as well as to the organization of syllables within a foot. Metrical analysis documents the arrangement of accented and unaccented syllables in different lines; it groups those lines according to the number of feet within them, classifies stanzas by rhyme schemes and the number of lines per stanza, etc. Scansion doesn't create rhythm; it reveals and visually represents it.

SEE ALSO *foot, meter.*

scop An Anglo-Saxon minstrel-poet, attached to the court of a chieftain or king, who both composed poems and sang or recited the traditional compositions of others. The earliest records of scops, who worked in preliterate societies, date to the fourth century, where they are referred to in early English poems. The scop was traditionally a harpist and poet-singer who had fully mastered the complex oral-formulaic materials of Old Germanic prosody. Only one poem definitely attributed to a specific scop has come down to us. This forty-two-line poem is recorded in *The Exeter Book,* a tenth-century compilation of Old English poetry, and traditionally called "Déor" after its reputed author.

Then I of myself / will make this known
That awhile I was held / the Héodenings' scop,
To my duke most dear / and Déor was my name. (lines 35–37)

(the novel of sensibility) and sentimental comedies (the drama of sensibility) characterized by the pathos of sensitivity, overly refined emotions, acute perceptions and responses. There is a turn from the restraints of neoclassicism and new sympathy for the Middle Ages, for Spenser, Shakespeare, and Milton, for archaic or "primitive" poetry, manifested in an awakened interest in ballads and other folk poetry, hence the vogue for the Ossian poems and Thomas Percy's *Reliques of Ancient English Poetry* (1765). Northrop Frye finds a new attention to the psychological view of literature as process rather than product, something more fragmentary, irregular, and unpredictable than the finished works of the Augustans, which helps account for the sudden emergence of a lyrical impulse in the age of sensibility, the era of Christopher Smart's "A Song to David," Thomas Chatterton's elegies, Robert Burns's songs, and William Blake's lyrics. "The poetry of process is oracular, and the medium of the oracle is often in an ecstatic or trance-like state," Frye writes. "Autonomous voices seem to speak through him, and as he is concerned to utter rather than to address, he is turned away from his listener, so to speak, in a state of rapt self-communion. The free association of words, in which sound is prior to sense, is often a literary way of representing insanity."

The excess of feeling in this lyrical poetry can be dizzying. In the age of sensibility, Marshall Brown remarks, "intense feelings for nature and humanity were accompanied by . . . intense anxieties about the integrity of the self," including the melancholy we find in Samuel Johnson and Thomas Gray, and the fear of madness — and the madness itself — we encounter in Smart, William Collins, and William Cowper, whose instabilities of selfhood vibrate into torrents of sorrow or rapture. In Collins's "Ode on the Poetical Character" (1747), Smart's *Jubilate Agno* (*Rejoice in the Lamb,* 1759–63), and Blake's *The Four Zoas* (1807), the soul, God, and nature are brought into what Frye calls "a white-hot fusion of identity, an imaginative fiery furnace in which the reader may, if he chooses, make a fourth."

In the twentieth century, T. S. Eliot formulated a doctrine of what he called "dissociation of sensibility," a supposed split between thinking and feeling that he traced to the seventeenth century. The task of modern poetry, Eliot thought, was to reunify sensibility. As a critical term, *sensibility* now has a more limited usefulness. When we speak of a poet's sensibility, we generally mean his or her characteristic way of responding to experience.

SEE ALSO *neoclassicism, pathos, Romanticism, sentimentality, the sublime, taste.*

sentimentality From the Medieval Latin word *sentimentum,* which derives from the Latin *sentire,* "to feel." The word *sentiment* has been employed in a variety of ways to refer to an attitude, thought, or judgment prompted by feeling, and thus was used to denote both emotion and opinion. The adjective *sentimental* began to be popularly used in the eighteenth century. Raymond Williams quotes Lady Bradshaugh (1749) — "*sentimental,* so much in vogue among the polite ... Everything clever and agreeable is comprehended in that word ... a *sentimental* man ... a *sentimental* party ... a *sentimental* walk" — and recognizes that the term encompasses both "a conscious openness to feelings" and "a conscious consumption of feelings." It was the latter that made the word *sentimental* especially vulnerable to criticism.

In the nineteenth century, *sentimentality* took on negative connotations from which it never recovered. It is a deliberately modern, self-reflexive term, and generally suggests a disproportionate emotional response. George Meredith defined sentimentalists as those who "seek to enjoy Reality without incurring the Immense Debtorship for a thing done" (*The Ordeal of Richard Feverel,* 1859), and Oscar Wilde said that "a sentimentalist is simply one who desires to have the luxury of an emotion without paying for it" (*De Profundis,* 1905). I. A. Richards brought the term into the twentieth-century critical discourse about poetry when he argued that "a response is sentimental if it is too great for the occasion" (*Practical Criticism,* 1929). Brian Wilke surveys ten basic handbooks on literature in his essay "What Is Sentimentality?" (1967) and concludes that all ten agree that the common keynote is the idea of disproportion or excess.

Sentimentality is frequently used as a term of condescension. "In some poems you're taking the risk of sentiment brimming over into sentimentality," an interviewer once told Philip Larkin, who replied, "Am I? I don't understand the word sentimentality. It reminds me of Dylan Thomas's definition of an alcoholic: 'A man you don't like who drinks as much as you do.' I think sentimentality is someone you don't like feeling as much as you do."

SEE ALSO *pathos, sensibility, taste.*

septenary, see "accentual-syllabic meter" in *meter.*

septet   The seven-line stanza, of varying meter and rhyme, has been utilized by a large number of English poets from Chaucer (ca. 1340–1400) and Lydgate (ca. 1370–ca. 1451) to William Morris (1834–1896) and John Masefield (1878–1967). The septet has an odd extra punch, a piercing last line, which moves past the symmetry of any even-numbered stanza. Here is a breathtaking stanza from Thomas Nashe's "A Litany in Time of Plague" (1600):

> Beauty is but a flower
> Which wrinkles will devour;
> Brightness falls from the air;
> Queens have died young and fair;
> Dust hath closed Helen's eye.
> I am sick, I must die.
>   Lord, have mercy on us!

The most historically interesting fixed form of the seven-line stanza is rhyme royal, an iambic pentameter stanza rhyming *ababbcc,* which was employed with great dignity by Chaucer in *Troilus and Criseyde* (ca. 1380s) and by Shakespeare in "The Rape of Lucrece" (1594). Something in the lucky number seven seems to lead to desperation or comedy.

SEE ALSO *rhyme royal, rondelet.*

sestet   The subdivision or last six lines of an Italian sonnet, following the first eight lines, the octave. It is also applied (along with the terms *sexain, sixain, sextain, sextet,* and *hexastich*) to the different varieties of the six-line stanza, such as that of the sestina and also the so-called Venus and Adonis stanza (iambic pentameter, rhyming *ababcc*), named after Shakespeare's poem. The sestet, which was first developed by Italian poets, is also called the *sesta rima.* It has an American lineage that runs from Anne Bradstreet's "Prologue"

(1650) and Edward Taylor's *Preparatory Meditations* (1682–1725) to Richard Wilbur's "A Wood" (1969) and Charles Wright's *Sestets* (2009).

The Spanish *sextilla* has six octosyllabic or shorter lines. It options two rhyme schemes: *aabccb* or *abbacc*. Robert Burns mastered the Scottish stanza, or Habbie stanza, a form found in medieval Provençal poems and in miracle plays of the Middle Ages, to such a degree that it came to be called the Burns stanza, or Burns meter. The Burns stanza intermingles two rhymes and meters: it rhymes *aaabab;* lines 1, 2, 3, and 5 are tetrameter, lines 4 and 6 are dimeter. Here are three central stanzas from "Epistle to John Lapraik, an Old Scottish Bard" (1785). Notice how the first three lines build to a crescendo, which is then punctuated by the punch of the fourth line and the epigrammatic cut of the sixth one.

> What's a' your jargon o' your schools,
> Your Latin names for horns an' stools;
> If honest Nature made you fools,
> > What sairs your Grammars?
> Ye'd better taen up spades and shools,
> > Or knappin-hammers.
>
> A set o' dull, conceited hashes,
> Confuse their brains in colledge-classes!
> They *gang in* stirks, and *come out* asses,
> > Plain truth to speak;
> An' syne they think to climb Parnassus
> > By dint o' Greek!
>
> Gie me ae spark o' Nature's fire,
> That's a' the learning I desire;
> Then tho' I drudge thro' dub an' mire
> > At pleugh or cart,
> My Muse, tho' hamely in attire,
> > May touch the heart.

SEE ALSO *sestina, sonnet, stanza.*

sestina The sestina, an intricate verse form created and mastered by the Provençal poets, is a thirty-nine-line poem consisting of half a dozen six-line stanzas and one three-line envoi ("send-off"). The six end-words are repeated, in a prescribed order, as end-words in each of the subsequent stanzas. The concluding tercet brings together all the end-words; each line contains two of them, one in the middle and one at the end.

The twelfth-century Provençal poet Arnaut Daniel is credited with inventing the sestina, a form widely practiced by Dante (1265–1321) and Petrarch (1304–1377), who followed the troubadours. Sir Philip Sidney put the form to good use in *Arcadia* (1590). The sestina has had particular fascination for Victorian and modern poets, perhaps because it generates a narrative even as it circles back on itself and recurs like a song. Ezra Pound compared it, in *The Spirit of Romance* (1910), to "a thin sheet of flame folding and infolding upon itself."

The numerical scheme, which once may have had magical significance, has the precision and elegance of musical (or mathematical) form:

Stanza one: 1, 2, 3, 4, 5, 6
Stanza two: 6, 1, 5, 2, 4, 3
Stanza three: 3, 6, 4, 1, 2, 5
Stanza four: 5, 3, 2, 6, 1, 4
Stanza five: 4, 5, 1, 3, 6, 2
Stanza six: 2, 4, 6, 5, 3, 1
Envoi: 1, 2; 3, 4; 5, 6

There are often variations on how the six words recur in the final tercet, such as 2, 5; 4, 3; 6, 1.

In this late nineteenth-century sestina, Edmund Gosse pays homage to Arnaut Daniel, who is cited in the epigraph as "the first among all others, great master of love [poetry]":

Sestina
Fra tutti il primo Arnaldo Daniello
Gran maestro d'amor — Petrarch

In fair Provence, the land of lute and rose,
Arnaut, great master of the lore of love,
First wrought sestinas to win his lady's heart,
Since she was deaf when simpler staves he sang,

And for her sake he broke the bonds of rhyme,
And in this subtler measure hid his woe.

"Harsh be my lines," cried Arnaut, "harsh the woe
My lady, that enthorn'd and cruel rose,
Inflicts on him that made her live in rhyme!"
But through the metre spake the voice of Love,
And like a wild-wood nightingale he sang
Who thought in crabbed lays to ease his heart.

It is not told if her untoward heart
Was melted by her poet's lyric woe,
Or if in vain so amorously he sang;
Perchance through cloud of dark conceits he rose
To nobler heights of philosophic love,
And crowned his later years with sterner rhyme.

This thing alone we know: the triple rhyme
Of him who bared his vast and passionate heart
To all the crossing flames of hate and love,
Wears in the midst of all its storms of woe, —
As some loud morn of March may bear a rose, —
The impress of a song that Arnaut sang.

"Smith of his mother-tongue," the Frenchman sang
Of Lancelot and of Galahad, the rhyme
That beat so bloodlike at this core of rose,
It stirred the sweet Francesca's gentle heart
To take that kiss that brought her so much woe
And sealed in fire her martyrdom of love.

And Dante, full of her immortal love,
Stayed his drear song, and softly, fondly sang
As though his voice broke with that weight of woe;
And to this day we think of Arnaut's rhyme
Whenever pity at the laboring heart
On fair Francesca's memory drops the rose.

Ah! sovereign Love, forgive this weaker rhyme!
The men of old who sang were great at heart,
Yet have we too known woe, and worn thy rose.

An anthology of late nineteenth- and twentieth-century examples might begin with Swinburne's "The Complaint of Lisa," a rhyming double sestina with twelve twelve-line stanzas and a six-line envoi. It would include examples by Rudyard Kipling, Ezra Pound, and W. H. Auden; by Elizabeth Bishop ("Sestina"), John Ashbery ("Farm Implements and Rutabagas in a Landscape"), Alan Ansen ("A Fit of Something Against Something"), Donald Justice ("Here in Katmandu"), Donald Hall ("Sestina"), Anthony Hecht ("The Book of Yolek"), Marilyn Hacker ("Untoward Occurrence at Embassy Poetry Reading"), and Deborah Digges ("Hall of Souls"). James Cummins adapts the form to American popular culture in his first book, *The Whole Truth* (1986), which consists of twenty-five sestinas revolving around the characters in the *Perry Mason* television series.

sexain, see *sestet.*

sextilla, see *sestet.*

shaman, shamanism   In tribal societies, a shaman is a medium between the visible and invisible worlds, an intermediary between the human and spirit worlds. Shamans practice magic or sorcery for purposes of healing, divination, and control over natural events. They have close associations with poetry. Mircea Eliade views the shaman as a "proto-poet" and "specialist of the sacred" who masters "techniques of ecstasy." In shamanic séances, the shaman goes into a trance and becomes possessed by a god or gods who speak through him or her. The shaman, who travels in supernatural worlds and speaks in an exalted or trancelike manner, embodies and enacts the idea of the poet as a prophet or seer. "It is likewise possible that the pre-ecstatic euphoria constituted one of the universal sources of lyric poetry," Eliade speculates. "In preparing his trance, the shaman drums, summons his spirit helpers, speaks a 'secret language' or the 'animal language,' imitating the cries of beasts and especially the songs of birds. He ends by obtaining a 'second state' that provides the impetus for linguistic creation and the rhythms of lyric poetry."

Nora Chadwick makes the case, in *Poetry and Prophecy* (1942), that the fundamental elements of the prophetic function of poetry operate in the same way all over the world:

Everywhere the gift of poetry is inseparable from divine inspiration. Everywhere this inspiration carries with it knowledge — whether of the past, in the form of history and genealogy; of the hidden present, in the form commonly of scientific information; and of the future, in the prophetic utterance in the narrower sense. Always this knowledge is uttered in poetry which is accompanied by music, whether of song or instrument. Music is everywhere the medium of communication with spirits. Invariably we find that the poet and seer attributes his inspiration to contact with supernatural powers, and his mood during prophetic utterance is exalted and remote from that of his normal existence. Generally we find that a recognized process is in vogue by which the prophetic mood can be induced at will. The lofty claims of the poet and seer are universally admitted, and he himself holds a high status wherever he is found.

Some researchers believe that the traditional shamans of northern and central Asia were the predecessors of the epic singers of ancient Greece. Ted Hughes called the shamanic flight "one of the main regeneration dramas of the human psyche: the fundamental poetic event."

SEE ALSO *inspiration, oral poetry, vatic.*

shan-shui Rivers-and-mountains poetry. Originating in the early fifth century, this Chinese tradition represents, as David Hinton puts it in his anthology *Mountain Home* (2002), "the earliest and most extensive literary engagement with wilderness in human history." The poetry embodies a deep physical and spiritual sense of belonging to the wilderness. Hsieh Ling-yün (385–433) is the founder of the rivers-and-mountains tradition, whereas T'ao Ch'ien (365–427) is the founder of the fields-and-garden tradition. Yet T'ao Ch'ien wrote, "Vast and majestic, mountains embrace your shadow; / broad and deep, rivers harbor your voice." The great T'ang dynasty poets all wove their consciousness into the wilderness. One thinks of Meng Hao-jan (689–740), Wang Wei (701–761), Li Po (701–762), and Tu Fu (712–770), who wrote, "The nation falls into ruins; rivers and mountains continue."

SEE ALSO *ecopoetry, nature poetry.*

shiᶜr From the Arabic verb *shaᶜara,* meaning "to know," "to understand," and "to perceive." The Arabic word for poetry. In *An Introduction to Arab Poetics* (1985), the poet Adonis explains, "We call the poet *shāᶜir* (literally, 'one who knows, understands, perceives') in Arabic because he perceives and understands (*yashʿuru*) that which others do not perceive and understand, that is he knows (*yaʿlamu*) what others do not know." In general, the term *poetry* refers to a special kind of speech regulated by rhyme and meter. The verb *shaʿara* has also come to have an additional meaning: "to feel."

shloka, sloka From the Sanskrit root *shru,* meaning "to hear." *Shloka* is sometimes translated as "poetry." In the Upanishads, the word is employed to mean "union." In classical Sanskrit literature, it is used for both "poem" (verse in any meter) and "fame." Tradition has it that in post-Vedic literature, meaning after the most sacred writings of Hinduism in early Sanskrit (the Samhitas, the Brahmanas, the Aranyakas, the Upanishads) had been written, Valmiki uttered the first *shloka,* the famous opening section of the Ramayana (fifth to fourth century B.C.E.). This stanza, two sixteen-syllable lines, was composed in the common epic meter called *anushtup* (made up of four *padas,* or feet, each eight syllables long), which in turn came to be called the *shloka* meter.

Shloka* is equated with Hindu prayer, in which it is heard as a kind of hymn chanted or sung in liturgy. It can also have a proverbial sense. The Kashmiri offshoot of *shloka* is *shrukh* ("wise sayings of a great man").

short meter, short measure A variation of the common meter found in hymns. Whereas in ballad meter the four-line stanza follows a pattern of alternating stresses (4, 3, 4, 3), the short meter foreshortens the first tetrameter line (3, 3, 4, 3). It is usually iambic. The stanza rhymes *abcb* or *abab*. The form is similar to poulter's measure, which consists of rhyming couplets that alternate iambic hexameter (twelve-syllable) and iambic heptameter (fourteen-syllable) lines. Emerson purposely employs the short measure of the hymnal in his quatrain "Poet" (1867):

> Tŏ clóthe thĕ fierў thóught
> Ĭn símplĕ wórds sŭccéeds,
> Fŏr stíll thĕ cráft ŏf génĭus ís
> Tŏ másk ă kíng ĭn wéeds.

SEE ALSO *ballad, hymn, long meter, poulter's measure.*

silvae   A collection of encomiastic odes, epigrams, and other kinds of short verse. *Silvae* means "woods" or "forest" but also "raw material" and, metaphorically, a miscellaneous collection. Statius's *Silvae* (ca. 89–96 C.E.), which sets the model, consists of thirty-two occasional poems that congratulate and thank friends, console mourners, admire monuments, describe memorable scenes. These rapid impromptu poems or "bits of raw material" created a vogue for deliberately rough, extemporaneous poems. Statius's contemporary Quintilian considered it a fault that certain writers "run over the material first with as rapid a pen as possible, extempore, following the inspiration of the moment: this they call *silva*" (*Institutio oratoria*, first century). The improvisatory sketch appealed to Renaissance writers, such as Poliziano (Angelo Ambrogini), who titled his verse lectures *Silvae* (1480–90), and Ben Jonson, whose note to *The Underwood* (1640) explains, "With the same leave, the ancients called that kind of body *Sylva*, or *Hylë*, in which there were works of divers nature, and matter congested; as the multitude call Timber-trees, promiscuously growing, a *Wood*, or *Forest:* so am I bold to entitle these lesser Poems, of later growth, by this of *Underwood*, out of the Analogy they hold to the *Forest . . .*"

   Some examples of the poetical *silvae* as a collection of occasional poetry: Pierre de Ronsard's *Bocages* (1554), Phineas Fletcher's *Silva Poetica* (1633), Abraham Cowley's *Sylva, or divers copies* (1636), Robert Herrick's *Hesperides* (1648), and John Dryden's *Silvae: or, the second Part of Poetical Miscellanies* (1693). Alastair Fowler points out that the *silvae* has maintained a tenuous tradition in such works as Samuel Taylor Coleridge's *Sibylline Leaves* (1817), Leigh Hunt's *Foliage; or, Poems Original and Translated* (1818), Walt Whitman's *Leaves of Grass* (1855), Robert Louis Stevenson's *Underwoods* (1887), Robert Lowell's *Notebook* (1967–68), and Edwin Morgan's *New Divan* (1977). "We tend to take for granted the idea of a collection of poems on various subjects and in different forms, without reflecting that such collections constitute a specific genre. It seems almost as if the genre were too dominant, too nonpareil, to have a name."

SEE ALSO *occasional poem.*

simile   The explicit comparison of one thing to another, using the word *as* or *like* — as when Robert Burns writes,

> My love is like a red, red rose
>> That's newly sprung in June:
> My love is like the melodie
>> That's sweetly play'd in tune.

The essence of simile is likeness and unlikeness, urging a comparison of two different things. A good simile depends on a kind of heterogeneity between the elements being compared. Similes are comparable to metaphors, but the difference between them is not merely grammatical, depending on the explicit use of *as* or *like*. It is a difference in significance. Metaphor asserts an identity. It says, "A poem is a meteor" (Wallace Stevens); it says A equals B, and in doing so relies on condensation and compression. By contrast, the simile is a form of analogical thinking. It says, "Poetry is made in a bed like love" (André Breton); it says A is like B, and thereby works by opening outward. There is a digressive impulse in similes that keeps extending to new things.

The simile asserts a likeness between unlike things, maintaining their comparability. It also draws attention to their differences, thus affirming a state of division. When Shakespeare asks, "Shall I compare thee to a summer's day?" ("Sonnet 18," 1609), he draws attention to the artificial process of figuration. So does the Hebraist who asserts, in the Song of Songs (1:9), "I have compared thee, O my love, to a company / of horses in Pharaoh's chariots." The reader participates in making meaning through simile, in establishing the nature of an unforeseen analogy, in evaluating the aptness of unexpected resemblance.

SEE ALSO *analogy, figures of speech, metaphor, rhetoric, trope.*

sincerity   *Sincerity,* which Lionel Trilling defines as "a congruence between avowal and actual feeling," was a negligible term in criticism until the second half of the eighteenth century, when it came into vogue with Jean-Jacques Rousseau's *Confessions* (1769) and Goethe's *Sorrows of Young Werther* (1774). The Romantic poets placed a high value on the uniqueness of individual experience. They made the expression of powerful emotion a crucial touchstone, a raison d'être for poetry itself. Romantic sincerity, like Romantic spontaneity, was an artful construction that gave the feeling of an utterly authentic relationship between the poet and his subject, without any intervening artifice. "There is nothing of the conventional craft of artificial writers," Leigh Hunt said about Keats's "The Eve of St. Agnes" (1819). "All flows out of sincerity and passion."

There are two countermovements related to sincerity in the second half of the nineteenth century. On one hand, Victorian poets and critics gave greater moral weight to the idea of sincerity. Writing from the heart, the appearance of sincerity, became a measure of poetic integrity. The most genuine poetry corresponded to the poet's deepest state of mind. Matthew Arnold spoke of "the high seriousness which comes from absolute sincerity." On the other hand, as Nietzsche said, "Every profound spirit needs a mask," and insincerity, the idea of a dramatic pose, also gained traction. Charles Baudelaire enshrined the idea of the dandy, a cultivated figure, and Robert Browning created the fictive speakers of the dramatic monologue, a type of poem that marginalizes the idea of poetic sincerity. The advantage of posing would culminate in Oscar Wilde's aphorism "Man is least himself when he talks in his own person. Give him a mask and he will tell you the truth." The modernist poets shifted the idea of sincerity away from self-expression, the honest transcription of feeling, toward verbal accuracy, artistic precision. Sincerity is reflected in making. Ezra Pound said, "I believe in technique as the test of a man's sincerity."

SEE ALSO *decadence, dramatic monologue, impersonality, neoclassicism, persona, Romanticism, sensibility.*

sirventes, serventes   A type of satirical poem in Provençal poetry. This partisan genre, filled with praise and blame, was usually employed to satirize the vices and follies of the age. It was common for a troubadour to borrow the tune for a sirventes from a more popular *chanso* ("love song"), which was considered the superior genre. The poems were usually topical, often exhortational, and they attacked any subject but love. Bertran de Born (ca. 1140s–1215) was considered the master of the sirventes, or political song.

The double sirventes consists of a pair of formally matching antithetical lyrics. It takes the strophic back-and-forth of the *tenson,* a debate poem, and develops it into whole lyrics. The most celebrated example of the *sirven-*

tes-tenson is the series of six exchanges between Sordello and Pierre Bremon between 1234 and 1240.

SEE ALSO *chanso, planh, poetic contest, satire, tenson, troubadour.*

skald, scald   This Old Norse word for "poet" is generally applied to Norwegian or Icelandic court poets from the ninth to the thirteenth century. The most credible etymology suggests that the word *skald* derives from a lost Germanic verb, *skeldan,* "to abuse verbally." Thus a *skald* may originally have meant "poet who abuses someone verbally." The skalds ("verse smiths") were proud of their craft and often compared themselves to artisans. They were experts at kennings (metaphoric compounds) and mastered complicated alliterative verse forms, such as the *dróttkvætt* ("lordly meter"). Skaldic poets were well-rewarded historians of their patrons, and much of their work had to do with praising their lords. The Scottish poet Hugh MacDiarmid identified with the passionate social role of the skald: "I have been a singer after the fashion / Of my people — a poet of passion," he wrote in "Skald's Death" (1934), which is engraved on the cairn beside his memorial.

SEE ALSO *kenning.*

Skeltonics, Skeltonic verse   A rough-and-tumble verse form named after its originator, John Skelton (1460–1529), who wrote in jumpy short lines with irregular rhythms. Skelton's lines had two or three stresses and any number of syllables, and his lyrics rhymed in irregular groups. He liked wordplay, alliterating couplets, and parallel constructions. Here is how he described his own verse in "Colin Clout" (1522):

> And if ye stand in doubt
> Who brought this rhyme about,
> My name is Colin Clout.
> I purpose to shake out
> All my connying bag.
> Like a clerkly hag;
> For though my rhyme be ragged,
> Tattered and jagged,
> Rudely rain beaten,

> Rusty and moth-eaten,
> If ye take well therewith,
> It hath in it some pith.

James VI called Skelton's lively, funny, doggerel-like poems "tumbling verse," and the energetic short lines and fast, frequent rhymes do tumble down the page. Skelton's "rude rayling" was praised by Wordsworth and Coleridge, and championed by such poets as W. H. Auden and Robert Graves, who asked, "What could be dafter / Than John Skelton's laughter?" ("John Skelton," 1918).

SEE ALSO *doggerel, light verse, tumbling verse.*

slam poetry A form of poetic boxing, a competition in which poets perform original work before an audience. Slam poetry returns poetry to its oral roots, though its subject matter is current and often focuses on social, racial, economic, and gender injustices. The poems are often memorized. They aren't meant to be read on the page, but performed. The judges are selected from the audience, which tends to be vocal. The competitors perform alone or in teams. Poetic contests are ancient, but the structure of the contemporary slam was started by Marc Smith at the Green Mill on Lawrence and Broadway in Chicago, Illinois, in 1986. He called his series "The Uptown Poetry Slam." The poetry slam quickly spread across the country.

SEE ALSO *poetic contests, spoken word poetry.*

slant rhyme, see *near rhyme.*

song A musical composition intended or adapted for singing. Song was originally inseparable from poetry, and poems were meant to be chanted and sung, sustained by oral tradition. Poetry is still considered song in many parts of the world, whether it is presented with or without musical accompaniment. The word *lyric* derives from the Greek *lyra,* or "musical instrument," and the Greeks spoke of lyrics as *ta mele,* "poems to be sung." Greek lyrics took the form of either monodies, sung by a single person, or choral odes, sung by choirs. Epic poems were considered *aoidé* ("singing"). The musical element is so intrinsic to poetry that one never forgets its origin in musical expression — in singing, chanting, and recitation to musical accompaniment.

Until the sixteenth century in Europe, poets were also composers and musicians. The poet was a performer — a bard, a skald, a scop, a troubadour. Heroic poems were sung (or chanted) and so were courtly love poems. There were professional and nonprofessional poets. One sang or listened to ballads, one shared hymns in church. Before the eighteenth century, writers or critics seemed to make little or no distinction between melodic lyrics, such as Thomas Campion's ayres or the songs of William Shakespeare's plays, and nonmusical written lyrics, such as Shakespeare's sonnets. Horace (65–8 B.C.E.) called the language of his satires, which are often close to daily speech, "singing." During the Renaissance, English writers first began to write their lyrics for readers rather than composing them for musical performance. The word *song* increasingly came to suggest a literary composition in verse form. Songs were still written for music, but the term *song* was also used metaphorically, as in Christopher Smart's "A Song to David" (1763) or William Blake's *Songs of Innocence and Experience* (1789), which are meant to be read.

SEE ALSO *air, aoidos, ballad, bard, chanson, epic, folk song, lyric, oral poetry, scop, skald, troubadour.*

songbook   A collection of verses set to music. *The Great American Songbook,* for example, refers to the vast repertoire of pre–World War II pop music, which includes such standards as "Alexander's Ragtime Band" (1911, Irving Berlin), "Someone to Watch Over Me" (1926, George and Ira Gershwin), "Ain't Misbehavin'" (1929, Fats Waller), "I've Got You Under My Skin" (1936, Cole Porter), and "My Funny Valentine" (1937, Richard Rodgers and Lorenz Hart).

There were various anthological *canzonierei,* or songbooks, in late medieval and Renaissance Italian poetry. These provided a lyrical prototype for Petrarch's *Il canzoniere* (*Songbook,* 1374), which is also called in Latin *Rerum vulgarium fragmenta* (*Fragments of Vernacular Poetry*), his own nickname for the collection, and in Italian *Rime sparse* (*Scattered Rhymes*). Ever since Petrarch, the songbook has been used metaphorically to capture the oral power of "song" for the written lyric.

SEE ALSO *ballad, canzone, chanson, madrigal, sestina, song, sonnet.*

sonnet From the Italian word *sonetto*, meaning "a little sound" or "a little song." The stateliness of this fourteen-line rhyming poem, invented in southern Italy around 1235, belies the word's modest derivation. The sonnet has had a durable life ever since its inception. It is a small vessel capable of plunging tremendous depths.

The spaciousness and brevity of the fourteen-line poem suit the contours of rhetorical argument, especially when the subject is erotic love. The form becomes a medium for the poet to explore his or her capacity to bring together feeling and thought, the lyrical and the discursive. The meter of the sonnet tends to follow the prevalent meter of the language in which it is written: in English, iambic pentameter; in French, the alexandrine; in Italian, the hendecasyllable. The two main types of sonnet form in English are the English, or Shakespearean, sonnet, which consists of three quatrains and a couplet, usually rhyming *abab, cdcd, efef, gg,* and the Italian, or Petrarchan, sonnet, which consists of an octave (eight lines, rhyming *abbaabba*) and a sestet (six lines, rhyming *cdecde*). The volta, or turn, refers to the rhetorical division and shift between the opening eight lines and the concluding six.

The Petrarchan sonnet probably developed out of the Sicilian *strambotto,* a popular song form consisting of two quatrains and two tercets. The sonnet was widely practiced throughout the later Middle Ages by all the Italian lyric poets, especially the *stilnovisti* — Guinizelli, Cavalcanti, and Dante — who used it to reinvent the love poem as a medium of quasi-religious devotion to a beloved lady. Petrarch's 317 sonnets to Laura are a kind of encyclopedia of passion. The Petrarchan sonnet invites an asymmetrical two-part division of the argument. Its rhyming is impacted and it tends to build an obsessive feeling in the octave, which is let loose in the sestet. "One of the emotional archetypes of the Petrarchan sonnet structure," Paul Fussell asserts, "is the pattern of sexual pressure and release."

Sir Thomas Wyatt and the Earl of Surrey imported the Petrarchan form to England early in the sixteenth century. Surrey later established the rhyme scheme *abab, cdcd, efef, gg.* George Gascoigne described this new version of the sonnet in 1575: "Sonnets are of fourteene lynes, every lyne conteyning tenne syllables. The first twelve do ryme in staves of foure lynes by crosse metre, and the last two ryming together do conclude the whole."

"SHAKE-SPEARE'S SONNETS. Neuer before imprinted" appeared in 1609, and these 154 sonnets comprise a high-water mark of English poetry. The Shakespearean sonnet invites a more symmetrical division of thought into three equal quatrains and a summarizing couplet. It is well balanced, well suited to calculation. The form enables a precision of utterance and freedom of forensic argument. "The sonnet of Shakespeare is not merely such and such a pattern, but a precise way of thinking and feeling," T. S. Eliot notes. It also offers more flexibility in rhyming, which is crucial since Italian is so much richer in rhyme than English. The poet using this logical structure can also create wild disturbances within the prescribed form. This seems to work especially well for closely reasoned and ultimately highly unreasonable and even obsessive subjects, like erotic love.

Over the centuries poets have proved ingenious at reinventing the formal chamber of the sonnet. The Elizabethan poet Edmund Spenser developed an interlacing version of the sonnet called the link, or Spenserian, sonnet. It interlinks rhymes and concludes with a binding couplet (*abab, bcbc, cdcd, ee*). The Miltonic sonnet retains the octave rhyme scheme of the Petrarchan sonnet, but doesn't turn at the sestet and varies its rhyme scheme, thus opening up the form. Milton further extended the form in a tailed sonnet, composed of twenty lines. He turned the sonnet away from love to occasional and political subjects ("When the Assault Was Intended to the City," 1642; "On the Late Massacre in Piedmont," 1655).

The sonnet was virtually extinct after 1650 until the Romantic poets revitalized it. Leigh Hunt said, "Every mood of mind can be indulged in a sonnet; every kind of reader appealed to. You can make love in a sonnet, you can laugh in a sonnet, can narrate or describe, can rebuke, can admire, can pray." How much poorer English poetry would be without Wordsworth's "Composed upon Westminster Bridge, September 3, 1802," Keats's "On First Looking into Chapman's Homer" (1816), and Shelley's "Ozymandias" (1818). So too in France the sonnet was revived by Gautier (1811–1872) and Baudelaire (1821–1867) and further developed by Mallarmé (1842–1898), Rimbaud (1854–1891), and Valéry (1871–1945). George Meredith lengthened the traditional sonnet to sixteen lines in his fifty-poem sequence *Modern*

Love (1862). Gerard Manley Hopkins invented a form he called a curtal sonnet — literally, a sonnet cut short to ten and a half lines, such as "Pied Beauty" (1877). Hopkins also experimented with metrics in "Spelt from Sibyl's Leaves" (1886; "the longest sonnet ever made"), which employs eight-stress lines.

There is a sense of permanence and fragility, of spaciousness and constriction, about the sonnet form that has always had poets brooding over it, as in John Donne's well-known lines from "The Canonization" (1633):

> We'll build in sonnets pretty roomes;
> As well a well wrought urne becomes
> The greatest ashes, as halfe-acre tombes . . .

Dante Gabriel Rossetti called the sonnet "a moment's monument" (*The House of Life,* 1881). In a way, every great sonnet is a moment's monument to the form itself. As Northrop Frye wrote about the Shakespearean sonnet, "The true father or shaping spirit of the poem is the form of the poem itself, and this form is a manifestation of the universal spirit of poetry."

SEE ALSO *alexandrine, courtly love, hendecasyllable, iambic pentameter, Petrarchism, sonnet cycle.*

sonnet cycle   The sonnet tends to be a compulsive form. As John Donne wryly put it, "The Spanish proverb informs me, that he is a fool which cannot make one sonnet, and he is mad which makes two." The sonnet cycle (or sonnet sequence) consists of a series of sonnets on a particular theme addressed to a particular person. Love is often the obsessive theme of this petition for emotional recognition. The great advantage of the cycle is that it allows the poet to record every aspect and mood of the experience, to explore feeling in detail, and to analyze the progress of attachment, the ups and downs of the affair. Yet each individual sonnet maintains its integrity. Thus the cycle combines the rhetorical intensity of the short poem with the thematic scope of the long poem or story.

Some key early examples: Dante's *Vita nuova* (1293), which has extensive prose links; Petrarch's *Canzoniere* or *Rime* (1360), a sequence of 317 sonnets and 40 other poems in praise of one woman, Laura; Ronsard's *Amours* (1552–84); Sidney's quasi-narrative *Astrophil and Stella* (1591); Spenser's *Amoretti* (1595); and Shakespeare's *Sonnets* (1609). There were no British sonnets before about 1530 and very few after 1650, until the Romantic revival of the form. Some key Romantic and post-Romantic examples of the sequence: Wordsworth's *Ecclesiastical Sonnets* (1822); Rossetti's *The House of Life* (1881); Elizabeth Barrett Browning's *Sonnets from the Portuguese* (1850); Dylan Thomas's ten-part "Altarwise by Owl-Light" (1936); W. H. Auden's "Sonnets from China" (1938); and Seamus Heaney's "Glanmore Sonnets" (1979).

One specialized version of the sonnet sequence is the corona, or crown, of sonnets, which consists of seven interlocked poems. The final line of each lyric becomes the first line of the succeeding one, and the last line of the seventh sonnet becomes the first line of the opening poem. The whole is offered as a crown (a panegyric) to the one addressed. The repetitions and linkages within the larger circular structure are well suited to obsessive reiterations of supplication and praise.

SEE ALSO *sonnet*.

sound poetry   Sound is crucial to poetry and thus, in one sense, all poetry is sound poetry, except, perhaps, deaf poetry. Sidney Lanier emphasized the idea of sound in poetry when he commenced his treatise *The Science of English Verse* (1880) with an "Investigation of Sound as Artistic Material": "When formal poetry, or verse . . . is repeated aloud, it impresses itself upon the ear as verse only by means of certain relations existing among its component words considered purely as sounds, without reference to their associated ideas."

Sound poetry generally refers to a type of poetry that aggressively foregrounds the sounds of words. It is performance oriented and seeks to override conventional denotative and syntactical values. It goes beyond the page so that sound alone dominates. Sound poetry has its roots in preliterate oral traditions, in tribal chants and magic spells. The more extreme that nonsense poetry becomes, repressing sense, the more it tends toward sound poetry. There is a mode of tribal poetry that uses instruments to mimic the human voice. Thus the media of poetry in tonal languages include drums, whistles, flutes, and horns. Whereas in American jazz, scat singers use their voices to create the equivalent of instrumental solos, in tribal poetries, musicians use their instruments to create the equivalent of human voices.

As a self-conscious avant-garde phenomenon, sound poetry dates to the early years of the twentieth century. The Russian futurists Aleksei Kruchenykh and Velimir Khlebnikov isolated the phonic aspects of language in their manifesto "The Word as Such" (1913), which insists that "the element of sound lives a self-oriented life." The Italian futurist F. T. Marinetti developed a poetic technique he called *parole in libertà* ("words in freedom"), which he used for his onomatopoetic *Bombardamento di Adrianapoli* (1913), to re-create the 1912 siege of Adrianople. Sound poetry was explicitly a Dadaist creation, and the movement radiated outward from Zurich and Berlin. Hugo Ball claimed to have invented it at the Cabaret Voltaire in 1916. The spontaneous desire to rescue language and return it to its origins helped motivate his "destruction of language." He said, "I invented a new genre of poems, verse without words, or sound poems. I recited the following: 'gadji beri bimba / glandridi lauli lonni cadori...'" Ball called these hypnotic nonce words *grammologues* ("magical floating words"). There is a strong element of shock in the way the Dadaists used sound poetry to attack notions of reason, order, and control. The Dadaists Raoul Hausmann (1861–1971) and Kurt Schwitters (1887–1948) both created their own versions of sound poems.

In 1921, Theo van Doesburg, the founder of the Dutch avant-garde movement De Stijl, published three "letter-sound images" and asserted, "To take away its past it is necessary to renew the alphabet according to its abstract sound values. This means at the same time the healing of our poetic auditory membranes, which are so weakened, that a long term phono-gymnastics is necessary!" As early as 1919, Arthur Pétronio (1897–1983) invented something he called *verbophonie,* which harmonized phonetic rhythms with instrumental sounds, and the French Lettrists of the 1940s created full-scale sonic texts, a "New Alphabet." Since the 1950s, poets around the world have continued to experiment with sound compositions and soundscapes, often relying on technology to create startling new effects. Some examples: Henry Chopin's *audiopoems,* Bernard Heidsieck's *poempartitions* and *biopsies,* the text-sound compositions of the Swedish Fylkingen's Group for Linguistic Arts, Bob Cobbing's *Concrete Sound,* Herman Damen's sonic genres *verbosony* and *verbophony,* Tera de Marez Oyens's *vocaphonies,* Jackson Mac Low's systematic chance operations. In the 1970s, the Four Horsemen, a group of

Canadian poets, started using their voices as instruments to celebrate vocal sound.

Sound poetry is performance poetry. "When did you start writing sound-poetry?" the interviewer asks in Edwin Morgan's poem "Interview" (ca. 1981). The answer comically enacts sound poetry itself:

> —Vindaberry am hookshma tintol ensa ar'er.
> Vindashton hama haz temmi-bloozma töntek.

SEE ALSO *abstract poetry, Dadaism, nonsense poetry, onomatopoeia, oral poetry, performance poetry, zaum.*

spell   An incantation or charm designed to produce magical effects. "It is exceedingly well / To give a common word the spell," the eighteenth-century poet Christopher Smart writes, punning on the word *spell.* Tribal peoples everywhere have believed that the act of putting words in a certain rhythmic order has magical potency, a power released when the words are chanted aloud.

SEE ALSO *chant, charm, incantation, oral poetry.*

Spenserian stanza   Edmund Spenser invented a nine-line pattern for his epic romance *The Faerie Queene* (1590–96). The Spenserian stanza consists of eight iambic pentameter lines with a hexameter (alexandrine) at the end. It rhymes *ababbcbcc.* The interweaving rhymes seem influenced by Chaucer's use of rhyme royal (seven-line stanzas rhyming *ababbcc*) and the Monk's Tale stanza (eight lines rhyming *ababbcbc*). It is also related to the eight-line or ottava rima stanza, which Ludovico Ariosto mastered in *Orlando furioso* (1516), but it goes one step further, since the last line has a conclusive or epigrammatic power. It is a stanza of great versatility and enables Spenser to be lusciously dreamy and vividly narrative; it is brisk enough for quickly sketched vignettes, slow enough for visual description and philosophic speculation.

> Help then, O holy virgin, chief of nine,
> Thy weaker novice to perform thy will;
> Lay forth out of thine everlasting scrine [chest for records]

The antique rolls [records], which there lie hidden still,
Of faery knights and fairest Tanaquill,
Whom that most noble Briton prince so long
Sought through the world and suffered so much ill
That I must rue his undeservèd wrong.
O help thou my weak wit, and sharpen my dull tongue.

The Spenserian stanza was dropped in the eighteenth century, but revived by the Romantic poets. A good shortlist of the second flowering would include Wordsworth's "Female Vagrant" (1798), Burns's "Cotter's Saturday Night" (1785–86), Scott's "Vision of Don Roderick" (1811), Byron's *Childe Harold's Pilgrimage* (1812–18), Keats's "The Eve of St. Agnes" (1819), and Shelley's "Revolt of Islam" (1817) and "Adonais" (1821).

SEE ALSO *Monk's Tale stanza, ottava rima, rhyme royal, terza rima.*

spirituals   Sacred songs. The word *spiritual,* applied to religious songs, was initially used to distinguish "godly" songs from secular or "profane" ones. The spiritual developed from the folk hymns of dissenters in colonial America. It generally refers to two closely connected bodies of music: white spirituals and African American spirituals. It was around the time of the Great Revival (1800) that *spiritual* became the name for revival hymns or camp-meeting songs. *The Standard Dictionary of Folklore, Mythology, and Legend* (1972) points out that "its special application to Negro religious song is of fairly recent date as a catch-all term for the 'hallies,' shouts, jubilees, carols, gospel songs, and hymns for regular services, prayer meetings, watches, and 'rock' services."

White spirituals began with the doleful psalm-singing of the Puritans. The tradition was later enlivened by many splinter sects of Baptists and Methodists, who added marching and dancing rhythms, ballad tunes, and colorful lines suitable to frontier camp meetings. The Holiness Revival, which started around 1890, added jazzy, syncopated rhythms. The songs are accompanied by instruments, such as the banjo and the guitar, once considered profane.

African American spirituals developed as the music of American slaves of African descent. In form they exemplify African American hybridity. They are spiritually the substance of African American Christianity. They tell a story of suffering, endurance, and triumph, history and eternity. They seek absolute or ultimate justice. They use biblical stories to express the longing for delivery out of slavery:

Go down Moses,
Way down in Egypt land,
Tell ole Pharaoh,
To let my people go.

African American spirituals were not collected until after the Civil War. Three northerners, William F. Allen, Charles P. Ware, and Lucy McKim Garrison, made the first systematic collection, *Slave Songs of the United States* (1867), which included some of the spirituals that are still best known, such as "Old ship of Zion," "Lay this body down," "Michael, row the boat ashore," and "We will march through the valley." Cornel West states that "the spirituals of American slaves of African descent constitute the first expression of American modern music. How ironic that a people on the dark side of modernity — dishonored, devalued and dehumanized by the practices of modern Europeans and Americans — created the fundamental music of American modernity."

SEE ALSO *blues*.

spoken word poetry   Poetry is an ancient oral art, but the spoken word movement developed in the late 1980s and early '90s as a particular phenomenon. The term *spoken word* is a catch-all that includes any kind of oral art, including comedy routines and prose monologues, such as those by Spalding Gray. Spoken word poetry refers to any kind of poetry recited aloud: hip-hop, jazz poetry, the poetry performed at slams or traditional poetry readings. Perhaps its Ur form is performance poetry, which is kindred to performance art. Performance poems tend to have a visceral spontaneity, a highly vocal, in-your-face quality. They are not meant to be read on the page, or sung.

The spoken word movement was inspired by the countercultural vitality of the Beat poetry of the 1950s. Allen Ginsberg stated categorically, "The spoken-word movement comes out of the Beats, but with rhyme added."

Both movements disdain the academy. Spoken word poetry often carries a strong social critique, aggressive political commentary. It speaks up for those who are mostly unheard in society. The setting is a key part of the experience, which can have an element of the carnivalesque. Its great strength is that it is driven by the human voice.

SEE ALSO *jazz poetry, oral poetry, performance poetry, poetry contest, slam poetry.*

spondee A poetic foot consisting of two equally accented syllables, as in the words *dáylíght* and *níghtfáll.* The Greek term for two spondees is *dispondee,* which we recognize in the words *hómemáde ártwórk.* The word *spondee* derives from *sponde* ("solemn libation"), and the Greek meter (two equally long syllables) was originally used in chants accompanying libations. It was a meter for making an offering, performing a rite. In accentual-syllabic poetry, spondees create an emphatic stress, a hammer beat, but seldom control an entire rhythm in English. The first, third, and fifth lines are spondaic in this anonymous nursery rhyme:

> Óne, twó
> Buckle my shoe;
> Thrée, fóur,
> Shut the door;
> Fíve, síx,
> Pick up sticks . . .

Since stress is always relative in English, there may be no perfect spondee.

SEE ALSO *foot, meter.*

sprung rhythm Gerard Manley Hopkins's term for a type of rhythm that depends solely on the number of stresses in a line. Sprung rhythm scans by counting accents and not syllables, like the accentual beat in Anglo-Saxon verse. It is a particular method of timing. Hopkins objected to the way that in most post-Renaissance English poetry, a stressed syllable is accompanied by a uniform number of unstressed ones. He thought this was musically deadening. "Why do I employ sprung rhythm at all?" Hopkins wrote to Robert Bridges. "Because it is the nearest to the rhythm of prose, that is the native and natural rhythm of speech, the least forced, the most rhetorical and emphatic of all possible rhythms." Hopkins believed sprung rhythm could better capture the musical rhythms of speech than traditional meters could.

SEE ALSO *counterpoint;* also "pure accentual meter" in *meter.*

stanza   The natural unit of the lyric: a group or sequence of lines arranged in a pattern. A stanzaic pattern is traditionally defined by the meter and rhyme scheme, considered repeatable throughout a work. A stanzaic poem uses white space to create temporal and visual pauses. The word *stanza* means "room" in Italian — "a station," "a stopping place" — and each stanza in a poem is like a room in a house, a lyric dwelling place. "The Italian etymology," Ernst Häublein points out in his study of the stanza, "implies that stanzas are subordinate units within the more comprehensive unity of the whole poem." Each stanza has an identity, a structural place in the whole. As the line is a single unit of meaning, so the stanza comprises a larger rhythmic and thematic sequence. It is a basic division comparable to the paragraph in prose, but more discontinuous, more insistent as a separate melodic and rhetorical unit. In written poems stanzas are separated by white space, and this division on the printed page gives the poem a particular visual reality. The reader has to cross a space to get from one stanza to another. *Stave* is another name for *stanza,* which suggests an early association with song.

A stanza that consists of lines of the same length is called an isometric stanza. A stanza that consists of lines of varying length is called a heterometric stanza.

A stanza of uneven length and irregular pattern — of fluid form — is sometimes called quasi-stanzaic or a verse paragraph.

The monostich is a stanza consisting of just one line. After that, there is the couplet (two-line stanza), tercet (three-line stanza), quatrain (four-line), quintet (five-line), sestet (six-line), septet (seven-line), and octave (eight-line). There are stanzas named after individual poets, such as the Spenserian stanza (the nine-line pattern Spenser invented for *The Faerie Queene,* 1590–96) and the Omar Khayyám quatrain (the four-line stanza the Persian poet employed in the eleventh century for *The Rubaiyat*). Each stanza has its own distinctive features, its own music, and its own internal history, which informs and haunts later usage.

SEE ALSO *couplet, heterometric stanza, isometric stanza, meter, monostich, octave, quatrain, quintet, rhyme, rubaiyat stanza, septet, sestet, Spenserian stanza, stichic, strophe, tercet, verse paragraph.*

stave, see *stanza.*

stich, stichos From the Greek word *stichos,* meaning a "row" or "line." A stich is a line of Greek or Latin verse. Half of a line is called a hemistich, a sole line (or a one-line poem) is called a monostich, and a couplet is called a distich.

SEE ALSO *couplet, hemistich, line, monostich, stichic.*

stichic A stichic poem is composed as a continuous sequence of lines without any division of those lines into regular stanzas. Contrasted to strophic organization, whose lines are patterned in stanzas, it is thus astrophic. *Paradise Lost* (Milton, 1667), *The Prelude* (Wordsworth, 1805, 1850), and *Four Quartets* (Eliot, 1943) are stichic; *The Faerie Queene* (Spenser, 1590–96), "Ode to a Nightingale" (Keats, 1819), and "Asphodel, That Greeny Flower" (Williams, 1955) are strophic. If subdivided at all, the blocks of a stichic poem are called stanzas of uneven length, or verse paragraphs. The tendency toward stichic verse is particularly strong in narrative and descriptive poetry, in long poems with the wide sweep of prose, such as A. R. Ammons's *Tape for the Turn of the Year* (1994), John Ashbery's *Flow Chart* (1991), and W. S. Merwin's *The Folding Cliffs: A Narrative* (1998).

SEE ALSO *descriptive poetry, narrative poetry, stanza, strophe, verse paragraph.*

strict-meter poetry, free-meter poetry In the first half of the fourteenth century, Einion the Priest divided all Welsh meters into three categories: *awdl, cywydd,* and *englyn.* Revised by Dafydd ab Edmwnd in 1450, this arrangement of the "twenty-four metres" into three classes has defined "strict-meter" poetry. All forms that fell outside the twenty-four meters were considered free-meter poetry. The breakdown of the bardic orders also led to the rise of the free meters. There is a strong nationalistic dimension to the resurgence of strict-meter poetry in modern Welsh poetry.

SEE ALSO *bard, cywydd.*

strophe From the Greek: "turning." A term for stanza or verse paragraph. A poem is traditionally considered strophic if its lines are arranged into stanzaic patterns, and astrophic or stichic when not. There is a strong tendency in some poetries to arrange poems into recognizable units of two, three, four, five, six, or more lines. European folk songs, for example, are strophic. The word *strophe* originally applied to the opening section (and every third succeeding section) of the Greek choral ode, which the chorus chanted while moving across the stage. This movement was followed by the antistrophe, an identical countermovement, and an epode, recited while the chorus was standing still.

SEE ALSO *antistrophe, epode, ode, stanza, stichic, verse paragraph.*

structure A structure is something built or constructed — a building, a bridge, a dam. Poetry borrows a term from architecture to account for the system of relations in a literary work. Structure is the developing or organizational means of a patterned work of art. The New Critics made the term one of the cornerstones of the attempt to differentiate the individual poem from a prose statement. Thus John Crowe Ransom advocated for a "structural understanding of poetry" and divided a poem into two constituent parts: "a central logic or understanding" and a "local texture" ("Criticism as Pure Speculation," 1941).

The term *structure* is sometimes misconstrued as the equivalent of *form*. Its meaning wavers because it takes a spatial metaphor and applies it to a temporal work. Ellen Bryant Voigt argues that "structure is the way all the poem's materials are organized, whether they are abstract or concrete, precise or suggestive, denoted or connoted, sensory or referential, singular or recurring." She calls structure "the purposeful order in which materials are released to the reader." Michael Theune defines structure as "*the pattern of a poem's turning*" and thus focuses on the skeletal part of a poem's structure.

A dramatic structure refers to the way that a play is organized, its unfolding plot. It has temporal divisions, a beginning, middle, and end. The New Critics applied the idea of dramatic structure to lyric poetry. Thus Robert Penn Warren describes dramatic structure as "a movement through action toward rest, through complication toward simplicity of effect" ("Pure and Impure Poetry," 1942). This involves, as Warren himself recognized, the active participation of the reader. In *Frame Analysis* (1974), the sociologist Erving Goffman took the idea of dramatic structure and applied it to social situations in everyday life.

SEE ALSO *form, sonnet, texture.*

style The manner of linguistic expression in a work of literature, the way in which something is said or done, expressed, written. Style is a quality of distinctive features — the choice of words, the figures of speech, the rhetorical devices, etc. — that belong to an individual, a group, a school, or an era. In classical theories of rhetoric, styles were traditionally classified according to three main types: high (or grand), middle (or mean), low (or plain). The level of style was matched to the speaker and the occasion. In poetry, styles are often classified according to the distinctive features of an individual writer (Chaucerian, Miltonic), an influential text (biblical style), or a literary period or tradition (metaphysical, Georgian). In the end, style cannot be separated from meaning. It is the way a work carries itself.

SEE ALSO *decorum, figures of speech, poetic diction, rhetoric.*

the sublime *The Oxford English Dictionary* defines *sublime* as "set or raised aloft, high up." The word derives from the Latin *sublimis,* a combination of *sub* ("up to") and *limen* ("lintel," the top piece of a door frame) and suggests nobility and majesty, the ultimate height, a soaring grandeur, as in a skyscraper or a mountain, or as in a dizzying feeling, a heroic deed, a spiritual attainment, a poetic expression — something boundless that takes us beyond ourselves, the transporting blow. "The essential claim of the sublime," Thomas Weiskel asserts in *The Romantic Sublime* (1986), "is that man can, in feeling and in speech, transcend the human." The sublime instills a feeling of awe in us, which can be terrifying. *The Oxford English Dictionary* also describes the effects of the sublime as crushing or engulfing, irresistible. The sublime is one of our large metaphors. As Weiskel puts it, "We cannot conceive of a literal sublime."

In the third century, Longinus inaugurated the literary idea and tradition of the sublime in his treatise *Peri hypsous* (*On the Sublime*). For him, the sublime describes the heights in language and thought. It is accessed through rhetoric, the devices of speech and poetry. It is a style of "loftiness," something we experience through words. "Sublimity is always an eminence and excellence in language," he claims. "It is our nature to be elevated and exalted by true sublimity. Filled with joy and pride, we come to believe we have created what we have only heard." The sublime is our "joining" with the great. Longinus raised the rhetorical and psychological issues that haunt the idea of the sublime, ancient and modern.

Longinus's treatise was translated into French by Boileau (1674) and passed quickly into English. Alexander Pope claimed that Longinus "is himself the great Sublime he draws" ("An Essay on Criticism," 1711). Edmund Burke took up the effects of the sublime in language in *A Philosophical Inquiry into the Origin of Our Ideas of the Sublime and Beautiful* (1756), where he argues that the sublime and the beautiful are mutually exclusive. He adds terror as a crucial component. "Whatever is fitted in any sort to excite the ideas of pain and danger, that is to say, whatever is in any sort terrible, or is conversant about terrible objects, or operates in a manner analogous to terror, is a source of the *sublime;* that is, it is productive of the strongest emotion which the mind is capable of feeling." There are subsequent philosophical investigations of the sublime in Kant (*Critique of Judgment,* 1790), Schopenhauer (the first volume of *The World as Will and Representation,* 1819), and Hegel (*Aesthetics: Lectures on Fine Art,* 1835). "In the European Enlightenment," Harold Bloom explains, the literary idea of the sublime "was strangely transformed into a vision of the terror that could be perceived both in nature and in art, a terror uneasily allied with pleasurable sensations of augmented power, and even of narcissistic freedom, freedom in the shape of that wildness that Freud dubbed 'the omnipotence of thought,' the greatest of all narcissistic illusions."

The Romantic poets were obsessed with sublimity; that is, with the idea of transcendence, with possible crossings between the self and nature, with the boundlessness of the universe. Each had a different idea of transcendence, as when Keats distinguished the true poetical character, which is selfless, from "the Wordsworthian or egotistical sublime," a sublime suffused with the self. Wordsworth himself called the elevation of the sublime a "visionary gleam." The Romantics transformed the sublime into a naturalistic key, internalizing it, which opened a space later entered by Freud, who was preoccupied with powerfully disruptive and uncanny moments.

The sublime has its own American genealogy and history. "How does one stand / To behold the sublime?" Wallace Stevens asks in "The American Sublime" (1936). In "Self-Reliance" (1841), Emerson takes up Longinus's idea of the reader's sublime when he declares that "in every work of genius we recognize our own rejected thoughts; they come back to us with a certain alienated majesty." Irving Howe spoke of "a democratized sublime," a space for schooling the spirit.

SEE ALSO *picturesque, rhetoric, the uncanny.*

surah, sura   The Koran is organized by surahs (chapters) and verses. There are 114 individually named surahs. Each consists of any number of verses and, except for surah 9, begins with the invocation "In the name of God, the merciful, the beneficent." The word *surah* is used exclusively to describe the Koran's divisions.

Surrealism   The convulsive phenomenon known as Dadaism was revitalized and transformed into the more durable movement of Surrealism in France in the 1920s. The term *surréaliste* was coined by Guillaume Apollinaire in 1917 to suggest a dramatic attempt to go beyond the limits of an agreed-upon "reality." André Breton used the term *Surrealism* ("superrealism," or "above reality") in 1924 in the first of three manifestoes. The Surrealists were apostles of what Breton called "beloved imagination." They hungered for the marvelous and believed in the revolutionary power of erotic desire and "mad love," of dreams, fantasies, and hallucinations. They sought to free the mind from the shackles of rational logic and explored the subterranean depths of the unconscious. They cultivated a condition of lucid trance and experimented with automatic writing—that is, writing attempted without any conscious control, as under hypnosis. The Surrealists courted disorder and believed in the possibilities of chance, of emotion induced by free association and surprising juxtapositions. Their true goal was inner freedom.

The major Surrealists in poetry: André Breton, Louis Aragon, Robert Desnos, Paul Éluard, Philippe Soupault, Benjamin Peret. Breton acknowledged that Surrealism was the "prehensile tail" of Romanticism. Surrealism dissolved as a cohesive movement in the late 1930s, but the United States benefited from the wartime presence of some of the leading Surrealist figures, such as Breton and Max Ernst. In a broad sense, Surrealism means a love of dreams and fantasies, a taste for strange marvels and black humor, an eagerness to take the vertiginous descent into the self in quest of the secret forces of the psyche, a faith in the value of chance encounters and free play, a belief in the liberating powers of eros, of beloved imagination.

SEE ALSO *automatic writing, Dadaism, imagination, Romanticism.*

sutra In Sanskrit, *sutra* literally means a "thread" (the word derives from a verbal root meaning "to sew") or line that holds things together. It generally refers to an aphorism or a collection of aphorisms in the form of a manual. In Hinduism, the sutras (500–200 B.C.E.) are treatises that deal with Vedic rituals and customary laws. They provide concise surveys of past literature in mnemonic, aphoristic form. In Buddhism, the term *sutra* generally refers to the oral teachings of the Buddha. The Beat poets loosely adapted the word *sutra* to refer to rules that hold an idea together, as in Allen Ginsberg's "Wichita Vortex Sutra" (1966) and "Sunflower Sutra" (1955).

syllable The smallest measurable unit of poetic sound. *Verse* is a monosyllabic word (composed of one syllable), *poetry* is a polysyllabic one (composed of multiple syllables). "English speech is carried on a stream of *syllables,* each one a little articulation of energy produced by the muscles that expel air out of the mouth, shaped by the vocal cords and the organs of the mouth," Derek Altridge writes in *Poetic Rhythm* (1995).

The syllable is the sole constituent in pure syllabic meter. Syllabic verse is common in languages that are syllable-timed, such as Japanese. It is less common in English, a stress-based language. Most traditional English poetry is thus accentual-syllabic; it counts both stresses and syllables. Pure syllabics, which counts only syllables, is rarer in English-language verse.

In English, syllabics is a numerical system the poet uses to structure the poem. It is a method of organization, a sort of game or puzzle, which has to do with counting. It is imposed but it doesn't necessarily *feel* imposed. Elizabeth Daryush (1887–1977) in England and Marianne Moore (1887–1972) in America pioneered the use of syllabic verse in modern poetry. They played with the expectations of iambic verse. In our era, such poets as Thom Gunn and Richard Howard have created a feeling of ease and flexibility, a natural-sounding verse in syllabics.

SEE ALSO *beat;* also "pure syllabic meter" in *meter.*

symbol From the Greek verb *symballein,* meaning "to put together," and the noun *symbolon,* meaning "mark," "emblem," "token," or "sign." In the classical world the *symbolon* was a half coin or half of a knucklebone carried by one person as a token of identity or a mark of obligation to someone holding the other half. It was a sign of agreement, a concrete object that represented a pledge. Each represented a whole. When the two halves were rejoined, they composed one coin or one knucklebone, a complete meaning.

Dr. Johnson defines a symbol as "that which comprehends in its figure a representation of something else." Thus a dove is both a graceful bird *and* a universal symbol of peace. A rose is both a literal flower *and* the most commonly used floral symbol in the West. "It is the paragon of flowers in Western tradition," as one dictionary of symbols explains — "a symbol of the heart, the centre and the cosmic wheel, and also of sacred, romantic, and sensual love."

Words are arbitrary symbols of meaning. They are also textured entities. Specific words are symbols that go beyond the literal. In poetry, it is critical to remember that *rose* is first of all a one-syllable, four-letter noun with a specific sound that ovals the mouth when you say it aloud. It has an acoustic impact, as when Wordsworth seals it as a rhyme in his ode "Intimations" (1807): "The Rainbow comes and goes, / And lovely is the Rose ..." The rose here is a word that stands for a literal flower, but it is also something more, like the transient rainbow. In a poem, the literal meaning and the literary symbol work together. We bring to our reading all the symbolic connotations and meanings available to us, but the symbol should first be understood in terms of how it works as a device within a poem itself.

The Princeton Encyclopedia of Poetry and Poetics (1974) summarizes that in literary usage, a symbol refers to "a manner of representation in which what is shown (normally referring to something material) means, by virtue of association, something more or something else (normally referring to something immaterial)." How a thing can be both itself and something else is one of the great mysteries of poetry. In poetry, a symbol offers a surplus of resonance, of significance, since a poem can have great suggestive power, like a dream. It can also have the strange precision of a dream, what Baudelaire termed "evocative bewitchment" and Yeats called "indefinable and yet precise emotions." In "The Symbolism of Poetry" (1900), Yeats called these lines by Burns, which he altered slightly in memory, "perfectly symbolical":

> The white moon is setting behind the white wave,
> And Time is setting with me, O!

Yeats said,

> Take from them the whiteness of the moon and of the wave, whose relation to the setting of Time is too subtle for the intellect, and you take from them their beauty. But, when they are together, moon and wave and whiteness and setting Time and the last melancholy cry, they evoke an emotion which cannot be evoked by any other arrangement of colours and sounds and forms. We may call this metaphorical writing, but it is better to call it symbolical writing.

SEE ALSO *allegory, symbolism.*

symbolism   A literary movement that thrived in France between the 1870s and '90s. It was initially called idealism. The leading symbolist poets, Paul Verlaine, Arthur Rimbaud, and Stéphane Mallarmé, along with the key figures Jules Laforgue and Tristan Corbière, were at the forefront of the modern poetic tradition. The symbolist poets opposed all forms of naturalism and realism. They craved a poetry of suggestion rather than direct statement and treated everything in the external world as a condition of soul. They sought to repress or obfuscate one kind of reality, the quotidian world, in order to attain a more permanent reality, a world of ideal forms and essences. They believed that a magical suggestiveness (what Rimbaud termed "*l'alchimie du verbe*") could best be achieved by synesthesia, fusing images and senses and bringing poetry as close as possible to music. Thus Verlaine's poem "Art poétique" (1874) advocates "music before everything." Walter Pater formulated a parallel doctrine in 1873 when he asserted, "All art constantly aspires towards the condition of music."

Baudelaire was one of the chief progenitors of the movement. His sonnet "Correspondances" (1857) envisioned nature as a "forest of symbols" and suggested a correspondence between the phenomenal world and the ideal one. He asserted in a prose piece that "everything, form, movement, number, color, perfume, in the *spiritual* as in the *natural* domain, is significant, reciprocal, converse, *corresponding*." Rimbaud followed Baudelaire and anticipated the Surrealists when he posited, "The poet makes himself a *seer* by a long, immense, and reasoned *derangement* of the senses." Correspondence was achieved through heightened concentration on the symbol, which had what Maeterlinck called a "*force occulte*." In 1891, Mallarmé defined symbolism:

> To name an object is to suppress three-quarters of the delight of the poem, which consists in the pleasure of guessing little by little; to *suggest* it, that is the dream. It is the perfect use of this mystery that constitutes the symbol: to evoke an object, gradually in order to reveal a state of the soul, or, inversely, to choose an object and from it identify a state of the soul, by a series of deciphering operations . . . There must always be enigma in poetry.

Enigma widens the space for daydreaming. It loosens the intellect and invites poetic reverie.

The symbolist movement reverberated around the globe and initiated poets into its mysteries. Some of the key figures it influenced: W. B. Yeats, Arthur Symons, Oscar Wilde, Ernest Dowson, and George Russell (Æ) in the British Isles; Stefan George and Rainer Maria Rilke in Germany; Hugo von Hofmannsthal in Austria; Innokenty Annensky, Alexander Blok, and Andrey Bely in Russia; Antonio Machado, Juan Ramón Jiménez, and Jorge Guillén in Spain; Rubén Darío in Nicaragua; T. S. Eliot, Ezra Pound, Amy Lowell, Hilda Doolittle (H. D.), Hart Crane, E. E. Cummings, and Wallace Stevens in the United States. Whoever believes in the occult or spiritual power of the poetic word is an heir to the symbolists.

SEE ALSO *decadence, modernism, modernismo, naturalism, symbol, synesthesia.*

synecdoche, see *metonymy, trope.*

synesthesia   A blending of sensations; the phenomenon of describing one sense in terms of another. The term *synesthesia* dates to only the late nineteenth century, but the device may be as old as literature itself. The *Iliad* (ca. eighth century B.C.E.) compares the voices of aged Trojans to the "lily-like" voices of cicadas; the *Odyssey* (ca. eighth century B.C.E.) evokes the "honey voice" of the Siren; the Bible refers to "seeing" a voice and "tasting" the word of God. Baudelaire popularized the notion of synesthesia with his idea that "the sounds, the scents, the colors correspond" ("Correspondances," 1857). In "Voyelles" ("Vowels," 1872), Rimbaud assigned colors to each of the vowels: "Black A, white E, red I, green U, blue O — vowels, / Someday I will open your silent pregnancies . . ." Rimbaud's lines exemplify the type of synesthesia known as *audition colorée,* wherein sounds are described as colors. Coleridge declares, in *Biographia Literaria* (1817), that "the poet must . . . understand and command what Bacon called the *vestigia communia* of the senses, the latency of all in each, and more especially . . . the excitement of vision by sound and the exponents of sound."

SEE ALSO *symbolism.*

synthetic rhyme   A rhyme that distorts a word, deleting, contracting, protracting, or otherwise wrenching letters into place to create a rhyme. This false rhyming, a weakness of bad poetry, is turned into a comic strength in light verse, as when Ogden Nash writes in "Spring Comes to Murray Hill" (1930), "I sit in an office at 244 Madison Avenue / And say to myself you have a responsible job, havenue?"

SEE ALSO *light verse, rhyme.*

T

tail rhyme Rhymes that answer each other across intervening stanzas. The form consists of a rhyming stanza, often a couplet or a triplet, followed by a line of a different length, usually shorter. The shorter lines (or tails) frequently rhyme with each other. At times, however, they rhyme with a line or lines in the preceding stanza; at times they don't rhyme at all; and at times they serve as refrains. Some refrains have the same formula (Tennyson's "Ask me no more"), while others vary it (Burns's "The Holy Fair").

In Medieval Latin, tail-rhyme stanzas were called *rhythmus caudatus* or *versus caudati,* in French *rime couée,* in Middle English *rime couwee.* The most popular medieval types were the six-line form, which George Saintsbury named Romance Sixes, and the twelve-line form, which predominated in romances. The tail-rhyme stanza was the favorite stanzaic form in thirteenth- and fourteenth-century poetry. Robert Herrick cleverly employs a tail rhyme to succeed and punctuate the triplets in "The White Island or Place of the Blest" (1648):

> There in calm and cooling sleep
> We our eyes shall never steep,
> But eternal watch shall keep,
>   Attending
>
> Pleasures such as shall pursue
> Me immortaliz'd, and you,
> And fresh joy, as never to
>   Have ending.

SEE ALSO *rhyme.*

tanka Also called *uta* or *waka*. The Japanese character for *ka* means "poem." *Wa* means "Japanese." Thus a *waka* is a Japanese poem. *Tan* means "short" and so a tanka is a short poem, thirty-one syllables long. It is unrhymed and has units of five, seven, five, seven, and seven syllables, which were traditionally printed as one unbroken line. In English translation, the tanka is customarily divided into a five-line form. It is sometimes separated by the three "upper lines" (*kami no ku*) and the two "lower ones" (*shimo no ku*). The upper unit is the source of the haiku. The brevity of the poem, and the turn from the upper to the lower lines, which often signals a shift in or expansion of subject matter, are two features that make the tanka comparable to the sonnet. A range of words, or *engo* ("verbal associations"), traditionally associate or bridge the sections. Like the sonnet, the tanka is also conducive to sequences, such as the *hyakushuuta,* which consists of one hundred tankas.

The tanka comprised the majority of Japanese poetry from the ninth to the nineteenth century; it is possibly the central genre of Japanese literature. It has prototypes in communal song, in oral literature dating back to at least the seventh century. The earliest anthology of Japanese poetry, *Man'yōshū* (*Collection of Ten Thousand Leaves,* ca. 759), contains more than forty-two hundred poems in the tanka form. The form gradually developed into court poetry and became so popular that it marginalized all other forms. The *renga* developed out of the tanka as a kind of court amusement or game. The *somonka* form consists of two tankas. They are relationship poems, exchange songs. In the first stanza, a lover conventionally addresses the beloved. In the second stanza, the beloved replies.

Tankas often appear inside or alongside longer prose or narrative works. Lady Murasaki Shikibu's *Tale of Genji,* which dates to the early eleventh century and is sometimes called the world's first novel, contains more than four hundred tankas. Many of the great tanka court poets were women, such as Akazome Emon (956–1041), Ono no Komachi (ca. 825–ca. 900), and Izumi Shikibu (ca. 970–1030). Starting in the nineteenth century, poets began to reconfigure and modernize the highly codified tanka form. This is evident in the work of the tanka poet Ishikawa Takuboku (1886–1912). The New Poetry Society, or Myōjō Poets (Morning Star Poets), and their chief rivals, the Negishi Tanka Society, brought tanka into the twentieth century. This traditional mood poem opened up to the currents of social and political life.

SEE ALSO *haiku, monostich, renga.*

taste   Aesthetic discernment. The metaphorical transfer from the physical sense of taste to the abstract quality of judgment, capitalized as Taste, took four centuries. Taste became an important critical and philosophical concept in eighteenth-century aesthetics. Joseph Addison defined it in his *Spectator* papers (1712) as "that faculty of the soul which discerns the beauties of an author with pleasure, and the imperfections with dislike." He also spoke of "rules . . . how we may acquire that fine Taste of Writing, which is so much talked of among the Polite World." Raymond Williams points out that taste had become equivalent to discrimination.

Eighteenth-century philosophers raised a variety of questions about taste and its relationship to beauty and sublimity. Is taste purely subjective? Can it be intersubjective? Is it limited to a single individual or group in one period of time? Is it a natural quality or a matter of cultivation? Is it an independent faculty? Is it culturally specific or cross-cultural? Can it be changed? How can we account for differences of taste? Are there universal canons of taste? David Hume sought the grounds for "a *Standard of Taste;* a rule, by which the various sentiments of men may be reconciled; at least, a decision, afforded, confirming one sentiment, and condemning another" (1757). Immanuel Kant treated taste as subjective but universal, since it is a response to the formal features of a work of art rather than to its content. "*Taste* is the ability to judge an object, or a way of presenting it, by means of a liking or a disliking *devoid of all interest*," he asserts in *Critique of Judgment* (1790). "The object of such a liking is called *beautiful.*"

The late eighteenth-century philosophical concept of taste was compromised by its association with cultivation, good manners, as in the difference between the tasteful and the tasteless, which is one reason Wordsworth attacked its superficiality in his preface to *Lyrical Ballads* (1800), where he mentions those "who will converse with us as gravely about a *taste* for Poetry, as they express it, as if it were a thing as indifferent as a taste for rope-dancing, or Frotiniac or Sherry."

Taste was renewed in the late nineteenth century as an important concept for those who opposed utilitarian notions of art. It was applied to aesthetic values. But the idea of taste was tainted by moral overtones and, as Williams argues, it "cannot now be separated from the idea of the consumer … and responses to art and literature … have been profoundly affected … by the assumption that the viewer, spectator or reader is a *consumer,* exercising and subsequently showing his taste."

SEE ALSO *sensibility, the sublime.*

tenor and vehicle, see *metaphor.*

tension   As a critical term, *tension* generally refers to the equilibrium achieved in a poem by balancing opposed tendencies, such as the literal and the metaphorical or the concrete and the abstract. In "Tension in Poetry" (1938), Allen Tate derived a special meaning of *tension* by "lopping the prefixes off the logical terms *ex*tension and *in*tension," and suggested that "the meaning of poetry is its 'tension,' the full organized body of all the extension and intension that we can find in it." Tate exhibited a New Critical preference for a poetry that embodies a dramatic interplay of opposing ideas.

tenson, tenzone, tencon   A type of debate poem developed by the Provençal poets in the twelfth century. The *tenson,* called *tenso* in Old Occitan, was a verbal contest between two poets. The invective was sometimes feigned. A poet could also use the *tenson* to oppose an imaginary adversary. It was called a *torneijamens* when more than two disputants participated. The *tenson* could take any metrical form, though the respondent was often challenged to reply in the same meter and rhyme scheme used by the challenger. It is the forerunner of the Scottish flyting.

The *tenson* later developed or specialized into the subgenre of the *partimen* (or *joc partit*), which eliminated the personal element. One poet proposed two hypothetical situations. The second poet chose one position and the initiator chose the other. The structure of each poem matched. The wandering troubadours carried the *tenson* to Italy and Sicily, where the *tenzoni* was commonly practiced by the poets of the *dolce stil novo.* In the Middle Ages the *tenson* adopted the new metrical scheme of the sonnet. Three of the sonneteers from the Sicilian court of Frederick — Giacomo da Lentino, Piero delle Vigne, and Jacopo Mostacci — wrote the first *tensons* in sonnet form. The subject was courtly love. Dante Alighieri and his one-time friend Forese Donati engaged in the earliest extant sonnet *tenson* ("Tenzone"), which consists of six rancorous and insulting sonnets traded back and forth between 1293 and 1296.

SEE ALSO *courtly love, débat, flyting, poetic contest, sonnet, troubadour.*

tercet   A verse unit of three lines. The tercet was historically defined as three lines containing rhyme, but most contemporary poets and critics use it as the name for any three-line stanza, with or without rhyme. It is a synonym for *triad* or *triplet,* the latter a word that is becoming antiquated.

There are many kinds of three-line stanzas. Think of three lines ending with the same rhyme word, as in this stanza from Robert Herrick's "Upon Julia's Clothes" (1648):

> Whenas in silks my Julia goes,
> Then, then, methinks, how sweetly flows
> That liquefaction of her clothes.

The interlocking three-line stanzas of terza rima are called tercets, as are the three-line stanzas in the villanelle. The ancient Hawaiian creation chant *The Kumulipo,* composed and transmitted through oral tradition, unfolds in triads, and so do many liturgical forms, such as the Kyrie prayer. William Carlos Williams exploited the tercet as a kind of descending staircase. The tercet has never been as widely employed as the couplet and the quatrain, but it seems distinctive because each stanza has a beginning, middle, and end. The number three has magical significance.

SEE ALSO *terza rima, variable foot, villanelle.*

terza rima   A verse form of interlocking three-line stanzas rhyming *aba, bcb, cdc,* etc. The terza rima form was invented by Dante Alighieri for the *Commedia* (*The Divine Comedy,* ca. 1302–5), using the hendecasyllabic (eleven-syllable) line common to Italian poetry. In *De vulgari eloquentia* (*On Eloquence in the Vernacular,* 1304–ca. 1307), Dante called rhyme *concatenatio* ("beautiful linkage"), and the triple rhymes beautifully link the stanzas.

Rhyming the first and third lines gives each tercet a sense of temporary closure; rhyming the second line with the first and last lines of the next stanza generates a strong feeling of propulsion. The effect of this chain-rhyme is both open-ended and conclusive, like moving through a series of interpenetrating rooms or going down a set of winding stairs: you are always traveling forward while looking back.

Chaucer introduced terza rima into English in the fourteenth century with "A Complaint to His Lady." Sir Thomas Wyatt's three *Satires* (1536) are the first sustained use of terza rima in our language. Shelley's "The Triumph of Life" (1824) is the finest English poem ever written in the form. The first eight lines capture its spiraling motion:

> Swift as a spirit hastening to his task
> Of glory and of good, the Sun sprang forth
> Rejoicing in his splendor, and the mask
>
> Of darkness fell from the awakened Earth —
> The smokeless altars of the mountain snows
> Flamed above crimson clouds, and at the birth
>
> Of light, the Ocean's orison arose,
> To which the birds tempered their matin lay.

Shelley also uses a terza rima sonnet for the five individual sections that comprise "Ode to the West Wind" (1819). The title poem of Randall Jarrell's *The Lost World* (1965) is a virtuoso piece of terza rima in three parts. Robert Pinsky capably uses slant rhymes to create what he calls "a plausible terza rima in a readable English" in his translation of Dante's *Inferno* (1994).

SEE ALSO *hendecasyllabics, tercet.*

tetrameter, see "accentual-syllabic meter" in *meter.*

texture   Modern poetry criticism has borrowed the term *texture* from the plastic arts. Texture tends to refer to the surface qualities of a work of art, as opposed to its general design, and to the concrete particulars of a poem, as opposed to its abstract ideas. In prosody, texture refers to the physical effects of sound, in poetics, to the tangible details inscribed in a poem. John Crowe Ransom made the term one of the cornerstones of his New Critical attempt to differentiate the incarnate poem from a prose statement. In "Criticism as Pure Speculation" (1941), Ransom advocates a "structural understanding of poetry" and divides a poem into two parts: "a central logic or situation," a so-called logical core, and a "local texture," which he characterizes as "excursions into particularity." The local texture gives a "sense of the real density and contingency of the world." For Ransom, then, a poem is "a logical structure having a local texture," and the "intent of the good critic becomes therefore to examine and define the poem with respect to its structure and its texture."

SEE ALSO *structure.*

theme A summary statement about a work, a condensation or salient paraphrase of its main line of thought or feeling. The concept of theme originated in classical rhetoric as the subject around which an orator constructed a speech. The idea of a proposed subject migrated to religion and by the Middle Ages had become a scriptural text that served as the basis for a sermon. In literature, theme became the idea, the topic or subject matter, the topos, on which a poet based a poem. In interpreting a medieval poem, Ernst Robert Curtius suggests, "we must ask, not on what 'experience' it was based, but what theme the poet set himself to treat." Theme was initially identified by the orator or author, but it followed that the listener or reader could identify and abstract a theme from a given work. In literary criticism, theme was considered synonymous with the "moral" or "message" of a work. In twentieth-century formalist literary criticism, such as New Criticism, theme was divorced from the idea of authorial intention, the moral of a work, and was grounded in close reading, in the particulars of a work of art. Criticism also borrowed from music the idea of theme as a principle of composition, which we recognize when critics speak of "theme and variations."

SEE ALSO *didactic poetry, invention, paraphrase, topos.*

threnody, see *elegy.*

tone An elusive poetic concept, tone is generally taken to indicate a writer's or speaker's sense of a given situation, sometimes an imagined one. The tone is in the inflection, how a thing is said, or seems to be said. The literary term *tone* is borrowed from the expression *tone of voice* and thus implies something spoken aloud. "Whenever a poem makes us conscious of some-one speaking, tone is a relevant conception," Hugh Kenner states. The reader establishes a tone, a complex of attitudes toward a subject, by determining how a speaker takes himself, and, more complicatedly, how the poet takes his speaker. This includes determining a speaker's attitude toward her subject (what she is addressing) as well as toward her audience (whom she is addressing). In oral poetry, the listener responds to the intonations of spoken words. In written poetry, spoken intonations must be inferred by readers; they hear the tones with an inner ear. The tonal range is vast and sometimes difficult to determine — is it aggrieved, beseeching, curious, determined, elevated, furious, grim, happy, ironic, or many of these things at once? A poem often shifts and develops a variety of shadings over the course of its movement from beginning to end.

Tone has been a key concept in modern critical discourse. In *Practical Criticism* (1929) I. A. Richards characterized tone as a literary speaker's "attitude to his listener" and argued that tone reflects "his sense of how he stands towards those he is addressing." The New Critics made tone one of their central analytic devices and focused on the discrepant tones of ambiguity, paradox, and irony. Mikhail Bakhtin argued that tone or intonation is "oriented *in two directions:* with respect to the listener as ally or witness and with respect to the object of the utterance as the third, living participant whom the intonation scolds or caresses, denigrates or magnifies."

SEE ALSO *ambiguity, drama, irony, paradox.*

topographical poetry   Samuel Johnson defined *topographical poetry* as "*local poetry,* of which the fundamental subject is some particular landscape … with the addition … of historical retrospection or incidental meditation." John Denham's "Cooper's Hill" (1642) brought the genre into vogue in English poetry for more than two centuries. Topographical poetry, which commences with a poet on a hill overlooking a river, "aims chiefly at describing *specifically named actual localities,*" as R. A. Aubin puts it in his history of the genre (1936). It re-creates a landscape or a generalized prospect, which is why C. V. Deane called it "prospect poetry." The "I" locates itself through the "eye."

The archaic term *chorography* (from the Greek: "writing about countries") is used interchangeably with *topographical poetry.* William Camden's Latin work *Britannia* (1586), the first county-by-county topographical survey of the entire British Isles, characterizes itself as a *chorographica descriptio* ("chorographic poem"). The Earl of Rochester wrote a mock topographical poem, "A Ramble in St. James Park" (1672), which brings together the beauty of the park with the depraved acts that people commit within it:

> Poor pensive lover, in this place
> Would frig upon his mother's face;
> Whence rows of mandrakes tall did rise
> Whose lewd tops fucked the very skies.
> Each imitative branch does twine
> In some loved fold of Aretine,
> And nightly now beneath their shade
> Are buggeries, rapes, and incests made.

In contemporary poetry, the genre is sometimes relabeled "site-specific poetry," as in "site-specific artwork," which consists of art made for a particular place.

SEE ALSO *ecopoetry, nature poetry.*

topos (plural *topoi*) From the Greek word for *place,* short for *commonplace.* A topos is a literary passage or expression that becomes a convention in subsequent literature. In *Latin Literature and the European Middle Ages* (1948), Ernst Robert Curtius took the idea of rhetorical commonplaces, standardized methods for constructing and treating arguments, and adapted it to literary concerns, so that a topos becomes a typical "intellectual theme suitable for development and modification." Topics are a stockroom of motifs, themes, and ideas. One topos would be "affected modesty," which medieval poets sometimes expressed as "trepidation before the matter at hand"; another would be the "inexpressibility topos," an emphasis upon the speaker's inability to cope with a subject ("What virtues are thine, if I could, I would gladly set forth," Fortunatus declares; "But little wit cannot relate great things"). Some writers treat the world as a stage, others consider it a book, but both are taking up traditional topics, or topoi.

SEE ALSO *convention, theme.*

tornada, see *envoi.*

tradition A handing down or handing over. Tradition suggests a consciousness of the past. The concept of tradition implies that we do not have our meaning entirely unto ourselves — rather, we are in relationship to what has come before us. Francis Bacon spoke of "the expressing or transferring our knowledge to others, which I will term by the general name of tradition or delivery" (1605). Tradition is not a passive accumulation of all previous works; it is an active process of selection, of losses and gains, renewals. Poets, readers, critics, and editors are all part of the process. Something from the past — a body of work, a style or convention, a set of beliefs — is excluded or lost; something else is chosen, renewed, and passed on. It would be more accurate to speak of traditions rather than tradition, since there are many different lines of descent, many separate inheritances. The idea that there is a single trajectory, one literary tradition that comprises the whole history of poetry, is a fantasy.

Tradition, in one sense, relates to culture and society. We speak of traditional cultures, which are bound to the established ways of the past. One type of poem, such as the traditional ballad, is handed down from one generation to another. A tradition in poetry may refer to a specific form, as when we speak of the tradition of the sonnet, or a line of inheritance, as when we speak of the Romantic tradition or the neoclassical tradition. The concept of tradition has sometimes been equated with an idea of respect, duty, and ceremony. Traditionalism takes a conservative bent and makes an ideology out of doing things as others have done them before us. It defines itself by adhering to previous doctrines, preordained values, and opposes what is progressive.

T. S. Eliot was responsible for bringing the concept of tradition into modern poetry. In "Tradition and the Individual Talent" (1919), he argues that for the individual writer with a historical sense, "the whole of the literature of Europe from Homer and within it the whole of the literature of his own country has a simultaneous existence and composes a simultaneous order." For Eliot, the "existing monuments form an ideal order among themselves, which is modified by the introduction of the new (the really new) work of art among them." This leads him to the formulation that "art never improves, but that the material of art is never quite the same." Eliot posits a cultural unity, "the mind of Europe," which has an almost spiritual authority over the individual. But there is no singular mind of Europe or timeless European tradition. Some critics dream of an ideal realm, a total library, which includes all the oral and written works ever created. Tradition consists of selections from that library.

SEE ALSO *canon, impersonality.*

tragedy From the Greek: "goat-song." Tragedy originated in ritual hymns sung during the sacrifice of a goat at Dionysian festivals. Goats were sacred to the god Dionysus, who made them his chosen victims (Euripides, *The Bacchae,* 405 B.C.E.). Sacrifice was a process of identification, and the goat was the embodiment of the god. The speaking/dancing chorus performed poems devoted to Dionysus, and, according to Aristotle, Greek drama grew out of these choral rites. Tragedy, which Aristotle considered the supreme form of poetry, developed as an interaction between a partly detached speaker and the rest of the chorus. In time the choral drama — the true relations were between the actor and the chorus — loosened the connection to Dionysus, and the choral element was discarded. Greek tragedy was chanted, sung, and danced in verse, a heightened verbal mode. The thirty-two plays that survive by Aeschylus (525–456 B.C.E.), Sophocles (ca. 496–406 B.C.E.), and Euripides (ca. 480–406 B.C.E.), which revolve around fate, necessity, and the nature of the gods, are the foundational achievement of European drama.

In the *Poetics* (350 B.C.E., 4 C.E.), Aristotle gave this definition of tragedy:

> Tragedy, then, is the imitation of an action that is serious and also, as having magnitude, complete in itself; in language with pleasurable accessories, each kind brought in separately in the parts of the work; in a dramatic not in a narrative form; with incidents arousing pity and fear, wherewith to accomplish its catharsis of such emotions.

Aristotle identified three elements of the tragic plot: *anagnorisis,* or recognition; *peripeteia,* or surprising reversal; and *pathos,* which he characterizes as "that act involving destruction or pain." The tragic hero is brought down by *hamartia,* the tragic flaw. Aristotle considered the response of an audience, its sense of "pity and fear," essential to tragedy.

Tragedies end badly; comedies end well. Tragedy is high, serious, dignified. Greek tragedy dealt with elevated figures in performance and referred exclusively to drama, or characters in action, as opposed to the epic, a poem narrated by a solo performer, a singer of tales. By the Middle Ages the term had become generalized to refer to the pattern of a narrative. Diomedes characterized it in the fourth century as "the narrative of heroic (or semi-divine) characters in adversity." Tragedy thus formulates a dramatic story, the narrative of a fall. Chaucer defines its characteristic movement in the prologue to "The Monk's Tale" (ca. 1387–1400):

> Tragedie is to seyn a certeyn storie,
> As olde bokes maken us memorie,
> Of him that stoode in greet prosperitee
> And is y-fallen out of heigh degree
> Into miserie, and endeth wrecchedly.

The Renaissance brought the idea of tragedy back to theater. There is a sense of fatal necessity worked out in dramatic tragedies. Something has been set in motion that cannot be stopped. Thomas Kyd's *Spanish Tragedy* (1592) inaugurated the bloodthirsty Elizabethan and Jacobean genre of the revenge tragedy, in which a leading character struggles to avenge the murder of a loved one. Some of the great "tragedies of blood," in which a wronged man sets out to do something terrible for a good reason: William Shakespeare's *Hamlet* (1603), *The Revenger's Tragedy* (published anonymously in 1607), Cyrill Tourneur's *The Atheist's Tragedy* (1611), John Webster's *The Duchess of Malfi* (1612), and John Ford's *'Tis Pity She's a Whore* (1633).

There was an eighteenth-century effort to apply the formula of classical tragedy to the domestic interior. George Lillo (1693–1739) in England, Gotthold Ephraim Lessing (1729–1781) in Germany, and Louis-Sébastien Mercier (1740–1814) in France all contributed to the genre known as domestic tragedy (*tragédie bourgeoise*).

One major offshoot of tragedy is the hybrid genre of tragicomedy. It typically contains comic elements but tells a story that is inherently tragic. Pierre Corneille's enormously popular *Le Cid* (1636) exemplifies this type of drama. It sparked a heated polemic (the Querelle du Cid) over the way it defied the classical unities.

SEE ALSO *comedy, pathos, tragicomedy.*

tragicomedy   Plautus (ca. 254–ca. 184 B.C.E.) coined the word *tragico- comoedia* to denote a play in which gods and mortals, masters and slaves, reverse traditional roles. Here is the passage from his play *Amphitruo* (ca. 206–186 B.C.E.):

> MERCURY: What's that? Are you disappointed
> To find it's a tragedy? Well, I can easily change it.
> I'm a god, after all, I can easily make it a comedy,
> And never alter a line. Is that what you'd like? . . .
> But I was forgetting — stupid of me — of course,
> Being a god, I know quite well what you'd like,
> I know exactly what's in your minds. Very well.
> I'll meet you half-way, and make it a *tragicomedy.*

Ever since, the hybrid genre of the tragicomedy has incorporated elements of both tragedy and comedy, as in Shakespeare's *Troilus and Cressida* (1602). Modern tragicomedy tends to be interchangeable with absurdist drama.

SEE ALSO *comedy, tragedy.*

translation   From the Latin word *translatio,* which in turn comes from *trans-* and *fero,* meaning "to carry across" or "to bring across." Translation is the transfer of meaning from one language to another. Strictly speaking, total translation is impossible, since languages differ and each language carries its own complex of linguistic resources, historical and social values. This is especially true in poetry, the maximal of language. In a poem there is no exact equivalent for the valences of sound, the intonations and sequences of words, the rhythm of separate lines, the weight of accruing stanzas, the totality of musical effects. That's why its untranslatability has been one of the defining features of poetry. Coleridge coined the word *untranslatableness.* Robert Frost asserted, "Poetry is what gets lost in translation." An Italian pun captures the idea: *traduttore/traditore,* translator/traitor.

Yet translation is also a necessity, the only way of bridging the barriers of language. It brings the world to our doorstep. For who among us can read everything in the original? George Steiner quotes Goethe's letter to Carlyle — "Say what one will of its inadequacy, translation remains one of the most important, worthwhile concerns in the totality of world affairs" — and adds, "Without it we would live in arrogant parishes bordered by silence."

There is a scale in translating poetry from the strictest literalism to the freest adaptation. The literalists argue that the only faithful translation is an interlinear trot, or prose paraphrase. This is Vladimir Nabokov's position: "The clumsiest literal translation is a thousand times more useful than the prettiest paraphrase." The argument against the strict trot is that it serves as an auxiliary to a poem while losing the poem itself, or at least what is most crucial about it. It is a useful but distant pointer and never provides a direct experience.

Another freer mode of translating poetry involves imitation (from the Latin *imitatio*), the art of modeling, the act of following a prototypical source. In *Preface to Fables* (1700), John Dryden characterized the art of imitation as a kinship between authors. Here an imitation takes on the force of a refashioning of a previous poem. Dryden explains that "in the way of imitation, the translator not only varies from the words and sense, but forsakes them as he sees occasion; and, taking only some general hints from the original, runs diversions upon the groundwork." An imitation is different than a literal rendition. It takes greater license and moves in more ambiguous literary space. It is interpenetrated by its source.

Imitation widens out into a greater departure from the original, an adaptation. As Michael Hamburger states, "Imitation in classical practice was the taking-over and renewal of past conventions and kinds — as the Romans took over and renewed Greek models, generations of later poets took over and renewed the Latin and Greek. What mattered in that was not the individuality of the poets imitated, but the perpetuation of exemplars, conventions, and kinds." The translation of poetry inevitably strives to re-create a totality that can never be fully recovered. But something else emerges. Joseph Brodsky reformulated Frost's position: "Poetry is what is gained in translation."

SEE ALSO *imitation, ode.*

triadic line   A line of Hebrew verse that contains three parallel units or half-lines, which are called versets, as in 2 Samuel 22:9, when the Lord descends to do battle: "Smoke came out of his nostrils, / fire from his mouth consumed, / coals glowed round him." William Carlos Williams's use of what he called a variable foot is sometimes called a three-ply or triadic line because it unfolds in three descending parts.

SEE ALSO *tercet, variable foot, verset.*

trimeter, see "accentual-syllabic meter" in *meter.*

triolet   From the French: "little trio." An eight-line poem with two rhymes and two refrain lines, *ABaAabAB* (the capital *A* and *B* represent the repeated lines). Here is W. E. Henley's light self-describing triolet from the late nine-teenth century:

> Easy is the triolet,
> If you really learn to make it!
> Once a neat refrain you get,
> Easy is the triolet.
> As you see! — I pay my debt
> With another rhyme. Deuce take it,
> Easy is the triolet,
> If you really learn to make it!

An intricate, playful, and melodious form, the triolet was originally a medieval French verse form, which dates to the thirteenth century and comes from the same family as the rondeau. The first triolets in English were prayers written by Patrick Carey, a seventeenth-century Benedictine monk. Robert Bridges reintroduced the form into English in the late nineteenth century. Edmund Gosse said that "nothing can be more ingeniously mischievous, more playfully sly, than this tiny trill of epigrammatic melody, turning so simply on its own innocent axis" ("A Plea for Certain Exotic Forms of Verse," 1877).

The triolet has a strict formality. The first two lines establish the subject. The repetition of the fourth line creates a moment of lyric intensity. The fifth and sixth lines take on a sudden air of freedom and expand the subject matter. The final lines knit the conclusion. A key feature of the triolet is how the poet plays with the repeated lines to change the meaning as the poem proceeds. French poets have tended to stick to eight-syllable lines (octosyllables), but poets in English have tended to rely on more open-ended line lengths and meters. A good anthology of triolets would include poems by Alphonse Daudet, Stéphane Mallarmé, Arthur Rimbaud, Austin Dobson, Arthur Symons, Wendy Cope, and Sandra McPherson.

SEE ALSO *octosyllabic verse, rondeau.*

triple meter   (1) Any poetic measure consisting of three units, such as anapestic and dactylic feet. The distinctive 1–2–3 movement spaces the stresses fairly evenly and the insistent rhythm now seems mostly suitable for light verse. (2) Any larger unit consisting of three feet or measures, such as the tripody, a Greek quantitative measure that treats three metrical feet as a single unit.

SEE ALSO *anapest, dactyl, light verse, meter.*

triple rhyme, see *rhyme.*

triplet, see *tercet.*

trochee   A metrical foot of two syllables, the first stressed, the second unstressed, as in the word *lúcky*. The trochee starts with a downbeat, as in the word *póet*. There are thus two trochees (a *di-trochee*) in the title of Hugh MacDiarmid's autobiography, *Lucky Poet* (1943). Longfellow's "Song of Hiawatha" (1855) is a celebrated example of trochaic meter, an insistent rhythm that encourages chanting:

> Should you ask me, whence these stories?
> Whence these legends and traditions,
> With the odors of the forest,
> With the dew and damp of meadows,
> With the curling smoke of wigwams,
> With the rushing of great rivers,
> With their frequent repetitions,

And their wild reverberations,
As of thunder in the mountains?

Longfellow was inspired by the national epic of Finland, the *Kalevala*,
compiled in the nineteenth century, which was created in what amounts to a
loose trochaic tetrameter. Finnish is essentially a trochaic language, since the
stress falls on the first syllable of each word and then all the other syllables
trail after.

Since the sixteenth century the trochee, the opposite of the iamb, has been
mostly employed to provide emphasis, substitution, and variation in iambic
lines, as in John Milton's companion poems "L'Allegro" and "Il Penseroso"
(both 1645). The trochee is the most common substitution for the first foot
of an iambic line, as in Shakespeare's "Sonnet 94" (1609): "They that have
power to hurt and will do none." It is the foot of reversal.

SEE ALSO *foot, iamb, iambic pentameter, meter.*

Troilus stanza, see *rhyme royal.*

trope   A figure of speech. A trope provides a way of extending the mean-
ing of words beyond the literal. *Turn* is an older English word for *trope,* and
tropes have the capacity to turn, to change and deepen our sense of words
and things. They can radically alter our sense of language and experience, and
thus of ourselves. It's commonly said that figurative language — saying one
thing and also meaning another — is an important resource for poetry, but it
is much more than that because it is at the heart of poetic thinking.

The master tropes, which include metaphor, simile, and synecdoche, have
been considered and taught for at least twenty-five centuries. Metaphor, the
most crucial and widely employed type of trope, creates an imaginary iden-
tity between different things, as when Dickinson says, "'Hope' is the thing
with feathers." A simile is an explicit comparison between two different
things, using the word *as* or *like,* as when Wordsworth remembers, "I wan-
dered lonely as a cloud." Synecdoche, a form of metonymy, substitutes the
name of one thing with something else closely associated with it, as when we
say "the heart" and mean "the emotions." The Roman rhetorician Quintilian
described synecdoche as "letting us understand the plural from the singular,

the whole from a part, a genus from the species, something following from something preceding; and *vice versa*" (*Institutes,* book 9, ca. 95 C.E.). Christopher Marlowe employs a synecdoche in *Doctor Faustus* (1604) when he asks, "Was this the face that launched a thousand ships / And burnt the topless towers of Ilium?" Tropes depend on a collaborative interpretive process between writer and reader. They rely on personal impressions and interpretations that readers discover and experience for themselves.

The word *trope* took on a special meaning in the Middle Ages when it came to refer to a phrase, sentence, verse, or strophe inserted into the liturgy. These verbal amplifications of passages in the authorized liturgy ornament, enforce, and enlarge the text. The elaboration of the prayer Kyrie eleison (Lord, have mercy) is a notable early example: "Kyrie / magnae Deus potentiae, / liberator hominis, / transgressoris mandati, / eleison." The most well known of all, the *quem quaeritis* trope, the introit of the Easter mass, developed into resurrection plays, medieval liturgical and pageant drama.

SEE ALSO *figures of speech, metaphor, metonymy, personification, rhetoric, simile.*

troubadour From the Provençal word *trobar,* meaning both "to find" and "to invent." The troubadours were poets who traveled from one court to another and flourished in southern France, northern Italy, and Spain between 1100 and 1350. Their language was Provençal, or langue d'oc. They are akin to trouvères (court poets who thrived in northern France at the same time) and minnesingers (wandering lyricists who flourished in Germany between the twelfth and fourteenth centuries). They are related to, though more elite than, jongleurs (itinerant minstrels, jugglers, and acrobats who entertained at the courts of medieval France and Norman England).

"Song again did not awake until the troubadour viol aroused it," Ezra Pound declared in *The Spirit of Romance* (1910). There are some 450 troubadours known by name. The first troubadour whose work has survived was William IX, Duke of Aquitaine, also known in Occitan as Guilhèm de Peitieus and in French as Guillaume de Poitiers (1071–1127). Bernart de Ventadorn (ca. 1130–1200), the acknowledged master of the *canso,* or love song, established the classical form of courtly love poetry. Bertran de Born (ca. 1140–1215) was the recognized master of the sirventes, or political song. Dante portrays him in the *Inferno* (1304–9) as one of the sowers of discord, holding up his severed head like a lantern. Women troubadours were called *trobairitz,* the first female composers of secular music in the Western tradition.

The twelfth-century troubadour Arnaut Daniel, the inventor of the sestina, was praised by Dante as *il miglior fabbro* ("the finer craftsman"), a dedicatory phrase that T. S. Eliot borrowed for "The Waste Land" (1922). Dante has this troubadour introduce himself in *Purgatorio* (1308–12, canto 26): "I am Arnaut, who weeps and goes on his way singing." Petrarch called him "the Grand Master of Love," and Ezra Pound deemed him the greatest poet who ever lived.

The troubadours wrote amorous poems of stunning technical virtuosity. Their field was the lyric; they did not write narrative poems. They composed in two competing styles: *trobar leu* (the plain or open style) and *trobar clus* (the hermetic or deliberately intricate style). Their creations were largely responsible for the phenomenon of courtly love. There is a great tension in their work between the poet/lover's allegiance to his lady and his allegiance to God. The troubadours have been called "the inventors of modern verse."

SEE ALSO *aubade, chanso, courtly love, jongleur, minnesinger, sestina, trouvère.*

trouvère   Akin to the medieval troubadours, the trouvères were court poets who thrived in northern and central France during the twelfth and thirteenth centuries and wrote in langue d'oïl, which became the French language. They were aristocratic poet-composers. The first known trouvère was Chrétien de Troyes, remembered for his five Arthurian romances. The most famous was Thibaut de Champagne, who became king of Navarre. Sixty-six of his charmed songs survive. Many trouvères, such as Gace Brulé, were knights. The repertoire of the trouvères was much like that of the troubadours. They excelled in the *grande chant* or *grande chanson courtoise* (courtly love songs) and also composed chansons de geste (songs of heroic deeds). Together, the troubadours and the trouvères created one of the greatest repertoires of love songs.

SEE ALSO *chansons de geste, chivalric romance, courtly love, troubadour.*

truncation, also called **catalexsis**   The omission of a final syllable or syllables in a metrical line of verse. A line that lacks one syllable is called catalectic. A normal line of poetry (i.e., a line that has the full number of syllables) is acatalectic. A line foreshortened by more than one syllable is called brachycatalectic. A line with one syllable too many, thus going "beyond the last metrical foot," is called hypercatalectic ("To be or not to be, that is the question"). The term *initial truncation* describes the omission of the first syllable in a line (an acephalous line). All of these variations can be used to create certain effects. Here are two stanzas from Shakespeare's octosyllabic poem "The Phoenix and the Turtle" (1601). Every line in the first stanza is acatalectic; every line in the second stanza is catalectic, pointedly truncated. The truncation seems to enact the feeling of reason being puzzled and confounded.

> Reason, in itself confounded,
> Saw division grow together;
> To themselves yet either neither,
> Simple were so well compounded,

> That it cried, "How true a twain
> Seemeth this concordant one!
> Love hath reason, reason none,
> If what parts can so remain."

tumbling verse   King James VI of Scotland coined this term in his treatise on verse, *Rules and Cautions* (1585). It refers to a four-stress, loosely anapestic accentual verse. James contrasts tumbling verse to "flowing" or smooth verse, which suggests that tumbling verse is rougher and more irregular, like doggerel. He also called it *rouncefallis,* connected it to the dueling form of the flyting, and gave an alliterative example from Montgomerie's "Flyting," which dates to the early 1580s: "Fetching fude for to feid it fast furth of the Farie." Tumbling verse has roots in Anglo-Saxon alliterative meter. Thomas Tusser's *Some of the Five Hundred Points of Good Husbandry* (1557, 1573) is a well-known extended example. The term also applies to the type of verse that John Skelton invented, known as Skeltonics.

SEE ALSO *doggerel, flyting, meter, Skeltonics.*

U

ubi sunt From the Latin: "where are they?" *Ubi sunt* is used as the opening line or refrain in a telling number of Medieval Latin poems. The phrase encapsulates the poignant disappearance of beloved people and things. Poets used the motif to catalog the names of those dead and gone, meditating on the fragility of beauty and the transitory nature of life. François Villon's "Ballade des dames du temps jadis" (1450) is the greatest medieval example, with its well-known refrain line:

> Mais où sont les neiges d'antan?

Dante Gabriel Rossetti rendered it memorably in his translation "The Ballad of Dead Ladies" (1870):

> But where are the snows of yester-year?

The *ubi sunt* theme — the perennial question *where are they now?* — recurs in American poetry such as Edgar Lee Masters's *Spoon River Anthology* (1915) and Robert Hayden's "Elegies for Paradise Valley" (1978).

the uncanny The uncanny has to do with the mysterious or strange, with experiences that are weird or ghostly, possibly supernatural. It is a warp in time, a crisis in normalcy. *Webster's Dictionary* defines the adjective *uncanny* as "(1) Having or seeming to have a supernatural or inexplicable basis; beyond the ordinary or normal; extraordinary; (2) Mysterious; frightening, as by superstitious dread; uncomfortably strange." Sigmund Freud's essay "Das Unheimliche" ("The Uncanny," 1919), which claims that the uncanny is concerned with "the theory of qualities of feeling," teaches us to see ourselves as split beings, to look for what is most foreign in ourselves. "We are all haunted houses," H. D. wrote, in her *Tribute to Freud* (1956).

The word *uncanny* dates back to eighteenth-century Scotland. Robert Fergusson's "An Eclogue. To the Memory of DR. WILLIAM WILKIE, late Professor of Natural Philosophy in the University of St. Andrews" (*Poems,* 1773) contains the earliest instance of the word. The uncanny reminds us of the resistant strangeness of literature itself. In a letter, Emily Dickinson recognizes the power of the uncanny: "Nature is a Haunted House — but Art — a House that tries to be haunted."

SEE ALSO *the sublime.*

unity From the Latin: "oneness, sameness." The idea that a work of art is self-contained and coherent, the parts are interdependent, and each part relates to the whole. Nothing can be taken away, nothing added. The crucial but contentious idea of artistic unity has a philosophical history that runs from Plato (ca. 427–ca. 347 B.C.E.) to Jacques Derrida (1930–2004). In the *Phaedrus,* Plato had Socrates argue that every composition should resemble a living organism. In the *Poetics* (350 B.C.E.), Aristotle expanded on this idea and argued that tragedy and epic should have a kind of "oneness." Each work should have a unity of action that is whole and complete. Homer "made the *Odyssey,* and likewise the *Iliad,* to center round an action that in our sense of the word is one," he said.

> As therefore, in the other imitative arts, the imitation is one when the object imitated is one, so the plot, being an imitation of an action, must imitate one action and that a whole, the structural union of the parts being such that, if any one of them is displaced or removed, the whole will be disjointed and disturbed. For a thing whose presence or absence makes no visible difference, is not an organic part of the whole.

Aristotle also argues that the epic "will thus resemble a living organism in all its unity, and produce the pleasure proper to it." In *Ars poetica* (ca. 19–18 B.C.E.), Horace denounced poets and painters who joined unharmonious parts together and followed Aristotle with a notion of unity: "In short, create what you wish, as long as it is a single harmonious whole."

Until the eighteenth century, most theories of literary unity dealt with drama and, occasionally, epic. Unity concerned formal rules, methods of plot construction. The French neoclassical writers expanded and rigidified Aristotle's "unity of action" into the so-called Three Unities (action, place, and time); writers from John Dryden (1631–1700) to T. S. Eliot (1888–1965) commended these norms, yet they never quite caught on in English, mostly because Shakespeare (1564–1616) frequently defied them.

The Romantic poets and critics expanded the idea of artistic unity to apply to lyric and shorter narrative poetry. They spoke of unity of feeling, unity created by the poet's mind in the act of creation, unity that grew organically from within a work, unity forged by the shaping and reconciling powers of the imagination. W. B. Yeats (1865–1939) was continually chiding himself to "hammer your thoughts into unity," obsessed by his own fragmented thinking, and seeking an elusive, even impossible unity of being. The discontinuities and fissures of modernism forced critics to think about unity in wider and more various ways. Many types of twentieth-century literary criticism depend on an expanded idea of artistic unity, more open to ambiguity, paradox, and contradiction, a reconciliation of discordant elements and parts.

Postmodern Continental theorists have mounted a sustained critique of the idea of unity as a postulated whole. Michel Foucault made the case against the repressive structures of continuity and unity in our thinking. Jacques Derrida turned the assault on unity into one of the fundamentals of deconstruction, which challenges the idea of structure as an organic whole, a fiction that limits the field of "freeplay." Derrida replaced structural closure or unity with a vision of unlimited textual freedom. Paul de Man leveled his attack against Anglo-American aesthetics, especially the New Critical idea, adapted from Coleridge, that a poem has a formal unity analogous to a living organism. By pushing the interpretive process as far as they did, de Man contended, the New Critics "exploded" the metaphor and thereby confirmed "the absence of the unity [they] had postulated." If unity can ever be resurrected as a desirable or necessary feature of poetry, the argument must take into account these critiques and suspicions, demonstrating that the open-endedness of poetic language can be part of its radical coherence.

SEE ALSO *ambiguity, archetype, imagination, imitation, organic form, paradox, postmodernism.*

universality   The loose and baggy idea of universality, of poetry that appeals to all worldwide, has a long, contentious history and limited usefulness. Yet it keeps cropping up, like the controversial and old-fashioned idea of our common humanity. One problem with the notion of universality is that it is used in such a wide variety of ways. In *Literary Criticism: A Short History* (1970), Wimsatt and Brooks distinguish nine distinct meanings of the term in the neoclassical era. The concept of universality migrated to literary criticism from philosophy, which distinguishes universals (abstract propositions and relations) from particulars (concrete objects that exemplify them). In literature, the "universal" has inevitably been associated with the "general" and the "abstract" and placed in opposition to the "concrete" and the "particular." These terms, which Hegel tried to reconcile with the idea of the concrete universal, are dialectical and complementary.

Sheldon Zitner explains that "cultural moments of conformity and consolidation like the neoclassical emphasize universals in discussions of both the form and aim of literature, and moments of skepticism and iconoclasm like the Romantic period or our own ignore them." We are relativists. Yet he also recognizes that the Romantics, who rejected aesthetic universals, also believed in a universal human nature. Thus Wordsworth wrote in 1800, "The Poet binds together by passion and knowledge the vast empire of human society, as it is spread over the whole earth." Goethe told Eckermann in 1827, "I am more and more convinced that poetry is the universal possession of mankind." In "The Poet and Time" (1932), the Russian poet Marina Tsvetaeva defined a universal work as "one which, translated into another language and another age, translated into the language of another age — least of all then — loses nothing. Having given everything to its own age and land, it gives everything once again to all lands and all ages. Having revealed its own place and age, up to the furthest bounds, it boundlessly reveals all that is not-place, not-age: for all ages."

There is no longer any cultural consensus. All centuries have had their cataclysms, but the historical realities of the twentieth and twenty-first centuries especially call into question the idea of universal standards of behavior and common values. The idea of universality, of the general over the particular, seems to deny or at least repress the historical conditions under which poetry is written, how it is created at a specific time in a specific place by specific people. Feminist and minority critics have also argued that canons of universality are Eurocentric and exclusive, naive at best. It may no longer be possible or even desirable to believe the Enlightenment idea that the One is the All, or that human nature is unchanging, or that, as Longinus contended in *On the Sublime* (100 C.E.), "lofty and true greatness in art pleases all men in all ages." Yet we continue to need some idea of shared humanity. And poetry itself, however different its aims and ends, is a universal of culture.

SEE ALSO *neoclassicism, postmodernism, Romanticism, translation.*

uta, see *tanka.*

utaawase A Japanese poetry match. A nineteenth-century Japanese-English dictionary defines *utaawase* as "to cause or let sing," as in the phrase *hito ni uta-awase kiku,* "to get another to sing that we may hear." Dividing into two groups, poets were assigned fixed topics (*dai*) and competed before judges. The earliest extant formal *utaawase* is the Zaiminbukyōke of 804. The *utaawase* was at first a frivolity, but later became a serious occasion that enabled poets to demonstrate their technical virtuosity. There were a set number of rounds in the typical medieval poetry match. Each round consisted of two poems on the same topic, which were pitted against each other, and then rated as winners (*kachi*), losers (*make*), or draws (*ji*). The poems were formal (*hare no uta*) and the topics were handed out in advance for such major competitions as Roppyakuban Utawaase, or Poetry Contest in 600 Rounds (1193), and the Sengohyakuban Utaawase, or Poetry Contest in 1,500 Rounds (1201).

The *jikaawase,* or personal poetry competition, which developed in the twelfth century, was a poetry match against oneself. The poet would select a topic and then compose one or two rounds of poems, pitting them against each other for comparison. The poet-priest Saigyō' compiled two such sequences: *Poetry Contest at the Mimosuso River* (1187) and *Poetry Contest at the Miya River* (1189).

SEE ALSO *poetic contests, tanka, waka, yūgen.*

ut pictura poesis Horace coined the Latin formula *ut pictura poesis* ("as in painting, so in poetry") in his *Ars poetica* (ca. 19–18 B.C.E.) to suggest that painting and poetry are parallel arts. But the principle of associating poetry and painting operated for centuries before him. Plato asserted in *The*

Republic (ca. 380 B.C.E.) that "the poet is like a painter." Aristotle referred to painting five times in the *Poetics* (350 B.C.E.): "It is the same in painting." And in "De gloria Atheniensium" (*Moralia,* first century), Plutarch attributed this statement to Simonides of Ceos (ca. 556–467 B.C.E.): "Painting is mute poetry, and poetry a speaking picture." Laurence Binyon claimed that "a precisely identical saying is proverbial among the Chinese."

Horace's motto was fiercely debated over the centuries. It established kinship between the arts and raised the question of literary pictorialism. Simonides's statement came to England in 1586 through Hoby's translation of Coignet, called *Politique Discourses:* "For as Simonides saide: Painting is a dumme Poesie, and a Poesie is a speaking picture; & the actions which the Painters set out with visible coulours and figures the Poets recken with words, as though they had been perfourmed." So too the sixteenth-century Portuguese poet Luís de Camões characterized painting as "*muda poesia,*" and the polymath Leonardo da Vinci (1452–1519) declared, "Painting is poetry which is seen and not heard, and poetry is a painting which is heard but not seen. These two arts (you may call them both either poetry or painting) have here interchanged the senses by which they penetrate to the intellect."

Horace's almost offhanded dictum was repeated so often that it became one of the keystones of Renaissance criticism. Charles-Alphonse du Fresnoy's poem "De arte graphica" ("The Art of Painting," 1665) was modeled on Horace's *Ars poetica.* It was translated into English in the mid-eighteenth century and had a great vogue, especially the line "A poem will be like a picture, and let a picture be similar to a poem."

The linkage between the verbal and visual arts began to fray in the eighteenth century. Edmund Burke attacked the connection in "A Philosophical Inquiry into the Origin of Our Ideas of the Sublime and the Beautiful" (1757): "So little does poetry depend for its effect on the power of raising sensible images, that I am convinced it would lose a very considerable part of its *energy,* if this were the result of all necessary description. Because that union of affecting words, which is the most powerful of all poetical instruments, would frequently lose its force, along with its propriety and consistency if the sensible images were always excited."

Gotthold Lessing also made a revisionary statement in *Laocoön* (1766) by distinguishing visual and verbal art. It was no longer axiomatic that poetry should be pictorial. The use of painting to illuminate poetry virtually disappeared during the Romantic era. Music and poetry were increasingly allied as sister arts. As an analogy for poetry, painting, a spatial art, was in effect replaced by music, a temporal one.

SEE ALSO *ekphrasis, imagism, picturesque.*

V

variable foot William Carlos Williams (1883–1963) coined this term to explain the three-step line that he developed in his later work. Williams claimed that the traditional fixed foot of English prosody needed to be altered to represent idiomatic American speech rhythms. He was seeking metrical relativity, a more intuitive cadence based on speech. The variable foot, he said, "rejects the standard of the conventionally fixed foot and suggests that measure varies with the idiom by which it is employed and the tonality of the individual poem. Thus, as in speech, the prosodic pattern is evaluated by criteria of effectiveness and expressiveness rather than mechanical syllable counts. The verse of genuine poetry can never be 'free,' but free verse, interpreted in terms of the variable foot, removes many artificial obstacles between the poet and the fulfillment of the laws of his design." Williams favored the *triversen* stanza, which consists of three lines that comprise a complete sentence. Each third of the sentence is a line. Each step is located farther from the left margin and lower on the page. "Each segment of a triadic cluster is a foot," Denise Levertov contends, "and each has the same *duration*." Williams was transforming the rhetorical tricolon — a sentence with three clearly defined parts (cola) of equal length — into a new American measure.

SEE ALSO *free verse, measure, tercet, vers libre.*

variorum From the Latin word *variorum,* meaning "of the various," and derived from the longer phrase *edito cum notis variorum,* "an edition with notes of various editors." A work that collates all the known variants of a text. A variorum edition was originally a text that included annotations from a variety of editors, critics, and commentators. It is now considered a work that presents a suggested text, as definitively as possible, with readings from dif-

ferent successive editions. It often includes the editor's notes as well as con-
jectural emendations proposed by previous editors.

SEE ALSO *textual criticism.*

vatic From the Latin word *vates,* meaning "prophet." The word *vatic* means
"inspired with the power of prophecy." From earliest times, prophecy has
been connected to rhythmical speech. The poet has often been considered a
divinely inspired seer, a *vates.* There may have been a caste of *vates* among the
Celts, or so the first-century geographer Strabo thought:

> ... there are generally three divisions of men especially reverenced, the Bards,
> the Vates, and the Druids. The Bards composed and chanted hymns; the Vates
> occupied themselves with the sacrifices and the study of nature; while the Dru-
> ids joined to the study of nature that of moral philosophy.

The vatic impulse is signaled in poetry whenever a poet speaks in a pro-
phetic voice beyond the social realm, as a vehicle — as when Shelley calls out
to the west wind, "Be thou, Spirit fierce, / My spirit! Be thou me, impetuous
one!" ("Ode to the West Wind," 1819) or as D. H. Lawrence testifies, "Not
I, not I, but the wind that blows through me!" ("Song of a Man Who Has
Come Through," 1917).

SEE ALSO *bard, fili, inspiration, verset.*

vehicle, see "tenor and vehicle" in *metaphor.*

Venus and Adonis stanza, see *sestet.*

verse From the Latin word *vertere,* meaning "to turn," or alternatively, from
the Latin word *versus,* meaning a "line, row, or furrow." A metrical composi-
tion. The plow as a metaphor for writing dates to antiquity. Verse is metrical
writing, a way of rhythmically marking time. Such formal writing is mark-
edly different from prose. "Verse," Sir Philip Sidney wrote, "being in its selfe
sweete and orderly, and being best for memory, the only handle of knowl-
edge, it must be in jest that any man can speak against it."

Verse has been generally distinguished from prose, but it has also some-
times been differentiated from poetry. Thus Sidney also spoke of verse as

being but an ornament and no cause to poetry, since there have been many
most excellent poets that never versified, and now swarm many versifiers that
need never answer to the name of poets ... It is not rhyming and versing that
maketh a poet — no more than a long gown maketh an advocate, who though
he pleaded in armour should be an advocate and no soldier.

In "The Defence of Poesy" (ca. 1582), Sidney was intent on distinguish-
ing genuine poetry from its facsimile, true poets from mere dabblers, neces-
sary words from ornamental ones, and yet it gives me a minor jolt when poets
use the term *verse* in a negative or somewhat derogatory way. It is not the fault
of verse, a demanding art of its own, that it has been misused. The formal
deliverance of poetry gives it ceremonial authority, a way of inhabiting and
marking us. Sidney also acknowledged that "the senate of poets hath chosen
verse as their fittest raiment." Joseph Brodsky asserts, "The one who writes a
poem writes it above all because verse writing is an extraordinary accelerator
of consciousness, of thinking, of comprehending the universe."

Verse is also used to refer to a single line of poetry, or to a single stanza,
especially of a hymn or song.

SEE ALSO *line, meter, prosody.*

verse drama, see *drama.*

verse epistle, see *letter poem.*

verse essay From the French word *essayer,* meaning "to try" or "to attempt." A
short expository composition in verse. Michel de Montaigne essentially invented
the essay form in *Essais* (1580). Francis Bacon's *Essays* (1597) brought the
short prose discourse into English. Consequently, the verse essay, which was
once directed to a general audience, brought some of the didactic sweep and
discursive power of the essay to lyric poetry. It is self-consciously rhetorical.
Alexander Pope adopted the essayistic stance for his two poems in heroic
couplets, "An Essay on Criticism" (1711) and "An Essay on Man" (1733–34);
the latter seeks to "vindicate the ways of God to man." There weren't many
advocates for the verse essay after the eighteenth century, but the blurring
of genres between lyric poetry and expository prose has interested contem-
porary poets. Karl Shapiro took up the mantle for his discussion of poetics,

Essay on Rime (1945). Charles Bernstein prefaces his book *My Way: Speeches and Poems* (1999) with the questions "What is the difference between poetry and prose, verse and essays? Is it possible that a poem can extend the argument of an essay or that an essay can extend the prosody of a poem?"

SEE ALSO *didactic poetry, discursive, neoclassicism, rhetoric.*

verse novel　A novel in poetry. A hybrid form, the verse novel filters the devices of fiction through the medium of poetry. There are antecedents for the novelization of poetry in long narrative poems, in epics, chronicles, and romances, but the verse novel itself, as a distinct nineteenth-century genre, is different than the long poem that tells a story because it appropriates the discourse and language, the stylistic features of the novel as a protean form. Alexander Pushkin's *Eugene Onegin* (1831) established the verse novel as a new type of poem in chapters and a new kind of novel in stanzas. Adam Mickiewicz's twelve-book verse novel *Pan Tadeusz* (1834) stands at the top of nineteenth-century Polish literature. In English literature, the verse novel took different forms in the 1850s and '60s: in Elizabeth Barrett Browning's fictional autobiography *Aurora Leigh* (1856); in Arthur Clough's epistolary fiction *Amours de Voyage* (1857); in George Meredith's sequence of sixteen-line sonnets, *Modern Love* (1962); and in Robert Browning's series of dramatic monologues, *The Ring and the Book* (1868–69). Unlike the Victorians, the modernist poets showed little interest in the verse novel, but contemporary poets have used it to gain for poetry some of the sweep and sensibility of prose fiction.

SEE ALSO *epic, narrative poetry, romance.*

verse paragraph　A self-contained unit of lines, a type of paragraph in verse. It is irregular in length and tends to be used in longer narrative and dramatic poems, often in blank verse. The word *stanza* was once reserved for units of equal length. A stanzaic poem was symmetrical and a poem in verse paragraphs was asymmetrical. Thus Matthew Arnold's poem "The Scholar-Gypsy" (1853) consists of stanzas while his poem "Dover Beach" (1867) consists of verse paragraphs. John Milton used the verse paragraph so powerfully that it is virtually synonymous with *Paradise Lost* (1667). Robert Frost managed "the sound of sentences" in the verse paragraphs of the long narrative poems in *North of Boston* (1914). Since the 1960s, the word *stanza* has been increasingly used to name both regular and irregular units within a poem. To understand the formal organization of a poem, it is still necessary to distinguish symmetrical stanzas and asymmetrical paragraphs, but the term *verse paragraph* is becoming antiquated.

SEE ALSO *stanza, stichic, strophe.*

verset A short verse, especially from a sacred book, as in the biblical Song of Songs and the Psalms. It also refers to a form based on such biblical models. The verset is one of two or three subunits that comprise a line of Hebrew poetry. Each verset contains a minimum of two and a maximum of ten syllables. The first line of the Psalm 1 has three parallel members, or versets: "Blessed *is* the man that walketh not in the counsel of the ungodly / nor standeth in the way of sinners, / nor sitteth in the seat of the scornful." This tripartite structure, a tricolon, is used sparingly. The prevalent pattern in Hebrew poetry contains two parallel versets, as in the second line of the Psalm 1: "But his delight *is* in the law of the LORD; / and in his law doth he meditate day and night." Each half of the line is also referred to as a bicolon, or hemistich.

Versets anticipate free verse in the wide sweep of their emotional expression. The form was first adapted for religious and mystical texts. Over the centuries it has been periodically redeployed to create a prophetic feeling. Paul Claudel's quasi-biblical mixture of long-lined free verse and prose is called the *verset claudélien.* The verset is also a structural device in the German poetry of Friedrich Hölderlin (1770–1843), the Polish poetry of Adam Mickiewicz (1798–1855), the French poetry of Arthur Rimbaud (1854–1891), and the English poetry of D. H. Lawrence (1885–1930). It has been used in vatic American poetry from Walt Whitman (1819–1892) to Allen Ginsberg (1926–1997).

SEE ALSO *alliteration, anaphora, assonance, free verse, hemistich, parallelism, stichic, vatic, verse paragraph.*

versicle This liturgical term can mean (1) a short sentence said or sung antiphonally (that is, in a call-and-response pattern); (2) a small verse; (3) a single verse of the Psalms or other part of the Bible; (4) a short or lone metrical line.

versification   The term *versification* has three meanings: (1) the making of verses; (2) the internal features, especially the metrical structure or style, of verse; and (3) the transformation into verse of something that was composed in prose.

SEE ALSO *prosody, verse.*

vers libre   From the French: "free verse." *Vers libre* was a radical innovation of French poetry dating to the 1870s, when the classically ordered language of poetry began to break down. One impulse of *vers libre* was to rupture strictly prescribed metrical patterns and rules, especially to break the stranglehold of the conventional twelve-syllable alexandrine verse line that dominated French poetry from the mid-seventeenth century onward. In the poetry of Paul Verlaine and Tristan Corbière, Arthur Rimbaud and especially Jules Laforgue, a symmetrical prosody gives way to the irregular surges and pauses of a new rhythm. The poets who investigated *vers libre* sought fresh verbal music suited to a distinct subject matter. The dream of *vers libre:* that every poem would have its own originary music perfectly suited to its subject. The use of free verse in American poetry predated the use of free verse in French literature, and yet the French practice of *vers libre,* especially the work of Laforgue, had terrific impact on the modernists T. S. Eliot, Ezra Pound, D. H. Lawrence, Hart Crane, William Carlos Williams, and others, and thus greatly influenced the development of free verse in English in the early twentieth century.

SEE ALSO *alexandrine, free verse, prose poem.*

villanelle   A French form codified in the sixteenth century, the villanelle has its roots in Italian folk song and was originally associated with pastoral verse (the name derives from *villa,* a "farm" or "country house"). It consists of nineteen lines divided into six stanzas — five tercets and one quatrain. The first and third lines become the refrain lines of alternate stanzas and the final two lines of the poem. They rhyme throughout, as do the middle lines of each stanza. The entire poem builds around two repeated lines and turns on two rhymes. Here is the schema:

A1 (refrain)
b
A2 (refrain)

a
b
A1 (refrain)

a
b
A2 (refrain)

a
b
A1 (refrain)

a
b
A2 (refrain)

a
b
A1 (refrain)
A2 (refrain)

The villanelle entered English poetry in the nineteenth century as a form of light verse, but it has had a more majestic life in the twentieth century. Many modern and contemporary poets have intuited how the compulsive returns of the villanelle could be suited both to a poetry of loss ("The art of losing isn't hard to master," Elizabeth Bishop wryly acknowledges in "One Art," 1976) as well as to a poetry speaking up against loss ("Do not go gentle into that good night," Dylan Thomas insists, 1951). My gathering of modern American villanelles would include Theodore Roethke ("The Waking," 1953), Weldon Kees ("Five Villanelles," 1947), Sylvia Plath ("Mad Girl's Love Song," 1951), James Merrill ("The World and the Child," 1962), Richard Hugo ("The Freaks at Spurgin Road Field," 1975), Howard Nemerov ("Equations of a Villanelle," 1975), Donald Justice ("In Memory of the Unknown Poet, Robert Boardman Vaughn," 1987), Mark Strand ("Two de Chiricos," 1998), Marilyn Hacker ("Villanelle," 1974), and Deborah Digges

("The Rockettes," 1989). Here is Edwin Arlington Robinson's "The House on the Hill" (1894):

> They are all gone away,
>   The House is shut and still,
> There is nothing more to say.
>
> Through broken walls and gray
>   The winds blow bleak and shrill:
> They are all gone away.
>
> Nor is there one to-day
>   To speak them good or ill:
> There is nothing more to say.
>
> Why is it then we stray
>   Around the sunken sill?
> They are all gone away,
>
> And our poor fancy-play
>   For them is wasted skill:
> There is nothing more to say.
>
> There is ruin and decay
>   In the House on the Hill:
> They are all gone away,
> There is nothing more to say.

SEE ALSO *refrain.*

virelay, vereli (also called *chanson baladée*) The name suggests that the virelay is a song (*lai*) that turns or twists (*virer*). Along with the ballade and the rondeau, it was one of the three fixed forms that predominated in French poetry and song in the fourteenth and fifteenth centuries. It may have originated as a dance or derived from Arabic songs transmitted by the troubadours in the twelfth century.

The virelay had a simple musical structure, but there were so many variations and options that it is now difficult to define. One common version begins with a refrain. This is followed by a four-line stanza; the first two lines of the quatrain have a repeated musical line different from the refrain.

The next two lines repeat the refrain. The initial refrain is then sung again. The alternating stanzas usually repeat for two more stanzas. Some of the great practitioners were Guillaume de Machaut (ca. 1300–1377), Jean Froissart (ca. 1337–ca. 1405), Christine de Pisan (1367–ca. 1430), and Eustace Deschamps (1340–1406), who defined the virelay in *Arte de dictier* (1392), the first treatise on French versification.

A virelay with only one stanza was called a *bergerette*. The Italian *balata* and the Spanish *cantiga* follow the same form. The virelay was severed from music in the fifteenth century and died out at the beginning of the sixteenth century. It never caught on in English. A virelay sometimes attributed to Richard Beauchamp, Earl of Warwick (1382–1439), begins, "I cannot half the woo compleyne / That dothe my woful hert streyne / With bisy thought and grevous payne . . ." Thomas Percy printed a "Balet," or virelay, attributed to Anthony Woodville, second Earl Rivers (ca. 1440–1483), in *Reliques of Ancient English Poetry* (1765).

SEE ALSO *ballade, formes fixes, lai, rondeau*.

virgule   A diagonal mark (/). In poetry, the slash is used to mark either foot divisions within a line of verse or a line ending.

SEE ALSO *scansion*.

visual poetry, see *concrete poetry*.

voice   The human voice — the sound produced by the vocal organs, our ability to produce such sounds — is the instrument of poetry. Poetry is made out of sound. It comes out of silence and ends in silence. It emerges from the body. The human voice ranges from the lowest murmur to the loudest shout, from chanting to singing. Human beings are speaking animals. We speak because we are not alone. Speech is social, language is collective. The first poetry is oral poetry, the artful use of language, which is spoken, chanted, or sung aloud. It is sound that draws attention to itself. Voice is an active, physical thing in oral poetry. That voice can speak directly (the poet speaks in his own voice) or indirectly (the poet speaks as someone else), but it must be sounded. It thrives in live connection.

Voice is found in both speaking and writing, but the nature of voice in written poetry must be metaphorical; it cannot be literal. The material qualities and acoustic range of voice (its tone, timbre, volume, and register) can only be invoked and inscribed. "The desire for live voice dwells in all poets," Paul Zumthor writes in *Oral Poetry* (1990), "but it is in exile in writing." The written poem appeals to the inner ear, the practice of aural reading. Every speaker requires a listener, every voice needs an ear, and the printed voice must imagine that listener, its addressee, because it is a communicative act between two people who are not physically present to each other. It therefore textualizes its voice, which is represented in language, recalled through sound. Garrett Stewart calls the complicated act of responding to the written poem "reading voices," a zone of "evocalization." When you recite a poem aloud, however, it is no longer disenfranchised from vocalized sound because your own voice becomes the instrument by which it comes alive. The poem voices itself through you.

Critics speak of "the voice" in a poem to mean its characteristic sound, style, manner, and tone, its implied attitude. To speak of "a poet's voice" becomes a metaphor for his or her distinctive way of speaking.

SEE ALSO *oral poetry, song, sound poetry*.

volta, volte, see *sonnet*.

W

waka The Japanese use w*aka* to refer to all serious poetry written in Japanese from the earliest literate times. It references poetry as a native possession of Japan. In contrast to popular or religious songs, *waka* refers to the forms of court poetry, such as the tanka. *Waka* is also used in modern times as a synonym for tanka, in which case it refers to a traditional verse form consisting of five phrases, each with a set number of syllables: 5–7–5–7–7. A comic *waka* is called a *kyōka*.

Japanese poetry is syllabic, and all traditional forms of Japanese poetry involve five- and seven-syllable lines. Some scholars think the model derives from Chinese poetry; others speculate that the alternating line lengths suited archaic patterns of singing. No one knows precisely why this syllabic pattern defines traditional Japanese poetry.

Kakekotoba is a "pivot-word," a type of wordplay crucial to *waka*. Pivot-words use sounds that mean two things at once by different parsings. A *makurakotoba* ("pillow-word") modifies the words it follows in various and sometimes ambiguous ways. There are two basic terms in Japanese poetics. *Kotoba* refers to the materials of poetry and includes such things as syntax and prosody, diction and imagery, quality of sound and phrasing. *Kokoro* refers to the spirit and feeling, the heart of poetry. Thus *kokoro naki* is poetry without "heart," *kokoro ari* is poetry with a conviction of feeling.

Ki No Tsurayuki's preface to the *Kokinshū* (ca. 905) expresses his belief in the naturalness and human feeling at the heart of Japanese poetry:

> The poetry of Japan has its roots in the human heart and flourishes in the countless leaves of words. Because human beings possess interest of so many kinds, it is in poetry that they give expression to the meditations of their hearts in terms of the sights appearing before their eyes and the sounds coming to their ears. Hearing the warbler sing among the blossoms and the frog in his fresh waters — is there any living being not given to song? It is poetry which,

without exertion, moves heaven and earth, stirs the feelings of gods and spirits invisible to the eye, softens the relations between men and women, calms the hearts of fierce warriors.

SEE ALSO *tanka.*

wedding songs, see *epithalamium.*

wisdom literature The ancient Near East had an elastic genre of literature and a wide corpus of works known as wisdom literature, much of it poetry. These works deal with ethical and religious topics, moral precepts, and the nature of divinity. The Book of Proverbs, which treats wisdom as something teachable in language, is the central biblical example of ancient Near Eastern wisdom literature. Some early Christian writers simply called it "Wisdom," and it was referred to in the Roman Missal as a "Book of Wisdom."

> A wise man will hear, and will increase learning; and a man
>   of understanding shall attain unto wise counsels:
> To understand a proverb and the interpretation; the words of the wise,
>   and their dark sayings. (Proverbs 1:5–6)

Wisdom literature includes the Book of Job, Ecclesiastes, and the Song of Songs from the Hebrew Bible, as well as the books of the Apocrypha known as the Wisdom of Solomon and Ben Sira, or Ecclesiasticus.

Biblical scholars coined the term *wisdom literature* for a genre of works embodying *hokmah* ("wisdom"). The term was subsequently adapted to other ancient Near Eastern works, such as the Mesopotamian corpus of wisdom texts, which seek to teach the art of leading a successful life in harmony with the divine. It is generally recognized that Proverbs 22:17–24:22 (the "Words of the Wise") borrows from the ancient Egyptian *Instruction of Amenemope* (ca. 1100 B.C.E.), which belongs to the primary didactic literary genre of *sebayt* ("instruction") and derives from the royal court. Admonitions, a subcategory of wisdom texts, were used to warn against social and moral evils. The word for wisdom in Sumerian is *nam-ku-zu,* which means "pure, sacred knowledge." This sacred knowledge, embodied in proverbs, fables, instructions, disputations, and dialogues, was passed on by master scribes to their pupils through such "rhetorical collections" or "scribal training literature" as *The Instructions of Shuruppak* (ca. 2500 B.C.E.), the most significant piece of Sumerian wisdom literature. It is a carefully constructed collection of poetic instructions on the proper way to live. The Akkadian word for sacred knowledge is *nēmequ,* which appears in the most well-known work of Babylonian wisdom literature: "Let me praise the Lord of Wisdom" (late second millennium B.C.E.). There are two main types of Babylonian wisdom literature. One contains practical advice on how to live, what to do. These are frequently addressed to "my son." The other type reflects more generally on human experiences.

SEE ALSO *didactic poetry, gnome, proverbs.*

wit The ability to make quick, clever connections with verbal deftness, to perceive the likeness in unlike things, relating incongruities and thus awakening the intelligence. *Wit* is a term with a long critical history. In his treatise *Rhetoric* (ca. 335–330 B.C.E.), Aristotle treated *asteia* ("wit") as the ability to make apt comparisons as well as a form of "well-bred insolence." Classical rhetoricians used it to mean "cleverness" or "ingenuity." The Latin writers termed it *urbane dicta* ("clever or witty sayings"). To the Renaissance, the word meant "intelligence" or "wisdom." During the seventeenth century, wit was associated with the metaphysical poetry of John Donne and others, and identified with the ability to create startling, far-fetched figures of speech. "Tell me, O tell, what kind of thing is *Wit,* / Thou who *Master* art of it," Abraham Cowley writes in his witty "Ode of Wit" (1656). Reacting against the metaphysical mode, Dr. Johnson attacked Cowley for "heterogeneous ideas . . . yoked by violence together," a criticism that would later be considered a compliment.

Once viewed as an essential feature of poetry, wit was defined by the philosopher John Locke as "the Assemblage of Ideas, and putting those together with quickness and variety." John Dryden characterized it as "sharpness of conceit," thereby emphasizing the shared self-consciousness between the poet and the reader. In "An Essay on Criticism" (1711), Alexander Pope famously contrasted "true wit," guided by judgment, with mere fanciful writing: "True Wit is Nature to advantage dressed, / What oft was thought, but ne'er so well expressed."

Rebelling against the association of wit with reason and common sense, the Romantic poets employed the concept of imagination to designate the ability to invent and perceive relations. Wit was degraded to a form of levity, from which it has never entirely recovered. In rediscovering the metaphysical poets, T. S. Eliot revived the concept of wit, which he described in an essay on Andrew Marvell as a "tough reasonableness beneath the slight lyric grace."

SEE ALSO *conceit, imagination, metaphysical poets.*

work song The song to accompany work is an oral phenomenon, an ancient, rhythmic, utilitarian form of verse. The work song increases labor efficiency by setting a steady pace for a group, timing its strokes. Tomb inscriptions from Egypt (ca. 2600 B.C.E.) include work songs for shepherds, fishermen, and chairmen. There are songs of the well-diggers in Numbers (21:17–18). In ancient Greece, there were songs for making rope and drawing water (fountain songs), for stamping barley and treading grapes, for spinning wool and herding sheep. The earliest French lyrics, called *chanson de toile* and dating from the twelfth century, were short poems to accompany needlework and tapestry weaving. It has been plausibly theorized that the rhythm of Anglo-Saxon poetry was based on the slow pull and push of the oar, whereas the Irish tradition developed a rhythm based on the pounding of hammer and anvil. If so, then English verse, which has a qualitative meter, has its origins in the physical action of work. Whenever the rhythm of certain tasks has become set — sowing, reaping, threshing, washing clothes, milking cows, rowing, hauling and pulling down sail, etc. — then there are accompanying songs that preserve those rhythms.

African traditional poetry includes songs to accompany such occupations as canoe paddling, milling of rice, marching, and nursing children. The call-and-response pattern of these songs, the interplay between a leader and a chorus (*dokpwe* in Dahomey), carried over to the New World in the form of field hollers and other songs improvised by people forced into slavery, in the lyrics of woodcutters and fishermen, of rural and prison road gangs. In the African American work song, a leader provides a strong rhythmic cue with two or three bars, which are then answered in the ejaculatory word or words of moving workers. The rhythmic interaction makes both poetry and music a participatory activity. The West African pattern also influenced the agricultural songs of Trinidad (*gayap*) and Haiti (*combite*).

Some folklorists argue that the work song challenges the nature of work by changing the mindset of the workers. The singer supplies a beat and relieves the tedium, transposing the space, creating a different relationship to time. The rhythm of the words — the work that poetry does — actively restructures time. It induces a kind of ritualistic hypnosis, a rhythmic ecstasy.

SEE ALSO *folk song, oral poetry, rhythm, sea shanties.*

wrenched accent, wrenched rhyme At times the requirements of metrical stress prevail over the natural accent of a word or words. The rhythms of folk songs, for example, do not always correspond to speech rhythms. Folksingers seem to find wrenched accents quite "natural" in performing ballads, as in this stanza from "Sir Patric Spens," which changes the emphasis on the word *máster* to *mastér:*

> Late late yestreen I saw the new moone,
>> Wi the auld moone in hir arme,
> And I feir, I feir, my deir master,
>> That we will cum to harme.

A rhyme that depends on a wrenched accent is called a wrenched rhyme. It rhymes a stressed with an unstressed syllable, as in the tenth stanza of the anonymous ballad "Mary Hamilton," which wrenches together the words *sae* and *free* so that they rhyme with the word *ladie:*

> When she cam down the Cannongate,
>> The Cannongate sae free,
> Many a ladie lookd oer her window,
>> Weeping for this ladie.

SEE ALSO *accent, folk song, meter, prosody, rhyme, scansion.*

Y

yūgen   This elusive Japanese term suggests mystery, subtlety, and depth. There is no exact equivalent in English for the deep aesthetic ideal of elegance and grace. *Yūgen* was originally a Buddhist term that referred to the dark or obscure meanings of the Buddhist Sutras. It means "difficult" or "obscure" in Ki no Yoshimochi's classical Chinese preface to the imperial anthology *Kokinshū* (ca. 905). The term *yūgen* was later applied to poetry and the other arts. It has had a bewildering number of critical interpretations over the centuries. The poet and nobleman Shunzei (1114–1204) was the first to advocate *yūgen* as a major poetic ideal. As he said, in the Jūzenshi postscript to the poetry contest that he judged in 1198 or so,

> In general, a poem need not always attempt clever conceits nor present its ideas fully and systematically. Yet when it is recited, whether it is simply read aloud or is formally intoned, there must be something about it which resounds with allure [*en*] and with profundity [*yūgen*].

The term *yūgen* evolved over time to suggest an elusive kind of beauty. It was the aesthetic ideal of the Nō drama, the masked dance-drama of medieval Japan, which was perfected by Zeami (1363–1443), who believed the actor must develop a poetic sensibility, elegant and suggestive. Robert Brower and Earl Miner point out that despite the critical, historical, and semantic vicissitudes of the term, "the core of yūgen remained the ideal of an artistic effort both mysterious and ineffable, of a subtle, complex tone achieved by emphasizing the unspoken connotations of words and the implications of a poetic situation." As a Zen concept, *yūgen* suggests the paring down of things to their essence. The symbol for *yūgen* is a swan with a flower in its bill. It is a poetic ideal of intensity and restraint, something mysterious and strange.

SEE ALSO *renga, utaawase, waka, Zen poetry.*

Z

zaum, zaoum   The Russian futurists Aleksei Kruchenykh (1886–1968) and Velimir Khlebnikov (1885–1922) were exponents of *zaum,* a coined word that means something like "trans-rational" or "beyond-sense." Trans-rational language (*zaumnyj jazyk,* or *zaum*) refers to a kind of sound poetry, a disruptive poetic language focused on the materiality of words. "It was a language of new words based on Slavic roots and the sounds indicated by individual letters of the alphabet," the translator Paul Schmidt explains. Khlebnikov especially loved puns and palindromes, neologisms, obsessive wordplay, and the magical language of shamans. He found eerie wisdom in separate linguistic sounds, such as "sh," "m," and "v." He believed that universal truths are secreted in "the self-same word" (*samovitoe slovo*), and he sought to access them through spells and incantations, magic words, folk etymologies, archaic sounds. The impulse was to test the relationship between sound and sense, to wrench words from their habitual meanings.

The Russian futurists wanted to create an extreme poetic language that could transcend common sense and the restrictive features of rational intellect. "If we think of the soul as split between the government of intellect and a stormy population of feelings," Khlebnikov wrote in his essay "On Poetry" (1919), "then incantations and beyonsense language are appeals over the head of the government straight to the population of feelings, a direct cry to the predawn of the soul."

The Russian formalists, especially the literary scholar Viktor Shklovsky and the linguist Roman Jakobson, wondered whether or not all poetry aspired to become "trans-sense poetry." In "The New Russian Poetry" (1919), Jakobson explains that "poetic language strives, as to its limit, toward the phonetic word, or more exactly, inasmuch as the corresponding set is present, toward the euphonic word, toward trans-sense speech."

SEE ALSO *chant, palindrome, pun, shaman, sound poetry, spells.*

zéjel   A Spanish poetic form, which is called *zajal* in Arabic and *zadjal* in French. The *zéjel* begins with an introductory stanza, a brief initial *estribillo* (refrain) that presents the theme of the poem. This is followed by a tercet, which is called a *mudanza* (i.e., a changing verse, from *mudar,* "to move or change") with a single rhyme (*monorrimo*). The *mudanza,* which at times also had internal rhymes, is followed by the repetition of one or more lines, a *vuelta* — the word means "turn" or "return" — rhyming with the initial stanza. The final line of the *estribillo* and that of the *vuelta* were sometimes shorter than the other lines. It is typically written in eight-syllable lines. The simplest and most common rhyme scheme is *aa, bbba, ccca, ddda,* and so forth.

The *zéjel* most likely was invented by the Hispano-Muslim poet Mucaddam ben Muafa, who was born in Cabra (Córdoba) in the mid-ninth century and died around 902. No *zéjels* by Mucaddam survive, but the invention of the form was reported by Aben Bassám de Santarem in 1109 and Aben Jaldún de Túnez in the fourteenth century. The troubadours picked up the *zéjel* form in the eleventh and twelfth centuries after crossing into Spain, and it was adopted early on by Macabru (fl. 1129–1150) and his patron, William IX, Duke of Aquitaine (1071–1150). The form is several centuries older than the French virelay and the Italian *lauda,* which have similar traits, and it most likely served as a model for these quintessential European forms.

The *zéjel* is closely related to the Arabic form *muwashshah.* The major difference is that the *zéjel* is written in vernacular Spanish and the *muwashshah* is written in classical Arabic, though the secular *muwashshah* typically closes with an envoi, or closing couplet, which is usually written out in the Arabic or romance vernacular (*kharja*). Both forms are closely associated with music. The word *zéjel* means *bailada,* which comes from the word *bailar,* "to sway back and forth, to dance."

Both the *zéjel* and the *muwashshah* were cultivated by Arabic and Jewish poets and musicians in medieval Andalusia. The *zéjel* especially thrived in the thirteenth century, but over the centuries, many poets among the Arabic peoples of the Mediterranean have continued to create *zéjels.* As Tomás Navarro reports in *Métrica española* (1956), "The writer Aben Said, who died in 1274, said that more zéjels [by Aben Guzmán] were remembered and sung in Baghdad than in the Andalusian cities. The tradition is still alive in the Arab countries; in Tunisia the name *canto granadino* reflects the Spanish origin of the zéjel."

SEE ALSO *muwashshah, octosyllabic verse, troubador, virelay.*

Zen poetry   Zen poetry tries to communicate the ineffable — the world of No-thing — through suggestion. The Japanese word *Zen* (*Chan* in Chinese) literally means "meditation," which Zen Buddhists believe is the Way of satori (awakening), the path to enlightenment. Zen originated in India and spread to China in the sixth century and then to Japan in the eighth century. Chinese Zen monks began to write poetry as an extension of their meditative practices. Zen poetry has no single formal property, though the Chinese Zen poets wrote quatrains with lines of equal length, and the seventeenth-century master Matsuo Bashō turned haiku into the quintessential Zen art. Zen poetry can be written in any language, though no language is adequate to express its truths, since there is, in essence, no room in Zen for letters or words. There is something helpless in Zen poetry, which tries to express the inexpressible, the realm of the absolute, primordial nothingness that cannot be named. Yet no Zen master poet doubts that this nothingness is present.

SEE ALSO *haiku, yūgen.*

Index

"A" (Zukofsky), 98, 116

"A Ballade of the Scottysshe Kynge" (Skelton), 33–34

"An A.B.C." (Chaucer), 1, 186–87

Absalom and Achitophel (Dryden), 160–61, 235, 277

"Adonais" (Shelley), 86, 90, 302

Aeneid (Virgil), 8, 30, 38, 88, 97, 127, 154, 191

"The Aeolian Harp" (Coleridge), 31, 59

Aetia (Callimachus), 191

"Against Women Unconstant" (Chaucer), 260

"Ah! Sun-flower" (Blake), 12

"Alba" (Pound), 21

Alcaeus, 4
    "Ode to Castor and Polydeuces," 202–3

"Alcaics" (Clough), 5

Alciati, Andrea: *Emblematum liber*, 92

Alcott, A. Bronson: *Sonnets and Canzonets*, 40

"Alexander's Feast" (Dryden), 80

"L'Allegro" (Milton), 63, 332

Al Que Quiere! (Williams), 66

"The Altar" (Herbert), 92

"Altarwise by Owl-Light" (Thomas), 299

América (Bello), 121

"The American Sublime" (Stevens), 310

Ammons, A. R.: *Tape for the Turn of the Year*, 306

"Among School Children" (Yeats), 201, 210

Amores (Ovid), 99

Amours de Voyage (Clough), 346

Amphitruo (Plautus), 328

Anacreon, 10

Anathemata (Jones), 98

Anderson, Jon: "The Blue Animals," 265

"Andrea del Sarto" (Browning), 84

"And *Ut Pictura Poesis* Is Her Name" (Ashbery), 49

"Anglo-Saxon Rune Poem," 273

"Annabel Lee" (Poe), 12, 258

"Antiphon (I)" (Herbert), 14

Antony and Cleopatra (Shakespeare), 234

"The Apparition of His Mistresse Calling Him to Elizium. Dezunt Nonulla—" (Herrick), 10

Arcadia (Sydney), 17, 193, 285

Archpoet: "Estuans intrinsecus," 123–24

Arensberg, Walter Conrad: "For Shady Hill," 66

"The Argument" (Jonson), 3

Ariosto, Ludovico: *Orlando furioso*, 44, 97, 301

Aristophanes
    The Clouds, 51, 160, 228
    The Frogs, 160, 228
    The Wasps, 79

"Arms and the Boy" (Owen), 257

Arnold, Matthew
    "The Scholar-Gypsy," 346
    "Thyrsis," 86, 90

Ars poetica (Horace), 19

"*Ars Poetica?*" (Milosz), 19

"Art poétique" (Verlaine),
314
Ashbery, John
"And *Ut Pictura Poesis* Is
Her Name," 49
"The Dong with the
Luminous Nose," 43
Flow Chart, 306
"Litany," 166
A Wave, 125
"Ask me no more"
(Tennyson), 316
"Asphodel, That Greeny
Flower" (Williams),
306
"Astrophel" (Spenser), 90
Astrophil and Stella
(Sidney), 180, 222,
246
*An Atlas of the Difficult
World* (Rich), 240
"Aubade" (Larkin), 22
Aucassin and Nicolette, 38
Auden, W. H.
"The Hidden Law," 270
"In Memory of Sigmund
Freud," 5, 90
"Letter to Lord Byron,"
162, 261
"New Year Letter," 131
"Sonnets from China,"
299
Augustine of Hippo:
"Psalmus contra
partem Donati," 1
Aurora Leigh (Browning),
346
"The Author to Her Book"
(Bradstreet), 16

"Autumn: A Dirge"
(Shelley), 77
"Autumn Sequel"
(MacNeice), 188

Bacchylides, 102
"Ballade at Thirty-Five"
(Parker), 28
"Ballade des dames du
temps jadis" (Villon),
27, 336
"Ballade des pendus"
(Villon), 27
"Ballade des proverbes"
(Villon), 242
"Ballade of Unfortunate
Mammals" (Parker),
28
Barnes, Barnabe: "Sestine
4," 85
Bashō, Matsuo, 126
*Hut of the Phantom
Dwelling,* 125
Bashō's Ghost (Hamill),
125
Batrachomyomachia, 184
Baudelaire, Charles
"Correspondances," 314
Les fleurs du mal, 72
"Mon coeur mis à nu," 57
Petits poèmes en prose,
239
Beauchamp, Richard: "I
cannot half the woo
compleyne," 351
Beckett, Samuel: *Waiting
for Godot,* 52
Beddoes, Thomas Lovell:
"Dirge," 77

"Before the Beginning of
Years" (Swinburne),
12
The Beggar's Opera (Gay),
35
Bello, Andrés: *América,* 121
"The Bells" (Poe), 273
Bentley, Edmund
Clerihew: "Geoffrey
Chaucer," 48
Beowulf, 94–95, 109, 155,
178, 188
Beppo: A Venetian Story
(Byron), 191–92
Bishop, Elizabeth: "One
Art," 349
"The Bishop Orders His
Tomb at St. Praxed's
Church" (Browning),
84
Blackburn, Paul: "Listening
to Sonny Rollins at
the Five-Spot," 151
"Black Rook in Rainy
Weather" (Plath),
265
Blake, William
"Ah! Sun-flower," 12
The Four Zoas, 281
"Proverbs of Hell," 11,
242
"The Sick Rose," 16
*Songs of Innocence and
Experience,* 295
"Spring," 65
"Blazon du beau tétin"
(Marot), 32
"The Blue Animals"
(Anderson), 265

Bogan, Louise: "Portrait,"
 276
Boileau-Despréaux,
 Nicolas: *Le lutrin*, 35
Boland, Eavan: "Envoi," 188
Bolardo, Matteo: *Orlando
 inamorato*, 44
Book of Proverbs, 354
Book of Songs, 193
Book of the Dead, 249–50
"The Book of the Duchess"
 (Chaucer), 202
Bradstreet, Anne
 "The Author to Her
 Book," 16
 *Exact Epitome of the
 Four Monarchies*,
 98
 "Prologue," 283–84
"The Bridge of Sighs"
 (Hood), 257
Bridges, Robert: "Song:
 Chorus to Demeter,"
 5
"A Broadway Pageant"
 (Whitman), 12–13
Brodsky, Joseph: "A Martial
 Law Carol," 41
Browning, Elizabeth
 Barrett
 Aurora Leigh, 346
 "Say over again, and yet
 once over again," 13
Browning, Robert
 "Andrea del Sarto," 84
 "The Bishop Orders His
 Tomb at St. Praxed's
 Church," 84
 Dramatic Idylls, 136

"A Grammarian's
 Funeral," 258
"Lost Leader," 108
"My Last Duchess,"
 84
Pippa Passes, 49
The Ring and the Book,
 181, 346
"Toccata of Galuppi's,"
 180
"Build Soil—A Political
 Pastoral" (Frost),
 86–87
Bunyan, John: *Pilgrim's
 Progress*, 7
Burns, Robert
 "Cotter's Saturday
 Night," 302
 "Epistle to John Lapraik,
 an Old Scottish
 Bard," 284
 "The Holy Fair," 316
 "My love is like a red, red
 rose," 290–91
 "Tam o'Shanter," 91,
 202
Butler, Samuel: *Hudibras*,
 63, 130–31
Byron, George (Lord)
 Beppo: A Venetian Story,
 192
 *Childe Harold's
 Pilgrimage*, 302
 "The Corsair," 202
 Don Juan, 36, 97–98,
 149, 210
 "The Giaour. A
 Fragment of a
 Turkish Tale," 116

Manfred, 49
"The Destruction of
 Sennacherib," 12

"Caedmon's Hymn," 127
"Caelica 6" (Greville), 276
"The Call" (Herbert), 60
Callimachus: *Aetia*, 191
Camões, Luís de: *Lusiads*,
 97
Campion, Thomas
 "Rose-Cheeked Laura,"
 275
 "Thrice tosse these
 Oaken ashes in the
 ayre," 46
 Two Books of Ayres, 4
 "With broken heart and
 contrite sigh," 157
"The Canonization"
 (Donne), 37, 298
The Canterbury Tales
 (Chaucer), 63,
 180–81, 191, 260
"Canto LXXX" (Pound),
 273
The Cantos (Pound), 39, 50,
 98, 116
Canzonettas (Saba), 40
Canzoni (Pound), 40
Carew, Thomas: "To
 Saxham," 62
Carmina (Catullus),
 40–41, 103
Carmina Anacreontea, 10
Carmina Burana, 123
"Carol" (Thomas), 41
"A Carol" (Hall), 41
"A Carol" (Lewis), 41

"Carol of the Three Kings"
(Merwin), 41
"Carpe Diem" (Collins), 42
Carroll, Lewis, 2, 10
"Jabberwocky," 197
"Rules and Regulations,"
108–9
Catullus
Carmina, 40–41, 103
"Catullus 101," 99
"Causes" (Van Duyn), 265
The Cenci (Shelley), 49
Cento virgilianus (Proba),
43
Certain Epistles (Daniel),
162
*The Changing Light at
Sandover* (Merrill),
49–50, 98
"Chanson Dada" (Tzara),
69
La chanson de Roland, 20,
44, 72, 96, 158–59,
191
"Charge of the Light
Brigade" (Tennyson),
69
Chatterton, Thomas:
"Minstrel's
Roundelay," 272
Chaucer, Geoffrey
"An A.B.C.," 1, 186–87
"The Book of the
Duchess," 202
The Canterbury Tales,
63, 180–81, 191, 260
"The Complaint of
Chaucer to His
Purse," 16, 27, 53

"A Complaint to His
Lady," 321
"Franklin's Tale," 158
"The House of Fame,"
202
"The Knight's Tale," 180
"Merciles Beaute: A
Triple Roundel," 271
"The Miller's Tale," 107
"The Monk's Tale," 327
Parlement of Foules, 260
"The Prologue to the
Legend of Good
Women," 63
"The Reeve's Tale," 107
"Tale of Sir Thopas," 80
Troilus and Criseyde, 64,
213, 242, 260, 283
Le chevalier de la charrette
(Troyes), 64
Child ballads, 25
Childe Harold's Pilgrimage
(Byron), 302
A Choice of Emblemes
(Whitney), 92
"Choriambics"
(Swinburne), 47
"The Chosen People"
(Ewer), 257
"Christabel" (Coleridge),
63, 178, 202
"A Christmas Carol"
(Coleridge), 41
"A Christmas Note for
Geraldine Udell"
(Rexroth), 235
"The Circus Animals'
Desertion" (Yeats),
210

"Cleis" (Hacker), 276
"The Cloud" (Shelley), 12
The Clouds (Aristophanes),
51, 160, 228
Clough, Arthur
"Alcaics," 5
Amours de Voyage,
346
Coleridge, Samuel Taylor
"A Christmas Carol," 41
"The Aeolian Harp,"
31, 59
"Christabel," 63, 178, 202
"Dejection: An Ode,"
59–60
"Fears in Solitude," 59
"Frost at Midnight,"
31, 59
"Kubla Khan: or a
Vision in a Dream. A
Fragment," 116
"Metrical Feet," 10, 65,
113
"The Nightingale. A
Conversation Poem,"
59
"The Ovidian Elegiac
Metre," 129
"Reflections on Having
Left a Place of
Retirement," 59
"The Rime of the
Ancient Mariner," 18
"This Lime-tree Bower
My Prison," 59
"To William
Wordsworth," 59–60
"What is an epigram?,"
100

"Colin Clout" (Skelton), 81, 293–94

Collins, Billy: "Carpe Diem," 42

Collins, William: "Ode on the Poetical Character," 281

The Comedy of Errors (Shakespeare), 52

Commedia (Dante). *see Divine Comedy* (Dante)

"A Complaint by Night of the Lover Not Beloved" (Earl of Surrey), 53

"The Complaint of Chaucer to His Purse" (Chaucer), 16, 27, 53, 260

"The Complaint of Conscience" (Percy), 53

"Complaint of Henry, Duke of Buckingham" (Sackville), 53

Complaints (Spenser), 235

"A Complaint to His Lady" (Chaucer), 260, 321

"Complaint unto Pity" (Chaucer), 260

"Complaynt of Our Soverane Lordis Papyngo" (Lyndsay), 53

"Complaynt to the King" (Lyndsay), 53

"Composed upon Westminster Bridge, September 3, 1802" (Wordsworth), 297

Confessio Amantis (Gower), 106, 202

Congreve, William: *Way of the World*, 52

Consolatio ad Liviam, 58

Consolatio ad uxorem (Plutarch), 57–58

Convivio (Dante), 39–40

"Coole Park and Ballylee" (Yeats), 210

"Cooper's Hill" (Denham), 193, 323

Cope, Wendy: "Rondeau Redoublé," 270

Corkery, Daniel: *The Hidden Ireland*, 5

Corneille, Pierre, 6

"Correspondances" (Baudelaire), 314

"The Corsair" (Byron), 202

"Cotter's Saturday Night" (Burns), 302

Cowley, Abraham, 10
   Davideis: A Sacred Poem of the Troubles of David, 98
   "Ode of Wit," 355

Cowper, William
   "Lines Written During a Period of Insanity," 275
   The Task, 31, 121

Crabbe, George: *The Village*, 9, 218

Crane, Hart: "Proem: To Brooklyn Bridge," 238

Crapsey, Adelaide: "November Night," 47

Daniel, Samuel
   Certain Epistles, 162
   Letter from Octavia to Marcus Antonius, 162

Dante Alighieri
   Convivio, 39–40
   Divine Comedy, 38, 51, 97, 128, 320
   Inferno, 8, 333–34
   Purgatorio, 88

Davideis: A Sacred Poem of the Troubles of David (Cowley), 98

Davidson, John: "The Gleeman," 122

Davies, John: "Some blaze the precious beauties of their loves," 32

Davis, Dick: "A Letter to Omar," 273

"The Day Lady Died" (O'Hara), 151

"The Day of Judgment" (Watts), 276

"Dear John, Dear Coltrane" (Harper), 151

"De arte graphica" (Fresnoy), 341

"Death's Valley" (Whitman), 49

"Débat du coeur et du corps" (Villon), 70

"Dedication" (Frost), 201

"Débat du cors et du l'âme," 70

"Dejection: An Ode" (Coleridge), 59–60

Denham, John: "Cooper's Hill," 193, 323

"Déor," 278

"Deor's Lament," 53, 160

De rerum natura (Lucretius), 76

"Desert Places" (Frost), 273

"The Destruction of Sennacherib" (Byron), 12

Dhlomo, Herbert I. E.: *Valley of a Thousand Hills,* 240

"A Dialogue, Between the Resolved Soul and Created Pleasure" (Marvell), 70–72

"A Dialogue Between the Soul and Body" (Marvell), 70–71, 75

"A Dialogue of Self and Soul" (Yeats), 75–76

Dickinson, Emily
"'Hope' is the thing with feathers," 332
"Nature is a Haunted House," 337
"Tell all the Truth but tell it slant," 19
"There's a certain Slant of light," 147

"Dinky" (Roethke), 157

"Dirge" (Beddoes), 77

"Dirge" (Emerson), 77

"A Dirge for McPherson" (Melville), 77

"Dirge for Two Veterans" (Whitman), 77

"Dirge in Woods" (Meredith), 77

"The Discursive Mode" (Hope), 77

"Le dit de l'herberie" (Rutebeuf), 79

"Ditiee de Jehanne d'Arc" (Pisan), 79

"A Ditty" (Sidney), 103

Divine Comedy (Dante), 38, 51, 97, 128, 320, 334

Doctor Faustus (Marlowe), 333

"The Dong with the Luminous Nose" (Ashbery), 43

Don Juan (Byron), 36, 97–98, 149, 210

Donne, John
"The Canonization," 37, 298
"A Hymne to God the Father," 243–44
"A Litany," 166
"The Paradox," 215
"Song," 129
"The Sun Rising," 16, 22, 109

Doolittle, Hilda ("H. D.")
Helen in Egypt, 98, 212
Tribute to Freud, 336

"Do Not Go Gentle into That Good Night" (Thomas), 211, 349

d'Orléans, Charles:
"Rondeau," 270

Dowland, John: *The first Booke of Songs or Ayres,* 4

Dramatic Idylls (Browning), 136

Drayton, Michael: "To His Coy Love: A Canzonet," 40

"The Dream of the Rood," 222

"The Dreme" (Lyndsay), 53

Dryden, John
Absalom and Achitophel, 160–61, 235, 277
"Alexander's Feast," 80
The Hind and the Panther, 35
Mac Flecknoe, 277
"To the Pious Memory of the Accomplished Young Lady, Mrs. Anne Killigrew," 203

"The Dry Salvages" (Eliot), 210

Duino Elegies (Rilke), 90

Dunbar, Paul Laurence: "We Wear the Mask," 270

Dunbar, William: "Lament for the Makers," 157, 226

The Dunciad (Pope), 277

The Dynasts (Hardy), 49

"Earl Brand," 25

Earthly Paradise (Morris), 192, 261

"Easter, 1916" (Yeats), 257

Eclogues (Virgil), 16–17, 86, 99, 135, 218

"An Eclogue. To the Memory of Dr. William Wilkie, late Professor of Natural Philosophy in the University of St. Andrews" (Fergusson), 336–37

Eddica minora, 88

"Effort at Speech" (Meredith), 276

Egyptian Book of the Dead, 249–50

Elder Edda, 88

"Elegiac Verse" (Longfellow), 89

"Elegies for Paradise Valley" (Hayden), 336

"An Elegy" (Jonson), 143

"An Elegy upon the Death of that Holy and Reverend Man of God, Mr. Samuel Hooker" (Taylor), 152

"Elegy Written in a Country Churchyard" (Gray), 89, 90, 128, 247

"Eleventh Song" (Sidney), 247–48

Eliot, T. S.
  "The Dry Salvages," 210
  "First Debate Between the Body and Soul," 75
  Four Quartets, 306

"The Love Song of J. Alfred Prufrock," 117

"The Waste Land," 50, 91, 116, 186, 334

"Eloisa to Abelard" (Pope), 162

Emblematum liber (Alciati), 92

Emblemes (Quarles), 92

Emerson, Ralph Waldo
  "Dirge," 77
  "Merlin I," 28
  "The Poet," 28, 289
  "Self-Reliance," 310

Empson, William: *The Structure of Complex Words,* 7

Endymion (Keats), 63

"Enigma" (Poe), 3

"Envoi" (Boland), 188

Epic of Gilgamesh, 95, 191, 205

Epic of King Gesar, 97

"Epigram Engraved on the Collar of a Dog which I gave to His Royal Highness" (Pope), 62

"Epigram from the French" (Pope), 100

Epigrams (Martial), 99

"Epistle to John Lapraik, an Old Scottish Bard" (Burns), 284

Epistolae (Horace), 228–29

Epistulae ex ponto (Ovid), 99

Epistulae metricae (Petrarch), 162

Epithalamion (Spenser), 31, 103

Epodon libor (Horace), 104

"Erinna to Sappho" (Wright), 276

"An Essay on Comedy" (Meredith), 278

"An Essay on Criticism" (Pope), 6, 19, 49, 76, 193, 197, 345, 355

"An Essay on Man" (Pope), 76, 345

"Estuans intrinsecus" (Archpoet), 123–24

Eugene Onegin (Pushkin), 192, 346

Euripides: *The Frogs,* 51

"The Eve of Saint Agnes" (Keats), 192, 292, 302

Everyman, 7

Every Man in His Humour (Jonson), 52

Ewer, W. N.: "The Chosen People," 257

Exact Epitome of the Four Monarchies (Bradstreet), 98

Exequy (King), 77

The Exeter Book, 278

Façade (Sitwell), 2

The Faerie Queene (Spenser), 6, 18, 46, 92, 97, 181, 301–2, 305

"Farewell Performance" (Merrill), 276

Faulkner, William: "Sapphics," 275–76

Faust (Goethe), 49, 156
"Fears in Solitude"
    (Coleridge), 59
"Female Vagrant"
    (Wordsworth), 302
Fergusson, Robert: "An
    Eclogue. To the
    Memory of Dr.
    William Wilkie, late
    Professor of Natural
    Philosophy in the
    University of St.
    Andrews," 336–37
"The Figure of the Youth
    as Virile Poet"
    (Stevens), 188
"Finland" (Graves), 273
*The first Booke of Songs or
    Ayres* (Dowland), 4
"The Fish" (Moore), 259
Les fleurs du mal
    (Baudelaire), 72
Flow Chart (Ashbery),
    306
"The Flyting of Dunbar
    and Kennedy," 109
*The Folding Cliffs: A
    Narrative* (Merwin),
    306
Folengo, Teofilo:
    Macaronea, 170
The Forest (Jonson), 162
"For Once, Then,
    Something" (Frost),
    128
"For Shady Hill"
    (Arensberg), 66
"Fortune" (Chaucer), 260
Four Quartets (Eliot), 306

"Fourth Satire of Dr. John
    Donne, Dean of
    St. Paul's Versified"
    (Pope), 259
"Four-Word Lines"
    (Swenson), 60
The Four Zoas (Blake), 281
"Franklin's Tale" (Chaucer),
    158
Fresnoy, Charles-Alphonse
    du: "De arte
    graphica," 341
The Frogs (Aristophanes),
    160, 228
The Frogs (Euripides), 51
Frost, Robert
    "Build Soil—A Political
        Pastoral," 86–87
    "Dedication," 201
    "Desert Places," 273
    "For Once, Then,
        Something," 128
    "The Gift Outright,"
        13, 201
    North of Boston, 76,
        346–47
    "Stopping by Woods on
        a Snowy Evening,"
        43, 273
    A Way Out, 84
"Frost at Midnight"
    (Coleridge), 31, 59
Frye, Northrop, 7
Funikov, Ivan: "Message
    of a Nobleman to a
    Nobleman," 162

"The Garden" (Marvell),
    219

Gay, John: *The Beggar's
    Opera,* 35
"Gentilesse" (Chaucer),
    260
"Geoffrey Chaucer"
    (Bentley), 48
Georgics (Virgil), 9, 76,
    120–21
"Get Em High" (West),
    130
"The Giaour. A Fragment
    of a Turkish Tale"
    (Byron), 116
"The Gift Outright"
    (Frost), 13, 201
Ginsberg, Allen
    "Kaddish," 166
    "Sunflower Sutra," 311
    "Wichita Vortex Sutra,"
        311
Gizzi, Peter: "Ode: Salute
    to the New York
    School," 43
"Glanmore Sonnets"
    (Heaney), 299
"The Gleeman"
    (Davidson), 122
"God's Controversy with
    New England"
    (Wigglesworth),
    151
Goethe, Wolfgang von
    Faust, 49
    "The Poetical Mission of
        Hans Sachs," 156
    West-East Divan, 122
Goldsmith, Oliver
    "New Simile, in the
        Manner of Swift," 131

"On the Use of Hyperbole," 133

González, Gregorio Gutiérrez: *Memoir on the Cultivation of Maize in Antioquia,* 121

"Good Morning, America" (Sandburg), 242

Gosse, Edmund: "Sestina," 285–86

Gower, John
Confessio Amantis, 106, 202
In Praise of Peace, 260–61

"A Grammarian's Funeral" (Browning), 258

Graves, Robert
"Finland," 273
"John Skelton," 294

Gray, Thomas
"Elegy Written in a Country Churchyard," 89, 90, 128, 247
"Ode on the Death of a Favourite Cat, Drowned in a Tub of Gold Fishes," 203

Greek Lyrics (Lattimore), 5

Greene, Robert: *Menaphon,* 32

Greville, Fulke: "Caelica 6," 276

Grossman, Allen: "Summa Lyrica," 31

Guillaume d'Angleterre, 161
Gylfaginning, 87–88

Hacker, Marilyn: "Cleis," 276

"Had we but World enough, and Time" (Marvell), 42

"The Hag of Beare," 160

Hall, Donald: "A Carol," 41

Hamill, Sam: *Bashō's Ghost,* 125

Hamlet (Shakespeare), 200, 327

Hammond, James: *Love Elegies,* 128, 247

Hardy, Thomas
The Dynasts, 49
"The Ruined Maid," 12
"The Temporary the All," 5, 276
"The Voice," 69

Harper, Michael: "Dear John, Dear Coltrane," 151

Háttatal, 88

Hayden, Robert: "Elegies for Paradise Valley," 336

Hayman, Robert: *Quodlibets,* 101

Heaney, Seamus: "Glanmore Sonnets," 299

"Heaven" (Herbert), 85–86

Helen in Egypt (Doolittle), 98, 212

"Hendecasyllabics" (Swinburne), 128

"Hendecasyllabics" (Tennyson), 128

Henley, W. E.: "The Triolet," 330

Henry IV (Shakespeare), 106

Henry V (Shakespeare), 188

Herbert, George
"The Altar," 92
"Antiphon (I)," 14
"The Call," 60
"Heaven," 85–86
"A Paradox: that the sicke are in a *better case,* then the Whole," 215

Herbert of Cherbury (Lord): "Ode upon a Question Moved, whether Love Should Continue for ever," 143

"Hero and Leander" (Marlowe), 62, 191

Herrick, Robert
"His Litany, to the Holy Spirit," 166
"Rules for Our Reach," 48
"The Apparition of His Mistresse Calling Him to Elizium. Dezunt Nonulla—," 10
"To the Virgins, to Make Much of Time," 42
"Upon His Departure Hence," 180

Herrick, Robert (*cont.*)
  "Upon Julia's Clothes,"
    320
  "The White Island or
    Place of the Blest," 316
Herzog Ernst, 96
Hesiod
  Theogony, 76, 188, 238
  Works and Days, 76, 120
The Hidden Ireland
    (Corkery), 5
"The Hidden Law"
    (Auden), 270
"The Hieroglyph of
    Irrational Space"
    (Wright), 44
Hikmet, Nazim: *Human
    Landscapes from My
    Country,* 98
The Hind and the Panther
    (Dryden), 35
"His Litany, to the Holy
    Spirit" (Herrick), 166
"The Holy Fair" (Burns), 316
"Home Is So Sad" (Larkin),
    47
Homer
  Iliad, 42, 88, 94, 99, 103,
    188, 205, 315
  Odyssey, 8, 15, 28, 94, 188,
    205, 315
Hood, Thomas: "The
    Bridge of Sighs," 257
Hope, A. D.: "The
    Discursive Mode," 77
"'Hope' is the thing
    with feathers"
    (Dickinson), 332
Hopkins, Gerard Manley
  "Pied Beauty," 297–98

"Spelt from Sibyl's
    Leaves," 298
  "The Starlight Night," 93
  "The Windhover," 7–8,
    212
  "The Wreck of the
    Deutschland," 67
Horace, 102
  Ars poetica, 19
  Epistolae, 228–29
  Epodon libor, 104
  Odes, 5, 41–42, 99
  Satires, 276–77
"Horatian Ode upon
    Cromwell's Return
    from Ireland"
    (Marvell), 201, 302
"The House of Fame"
    (Chaucer), 202
"The House on the Hill"
    (Robinson), 350
Howard, Richard: *Two-
    Part Inventions,* 50
Hudibras (Butler), 63,
    130–31
Hughes, Langston
  "Jazzonia," 150
  "The Weary Blues," 150
"Hugh Selwyn Mauberley"
    (Pound), 186
Hugo, Victor: *Les
    orientales,* 215
*Human Landscapes
    from My Country*
    (Hikmet), 98
*Hut of the Phantom
    Dwelling* (Bashō), 125
"A Hymne to God the
    Father" (Donne),
    243–44

Hymns to Aphrodite, 228
Hymn to Apollo, 228
"Hymn to Proserpine"
    (Swinburne),
    145–46, 258
"Hymn to the Sea"
    (Watson), 252
"Hyperion. A Fragment"
    (Keats), 116

"I Am Disquieted When
    I See Many Hills"
    (Plutzik), 276
Ibn Avitor, Yosef: "Lament
    for the Jews of Zion,"
    160
Ibn Ezra, Avraham:
    "Lament for
    Andalusian Jewry,"
    160
"I cannot half the woo
    compleyne"
    (Beauchamp), 351
"Icelandic Rune Poem,"
    273
Idyll (Theocritus), 103
Idylls of the King
    (Tennyson), 136, 192
"I Knew a Woman"
    (Roethke), 261
Iliad (Homer), 42, 88, 94,
    99, 103, 188, 205, 315
"Il Penseroso" (Milton), 63,
    202, 332
Inferno (Dante), 8, 333–34
"In Flanders Field"
    (McCrae), 270
Inge, William Ralph, 6
In Memoriam (Tennyson),
    16, 90, 143, 238, 259

"In Memory of Major
Robert Gregory"
(Yeats), 89, 136
"In Memory of Sigmund
Freud" (Auden), 5,
90
In Praise of Peace (Gower),
260–61
"Insensibility" (Owen), 58
"Interview" (Morgan), 301
"Intimations"
(Wordsworth), 312
"It Must Be Abstract"
("Notes Toward a
Supreme Fiction")
(Stevens), 2

"Jabberwocky" (Carroll),
197
James I (king of Scotland):
"The Kingis Quair,"
261
Jarrell, Randall: "The Lost
World," 321
"Jazzonia" (Hughes), 150
"John Skelton" (Graves),
294
Johnson, Robert: "Me and
the Devil Blues," 32
Johnson, Ronald: *Radi
os,* 105
Johnson, Samuel
"Let Observation with
extensive View," 63
"The Vanity of Human
Wishes," 70, 90
Jones, David, 8
Anathemata, 98
Jonson, Ben
"An Elegy," 143

*Every Man in His
Humour,* 52
The Forest, 162
"The Argument," 3
"To Penshurst," 62
"To the Imortall
Memorie and
Friendship of That
Noble Paire, Sir
Lucius Cary and Sir
H. Morison," 203
Jubilate Agno (Smart), 109,
117, 281
"June Thunder"
(MacNeice), 276
Justice, Donald: "Pantoum
of the Great
Depression," 215

"Kaddish" (Ginsberg), 166
Kalevala, 96, 332
Kalevipoeg, 96
Kazantzakis, Nikos: *The
Odyssey: A Modern
Sequel,* 98
Keats, John
Endymion, 63
"The Eve of Saint
Agnes," 192, 292, 302
"Hyperion. A Fragment,"
116
"Lamia," 192
"Ode to a Nightingale,"
105, 202, 306
"On First Looking into
Chapman's Homer,"
297
"To Autumn," 72, 75, 105
"The Keening of the Three
Marys," 154

Khayyám, Omar: *The
Rubaiyat,* 272–73, 305
"Kindly Unhitch That Star,
Buddy" (Nash), 259
"The Kind of Poetry
I Want"
(MacDiarmid), 19, 67
King, Henry: *Exequy,* 77
"The Kingis Quair"
(James I), 261
Kingsley, Charles: "The
Sands of Dee," 218–19
Kipling, Rudyard:
"Tommy," 180
"The Knight's Tale"
(Chaucer), 180
Knox, Ronald:
"Lamentations of the
Prophet Jeremiah:
An Alphabet of
Patience in Misery," 1
Kochanowski, Jan:
Laments, 160
König Rothar, 96
"Kubla Khan: or a Vision in
a Dream. A Fragment"
(Coleridge), 116
The Kumulipo, 320

"Lak of Steadfastness"
(Chaucer), 260
Lal, Lallu: *Prem Sagar,* 260
"Lamentations of the
Prophet Jeremiah:
An Alphabet of
Patience in Misery"
(Knox), 1
"Lament for Andalusian
Jewry" (Ibn Ezra),
160

"Lament for Art O'Leary" (Ní Chonaill), 160

"Lament for Eridu," 159

"Lament for Nippur," 159

"Lament for Sumer and Ur," 159

"Lament for the Destruction of Ur," 159

"Lament for the Jews of Zion" (Ibn Avitor), 160

"Lament for the Makers" (Dunbar), 157, 226

"Lament for the South" (Yü), 119

"Lament for Uruk," 159

Laments (Kochanowski), 160

"Lamia" (Keats), 192

Lancelot (Troyes), 46

Larkin, Philip
"Aubade," 22
"Home Is So Sad," 47

Lattimore, Richmond: *Greek Lyrics,* 5

"Law Clerk, 1979" (Leithauser), 273

Lawrence, D. H.: "Song of a Man Who Has Come Through," 344

The Lay of Havelok the Dane, 63

The Lay of the Last Minstrel (Scott), 158

Leaves of Grass (Whitman), 12–13, 42, 290

"Leaving Barra" (MacNeice), 215

Leithauser, Brad: "Law Clerk, 1979," 273

"Let Observation with extensive View" (Johnson), 63

Letter from Octavia to Marcus Antonius (Daniel), 162

"Letter to Lord Byron" (Auden), 162, 261

"A Letter to Omar" (Davis), 273

Lewis, C. Day: "A Carol," 41

"Lines Written During a Period of Insanity" (Cowper), 275

"Listening to Sonny Rollins at the Five-Spot" (Blackburn), 151

"Litany" (Ashbery), 166

"A Litany" (Donne), 166

"A Litany in Time of Plague" (Nashe), 90, 283

"Le livre dou voir dit" (Machaut), 79

Longfellow, Henry Wadsworth
"Elegiac Verse," 89
"Song of Hiawatha," 108, 331–32

"Lord Randal," 142

"Lost in Translation" (Merrill), 273

"Lost Leader" (Browning), 108

"The Lost World" (Jarrell), 321

"The Lotos-Eaters" (Tennyson), 19–20

Love, Dishonor, Marry, Die, Cherish, Perish (Rakoff), 12

"The Love Complaineth the Unkindness of His Love" (Wyatt), 248

Love Elegies (Hammond), 128, 247

"The Love Song of J. Alfred Prufrock" (Eliot), 117

Lucan: *Pharsalia,* 98

Lu Chi: "Wen-fu," 119

Lucretius: *De rerum natura,* 76

Lugones, Leopoldo: *Secular Odes,* 121

Lusiads (Camões), 97

Le lutrin (Boileau-Despréaux), 35

"Lycidas" (Milton), 90, 135, 193

Lycophron, 10–11

Lyly, John, 105–6

Lyndsay, David: "The Dreme," 53

Macaronea (Folengo), 170

Macbeth (Shakespeare), 30

Mac Con Midhe, Giolla Bríghde, 110

MacDiarmid, Hugh
"The Kind of Poetry I Want," 19, 67
"Skald's Death," 293

Mac Flecknoe (Dryden), 277

Machaut, Guillaume de
"Le livre dou voir dit,"
79
MacNeice, Louis
"Autumn Sequel," 188
"June Thunder," 276
"Leaving Barra," 215
"The Making of Man"
(Tennyson), 212
Le malade imaginaire
(Molière), 52
Malory, Thomas: *Le morte
d'Arthur,* 46
Manas, 97
Manfred (Byron), 49
"The Man with the Blue
Guitar" (Stevens),
19
"March: An Ode"
(Swinburne), 201
Margival, Nicole de:
"Story of the
Panther," 45
Marlowe, Christopher
Doctor Faustus,
333
"Hero and Leander,"
62, 191
"The Passionate
Shepherd to His
Love," 86
Marot, Cleement: "Blazon
du beau tétin,"
32
Martial
Epigrams, 99
"Sabinus, I don't like
you," 100
"A Martial Law Carol"
(Brodsky), 41

Marvell, Andrew
"A Dialogue, Between
the Resolved
Soul and Created
Pleasure," 70–71
"A Dialogue Between
the Soul and Body,"
70–71, 75
"The Garden," 219
"Had we but World
enough, and Time,"
42
"Horatian Ode upon
Cromwell's Return
from Ireland," 201,
203
"Mower" poems, 86
"To His Coy Mistress,"
63, 180
"Upon Appleton
House," 62, 215
"Mary Hamilton," 357
Masefield, John: "The
Widow in the Bye
Street," 261
The Mask of Anarchy
(Shelley), 235
Masters, Edgar Lee: *Spoon
River Anthology,* 102,
336
The Maximus Poems
(Olson), 98
McCrae, John: "In Flanders
Field," 270
McGrath, Thomas:
"Ode for the
American Dead in
Korea," 235
"Me and the Devil Blues"
(Johnson), 32

Melville, Herman: "A
Dirge for
McPherson," 77
*Memoir on the Cultivation
of Maize in Antioquia*
(González), 121
Menaphon (Greene), 32
"The Merchant's Son" (Ó
Raithille), 5
"Merciles Beaute: A Triple
Roundel" (Chaucer),
271
Meredith, George
"Dirge in Woods," 77
"An Essay on Comedy,"
278
Modern Love, 297, 346
Meredith, William: "Effort
at Speech," 276
"Merlin I" (Emerson), 28
Merrill, James
*The Changing Light
at Sandover,* 49–50,
98
"Farewell Performance,"
276
"Lost in Translation," 273
"A Renewal," 265
Merwin, W. S.
"Carol of the Three
Kings," 41
*The Folding Cliffs: A
Narrative,* 306
"Planh for the Death of
Ted Hughes," 226
"Metrical Feet"
(Coleridge), 10, 65,
113
Mickiewicz, Adam: *Pan
Tadeusz,* 346

Midsummer Night's Dream
(Shakespeare), 35,
137, 172
"The Miller's Tale"
(Chaucer), 107
Milosz, Czeslaw: "*Ars
Poetica?,*" 19
Milton, John, 6
"L'Allegro," 63, 332
"Il Penseroso," 63, 202,
332
"Lycidas," 90, 135, 193
"On the Late Massacre
in Piedmont," 297
"On the Morning of
Christ's Nativity,"
203
Paradise Lost, 15, 30, 78,
85, 97, 99, 105, 135,
147, 182, 191, 210, 306,
346
Paradise Regained, 98
Samson Agonistes, 49, 61
"When the Assault
Was Intended to the
City," 297
"Minstrel's Roundelay"
(Chatterton), 272
"Mnemosyne" (Stickney),
250
Modern Love (Meredith),
297, 346
Molière: *Le malade
imaginaire,* 52
"Mon coeur mis à nu"
(Baudelaire), 57
"The Monk's Tale"
(Chaucer), 327
"The Moon and the Yew
Tree" (Plath), 222

Moore, Marianne
"The Fish," 259
"Poetry," 19
Moore, Thomas: *Odes of
Anacreon,* 10
Moral Essays (Pope), 76
Moralia (Plutarch), 7
Moral Lessons (Stevenson),
92
Morgan, Edwin:
"Interview," 301
Morris, William: *Earthly
Paradise,* 192, 261
Le morte d'Arthur (Malory),
46
"Mower" poems (Marvell),
86
Der Münchener Oswald, 96
"My Last Duchess"
(Browning), 84
"My love is like a red, red
rose" (Burns), 290–91

Nash, Ogden
"Kindly Unhitch That
Star, Buddy," 259
"Spring Comes to
Murray Hill," 315
Nashe, Thomas: "A Litany
in Time of Plague,"
90, 283
"Nature is a Haunted
House" (Dickinson),
337
"New Simile, in the
Manner of Swift"
(Goldsmith), 131
"New Year Letter"
(Auden), 131
Nibelungenlied, 95–96

Ní Chonaill, Eibhlín
Dubh: "Lament for
Art O'Leary," 160
"The Nightingale. A
Conversation Poem"
(Coleridge), 59
Night Thoughts (Young),
90
North of Boston (Frost), 76,
346–47
"Norwegian Rune Poem,"
273
"No Second Troy" (Yeats),
256
"November Night"
(Crapsey), 47
Nowak, Mark: *Shut Up
Shut Down,* 125

"Ode for the American
Dead in Korea"
(McGrath), 235
"Ode of Wit" (Cowley), 355
"Ode on the Death of
a Favourite Cat,
Drowned in a Tub of
Gold Fishes" (Gray),
203
"Ode on the Death of the
Duke of Wellington"
(Tennyson), 202
"Ode on the Poetical
Character" (Collins),
281
Odes (Horace), 5, 41–42, 99
"Ode: Salute to the New
York School" (Gizzi),
43
Odes of Anacreon (Moore),
10

"Ode to a Nightingale" (Keats), 105, 202, 306

"Ode to Aphrodite" (Sappho), 202–3

"Ode to Castor and Polydeuces" (Alcaeus), 202–3

"Ode to the West Wind" (Shelley), 203, 256, 321

"Ode upon a Question Moved, whether Love Should Continue for ever" (Lord Herbert of Cherbury), 143

Odyssey (Homer), 8, 15, 28, 94, 188, 205, 315

The Odyssey: A Modern Sequel (Kazantzakis), 98

"The Offense" (Wright), 128

"Of the Anagrame, or Posy transposed" (Puttenham), 11

O'Hara, Frank
"The Day Lady Died," 151
"To the Poem," 265

Olson, Charles: *The Maximus Poems*, 98

Omeros (Walcott), 98

"One Art" (Bishop), 349

One Thousand and One Nights, 38, 260

"On First Looking into Chapman's Homer" (Keats), 297

"On the Late Massacre in Piedmont" (Milton), 297

"On the Morning of Christ's Nativity" (Milton), 203

"On the Use of Hyperbole" (Goldsmith), 133

Ó Raithille, Aodhagán:
"The Merchant's Son," 5

Orendel, 96

Les orientales (Hugo), 215

Orlando furioso (Ariosto), 44, 97, 301

Orlando inamorato (Bolardo), 44

"Out of the Cradle Endlessly Rocking" (Whitman), 194

Ovid
Amores, 99
Epistulae ex ponto, 99
Remedia amoris, 213
Tristia, 161

"The Ovidian Elegiac Metre" (Coleridge), 129

Owen, Wilfred
"Arms and the Boy," 257
"Insensibility," 58

The Owl and the Nightingale, 70

"Ozymandias" (Shelley), 297

Panchatantra, 38

Pan Tadeusz (Mickiewicz), 346

"Pantoum of the Great Depression" (Justice), 215

Paradise Lost (Milton), 15, 30, 78, 85, 97, 99, 105, 135, 147, 182, 191, 210, 306, 346

Paradise Regained (Milton), 98

"The Paradox" (Donne), 215

"A Paradox: that the sicke are in a *better case,* then the Whole" (Herbert), 215

Parker, Dorothy
"Ballade at Thirty-Five," 28
"Ballade of Unfortunate Mammals," 28

Parlement of Foules (Chaucer), 260

"The Passionate Shepherd to His Love" (Marlowe), 86

"Pastorals" (Pope), 86

Paterson (Williams), 98

Pearse, Pádraic: "A Woman of the Mountain Keens Her Son," 154–55

Pembroke, Countess of: "Psalm 120," 5

Penlycross: "Without a distich," 78

Percy, Thomas: "The Complaint of Conscience," 53

Petits poèmes en prose (Baudelaire), 239

Petrarch
  Epistulae metricae, 162
  Rime sparse, 31, 223
Phaedrus (Plato), 213
"Phanetai moi" (Sappho),
  275
Pharsalia (Lucan), 98
"The Phoenix and
  the Turtle"
  (Shakespeare), 335
"Pied Beauty" (Hopkins),
  297–98
Piers Plowman, 8, 178, 191
Pilgrim's Progress (Bunyan),
  7
Pindar, 101–2
Pippa Passes (Browning),
  49
Pisan, Christine de: "Ditiee
  de Jehanne d'Arc," 79
"Planh for the Death of Ted
  Hughes" (Merwin),
  226
"Planh for the Young
  English King"
  (Pound), 226
Plath, Sylvia
  "Black Rook in Rainy
    Weather," 265
  "The Moon and the Yew
    Tree," 222
Plato: *Phaedrus,* 213
Plautus: *Amphitruo,* 328
Plutarch
  Consolatio ad uxorem,
    57–58
  Moralia, 7
Plutzik, Hyam: "I Am
  Disquieted When I
  See Many Hills," 276

Poe, Edgar Allan
  "Annabel Lee," 12, 258
  "The Bells," 273
  "Enigma," 3
  "The Raven," 201, 250
Poema de mío, 96
Poem of Aqhat, 193
"The Poet" (Emerson),
  28, 289
"The Poetical Mission
  of Hans Sachs"
  (Goethe), 156
"Poetry" (Moore), 19
Pope, Alexander
  "An Essay on Criticism,"
    6, 49, 76
  The Dunciad, 277
  "Eloisa to Abelard," 162
  "Epigram Engraved on
    the Collar of a Dog
    which I gave to His
    Royal Highness," 62
  "Epigram from the
    French," 100
  "Essay on Criticism," 19,
    193, 197, 345, 355
  "An Essay on Man," 76,
    345
  "Fourth Satire of Dr.
    John Donne, Dean of
    St. Paul's Versified,"
    259
  Moral Essays, 76
  "Pastorals," 86
  "Prologue to Mr.
    Addison's 'Cato,'"
    134
  The Rape of the Lock,
    184, 277
"Portrait" (Bogan), 276

Pound, Ezra
  "Alba," 21
  "A Retrospect," 2
  "Canto LXXX," 273
  The Cantos, 39, 50, 98,
    116
  Canzoni, 40
  "Hugh Selwyn
    Mauberley," 186
  "Planh for the Young
    English King," 226
  "A Retrospect," 36, 117
  "The Return," 117–18
  "The River-Merchant's
    Wife: A Letter," 162
  "The Seafarer," 178
  The Spirit of Romance, 21
  "The Return," 4
The Prelude (Wordsworth),
  19, 86, 138, 181, 238,
  306
Prem Sagar (Lal), 260
Preparatory Meditations
  (Taylor), 283–84
The Princess (Tennyson),
  161
Proba: *Cento virgilianus,* 43
Probyn, May: "Say what
  you please," 271
"Proem: To Brooklyn
  Bridge" (Crane),
  238
"Prologue" (Bradstreet),
  283–84
"Prologue to Mr. Addison's
  'Cato'" (Pope), 134
"The Prologue to the
  Legend of Good
  Women" (Chaucer),
  63

Prometheus Unbound
(Shelley), 49
"Prothalamion" (Spenser),
103
"Proverbs of Hell" (Blake),
11, 242
Psalm 8, 94
"Psalm 120" (Countess of
Pembroke), 5
"Psalmus contra partem
Donati" (Augustine
of Hippo), 1
Purgatorio (Dante), 88
Pushkin, Alexander:
Eugene Onegin, 192,
346
Puttenham, George:
"Of the Anagrame,
or Posy transposed,"
11

Quarles, Francis: *Emblemes,*
92
Quodlibets (Hayman), 101

Racine, Jean, 6
Radi os (Johnson), 105
Rakoff, David: *Love,
Dishonor, Marry, Die,
Cherish, Perish,* 12
Raleigh, Walter: "A Vision
upon the Fairy
Queen," 246
Ramayana, 95
"A Ramble in St. James
Park" (Earl of
Rochester), 324
"The Rape of Lucrece"
(Shakespeare), 261,
283

The Rape of the Lock
(Pope), 184, 277
"The Raven" (Poe), 201,
250
"The Recluse"
(Wordsworth), 268
"The Red Wheelbarrow"
(Williams), 60
"The Reeve's Tale"
(Chaucer), 107
"Reflections on Having
Left a Place of
Retirement"
(Coleridge), 59
Régnier, Mathurin: *Satire
14,* 277
Remedia amoris (Ovid), 213
"A Renewal" (Merrill), 265
"Resolution and
Independence"
(Wordsworth), 261
"A Retrospect" (Pound), 2,
36, 117
"The Return" (Pound), 4,
117–18
The Revenger's Tragedy, 327
"Revolt of Islam" (Shelley),
302
Rexroth, Kenneth: "A
Christmas Note for
Geraldine Udell,"
235
"Rhapsody on Mount Kao-
t'ang" (Sung), 118–19
Rich, Adrienne: *An Atlas
of the Difficult World,*
240
Rigsthula, 87
Rilke, Rainer Maria: *Duino
Elegies,* 90

Rimbaud, Arthur:
"Voyelles," 315
"The Rime of the
Ancient Mariner"
(Coleridge), 18
Rime sparse (Petrarch),
31, 223
The Ring and the Book
(Browning), 181, 346
"The River-Merchant's
Wife: A Letter"
(Pound), 162
Robinson, Edwin
Arlington: "The
House on the Hill,"
350
Rochester, Earl of: "A
Ramble in St. James
Park," 324
Roethke, Theodore
"Dinky," 157
"I Knew a Woman," 261
"The Waking," 211
Romance of Antar, 171
Romeo and Juliet
(Shakespeare), 21–22,
243
"Rondeau" (d'Orléans), 270
"Rondeau Redoublé"
(Cope), 270
"Rose-Cheeked Laura"
(Campion), 275
"The Roundel"
(Swinburne), 271–72
The Rubaiyat (Khayyám),
272–73, 305
"The Ruined Maid"
(Hardy), 12
"Rules and Regulations"
(Carroll), 108–9

"Rules for Our Reach"
(Herrick), 48
"Rune Poems," 273
Rutebeuf: "Le dit de
l'herberie," 79

Saba, Umberto:
Canzonettas, 40
"Sabinus, I don't like you."
(Martial), 100
Sackville, Thomas:
"Complaint of
Henry, Duke of
Buckingham," 53
"Sailing to Byzantium"
(Yeats), 210
Salman und Moralf, 96
Samson Agonistes (Milton),
49, 61
Sandburg, Carl: "Good
Morning, America,"
242
"The Sands of Dee"
(Kingsley), 218–19
Sanson Agonistes (Milton),
49
"Sapphics" (Faulkner),
276
"Sapphics" (Swinburne),
275–76
Sappho, 4
"Ode to Aphrodite,"
202–3
"Phanetai moi," 275
Satire 14 (Régnier), 277
Satires (Horace), 276–77
Satires (Wyatt), 321
"Say over again, and yet
once over again"
(Browning), 13

"Say what you please"
(Probyn), 271
Scarron, Paul: *Virgile
travesti,* 35, 184
"The Scholar-Gypsy"
(Arnold), 346
Scott, Walter
*The Lay of the Last
Minstrel,* 158
"Vision of Don
Roderick," 302
"The Seafarer" (10th
century), 90
"The Seafarer" (Pound),
178
The Seasons (Thomson), 31,
75, 121
Secular Odes (Lugones), 121
"Self-Reliance" (Emerson),
310
Sestets (Wright), 283–84
"Sestina" (Gosse), 285–86
"Sestine 4" (Barnes), 85
Shahnameh, 95
Shakespeare, William
Antony and Cleopatra,
234
The Comedy of Errors, 52
Hamlet, 200, 327
Henry IV, 106
Henry V, 188
Macbeth, 30
*Midsummer Night's
Dream,* 35, 137, 172
"The Phoenix and the
Turtle," 335
"The Rape of Lucrece,"
261, 283
Romeo and Juliet, 21–22,
243

"Sonnet 18," 54, 223, 291
"Sonnet 20," 246
"Sonnet 30," 136
"Sonnet 94," 332
"Sonnet 129," 91
"Sonnet 130," 54–55, 223
The Tempest, 34, 204
Troilus and Cressida, 328
"Venus and Adonis," 62
The Winter's Tale, 26
Shelley, Percy
"Adonais," 86, 90, 302
"Autumn: A Dirge," 77
The Cenci, 49
The Mask of Anarchy, 235
"Ode to the West Wind,"
203, 256, 321
"Ozymandias," 297
Prometheus Unbound, 49
"Revolt of Islam," 302
"Stanzas Written in
Dejection," 258
"The Cloud," 12
"To a Skylark," 129
"The Triumph of Life,"
321
The Shepheardes Calender
(Spenser), 9, 86, 135,
193
Shulman, David:
"Washington
Crossing the
Delaware," 10–11
Shut Up Shut Down
(Nowak), 125
"The Sick Rose" (Blake), 16
Sidney, Philip
Arcadia, 17, 193, 285
Astrophil and Stella, 180,
222, 246

"A Ditty," 103
"Eleventh Song,"
    247–48
Silvae (Statius), 99
Sïrat Banï Hiläl, 97
*Sir Gawain and the Green
    Knight,* 33, 46, 193
Sir Orfeo, 158
"Sir Patric Spens," 357
Sitwell, Edith: *Façade,* 2
"Skald's Death"
    (MacDiarmid), 293
Skáldskaparmál, 88
Skelton, John
    "A Ballade of the
        Scottysshe Kynge,"
        33–34
    "Colin Clout," 81,
        293–94
Smart, Christopher
    Jubilate Agno, 109, 117,
        281
    "A Song to David," 281,
        295
"Some blaze the precious
    beauties of their
    loves" (Davies), 32
*Some of the Five Hundred
    Points of Good
    Husbandry* (Tusser),
    335
"Song" (Donne), 129
"Song: Chorus to
    Demeter"
    (Bridges), 5
"Song: Go, lovely Rose"
    (Waller), 247
"Song of a Man Who Has
    Come Through"
    (Lawrence), 344

Song of Deborah, 142
"Song of Hiawatha"
    (Longfellow), 108,
    331–32
*The Song of Igor's
    Campaign: An Epic of
    the Twelfth Century,*
    96
"Song of Myself"
    (Whitman), 13, 19,
    166
Song of Songs, 291, 347
"Song of St. Alexis," 191
*Songs of Innocence and
    Experience* (Blake),
    295
"A Song to David" (Smart),
    281, 295
Son-Jara, epic of, 97
"Sonnet 18" (Shakespeare),
    54, 223, 291
"Sonnet 20" (Shakespeare),
    246
"Sonnet 30" (Shakespeare),
    136
"Sonnet 94" (Shakespeare),
    332
"Sonnet 129"
    (Shakespeare), 91
"Sonnet 130"
    (Shakespeare), 54–55,
    223
"Sonnets from China"
    (Auden), 299
"Spelt from Sibyl's Leaves"
    (Hopkins), 298
Spenser, Edmund
    "Astrophel," 90
    Complaints, 235
    Epithalamion, 31, 103

The Faerie Queene, 6, 18,
    46, 92, 181,
    301–2, 305
"Prothalamion," 103
*The Shepheardes
    Calender,* 9, 86, 135,
    193
The Spirit of Romance
    (Pound), 21
Spoon River Anthology
    (Masters), 102, 336
"Spring" (Blake), 65
"Spring and All"
    (Williams), 252
"Spring Comes to Murray
    Hill" (Nash), 315
"Stanzas Written in
    Dejection" (Shelley),
    258
"The Starlight Night"
    (Hopkins), 93
Statius: *Silvae,* 99
"Staying Alive" (Wagoner),
    265
Stein, Gertrude, 2
    Tender Buttons, 66
Stevens, Wallace
    "The American
        Sublime," 310
    "The Figure of the Youth
        as Virile Poet," 188
    "It Must Be Abstract"
        ("Notes Toward a
        Supreme Fiction"), 2
    "The Man with the Blue
        Guitar," 19
    "Of Modern Poetry,"
        19
Stevenson, Robert Louis:
    Moral Lessons, 92

Stickney, Trumbull:
"Mnemosyne," 250
"Stopping by Woods on
a Snowy Evening"
(Frost), 43, 273
"Story of the Panther"
(Margival), 45
*The Structure of Complex
Words* (Empson), 7
Suckling, John: "Why so
pale and wan, fond
lover?," 256
"Sumer is icumen in," 252
"Summa Lyrica"
(Grossman), 31
"Sunflower Sutra"
(Ginsberg), 311
Sung Yü: "Rhapsody on
Mount Kao-t'ang,"
118–19
"The Sun Rising" (Donne),
16, 22, 109
Surrey, Earl of: "A
Complaint by Night
of the Lover Not
Beloved," 53
Swenson, May: "Four-Word
Lines," 60
Swift, Jonathan, 103
*A Town Eclogue. 1710.
Scene, The Royal
Exchange,* 87
"Vanbrugh's House," 131
Swinburne, Algernon
"Before the Beginning of
Years," 12
"Choriambics," 47
"Hendecasyllabics," 128
"Hymn to Proserpine,"
145–46, 258

"March: An Ode," 201
"The Roundel," 271–72
"Sapphics," 275–76

Táin Bó Cúailnge, 96
"Tale of Sir Thopas"
(Chaucer), 80
"Tam o'Shanter" (Burns),
91, 202
Tape for the Turn of the Year
(Ammons), 306
The Task (Cowper), 31, 121
Taylor, Edward
"An Elegy upon the
Death of that Holy
and Reverend Man
of God, Mr. Samuel
Hooker," 152
Preparatory Meditations,
283–84
"Tell all the Truth but tell
it slant" (Dickinson),
19
The Tempest (Shakespeare),
34, 204
"The Temporary the All"
(Hardy), 5, 276
Tender Buttons (Stein), 66
Tennyson, Alfred (Lord), 5
"Ask me no more," 316
"Charge of the Light
Brigade," 69
"Hendecasyllabics," 128
Idylls of the King, 136, 192
"The Lotos-eaters,"
19–20
"The Making of Man,"
212
In Memoriam, 16, 90,
143, 238, 259

"Ode on the Death
of the Duke of
Wellington," 202
The Princess, 161
Theocritus: *Idyll,* 103
Theogony (Hesiod), 76,
188, 238
"There's a certain Slant of
light" (Dickinson),
147
"They Flee from Me"
(Wyatt), 261
"This Lime-tree Bower My
Prison" (Coleridge),
59
Thomas, Dylan, 8
"Altarwise by Owl-
Light," 299
"Do Not Go Gentle into
That Good Night,"
211, 349
Thomas, R. S.: "Carol,"
41
Thomson, James: *The
Seasons,* 31, 75, 121
"Thrice tosse these Oaken
ashes in the ayre"
(Campion), 46
"Thyrsis" (Arnold), 86, 90
"To a Skylark" (Shelley),
129
"To Autumn" (Keats), 72,
75, 105
"Toccata of Galuppi's"
(Browning), 180
"To Her Sea-Faring Lover,"
172
"To His Coy Love:
A Canzonet"
(Drayton), 40

"To His Coy Mistress"
(Marvell), 63, 180
"Tommy" (Kipling), 180
"Tom o'Bedlam," 247
"To Penshurst" (Jonson),
62
"To Saxham" (Carew), 62
"To the Imortall Memorie
and Friendship of
That Noble Paire,
Sir Lucius Cary and
Sir H. Morison"
(Jonson), 203
"To the Pious Memory of
the Accomplished
Young Lady, Mrs.
Anne Killigrew"
(Dryden), 203
"To the Poem" (O'Hara),
265
"To the Virgins, to Make
Much of Time"
(Herrick), 42
"To Toussaint L'Ouverture"
(Wordsworth), 235
"To William Wordsworth"
(Coleridge), 59–60
*A Town Eclogue. 1710.
Scene, The Royal
Exchange* (Swift),
87
Tribute to Freud
(Doolittle), 336
"The Triolet" (Henley),
330
Tristia (Ovid), 161
"The Triumph of Life"
(Shelley), 321
Troilus and Cressida
(Shakespeare), 328

Troilus and Criseyde
(Chaucer), 64, 213,
242, 260, 283
Troyes, Chrétien de
*Le chevalier de la
charrette,* 64
Lancelot, 46
"Truth" (Chaucer), 260
Tusser, Thomas: *Some of
the Five Hundred
Points of Good
Husbandry,* 335
Two Books of Ayres
(Campion), 4
Two-Part Inventions
(Howard), 50
Tzara, Tristan: "Chanson
Dada," 69

"Upon Appleton House"
(Marvell), 62, 215
"Upon His Departure
Hence" (Herrick),
180
"Upon Julia's Clothes"
(Herrick), 320

Valley of a Thousand Hills
(Dhlomo), 240
"Vanbrugh's House"
(Swift), 131
Van Duyn, Mona: "Causes,"
265
"The Vanity of Human
Wishes" (Johnson),
70, 90
"Venus and Adonis"
(Shakespeare), 62
Verlaine, Paul, 6
"Art poétique," 314

The Village (Crabbe), 9, 218
Villon, François
"Ballade des dames du
temps jadis," 336
"Ballade des pendus," 27
"Ballade des proverbes,"
240
"Débat du coeur et du
corps," 70
Virgil
Aeneid, 8, 30, 38, 88, 97,
127, 154, 191
Eclogues, 16–17, 86, 99,
135, 218
Georgics, 9, 76, 120–21
Virgile travesti (Scarron),
35, 184
A Vision (Yeats), 22
"Vision of Don Roderick"
(Scott), 302
"A Vision upon the Fairy
Queen" (Raleigh),
246
"The Voice" (Hardy), 69
"Voyelles" (Rimbaud), 315

Wagoner, David: "Staying
Alive," 265
Waiting for Godot
(Beckett), 52
"The Waking" (Roethke),
211
Walcott, Derek: *Omeros,*
98
Waller, Edmund: "Song:
Go, lovely Rose,"
247
"The Wanderer," 90
The Wandering Jew
(Goethe), 156

Warren, Rosanna, 5
"Washington Crossing
    the Delaware"
    (Shulman), 10–11
The Wasps (Aristophanes),
    79
"The Waste Land" (Eliot),
    50, 91, 116, 186, 334
Watson, William: "Hymn
    to the Sea," 252
Watts, Isaac, 132
    "The Day of Judgment,"
    276
    "When I survey the
    wondrous cross,"
    167
A Wave (Ashbery), 125
Way of the World
    (Congreve), 52
A Way Out (Frost), 84
"The Weary Blues"
    (Hughes), 150
"Wen-fu" (Lu), 119
West, Kanye: "Get Em
    High," 130
West-East Divan (Goethe),
    122
"Western wind, when
    wilt thou blow"
    (Anonymous), 247
"We Wear the Mask"
    (Dunbar), 270
"What is an epigram?"
    (Coleridge), 100
"When I survey the
    wondrous cross"
    (Watts), 167
"When Lilacs Last in the
    Dooryard Bloom'd"
    (Whitman), 90, 136

"When the Assault Was
    Intended to the City"
    (Milton), 297
"The White Island or
    Place of the Blest"
    (Herrick), 316
Whitman, Walt
    "A Broadway Pageant,"
    12–13
    "Death's Valley," 49
    "Dirge for Two
    Veterans," 77
    Leaves of Grass, 12–13,
    42, 290
    "Out of the Cradle
    Endlessly Rocking,"
    194
    "Song of Myself," 13, 19,
    166
    "When Lilacs Last in the
    Dooryard Bloom'd,"
    90, 136
Whitney, George:
    A Choice of
    Emblemes, 92
"Why so pale and wan,
    fond lover?"
    (Suckling), 256
"Wichita Vortex
    Sutra" (Ginsberg),
    311
"The Widow in the Bye
    Street" (Masefield),
    261
Wigglesworth, Michael:
    "God's Controversy
    with New England,"
    151
Wilbur, Richard: "A
    Wood," 283–84

Williams, William Carlos
    Al Que Quiere!, 66
    "Asphodel, That Greeny
    Flower," 306
    Paterson, 98
    "The Red
    Wheelbarrow," 60
    "Spring and All," 252
"The Windhover"
    (Hopkins), 7–8,
    212
The Winter's Tale
    (Shakespeare), 26
"With broken heart
    and contrite sigh"
    (Campion), 157
"Without a distich"
    (Penlycross), 78
"A Woman of the
    Mountain Keens
    Her Son" (Pearse),
    154–55
"A Wood" (Wilbur),
    283–84
Wordsworth, William
    "Composed upon
    Westminster Bridge,
    September 3, 1802,"
    297
    "Female Vagrant," 302
    "Intimations," 312
    The Prelude, 19, 86, 138,
    181, 238, 306
    "The Recluse," 268
    "Resolution and
    Independence," 261
    "To Toussaint
    L'Ouverture," 235
    "The World Is too Much
    with Us," 36–37

Works and Days (Hesiod), 76, 120

"The World Is too Much with Us" (Wordsworth), 36–37

"The Wreck of the Deutschland" (Hopkins), 67

Wright, Charles: *Sestets,* 283–84

Wright, James
  "Erinna to Sappho," 276
  "The Offense," 128

Wright, Jay: "The Hieroglyph of Irrational Space," 44

Wyatt, Thomas, 8
  "The Love Complaineth the Unkindness of His Love," 248
  Satires, 321
  "They Flee from Me," 261

Yeats, William Butler
  "Among School Children," 201, 210
  "The Circus Animals' Desertion," 210
  "Coole Park and Ballylee," 210
  "A Dialogue of Self and Soul," 75–76
  "Easter, 1916," 257
  "In Memory of Major Robert Gregory," 89, 136
  "No Second Troy," 256
  "Sailing to Byzantium," 210
  A Vision, 22

Young, Edward: *Night Thoughts,* 90

Younger Edda, 87–88

Yü Hsin: "Lament for the South," 119

Zukofsky, Louis: *"A",* 98, 116